GEORGE EASTMAN

George Eastman

GEORGE EASTMAN

BY
CARL W. ACKERMAN

WITH AN INTRODUCTION BY
EDWIN R. A. SELIGMAN, LL.D, Ph.D.

And with Illustrations

Boston and New York
HOUGHTON MIFFLIN COMPANY
The Riverside Press Cambridge
1930

The Riverside Press
CAMBRIDGE · MASSACHUSETTS
PRINTED IN THE U.S.A.

PREFACE

PROFESSOR EDWIN R. A. SELIGMAN urged Mr. Eastman in 1925 to publish an autobiography. Returning to Columbia University after a visit in Rochester, the distinguished economist wrote: 'You will pardon me for saying that what interested me more than anything else was your interesting reminiscences. I hope that you will take seriously to heart my advice to publish your autobiography.' [1]

In the course of years many similar suggestions were made. Although Mr. Eastman originated the world system of film photography and created an international industry, and, although Dr. Nicholas Murray Butler said he was 'a literally stupendous factor in the education of the modern world,' [2] he assiduously avoided personal recognition. This was in accordance with a deliberate policy on Mr. Eastman's part to direct attention to the institutions he founded or financed rather than to any one individual.

By 1928, however, Mr. Eastman had transferred the management of his business to his successors and had distributed the bulk of his fortune to educational institutions and employees. Although he had attained 'a somewhat more detached position in respect to human affairs,' he was engaged in advancing the movement to bring about an international fixed calendar and in the founding of a dental dispensary in London and a professorship at Oxford University.

At the same time, wide public and scientific interest in color and sound photography directed attention to the

[1] March 3, 1925.
[2] October 24, 1928.

limited information available relating to the history of film photography, and the writer suggested that he be permitted to assemble the facts from Mr. Eastman's personal archives. The reading of his correspondence proved again the truth of Emerson's observation that 'there is properly no history; only biography.'

Mr. Eastman's records have been preserved for more than sixty-one years, while from 1878 to the present there is an unbroken chain of more than one hundred thousand letters. These reveal significant additions to the general fund of information relating to the modern industrial policy of large-scale production at low costs; to chemical research; to the relationship of music, leisure, and preventive dentistry to the enrichment of community life; and to the rebuilding of two large institutions of higher education — the Massachusetts Institute of Technology and the University of Rochester.

In the construction of this book a definite attempt has been made to follow Bacon's rule, that 'it is the true office of history to represent the events themselves, together with the counsels, and to leave the observations and conclusions thereupon to the liberty and faculty of every man's judgement.'

CARL W. ACKERMAN

ROCHESTER, NEW YORK
October, 1929

CONTENTS

ILLUSTRATIONS

INTRODUCTION

THE life of every successful captain of industry presents a problem interesting alike to the psychologist and to the economist. What is the secret of the type that he represents? And what are the characteristics of the individual so far as he diverges in any respect from the type?

In considering the first point we are confronted by two significant problems, that of motives, and that of methods.

So far as motives are concerned, we are no longer content with the older explanation of the economic man. In modern discussion the urge to make profits has been supplemented by a variety of other incentives to economic action. So far, however, as we can infer from a perusal of recent biographies, the leading economic motives that have actuated the typical captain of industry may be reduced to three in number.

It is obvious that in our modern competitive society the earliest and the most significant urge on the part of the beginner in the economic struggle is to get on; and the most tangible evidence of his ability to get on is to be seen in his accumulation of profits. It may safely be accepted as almost the tritest of observations that in our modern society money-making is the earliest stimulus to economic activity.

After reasonable success, however, has been achieved in this direction, some individuals at least — although naturally by no means all — find that the quest for money as such begins somewhat to pall upon them. Yet in a society like that of the United States, well-nigh everyone who has started remains in the game and the question arises as to what the compelling motives for this actually are. It is comparatively easy to observe, and it has often been stated, that money as an objective is now replaced by power. A wealthy man will continue to develop his already large business chiefly because he is now actuated by the desire to augment his power — power over his competitors, power over his fellows in the community — with all for which that stands.

While this is undoubtedly often true, the question arises whether a more significant and a more easily intelligible incentive is not sometimes found. The real secret of life, after all, is that of self-expression; and when we are dealing with great empire builders such as our foremost captains of industry, it is perhaps needless to seek a more recondite explanation of their activity. The great industrialist, the great merchant, the great financier is confronted day by day with a new situation, with a new difficulty to be overcome, with a new solution to be achieved. What the big man does is very much what the little man does, except that it is translated into a wider sphere. What he desires is to attain his immediate end, to solve his problem, to reach the particular objective which presents itself to him in the course of his daily operations. Just as the artist or the intellectual worker finds his greatest thrill in creation, so the business man is moved fundamentally by the same consideration. Not money, not power, but creation, success, accomplishment — that is the real secret of the activity of the captain of industry.

The motives that distinguish the modern capitalist are, however, only one part of the explanation. Equally interesting are the methods that he employs.

Here again there are several problems that present themselves.

The first point is that of the originality or the independence of the successful business man. It is sometimes stated that the end is often achieved, as it were, vicariously; that the successful man attains success by purchasing the ideas of others, by sucking the lifeblood of those who are unable independently to develop their own conceptions. That this is true in some cases is probable. But the advantage of an honest and truthful biography is that it enables us to perceive the inaccuracy of this statement as a whole. The great man, whether he be a business man, a scholar, or an artist, shows his greatness primarily by his originality of conception, by his ability to visualize what a smaller man is unable to see. The creative sense is always a distinguishing mark of greatness, and this applies in every field of human endeavor. The success of the typical captain of industry is original and not derivative.

The second and more interesting problem, however, is that of the way in which the great man comes to determine his objective. Does he spend his time in worrying over small matters, or does he wake up in the morning with a sudden flash of inspiration which illumines the dark corners and dissipates the difficulties? Is it not true that the great man — no matter in what field — is great because he has what the French call the flair, the instinct which crystallizes itself in the sudden resolution? The business man, like the artist, to be truly great must be gifted with an imagination — the imagination to conceive, and the imagination to resolve.

This does not mean, however, that one can make short cuts to the end or that one can achieve merely spectacular results. It is perhaps even more true of the modern business man than it is of the modern lawyer or the modern scholar that meticulous attention to details may often be more important than genius, or rather that this itself constitutes genius. No individual, whatever his career, can afford to neglect the slow, steady, and patient attention to detail which, as we have learned from many a life, spells the difference between success and failure.

The most interesting part of the present biography and the one which will surely make its wider appeal is the light which it throws upon these fundamental problems of business life and of American success. The truth of each point in the foregoing analysis is amply attested on almost every page of this work.

So far as we know, Mr. Eastman was the first manufacturer in the United States to formulate and to put into practice the modern policy of large-scale production at low costs for a world market, backed by scientific research and extensive advertising.

In respect especially to chemical investigation, we think that when a study of scientific research in American industry comes to be written, it will be seen that Mr. Eastman ranks among the first few industrialists who employed chemists to devote their entire time to experiments and research.

But there is another side to the biography. What is typical in the life of the great captain of industry is clear. There are, however, other things which are not so obvious to the general reader and which must be sought for between the lines. What I refer to here is not so much the explanation of the type, as the secret of the man; and that, after all, is the most interesting of human problems.

The life of most rich men, at least in the United States, may be divided into three stages, which I should like to call the acquisitive, the possessive, and the distributive.

At the outset, as observed above, every struggler in the competitive field is concerned chiefly with acquiring wealth. Even when the money-making motive has been supplanted by the power motive or the success motive, he is still primarily interested in acquisition. Not a few individuals never emerge from this stage.

In the great majority of cases, however, the time comes when the acquisition of money as such loses some of its pristine charm. Wealth now comes to be regarded not so much as an end in itself as a means to something else. The individual now turns his attention to the conveniences, the comforts, and the luxuries that wealth brings. If he is properly attuned, he will gradually develop from the stage of mere material gratifications to that of the more immaterial ends. He may enjoy his mansion, his *cordon bleu*, his yacht; but he will not infrequently make an art collection or devote himself to some particular hobby. All of these phenomena may be subsumed under the head of gratification or possession. He no longer thinks primarily of acquiring money, he has reached the stage of enjoying money. He has emerged from the acquisitive and entered on the possessive stage.

In not a few cases, however, a third stage makes its appearance; and in some exceptional instances this final or distributive stage is encountered almost at the outset. The more finely grained the individual, the sooner does he become conscious of his social responsibilities and the more does he realize that, although he may in first instance owe his success to himself, yet in a larger way he has been able to achieve his goal, in part at least, through the coöperation of others. This realization of social obligation ordinarily assumes three forms — responsibility to one's associates, responsibility to one's employees, responsibility to the community.

The most common form of this sense of social obligation is to one's own immediate associates. Even though the conception may be his, the execution necessarily depends upon the faithfulness of his colleagues. For that reason, many a successful captain of industry finds his real pleasure to consist in advancing *pari passu* the fortunes of his colleagues. He distributes to them a part of what would otherwise be retained by him.

It is a step further to realize that a great business ultimately depends on the loyalty of the workers. Perhaps the most remarkable change that has come over modern American business is the acceptance by the forward-looking employer of the doctrine that has long been taught by economists, the theory of the economy of high wages. High wages are economical in a double sense. In the first place dearer commodities are in the end cheaper, because they yield more surplus, provided that their high price reflects their intrinsic qualities. And in the second place, since profits depend upon sales, the wider the market the better the chances. The increasing wages of the mass of the community spell a continually augmented purchasing power.

These considerations have led to the growing democratization of American industry which is scarcely second in importance to the characteristic features of integration and mass production. To enable one's workers to participate in the growing prosperity of a business is the second phase of the distributive stage.

Finally, as the circle constantly widens, the great employer includes in his purview not alone his colleagues and his employees, but the public at large. The public as consumers he will endeavor to benefit by reducing the price of his product. This is of course the great defence of private property and private initiative. For success will be in the long run achieved only through service. The reduction in price which enlarges the producer's market and increases his profits affords to the consumer a continually wider circle of satisfactions.

The great man, however, soon passes beyond this circle of consumers of his own services and reaches the community at large, of which he is perhaps so distinguished a part. When this final phase in his distributive philosophy is attained, he will find his greatest satisfaction in the real secret of life, in making society as a whole the better for his having lived. If he reaches only the first rungs of this final ladder, he will make large bequests to hospitals and asylums; if he becomes more perspicacious and climbs to a higher rung, he will bestow his largesses upon education and research. If he climbs still upward and achieves the widest horizon, he will include in his benefactions the arts and the furtherance of world-wide and universal ends.

The story of the emergence from the acquisitive through the possessive to the distributive stage cannot well be adequately told in a biography without incurring the hazard of fulsome flattery. But to those who peruse this book and who can read between the lines, enough will be evident to attest this onward march in the life history of a great man.

What is characteristic in the career of Mr. Eastman is not only the gradual unfolding of all these traits, culminating in a great business as well as in a daring and wide-flung philanthropy, but also the more rare and precious sense of beauty which has ever marked his progress. There has been a distinct æsthetic side in all his accomplishments, in his vocation as well as in his avocations. His wonderful home, his weekly musicals, his color photography — all these, which more or less unconsciously represent the deepest of his strivings, are the expression of a fundamental æsthetic sense. To him, as to few mortals, has been vouchsafed the gift of combining art and industry, beauty and efficiency, the artistic and the practical.

I esteem it a peculiar privilege and a high honor to be permitted to call attention to some of these larger aspects of a remarkable career.

EDWIN R. A. SELIGMAN

COLUMBIA UNIVERSITY, NEW YORK
December, 1929

GEORGE EASTMAN

GEORGE EASTMAN

. .

CHAPTER I

ANCESTRY AND YOUTH

THE first letter George Eastman wrote on the subject of his ancestry is characteristic of a lifelong attitude toward the Past.

ROCHESTER, NEW YORK
Jan 10, 1885

C. L. Eastman, Esq.,
Penn Yan, N.Y.

DEAR SIR:

In reply to your letter of 24 ult.

My grandfather was Harvey Eastman, Marshall Oneida Co. N Y who had two brothers Abram Dayton & Joseph, all sons of Elder Hezekiah Eastman.

You can get further information in relation to the Oneida Co. family from A. R. Eastman Waterville who is interested in the genealogy to a greater extent than
Yours truly

GEO EASTMAN

Thirty-two years later, when the family genealogy was published, Eastman learned for the first time that he was a direct descendant of two pioneer families which settled in Massachusetts and Connecticut in the early seventeenth century. His American progenitors were Roger Eastman and Thomas Kilborne, who came to this country from England in 1638 and 1635, respectively, so that the family names thread their way through the annals of the Western Hemisphere for nearly three hundred years.

In the folio record of the Augmentation Office, Rolls Court, Westminster Hall, London, the names of Thomas Kilborne, his wife Frances, their four daughters and one son,[1] appear below the following notation:

'15*th*. *Apr.* 1635. These parties hereafter are to be transported to New England, embarqued in the Increase, Robert Lea, master, having taken the oath of allegiance and supremacy, as also being conformable to the orders and discipline of the church, whereof they brought testimony per certificates from the Justices and Ministers where their abodes have lately been.'

Their destination was Wethersfield, Connecticut, six miles below the present city of Hartford, where the Dutch had established a trading-post in the virgin valley of the Connecticut River. This settlement irked the British Crown, and, in order to save the fertile meadows from the complete control of New Amsterdam, British subjects were encouraged to settle there. The Kilborne family constituted the vanguard in the migration which became more extensive during succeeding years.[2]

Exactly three years after Thomas Kilborne sailed for the New World, a young house carpenter from Wiltshire, Roger Eastman by name, boarded the ship Confidence at Southampton and departed for the Massachusetts Bay Colony. By 1640, when Salisbury was incorporated, he received lands in the first subdivision, married Sarah Smith, and built the first house in that community.

During the next century the descendants of these two

---

[1] This son, John, changed the spelling of the name to Kilbourn.

[2] 'The pioneer farms in this valley generally were larger (up to 300 acres) than those eastward and from the start devoted considerable attention to stock raising.' (From *Industries of America*, by Professor Malcolm Keir.)

BIRTHPLACE OF GEORGE EASTMAN, WATERVILLE, N.Y.

families wended their ways through the Indian trails in the wilderness to the new frontiers in New Hampshire,[1] Vermont, Maine, and New Jersey. During the Revolutionary War, Elder Hezekiah Eastman, a Baptist minister, who was the first pastor of the first church in Danby, Vermont, moved his family to Marshall, Oneida County, New York. Here his son Harvey married Anne Rundell and raised a family of ten sturdy children on the paternal farm. Their youngest son was George Washington Eastman, born September 9, 1815.

In 1806, Thomas Kilbourn, a lineal descendant of the first Thomas Kilborne, moved from Connecticut to a clearing in the forest near the town of Marshall, named by the original settlers 'Paris Hill.' Among the seven children born to his wife Mary was their youngest daughter, Maria Kilbourn. In the family Bible her birth is recorded on August 22, 1821.

Oneida County, in the early decades of the nineteenth century, was known, as were the neighboring counties Oswego, Cayuga, Seneca, Ontario, and Monroe, 'as the happy hunting ground of such remnants of the Six Nations as survived the chastisement of Sullivan.'[2] For more than two centuries the Eastman and Kilbourn families had survived the Indian massacres both in New England and New York State. The family history is replete with dramatic encounters, but these were only a part of the price the pioneers paid to settle a new continent and build a new nation. They had to fell the trees, hew the timber, and clear the land before it, in turn, could sustain them. Fortitude, in these days, was the chief inheritance passed on from one generation to the next.

[1] Captain Ebenezer Eastman was the first settler in Concord, New Hampshire, 1727.

[2] From the first Directory of the Village of Rochester, 1827.

The building of the Erie Canal and the railroads brought the inhabitants of this northern tier of counties into closer communication, and as trade and industry developed, Rochester, the county seat of Monroe County, became a thriving city by 1840.

Two years later, George W. Eastman came to Rochester, founding, in this growing community, 'Eastman's Commercial College,' the first training school in the country to introduce actual business transactions in its course of studies. Two pieces of the paper 'money' used, together with an early circular and the book on penmanship,[1] indicate the nature of the course of instruction which became the common practice in the 'business colleges' of the United States prior to the Civil War. It was 'the design of the [Eastman] Collegiate Course to qualify the pupil to act as book-keeper in the most extensive and diversified establishment.'

Within two years the business school was firmly established, and George W. Eastman returned to Oneida County to marry Maria Kilbourn. The union of these two early American families, September 25, 1844, transmitted to their only son a heritage that recognized neither obstacles nor frontiers. The first two children were daughters, Ellen Maria and Emma Kate, but while the family was living in Waterville, their son, George, was born July 12, 1854.

[1] This book was *Chirographic Charts*, by Levi S. Fulton and George W. Eastman, published May, 1848, by A. S. Barnes & Co., New York, and H. W. Derby & Co., Cincinnati. Herein appears the following:
'The homely stanza of the spelling book bard,

"My boy, be cool,
Do things by rule,
And then you'll do them right,"

certainly contains much more truth than poetry, and like most of these short sayings in the book wherein we learned our alphabet, has in it much of the "proverbial philosophy," and is of very general application.'

Waterville was a town of only a few hundred inhabitants, situated in an agricultural district devoted chiefly to the raising of hops. In the winter, when the weather-worn vine poles were stacked like wigwams and covered with snow, they appeared to be silent reminders of ancestral hardships. Within the brief span of a few generations this transition had taken place.

The one-story frame house where George was born was the only one of its type in the community, easily recognizable because of the diminutive colonial porch and the attic windows which appeared to be squeezed under the eaves. It faced the old plank road, the main highway to Utica, over which Mrs. Eastman drove to take her husband when he commuted to and from Rochester. In the next block, George's lifelong friend, Frank L. Babbott, was born,[1] while only a few miles away, in Clinton, Elihu Root was attending a public school.

In October, 1854, Eastman's Commercial College was moved to the fourth floor of the Reynolds Arcade in Rochester, the most important building in the city at the time,[2] while the Eastman family residence remained in Waterville. By 1860, however, the college was known throughout many cities along the Great Lakes, and George W. Eastman was able to move his wife and

[1] August 14, 1854.

[2] The following sequences of study and costs were announced in the circular:

'Commercial Penmanship and Book-keeping by Double-Entry, as practically used in the different departments of Trade and Commerce, including Wholesale, Retail, Commission, Banking, Manufacturing, Shipping and Steam-boating, individual Partnership and Compound Company business.

'Students being taught individually can enter at any time, and the full course is usually completed in from four to eight weeks. For Teacher's Course, including Ornamental Penmanship in all the Ancient and Modern Hands and Diploma: $30. For Collegiate Course and Diploma: $25. For a Course of Lessons in Book-keeping alone: $10. For 24 lessons in Penmanship: $5. . . . Graduates assisted to suitable situations.'

children to the leading commercial city in the Genesee Valley.

'I was only six years old when I left Waterville with my parents,' Eastman recalled.[1] 'My most vivid recollections of Waterville are connected with two incidents. One time when my father returned to Waterville from a visit he brought me as a present a toy rake, the teeth of which must have been cast iron, for when I used it, one after another of the teeth broke off. I can remember now the pang of sorrow that each broken tooth caused. I was nearly heartbroken when I could use the rake no longer.

'The other incident was of a different kind. At noon I used to like to play with the workmen in my father's nursery when they were eating their lunch and they were fond of telling me interesting stories. I remember one of them claimed to have lived with the Indians and had learned their methods of tracking their enemies. He said he could take a hatchet (which he called a tomahawk) and by putting it to his forehead and then to the ground where the enemy had sometimes stood, he could track him to his hiding-place. He said he could prove it and that if the other men would blindfold him, I could run and hide and then he would find me.

'I did this and hid under a pile of loose lumber, the other men helping to cover me up. When all was ready, this man let out a whoop and I could hear him moving around. Finally he came to the pile of lumber and said "here he is." This excited me greatly, and after that I had a great admiration for the "great Indian tracker."'

Young George, however, did not have an opportunity of living in a story-book world very long, for two years

[1] Letter to T. H. Townsend, editor of the *Waterville Times*, September 20, 1927.

GEORGE W. EASTMAN

after the family moved to Rochester, his father died,[1] and his mother began those years of struggle which created in him a fear of poverty beyond our power to-day to appraise. To eke out an income for her family, Mrs. Eastman was compelled to take boarders.

George continued in the public schools until 1868. During the winter months he and another boy 'sawed brackets' in their spare time. 'These brackets were cut out of black walnut in filigree design and were used as bookshelves.'[2] The five dollars he received was his first 'real money' and with it he opened his first bank account. Besides, it gave him encouragement, for he had a natural boyish pride in having reached the age when he could earn something.

One day Captain Cornelius Waydell, a well-known insurance agent who had offices in the Arcade Building, offered George a job. It was one of those occasions that come only once in a lifetime, and George experienced a thrill not uncommon to most American boys. Three dollars a week was the initial wage and on the 8th of March, 1868, he went to work.

At this time he started his first 'Cash a/c' book, wherein he itemized all receipts and expenditures each month and kept an annual inventory. During the first year there were only a few expenditures, chiefly for clothing and board, but under the item of sundries we find 'Ice Cream 65' (cents), bought July 12, 1868, his fourteenth birthday!

The first 'recapitulation' shows his 'assets' at the end of the year amounted to thirty-nine dollars, an 'increase' of thirty-four dollars over the first five dollars earned sawing wood.

[1] April 27, 1862.
[2] From the *Thrift Advocate*, Rochester Savings Bank, May, 1923.

Recapitulation		1868
1868 Rec'd during Year		($) 131.00
" Paid " "		
Clothes	39.00	
Board	22.22	
Sundries	16.35	
Shoes	8.05	
Underclothes &c	3.03	
Hats	3.35	
	92.00	
On hand	39.00	

Assets

1868 — Mar. 2d	($) 5.
1869 — Jan 1	39.
Increase	($) 34.

Photography is mentioned first under date of January 27, 1869. Thereafter occur frequent references in the notebooks to the purchase of 'pictures,' material for picture frames and photographs, the first one being recorded, 'Photo for S. S. teacher.' February 1 (1869) he purchased '8 photos.' April 1 he took his mother to a 'lecture.' In June he gave his mother $12.50 extra for gas and coal, for his 'salary' had just been raised to four dollars a week. This year, on his fifteenth birthday, his uncle, Horace H. Eastman, of Waterville, sent him ten dollars, and on the fifteenth of the month he went on his first 'excursion.' In August he bought a new jackknife,[1] spent a whole week's salary subscribing for 'Harper's Weekly' for a year,[2] bought more photos and gave his mother a 'Century plant.' In September he received another dollar a week

---

[1] 'I remember as a boy,' Eastman wrote J. J. Bausch, October 24, 1924, 'going to North Water Street to search in the rubbish thrown out from your factory [Bausch & Lomb] for disks of hard rubber which had been punched from the eyeglass frames and afterwards cutting them out with a jackknife into finger rings.'

[2] During 1869 the political interest of the Nation was centered in President Grant's quarrel with Charles Sumner and his Cabinet, first over the President's attempt to secure the annexation of Santo Domingo, and secondly over Grant's yielding to the spoilsmen. In 1869, the first transcontinental railroad line was completed. 'The iron bands they laid at length united East and West and heralded the advent of cities, farms and commonwealths.' (Professor John Spencer Bassett.)

raise and by the end of that year there appears another 'Recapitulation':

1869 Rec'd during year		($) 233.00	
Paid " "			
Clothes	74.50		
Board	32.50		
Shoes	24.85		
Sundries	24.80		
Underclothes &c	10.40		
Hats	3.75		
Gymnasium	12.00		
Vacation trip	8.20		
		191.00	
Surplus		42.00	
Bro't for'd — 1868		39.00	
Jan 1/70 On hand		81	

	Assets	
Jan 1 1870	($) 81.
" 1 1869	39.
Increase	42.

The year 1870 brought him two increases in salary with the new firm which employed him — Buell & Hayden, successors of Buell and Brewster, another insurance concern. The last increase placed George on a $35 a month basis and he began to study French, became interested in 'stereopticons,' attended more lectures and 'exhibitions,' paid $20 to his mother's physician, bought $40 worth of coal in the summer when it was cheap, went on two more excursions, and took 'Kate' for a ride! Still at the end of the year his 'assets' had increased $125.78 and he had $287.78 'on hand' or in the bank.

In March, 1871, he purchased a flute on the installment plan. But, after taking lessons for two years and practicing 'Annie Laurie,' he made such slow progress that years later, when he heard some one else play the song, he did not recognize the tune, so Colonel Henry A. Strong used to say.

In April there is an early indication of sympathetic generosity. An injured boy received a dollar plus the 'Doc & med' fees. In May his salary was increased and he took out his first life insurance policy. On his seventeenth birthday his mother gave him five dollars for his first set of tools and workbench. In September he went on a vacation visiting his cousin, Mary Eastman, and her father and mother at Kingsville, Ashtabula County, Ohio. Upon his return, September 28, he sent her the following letter, written in a clear, even and exact, oval type of penmanship, a style which became characteristic in all his early correspondence as a business man:

Dear Cousin:

I found myself at home Saturday afternoon at half past five, very glad to get there, and somewhat tired with my long ride. It was dustier on the cars than I have ever seen it before and by the time I got home I had about all I could carry in my nose, eyes and mouth.

It hardly seems possible that I have been gone three weeks. When I opened the office Monday morning it seemed just as though I had closed it as usual last Saturday night.

Cousin Minnie is here yet, she is not going back to Columbia, but expects to teach at Beloit, Wis. this winter.

Cousin Eliza Thompkins is staying here while her mother is in New York. She returns to Syracuse next Monday or Tuesday.

The weather is cloudy and chilly and just cold enough to require a fire and warm enough to make the fire uncomfortable, I speak of the office. At home the grate fire is very pleasant.

The Western New York Fair opens on Tuesday. It is held on ground about a mile south of the city on the Erie R.R. To-day is the big day, the city is full of strangers and has a very lively appearance.

I got Uncle Barnard's clock home without further mis-

MARIA KILBOURN EASTMAN

haps than the loss of the key as I got off the car, and it is now in running order.

How does Mr. Gage fill my place at the churn? Does he earn his board? I yearn to clasp the dasher of the churn to my bosom once more. The girl says she will give me a chance to wipe dishes here, but somehow or other I don't seem to hanker after it.

I feel a great deal better than before I went away and think that with the help of some exercise at the gymnasium I shall be able to stand it till my next vacation, then, if I do not have a month it will not be my fault.

Mr. Buell, my senior employer, celebrates his golden wedding a week from to-day. He is about 72 years old, his partner (in business, I mean) is 26; some difference in years and still more in looks.

Ellen sent an invitation by me for Miss Ella Newton to visit her, as I did not see Miss Newton I forgot to deliver it. Will you, when you see her, please tell her that Ellen wants her to come and see her?

Mother sends her love to all.

With a great deal of love to yourself, Cousin Carrie and the others,

I remain your

Adopted brother

GEORGE

Mary received another letter the following month, and with this record his adolescent correspondence ends.

ROCHESTER, N.Y. *Oct* 12/71

MY DEAR COUSIN.

I take this evening as the only opportunity I shall have for some time to answer your letter.

The Chicago fire has given us a job that will keep us

busy for a week or two. Several of the Companies represented by us have suspended, which necessitates the
making of new policies covering property to the amount
of three quarters of a million or more. I have had 30
minutes for dinner and thirty minutes for supper to-day
& expect to work till ten or eleven o'clock & ditto for the
rest of the week.

Just now there is a lull in the storm while 'the heads'
decide on a course of action, which I take advantage
of.

You mentioned Cousin Emeline's being in Chicago; I
trust she got away from there without accident. I have
thought of her a great many times since I got your letter
and hoped that she was safe at Kingsville.

I suppose Cousin Porter & Mr. Webster are among the
victims of the great fire. I hope their losses are small.
Was not the fire awful — but I suppose you know more
of the details than I, if Cousin Emeline has got home.

We had a very pleasant but short visit from Cousin
Delia & her mother. We wished we could have made it
pleasant for them to stay longer.

Every time I go up stairs to see Mrs. Ranney, she sets
me at work on her machine, says 'make yourself useful
as well as ornamental,' but I always think of you; I do
not consider that debt paid, but will call it even till I
come again.

I hope to hear from you before long. Kingsville news
will always interest me with such a Chronicler.

I have felt pretty well ever since I came home. My
lungs do not do exactly the fair thing by me but I guess
they will be all right when it comes cold weather.

How is Cousin Carrie? Has she commenced that tidy
she was going to make for me when I got married? Tell
her to make it alike on both sides.

Give my love to Mary Luce. Does she consider me a success as a Wart Doctor?

We have just received a letter from Ellen. She says the baby has gained a pound a week & is getting along nicely. Mother is always asking me who it looks like — as though a young one 3 weeks old looks like anything but a little monkey.

Mother joins me in love to all the relatives. With a great deal of love for yourself, I am, in haste,

Your brother

GEO

In November, George took his first dancing lessons, and for Christmas he framed a picture for his mother and, also, remembered Cousin Mary.

He began the year 1872 with $516.95 'on hand,' and in February made his first investment, withdrawing five hundred dollars from the savings bank to buy a mortgage bond. As his salary had increased to forty-seven dollars a month, he took out another life insurance policy in favor of his mother. More photographs were purchased, his tools were sharpened, and he began to do extra work at night. In July he made his first trip to Niagara Falls, bought an atlas, and in August took a three weeks' vacation, visiting Boston, Portland, Bath, and Squirrel Island, Maine, where he sailed and fished. Upon his return he made his first payment on his first adventure in real estate, 'lots in Brighton,' east of Rochester, which he lost eventually when the development failed. For the whole year the recapitulation showed assets for the first time above one thousand dollars.

During 1873 and 1874, George spent more time at his workbench, enlarged his tool kit, made a trip to Chicago, attended more lectures and concerts, sent 'Miss P' flowers, bought his first razor, took his mother out to dinner, indulged a little more in candy and figs, paid twelve dollars for a pair of trousers, and increased his payments for board and his Sunday School offerings. The next year he bought his first technical books, journeyed to Watkins Glen on his twenty-first birthday, bought 'cigars for the boys,' went to the local rifle gallery to learn to shoot, made his first checker board, and paid his first pew rent at Saint Luke's Episcopal Church.

Within these few years the boy had become a man. In April, 1874, he had left the insurance office to become a junior bookkeeper in the Rochester Savings Bank. By the summer of 1876 he was receiving $1400 a year, and his accounts show that he took over all the household financial responsibilities from his mother, superintended the 'spring cleaning,' purchased new carpets and furnishings, including more pictures and new frames. For a time the monthly expenditures for candy had been succeeded by medicine and doctors' bills. He needed more exercise. Bank work, combined with bench work at home at night or with reading and study, were too confining, so he took riding lessons and began to feel better.

In the mean time his savings had increased. January 1, 1877, he had $3600 invested and cash on hand. His mother was comfortable and happy and there was no immediate danger of poverty, but he was unsatisfied. Advancement in insurance and banking, the two careers he had experienced, resembled too much the 'covered wagon' days and not at all the advancing age of machinery. But no one, not even his mother, knew what was going on in his mind.

The summer of 1877 passed without a vacation, which was, in itself, unusual. Horseback riding and croquet games continued and so did the doctor's calls and the

CURRENCY USED IN THE EASTMAN COMMERCIAL COLLEGE

medicine, but tools were sharpened again, new 'science primers' were added to his workroom, while his inquisitive eyes and inquiring mind struggled with the possibilities of the future. Each day at the bank there was the same concentration. At home his mother noticed ever more application to his reading, nevertheless he was ready and willing to go out with her, or do whatever he thought would add to her happiness. Although he might jump from planet to planet in his own thinking, she was his fixed star.

By Thanksgiving the secret was out. His interest in pictures had been transferred to the cumbersome paraphernalia of picture-making. Purchasing $94.36 worth of 'sundries and lenses,' he arranged with George H. Monroe, a local photographer, to teach him the meticulous studio science called 'the art of photography.' [1]

Although experiments in photography had been progressing for at least three quarters of a century, there was as great a gap in results between 1802 and 1877 as there was between Franklin's lightning rod and Morse's telegraph. And there was as great an abyss between the telegraph and the radio as there was between 'wet plate' photography and the film system, as the high-lights and shadows of the early history of photography reveal.

In 1802, Wedgwood, an Englishman, utilized two discoveries of the sixteenth century to make silhouettes. The first was the 'camera obscura,' [2] a box with a lens covering a hole in one side, now commonly ascribed to an Italian physicist, Giovanni Battista della Porta, about 1553. The other discovery is attributed to J. H. Schultze, who observed that silver nitrate and other silver compounds were sensitive to light.

[1] 'Photography' is coined from two Greek words meaning 'light writing.'
[2] 'Camera obscura' is the Latin for 'dark room.'

Wedgwood's experiments were only partially successful, but they were followed by the work of another Englishman, Davy, who got better pictures. Yet even he had to lament at the end of his work: 'Nothing but a method of preventing the unshaded parts from being colored by exposure to the day is wanting to render this process as useful as it is elegant.' There was still no way to keep the light which made the picture from destroying it afterward.[1]

The problem of 'fixing' was solved in 1839, when Sir John Herschel recommended to Louis Jacques Mandé Daguerre his own discovery of twenty years earlier, hyposulphite of soda, since familiar to the photographic world as 'hypo.' Then, at last, pictures stayed as they were taken.

Daguerre was an artist who used the 'camera obscura' for sketching purposes. His reason for experimenting with photography was the desire to save labor — to catch the image photographically rather than by means of sketches. Joseph Nicephore Niepce, another Frenchman, was interested in finding a method of automatically copying designs upon lithographic stone. In 1839 they formed a partnership, and on August 19 of the same year presented a full description of the daguerreotype at a meeting of the Academy of Arts and Sciences in Paris.

Daguerre and Niepce used a copper plate, coated with

[1] 'It is difficult to give a date to the beginnings of photography. Perhaps the discovery was made by the man who first noticed that the skin is tanned by the summer sun. The sun's rays effect almost every known chemical to some extent.' (Charles R. Gibson in *Photography as a Scientific Instrument.*) In *Pencil and Nature* (1844), Fox Talbot wrote: 'Some time previously to the period of which I have been speaking (1838) I met with an account of some researches on the action of light by Wedgwood and Sir Humphry Davy. Their short memoir on this subject was published in 1802. ... It is curious and interesting and certainly establishes their claim as the inventors of the photographic art, though the actual progress they made in it was small.'

a sensitive surface of silver fumed with iodine. After exposure in the camera, the plate was held over a dish of warm mercury until the vapor clung to the parts of the plate where the light had acted. The silver iodide of the sensitive coating was then dissolved away by hyposulphite of soda and the light areas appeared mercury-white, while the dark parts retained the black metallic silver surface of the plate.

Daguerre's process was the first to cross the Atlantic, and in the famous diary of Philip Hone, of New York City, written in 1839, appears the most remarkable prophecy in the history of photography — of pictures that would record sound as well as light:

'I went this morning by invitation of Monsieur Francis-Gourand, to see a collection of the views made by the wonderful process lately discovered in France by Monsieur Daguerre, which is called by his name. Mr. Gourand is the pupil and friend of the inventor, and he comes to this country to make known the process.

'The pictures he has are extremely beautiful — they consist of views in Paris, and exquisite collections of the objects of still life. The manner of producing them constitutes one of the wonders of modern times, and, like other miracles, one may almost be excused for disbelieving it without seeing the very process by which it is created. Every object, however minute, is a perfect transcript of the thing itself; the hair of the human head, the gravel on a roadside, the texture of a silk curtain, or the shadow of the smaller leaf reflected upon the wall, are all imprinted as carefully as nature or art has created them in the objects transferred; and those things which are invisible to the naked eye are rendered apparent by the help of a mighty magnifying glass.

'It appears to me not less wonderful that light should

be made an active operating power in this manner, and
that some such effect should be produced by sound; and
who knows whether, in this age of invention and discoveries, we may not be called upon to marvel at the
exhibition of the human voice muttering over a metal
plate prepared in the same or some other manner the
words "tree," "horse," and "ship." How greatly ashamed
of their ignorance the bygone generations of mankind
ought to be!'

Among the early experimenters in this country were
Professor John W. Draper, of New York University, and
Professor Samuel F. B. Morse, inventor of the telegraph.
For several years there was a controversy over which
one took the first picture of a person with the eyes open.
It is now commonly attributed to Professor Draper. 'In
the scientific world,' he wrote,[1] 'it is recognized that
priority of publication shall be considered as establishing
priority of discovery or invention. I published in the
"London and Edinburgh Philosophical Magazine" in
March, 1840, an announcement that I had succeeded in
procuring portraits by the Daguerreotype, and shortly
afterwards in the same journal, gave a detailed account
of the whole operation. In these publications the invention, of course, was openly claimed by me and Prof.
Morse's name was never mentioned. He saw them while
they were in manuscript, and again after they were
printed, and put forth no counter claim. Indeed, I
believe he never published anything on daguerreotype
portraiture.

[1] *Scribner's Monthly*, October 20, 1873.
'Probably the first really successful celestial photograph was made in
1840 by J. W. Draper. He was able to obtain negatives of the moon, showing
the principal formations of her surface. Ten years later, in 1850, Bond and
Whipple made still better moon pictures at Harvard College.' (*New International Encyclopædia.*)

GEORGE EASTMAN AT THE AGE OF THREE

'As to experiments in the glass studio for the purpose of taking photographs with the eyes open, I can assure you that many very perfect portraits with the eyes open had been made by me long before that expense was encountered. Let me add that at this time Prof. Morse was completely occupied with the invention of his telegraph; he had his apparatus in my laboratory; he was not familiar either with chemical or optical science, and took an interest in photographic portraiture only from an artistic point of view, his earlier life having been devoted, as is well known, to painting as a profession.'

The Daguerreotype results 'were very beautiful,[1] but these early processes of photography required very great exposures so that at first the unfortunate subject had to sit for as long as ten minutes in the full sun without moving in order to impress the plate sufficiently. Although many experiments were made in an attempt to find substances more sensitive to light so that the exposure could be reduced, the only real solution was to find some method by which light had to do only a little of the work and the production of the image itself could be effected by chemical action instead of by the action of the light.

'A great step in this direction was taken by Fox Talbot in 1841. He found that if he prepared a sheet of paper with silver iodide and exposed it in the camera he got only a very faint image, but if after exposure he washed over the paper with a solution containing silver nitrate and gallic acid, a solution from which metallic silver is very easily deposited, then this solution deposited the silver where the light had acted and built up the faint image into a strong picture. This building up of a faint image or, indeed, of an image which is altogether invisible, into a picture is what is now called "development."

[1] From *The Fundamentals of Photography*, by Dr. C. E. K. Mees.

'Fox Talbot was not only the first to develop a faint or invisible image; he was also the first man to make a negative and use it for printing. . . . Of course, the paper was not transparent as our film is, but he made it more transparent by treating it with oil or wax.'

'The next step of great importance,' writes Gibson, the English authority, 'was the introduction of collodion. Although a method of nitro-cellulose had been discovered in 1846 by Schoenbein, and although its application to photography seems to have been suggested first by Le Grey of Paris, it was F. Scott Archer (an English architect) who first used it in the making of photographic negatives' (1848).[1] This was the 'wet collodion' process which was in vogue in 1877 when George Eastman began to study photography. It is clearly described in a contemporaneous magazine article, 'The Wonders of Photography':

'The negative, from which photographs are printed, is what you sit for while in the sky-light. It is so called, because the lights and shades therein are reversed from those in your figure. Or, in other words, if your hair and eyes and dress are dark, they will appear light in the nega-

[1] 'In 1848 Niepce de Saint-Victor, who was a nephew of the original Niepce, used a film of albumen on a sheet of glass to hold the sensitive compound. He coated the glass with white of egg and potassium iodide, and when this was dry he treated it with a solution of silver nitrate, and this was exposed either in the wet or dry state in the camera, and afterwards developed with gallic acid.

'It should be noted that in this method Niepce de Saint-Victor was the first to use a film on the glass for carrying the sensitive salts. Glass plates had been used some time previously (1840) by Sir John Herschel, but he had no supporting film, merely placing the silver salt solution on the glass.

'In 1840 Professor Joseph Petzval introduced his portrait lens. He was a professor of mathematics in the University of Vienna. . . . In 1845 W. H. F. Talbot published *Sun Pictures of Scotland*, a collection of photographs. In 1841 he patented the "Calotype" process, later called the "Talbotype." It is interesting to note that Queen Victoria and the Prince Consort practiced the art of Talbotype, having a dark-room equipped at Windsor.' (Gibson.)

tive, and vice versa. They appear in their proper place in the pictures, which are called positives.

'The negative is made on clear, crystal glass, first polished and well cleaned with powdered rotten-stone or alcohol, coated with a creamy mixture of ether, alcohol, gun-cotton, and sundry bromides and iodides, and dipped into a bath of pure water and nitrate of silver, after remaining in which a few moments, the collodion film becomes highly sensitive to the light, being impregnated with the silver solution, which makes it turn black whenever light is permitted to strike it. This fact may be proved by pouring a little nitrate of silver over a piece of paper and placing a leaf thereon; after exposure to the sun a while, an imprint of the leaf will be found on the paper, showing every vein and pore black, where the light has shone through, white where the substance of the leaf has covered the paper. In the same way are negatives made, and your image is fixed in the sensitized film by the sunbeams as they dance around you while you are sitting for your picture.

'After the sitting, the artist takes the negative into the mysterious little dark-room; we will go along and see what he does, provided you walk softly and make no dust, for dust is a great enemy to successful manipulation, and that is why "no admittance" is placed over every dark-room door, and why the doings inside are kept so mysteriously secret.

'You shall now see him pour a solution over your negative, which at first looks like a frost-covered window, and watching it a moment, you shall see your own image come up from the hoary surface and stand out in bold relief before you, an unmistakable likeness, but a negative. It is now well washed, fixed with another solution, dried, varnished, and placed in the hands of the printer.

'We pass through a room where several young ladies are at work, floating pure white sheets of paper upon a substance made of the white of eggs and called albumen. These sheets, after being hung over wooden rods until dry, are pressed, and taken into a second dark-room, where they receive treatment not unlike that of your negative. The sheet is floated upon a silver solution, dried thoroughly, placed in a closed box containing ammonia, where it is fumed a little while, after which it is ready for the printer. He places the paper and the negative face to face, presses them together in a wooden frame, and places both in the light. In a little while, if the light be strong, the paper becomes entirely changed in color, and your image, as you appeared to the operator, is plainly visible upon its surface. Expose it to the light, however, and it will soon grow black. To prevent this, the print must be washed well and then fixed, which requires the aid of yet another solution, composed of hyposulphate of soda and water.

'After fixing, it is again washed, but does not yet assume the proper tone and color. This is attained by another process, called toning, which consists in dipping the print in a solution of chloride of gold and other ingredients. A grand and final bath is now given the print, wherein it is made to whirl around and wash itself for several hours, by sundry saucy streams of water shooting at it all the time. From this bath it is taken, dried, neatly trimmed, pasted on a card, dried, pressed, polished, and delivered to you, after having whirled through at least twenty-five different pairs of hands or through the same hands as often.

'But Photography is not to be confined, nor is it, to taking the pictures of coarse, ugly men and capricious women. True, the way in which it accomplishes this is extremely wonderful, and enough for one art to accomplish, but it is not all. It is becoming daily of more and more importance, though yet in its infancy, and its uses and appliance are just beginning to be discovered.

'Men who would not be seen handling a box or dusting a shelf in their own store, boast of fingers and linen stained with nitrate of silver and odoriferous chemicals, and are not ashamed to carry their tents and other apparatus upon their backs up and down through the country, with dusty faces and perspiring brows, even at the risk of having the country children taking them for a hand-organ man and clamoring for music!'

The taking as well as the making of photographs in 1877 was a fastidious affair. The sensitive-coated glass plates had to be exposed in the camera while wet, in fact the development, too, had to be completed before the emulsion dried. When pictures were taken in the field, the common expression then for out-of-doors, the photographer had to lug a complete coating and developing outfit with him in a pack on his back, or in a wheelbarrow.

'But in those days, one did not "take" a camera; one accompanied the outfit of which the camera was only a part,' Eastman recalled.[1] 'I bought an outfit and learned that it took not only a strong but also a dauntless man to be an outdoor photographer. My layout, which included only the essentials, had in it a camera about the size of a soap box, a tripod, which was strong and heavy enough to support a bungalow, a big plate-holder, a dark-tent, a nitrate bath, and a container for water. The glass plates were not, as now, in the holder ready for use; they were what is known as "wet plates" — that is, glass which had

[1] This excerpt is from the first interview Eastman authorized, in *System*, October, 1920.

to be coated with collodion and then sensitized with nitrate of silver in the field just before exposure. Hence the nitrate of silver was something that always had to go along and it was perhaps the most awkward companion imaginable on a journey. Being corrosive, the container had to be of glass and the cover tight — for silver nitrate is not a liquid to get intimate with. The first time that I took a silver bath away with me, I wrapped it with exceeding great care and put it in my trunk. The cover leaked, the nitrate got out, and stained most of my clothing.

'This was in Grant's administration, and every one was talking about purchasing Samana Bay in Santo Domingo as a naval base. Santo Domingo struck my fancy, and, carefully figuring out the expense, the trip down there seemed feasible. I talked it over with a man at the bank who had been an assistant to the photographer of the famous Powell Survey, and he told me what a wonderful thing it would be to take a camera along and make a real record of the expedition.

'I did not go to Santo Domingo. But that did not matter so much because, in making ready, I had become wholly absorbed in photography — in spite of all the trouble involved and in spite of the fact that, wherever I set up my apparatus, a crowd drew around as though I were going to open a patent-medicine show. One burning hot day I set up my encampment to go about photographing the natural bridge at Mackinac and then disappeared into my little teepee to make the plates ready. When I came out, a party of tourists had draped themselves about the bridge in the engaging attitudes that were then thought necessary when one was photographed close to nature.

'I paid no attention to them, took several exposures,

and, when I had finished, one of the men came forward and inquired the price. I told him that I was an amateur making pictures for my own amusement and not for sale. He exploded:

' "Then why did you let us stand in the hot sun for a full half-hour while you fooled around with your contraptions! You ought to wear a sign saying that you are an amateur!"

'Being an amateur was, I suppose, arduous work, but one never finds a hobby hard riding and I went out taking photographs whenever I could, read everything that was written on the subject, and generally tried to put myself on the plane of the professional photographer without, however, any idea of going into the business of photography. Since I took my views mostly outdoors — I had no studio — the bulk of the paraphernalia worried me. It seemed that one ought to be able to carry less than a pack-horse load.'

At this time, in the course of his reading, Eastman came across an article in the 'Almanac' of the 'British Journal of Photography,' giving the formula for making a sensitive gelatine emulsion, with which the glass plates could be coated and used when dry.

'The English article started me in the right direction. I began in my spare time — for I was still working in the bank — to compose an emulsion [1] that could be coated

[1] To make an emulsion that would take good photographs was a tedious task as may be judged from the following account which Eastman sent a fellow amateur:

'You will have no difficulty in getting great rapidity with the following provided your light is all right. You will of course see it is essentially Bennett and I make no claim whatever beyond a slight change in proportions:

Gel 40 grs. Bro Am 23½ grs. Water ¾ oz.
Silver 40 grs. Water ¼ oz.

'Raise temperature of solution to 150° fahr. & unite slowly, shaking between additions of the silver. Then place in the bath and keep at 100° *five*

and dried on the glass plate and retain its properties long enough to be used in the field and thus avoid lugging around the dark-tent and silver bath. My first results did not amount to much, but finally I came upon a coating of gelatine and silver bromide that had all the necessary photographic qualities. . . . At first I wanted to make photography simpler merely for my own convenience, but soon I thought of the possibilities of commercial production.'

Eastman had been working at night, frequently all night long, sleeping mostly on Sundays. He was as 'thin as pie crust,' but he had an idea. He would make dry plates and market them as the Liverpool Dry Plate Company, Wratten & Wainwright, Ltd., and B. J. Edwards were doing in England! He would give up his clerkship at the bank and go into business! These thoughts stimulated him to action. In an hour of youthful exaltation he wrote to his Uncle Horace H. Eastman, disclosing his ideas, but when the postman brought the answer the young man read:

WATERVILLE 13*th* *Jan* 1878

DEAR GEORGE

Yours of the 10th inst is received. I regret that I cannot comply with your request. I would do anything for you in this respect that I would do for Harvey. [His own son.]

At my age my business acts must relate more to the present and not so much involve the uncertain future. I am now living on borrowed time, having already

---

days. Then precip. with 2 oz. 95% alcohol or wash in any desired way, one way being as good as another if you extract all the nitrate you can discover by testing and provided the wash water does not dilute the above to more than 1½ oz. finished emulsion. Add ¾ dr. alcohol and 10 m. of 8 gr. sol. chr. alum, filter and coat. Two days in the bath gives about wet-plate rapidity. Some kept 7 days was about five times as rapid.'

passed my three score & ten. When I reached this age I so arranged my business matters that I could not keep faith with others by becoming a party to any agreement the future fulfillment of which could in the slightest degree be uncertain or doubtful or depend upon future contingency, so you will see I decline not because I have not the most perfect confidence in your honesty & integrity — but because the objection is purely *personal to myself* and would apply in reference to any other person living.

Notwithstanding I do not hold out to you the coveted inducement to visit us — we shall be very glad to see you & hope you will give us an opportunity.

You said nothing about your mother. We shall expect a long visit from her when warm weather comes — Remember us to her.

Your uncle

HORACE

The refusal was final, of course, but not an insurmountable obstacle. He could start with his own savings on a smaller scale and work up. This he proceeded to do. He increased his purchases of photographic materials, cooked his own emulsions, coated the plates, took his own pictures, developed the negatives, and made his own prints. By July, things were progressing so well that he decided upon a trip to Lake Superior on his vacation to test his own product in a different locality. By January, 1879, he was so absorbed in his experiments and his reading of 'the state of the art' in the British and American photographic magazines that he decided to enlarge his reading by studying German and French. A teacher was engaged, grammars and 'keys' were bought, as well as cod liver oil and porous plasters! All of these details were faithfully recorded in his notebooks.

By June, 1879, he was not only making plates which were 'entirely successful,' but he had built an apparatus for coating them. Confident that 'nobody will coat plates by hand after they have seen the machine,' he withdrew four hundred dollars from his savings bank and made his first trip to England, the photographic center of the world. Here, during the reign of Queen Victoria, he received his first patent, July 22, 1879, and hurried home.

On September 9, 1879, through his patent attorney, George B. Selden, he made application for letters patent in the United States on 'an Improved Process of Preparing Gelatine Dry-Plates [1] for Use in Photography and in Apparatus therefor,' which were submitted to the Patent Office in Washington. Preparations were made immediately for registering the patent in France, Germany, and Belgium through Hazeltine, Lake & Co., patent agents he retained in London.

'In the preparation of gelatine dry-plates,' the specifications read, 'great difficulty has heretofore been encountered in spreading the gelatine emulsion evenly over the glass. This has ordinarily been accomplished by a glass rod, the action of which was assisted by inclining the plates slightly in different directions, causing the emulsion to flow toward the edges. It has been found difficult by this means to cover the margins of the glass or to secure an even coating on the whole surface, while the process of coating the plates in this way was necessarily slow and tedious, and therefore expensive.

'By my improved process plates are covered with a perfectly uniform coating of gelatine emulsion, extending entirely out to the edges of the plates, and this result is

[1] U.S. Patent Office, Letters Patent No. 226,503. Application filed: September 9, 1879. Issued: April 13, 1880.

PRINT FROM ONE OF 'G. EASTMAN'S FIRST GELATINE NEGATIVES
WINTER 1879-80'

accomplished very much more rapidly than inferior plates are produced by the old method.'

By fall he was in the midst of negotiations, as the letter-press copies of communications to his solicitors and prospective customers indicate.

One letter is of particular importance, as it forecasts his future business policy: [1]

[ROCHESTER]
Oct. 13/79

Messrs Mawson & Swan
     (Newcastle-on-Tyne)

GENTLEMEN:

I have definitely decided not to grant any further license to use my invention in England. While there in July I made no great effort to push it, thinking it would be better to wait than be in a hurry, hence I approached but two parties on the subject one of whom was a Mfg of Gel plates. The other did not have the cash to pay down, but made me a very good offer to work it on a royalty basis with a fair sum down besides. I accepted the offer more to get the machine working on a large scale than anything else, but I do not favor the plan generally, preferring to sell out the balance in a lump, for a sum which is much smaller than the sum represented by the royalty on the one license reserved.

I am not at liberty to give you a definite refusal, but I will say that if you are prepared to pay the price which I now ask, five hundred pounds cash, my solicitors, Messrs Hazeltine, Lake & Co., Southampton Bldgs, Chancery Lane, have full power to close the matter, provided they have not already done so with another party.

[1] All these early letters were written in longhand. Special ink was used, so that copies could be made in letter-press books.

I am as yet connected with photography as an amateur only but am making preparations to engage in the manufacture of Gelatine Plates on a *large scale* and expect my invention to enable me, if necessary, to *put* the *price down* to a point which will *prevent miscellaneous competition.*

If your Mr. Swan thinks of coming over to the States I should like to hear from you on the subject and perhaps we might be of some use to each other. I should also like to hear the merits of his process.

In the mean time believe me

Yours very truly,

GEORGE EASTMAN

By December, he had sold the English rights, but the pay was so slow he would have been financially embarrassed had he been dependent upon it. Instead, he went to work improving the machine and experimenting with emulsions. Like Thomas A. Edison, who had tested thousands of filaments for his electric light, Eastman had boiled and tested many emulsions and engaged in a detailed, technical correspondence with George H. Johnson, an amateur photographer of Bridgeport, Connecticut.

By April, 1880, Eastman had leased the 'entire third floor of a large building in the heart of the city' and was 'pretty well located,' he wrote Samuel Fry, of London. July 11 he sent him another enthusiastic letter: 'I have just ordered another application filed for an English patent. It is a big thing and I will write you about it hereafter.'

His second invention was a new machine which differed radically from the first one. 'It is not expensive to make, simple, easy to clean,' Eastman wrote, 'works as rapidly as anything heretofore devised, is adjustable to any size plate. In short it is an eminently practical apparatus for every one who uses emulsion in large or small quantities.'

August 18, 1880, he initiated his first merchandising effort outside his home city, with the following self-explanatory letter to E. & H. T. Anthony, the largest photographic house in New York City:

'Word came to me through Mr. Monroe that your Mr. E. Anthony, whom he saw at Alexandria Bay, desired me to write you before I placed my Gelatine plates upon the market.

'This I am now preparing to do and hence this letter.

'My formula is in very excellent condition and has been thoroughly tested through the hot weather both as regards manufacture and manipulation of the plates. I am also supplied with a stock of tested chemicals. Therefore I shall be prepared to commence manufacture as soon as my laboratory is fitted up, it being almost complete at this time.

'If you should desire to make any arrangements looking to the handling of the plates on the market — I should be very happy to hear from you, to furnish you with prints or negatives or to show you the great simplicity of the manipulation of my plates.

'The capacity of my works will be somewhat limited at first but with the aid of recently perfected apparatus and machinery will be capable of rapid expansion if the demand requires it.

'The apparatus spoken of will also materially *reduce the cost of manufacture upon a large scale.*'

A few days before Thanksgiving, 1880, exactly three years after he had become seriously interested in photography, Eastman was in business for himself. His laboratory was complete. Labels and developing directions were printed. Boxes were made in which the plates could be safely shipped. Anthony had placed orders to be filled in December totaling $1053.08. 'As soon as details of mfg.,' he wrote the New York Agency, 'are fully systematized, *I shall advertise extensively* in all the photo-journals *and put competent operators on the road to demonstrate* the working of the plates.'

Eastman's fame, too, had spread. British photographic journals recognized his inventions. Romain Talbot wrote from Berlin for the 'entire German rights.' The leading professional photographers in Chicago and Washington, D.C., had heard of his dry plates and after examining some of his prints and negatives pronounced them 'the best dry plate work' on the market and sent in their orders. The Smithsonian Institution and the United States Government bureaus also were making inquiries.

CHAPTER II

THE EPIC STORY OF FILM

THESE were epochal days in the United States.

The year 1876 had marked the end of the first century of the independence of the United States and the beginning of another period which was to witness the greatest economic and social revolution in the history of the world. From 1776 to the Philadelphia Centennial one hundred years later, political theory and practice dominated both this country and the world. From 1876 to the present, all of the fundamental human institutions, as far as civilization is concerned, have been changed by the operation of new economic forces which evolved from a series of great inventions beginning with the telephone and extending to the airplane.[1] Family life, private property, the State, the Church, and the University [2] have been altered completely and radically within the

[1] During the brief span of twenty-seven years, from 1876 to 1903, there were twelve basic inventions:
1. 1876, the telephone, by Alexander Graham Bell.
2. 1877, the talking machine, by Thomas A. Edison.
3. 1879, the electric light, by Edison.
4. 1879, the gasoline automobile, although the first practical car was not built until 1895.
5. 1884–87, the trolley car by Van Depoele & Sprague.
6. 1884, photographic film and roll-holder by Eastman and William H. Walker, followed by transparent film in 1889.
7. 1885, the linotype by Mergenthaler.
8. 1885, electric furnace reduction by Cowles.
9. 1888, the recording adding machine by Burroughs.
10. 1889, the motion-picture machine by Edison.
11. 1896, high frequency wireless by Marconi.
12. 1903, the airplane by Orville and Wilbur Wright.

[2] This is Dr. Nicholas Murray Butler's classification of the fundamental human institutions.

brief space of fifty-three years (1876–1929). While the thoughts which produced this peaceful upheaval were original with only a few men, their ideas, once planted in the minds of others, have been multiplied beyond all possibility of calculation. 'Every revolution,' said Emerson, 'was first a thought in one man's mind, and when the same thought occurs to another man, it is the key to the era.'

These extraordinary discoveries and developments of modern science were not foreseen in the administration of President Grant. Some of the reasons why may be more evident, perhaps, if reference is made to a few of the important subjects presented in the President's final annual message to the Congress, December 5, 1876. These reasons, too, will serve to convey an appreciation of national conditions when the industrial pioneers began their efforts at *new* construction, not the reconstruction with which Grant had struggled for eight years.

'At the beginning of my first administration the work of reconstruction, much embarrassed by the long delay, virtually commenced,' the Presidential message read, 'the country was laboring under an enormous debt . . . and taxation was so oppressive as to discourage production.' Since then 'the balance of trade has been changed from over $130,000,000 against the United States in 1869 to more than $120,000,000 in our favor in 1876 . . . and it is confidently believed . . . that the pledge of Congress to resume specie payments in 1879 will be easily accomplished.

'The international exhibition held in Philadelphia this year . . . has proven a great success, and will, no doubt, be of enduring advantage to the country. It has shown the great progress in the arts, sciences and mechanical skill made in a single century, and demonstrated that we

are but little behind older nations in any one branch,
while in some we scarcely have a rival. It has served, too,
not only to bring peoples and products of skill and labor
from all parts of the world together, but in bringing together people from all sections of our own country, which
must prove a great benefit in the information imparted
and pride of country engendered.'

Such was the state of the Union when the period of
inventions began which laid the foundations for a new
world. First came the telephone, which Professor Alexander Graham Bell exhibited at the Philadelphia Exhibition. 'The first man of consequence to befriend the
telephone was Lord Kelvin, then an untitled young
scientist.' [1] Returning to England, he became the champion of the instrument before the British Association for
the Advancement of Science, but as late as 1880 Herbert
Spencer wrote: 'The telephone is scarcely used at all in
London, and is unknown in the other English cities.'

The adoption of the telephone in this country was
equally slow. There was 'only one lonely idle telephone
in the White House, used by the servants' during the
administrations of Presidents Cleveland and Harrison.[2]
But all industries were small. Water and gas were the
only public utilities. Steel was an infant industry. In
1876 only 533,191 long tons of steel were produced in this
country.[3]

By 1878 'New England was peopling the Middle West,
whose restive resident settlers, in turn, were filling up the
vast grain territories beyond the Mississippi . . . Austria-
Hungary, Bohemia, Italy, and Poland were sending the
vanguard of the great army of laborers soon to fill the
manufacturing plants.

[1] Herbert N. Casson, in the *History of the Telephone*. [2] *Ibid.*
[3] Fifty years later the production totaled 48,293,736 long tons.

'Nearly five hundred railroads sold under foreclosure of mortgages during the preceding three years had been re-organized under plans which provided funds for recon-struction. Replacement of streaks of rust with new and heavy rails suddenly became an absolute necessity of the big combinations effected under the lead of the Penn-sylvania and Vanderbilt systems.

'Iron and steel factories could not resume operations rapidly enough to meet the demands.' [1]

Andrew and Thomas Carnegie, while active in the manufacture of steel, had not yet incorporated Carnegie Brothers and Company.[2] Andrew W. Mellon was just beginning his career in his father's bank in Pittsburgh.

In 1876, Joseph Pulitzer founded the 'St. Louis Post-Dispatch,' Melville E. Stone issued the first number of the 'Chicago Daily News,' and Cyrus H. K. Curtis moved from his birthplace in Maine to Philadelphia. Two years later, W. Duke Sons and Company were 'manufacturing and selling tobacco leaf bought from other farmers,' and in the following year F. W. Woolworth started his Five and Ten Cent business.[3] The United States had less than fifty million inhabitants, conditions in the South were still chaotic, and New York City 'was a comfortable, placid, provincial town where every one spoke English and knew every one else by his first name.' [4]

[1] From *Henry Clay Frick*, by George Harvey.

[2] This company was incorporated in 1881. This was the year Theodore Roosevelt first became a candidate for public office. Woodrow Wilson was teaching in the South and had not yet been called to his professorship at Bryn Mawr College, while Calvin Coolidge was a nine-year-old schoolboy in Vermont and Herbert Hoover, aged seven, was growing up in Iowa. These facts are of more than passing interest in view of the far-reaching importance of their public policies toward business during their respective administrations.

[3] It was not until 1885 that James B. Duke, 'the driver, went after volume and organization.' (From Forbes, *Men Who Are Making America*.)

[4] Statement by Ralph D. Blumenfeld, editor of the London *Daily Express*.

In 1876, after working as a newsboy and telegrapher in many parts of the United States and Canada, Edison had moved to Menlo Park, New Jersey. Here within three years he created the talking machine, followed by the electric light, which, on October 21, 1879, 'maintained its incandescence for over forty hours,' forcing a nation of skeptics to take to cover.

Boarding with Mrs. Eastman in these historic days were Colonel and Mrs. Henry A. Strong.[1] He was a well-to-do partner in Strong, Woodbury and Company, leading whip manufacturers. Up to 1880 he was only an interested observer, but Eastman's own carefully calculated confidence impressed him so greatly that he began to discuss the financial side of the business with him. The prospects of substantial profits were self-evident. Early in December, he decided to become a partner. Then he left on a business trip to the Middle West, and on December 14, 1880, we find the first of a long series of intimate letters exchanged between these two men.

DEAR GEORGE:

Your welcome letter of seventh instant received at Minneapolis and right glad was I to hear of your progress. I do not think you have reached bottom yet on price of glass so keep up your inquiries while your present stock lasts and be ready for the lowest man when it is time to order again. You will probably have the same experience in all the material you have to purchase. Dealers require constant watching and often when you are sure you have touched bottom, some darned fool will come along and knock the bottom clean out. I hope to reach home on

[1] Henry Alvah Strong was born in Rochester, August 30, 1838. In 1861 he enlisted in the Navy, became a paymaster, and served four years during the Civil War.

Sunday or Monday next or on Tuesday at the very latest. I was pretty confident that Anthony intended to obtain the monopoly of your goods, to which of course there is no objection, provided he binds himself to take all you can produce, but such a contract should be as firm, solid and sure as the rock of ages so that there would be no possible loophole of escape on their part. Hope you have discovered some good locations, so that you can grow promptly and rapidly.

But I must close. We both send you love and regards to you all,

Yours truly

HENRY

Two days before Christmas, the Strongs returned to Rochester and the Colonel invested his first one thousand dollars in George Eastman's enterprise.[1]

Meanwhile Edison was laying the foundation for the world's greatest public utility. In 1881 he opened business offices at 65 Fifth Avenue, New York City, and established the first commercial incandescent lamp factory at Harrison, New Jersey. On September 4, 1882, he commenced the operation of the first commercial central station in New York City for the distribution of electric current for light, power, and heat. The same year Eastman became one of his first customers,[2] and two years later, wrote a testimonial for the electric light:

[1] 'I retained my place in the Savings Bank until Sept. 1881, giving the business what attention I could between the hours of three P.M. and breakfast time.' (Eastman to William H. Walker, October 9, 1890.)

[2] 'On page 21 of the 14th Bulletin of the Edison Electric Light Company, 65 Fifth Avenue, dated October 14, 1882, the name of the Eastman Dry Plate Company (photographic materials) of Rochester, New York, appears with the entry, "16 lamps." The Bulletin stated: "There are now 123 Edison isolated plants aggregating 211,998 lamps, running or in process of installation in various parts of the United States. . . ." In Bulletin 16, dated February 2, 1883, on page 16, the Eastman Dry Plate Company appears as one of the

COLONEL HENRY ALVAH STRONG

December 2, 1884

Edison Co for Ins. Lgty

GENTLEMEN:

In reply to your favor Dec. 1st we would say that the plant you put in for us *over two years ago* is giving good satisfaction and answers the requirements of our business for a steady uniform light.

All of our chemical work is done by artificial light and we run your machine twelve or more hours per day. We usually run about twenty-five lights, and we have turned our armature down twice in the time that has passed since it was put in.

Yours truly

GEO EASTMAN, Treas.

This was the naïve beginning of one of the most far-reaching business relationships in the history of American industry, for seven years later, Edison became Eastman's customer when these two men working independently laid the foundations for one of the largest businesses in the world.

Fifty years ago large-scale or mass production was confined almost exclusively to bulk products such as oil, steel, coke, coal, or other minerals, which were being drawn in apparently inexhaustible quantities from a country fabulously rich in natural resources, and converted into finished products. On the other hand, large-scale or mass production of scientific or mechanical goods by machinery was, to our knowledge, confined entirely to the clock, sewing machine, and gun factories of New England. Rockefeller, Carnegie, and Frick were manu-

plants enlarged after trial, having increased their plant from "E" dynamo and 15 "A" lamps to "1–Z" dynamo and 60 "A" lamps.' (Edison Historical Research Department, Orange, New Jersey.)

facturers and distributors of minerals or mineral products manufactured from raw materials already existing in large quantities for markets yawning for their business.[1]

Bell, Edison, and Eastman, however, had first to originate a product or a utility. Then they, or others, had to create a demand before they could produce in quantity. But as far as continuous scientific application of human ingenuity and mechanical precision are concerned, the manufacture of a photographic emulsion, whether spread on paper, glass, or film, adaptable to all conditions of temperature and atmosphere in the hands of an amateur or a scientist, was in 1879, and is to-day, incomparable to all other scientific manufactures.

Electricity existed prior to Bell and Edison, as photography antedated Eastman, but each created a new science — telephony, electrical illumination, and film photography. They also originated new industries. These in turn brought new occupations, new policies, new professions, new publications, a wider distribution of knowledge, new channels of communications and understanding — perhaps, also, a new cycle of civilization.[2]

[1] In the mean time there were also significant developments in oil and transportation. 'By the eighties it had become common knowledge that the Standard Oil Company controlled more than ninety per cent of the country's refining business. How this control had been secured, how it was exercised, and whether the mechanism of control was within the law, were mysteries.' Although that was 'the original trust,' the word 'trust' as a name for a combination aiming at monopoly did not come into the language until 1882. (*Our Times*, by Mark Sullivan.)

[2] 'From the treatment accorded Bell and his associates, from the vicious attacks upon their fairly won and amply proved patents, there is no escaping the conclusion that business morals and commercial decency in the eighties were lower than they are to-day. Every innovation has to endure ordeal by competition; but there is present in our modern world more of the spirit of fair play in such tests than existed in the early eighties. Many causes have contributed to this elevation of the ethics of trade; a vast amount of cleansing water has gone over the dam of competition in fifty years; we have had our scandals and reforms, our muck-rakers and trust-busters, investigation and

But Bell, Edison, and Eastman differed from each other in their business viewpoints. Bell, besides being an inventor, had a remarkably accurate vision of the future. 'It is conceivable,' he prophesied in 1877, 'that cables of telephone wires could be laid underground or suspended overhead, connecting by branch wires with private dwellings, country houses, shops, manufactories, etc., etc., and also connecting cities and towns and various places throughout the country.' But Professor Bell lacked business ability, and the early financing and building of the company were entrusted entirely to Gardiner G. Hubbard, his father-in-law, Thomas Sanders, and Theodore N. Vail.

Edison was a wizard with little interest in those days in the commercial possibilities of his inventions, one of which he put away on a shelf for several years, unconcerned with its market potentiality. What Edison lacked in business acumen, however, the others supplied. In his tribute to Coffin, the first business genius in the electrical world, Edison himself declared: 'He was one of the greatest among the men who have so greatly contributed to the surprising increase in the wealth and prosperity of the United States.'

Eastman, however, was fascinated by the business possibilities of photography. We noted in the first chapter references in his early letters to large-scale production at low costs. The fact that he went to England before he started manufacturing in this country is evidence that he was after the European as well as the home market. Finally, his reference to extensive advertising shows that

---

legislation aplenty. Likewise we have had the benefit of certain shining examples of four-square business, in which success has been attained by fair means, and ideals of public service consistently maintained.' (Arthur Pound, in *The Telephone Idea*.)

by the winter of 1879–80 he had established four fundamental business principles, upon which he was to build
his own concern.

1. Production in large quantities by machinery;
2. Low prices to increase the usefulness of his products;
3. Foreign as well as domestic distribution; and
4. Extensive advertising as well as selling by demonstration.

These policies were to be tested sooner than the young
inventor realized. January 1, 1881, the Eastman-Strong
business association began, officially, with the manufacture of gelatine dry plates in a rented loft of a State
Street factory building.

Business grew rapidly. By fall, Colonel Strong had invested a total of five thousand dollars, while the younger
partner himself had contributed practically the same
amount. The force, originally consisting of one man, had
expanded, too. The output rose to about four thousand
dollars' worth of plates a month, all of which were shipped
to the wholesalers, who allowed the unsold ones to
accumulate during the winter.

Then, suddenly, the glass-plate business became a glass
house. Photographers began to complain that the Eastman plates were dead; that they had lost their sensitiveness! Eastman hurried to New York to see Anthony and
tested samples from the stock, discovering, what to that
period was unknown, that time dulls the sensitiveness of a
photographic emulsion. As Anthony also had no way
of knowing this, he had sold the fresh stock as it arrived
and permitted a supply of old plates to accumulate.
Here were thousands of dollars' worth of worthless goods
in the hands of the largest wholesaler in the country!

There was only one thing to do, and that was done.

Eastman recalled the stock and promised to replace all plates in the hands of Anthony or photographers which had not measured up to his promises.

But calamities, as is so well known, never come alone. Try as best he could the young inventor was unable to produce a good emulsion. Neither his formula nor any other would work. The tragic tale we find recorded on the worn pages of a notebook, stained with chemicals, soiled by constant fingering, and now brown with age. Emulsion upon emulsion was tried until the number of efforts reached four hundred and fifty-four. Then this note: 'Trials show slight red fog & slight veil. Rapid and fair intensity.' Eighteen more attempts at mixing, cooking, and testing finally yielded an emulsion 'free from red fog.' Then, the 'bottle broke & lost all.'

Throughout this time the factory was closed. Days, then weeks passed. Four hundred and sixty-nine experiments had ended in failure. Eastman was unable to sleep or rest, and found relaxation only by lying awake all night reading detective and cowboy stories.

March 11, 1882, two men from Rochester boarded the Germanic as she sailed for England. Henry A. Strong and George Eastman were making their first trip abroad together. On the 4th of April they returned. Experiments were resumed again in Rochester and after sixteen attempts the plates were again 'clear and good.'

The night of April 16, the two partners had their first sound sleep in many weeks, for the long investigation, the discouraging experiments, and the trip to England had disclosed that the trouble was due to the new supply of gelatine received direct from the manufacturers and not to the Eastman formula or to his machines.

But on the last page of the notebook appears this ominous memorandum:

'Apl 28th/82
'Note $600. 10 days.'

Eastman, for the first time in his life, was in debt. But he had learned two invaluable business lessons. Hereafter he would test samples of every chemical or ingredient before he purchased a supply, and, secondly, he would always 'control the alternative.' By this he meant that he would always 'control' more than one way of doing everything he undertook.

This last principle he added to his four business policies, for neither he nor Colonel Strong had lost faith. Eastman himself was thoroughly convinced that mass production, at low costs, extensive advertising, and international distribution, combined with this 'control of the alternative,' were sound business practices.

The Eastman Dry Plate Company had no difficulty resuming business after the shut-down. The policy of making good all merchandise which proved to be defective was an audacious if not an uncommon practice. Neither Anthony nor the trade knew much about Eastman's difficulties. The trade was so eager for his new supply that the six-hundred-dollar note was quickly liquidated and the company closed its first fiscal year with a profit of $14,889.88. The following year was equally successful, but other concerns were attracted to the field and the market was soon oversupplied. Prices fell; some competitors became discouraged, while others suffered such substantial financial losses that they gave up the business. Eastman, however, plowed the profits into his factory, machinery, chemicals, and investigations. He was just beginning.

Contemplating the future, which was now a habit, he recognized that the fundamental problem in photography might be stated in seven words: 'What could take the place of glass?'

This was not an original thought. Photographic journals had speculated upon the possibilities of a substitute
as early as 1870. Others had attempted to find a new
base for emulsion, because it was generally recognized
that glass was unsatisfactory, obviously fragile, wasteful,
and heavy. Glass, also, limited the utility of photography,
but, up to this time, no one had really done very much
about it. It was a good theory awaiting the attention of
some one who would make a practical product, commercially available everywhere.

Collodion had always fascinated Eastman. Here was
a substance made from cotton and nitric acid, the latter
composition being named by the Swiss inventor 'nitro-
cellulose,' but commonly called gun-cotton. The fact
that such a chemical union produced both collodion and
an explosive had natural attractions for a man who had
experimented as much as Eastman had with both 'wet'
and 'dry' plates, in which the handling of collodion was
one of the keys to success.

The beginning of these experiments is recorded in a
letter to one of his attorneys.

'I first conceived the process of making Transparent
Film by coating a support with a solution of Nitro
Cellulose, and then coating it with emulsion and afterwards stripping it off — early in the year 1884, not later
than Feb. or Mch. During the first half of that year I
made many experiments in which I used both paper and
glass as a temporary support. I used ordinary soluble
gun cotton dissolved in concentrated Sulphuric ether and
grain alcohol equal parts, 10 grains of cotton to the ounce
of the solvent. I sometimes added a small quantity of
castor oil to the solution in order to give it more body.
I coated this solution first on glass, prepared by rubbing
with Talc. I then poured on the glass as much of the

solution of Nitro Cellulose as it would hold in a level position and allowed it to dry.

'I was unable with one coating to get a sufficiently heavy skin or Pellicle to serve as a final support for the emulsion, so I poured on top of the first coating a solution of rubber in benzine. After drying I poured on another portion of Nitro Cellulose solution and let that dry. I repeated these successive coatings eight or ten times endeavoring to get sufficient body to the pellicle.

'I also made experiments by using paper as a temporary support and coating the Cellulose immediately upon the paper, and afterwards coated it with the emulsion. I had no difficulty in stripping the Cellulose from the paper, the cellulose adhered to the emulsion and separated from the paper. The pellicle was not heavy enough to form a reliable final support for the emulsion. I investigated various publications, endeavoring to find a method for making a thick enough solution of cellulose in order to get a thicker coating, but I was unable to find any directions for obtaining a solution containing more than 10 or 12 grains to the ounce. The experiments that I made produced films upon which I was able to make pictures by leaving the films upon the paper support during the exposure and development, and stripping them afterwards.'

In this matter-of-fact manner the inventor described the creation of the first practical 'skin' or film in the history of photography.

The development of this new product, for which an application for letters patent was filed March 4, 1884, raised innumerable technical as well as chemical problems. A new mechanism had to be designed to hold the film in the camera. Both Eastman and William H.

Walker [1] worked on this problem and produced, in short order, the roll-holder, a light-weight mahogany frame which could be fitted to the back of any standard camera on the market. A continuous roll of the new film could be fastened to spools, revolved by means of a clock key on the outside. This mechanism took the place of, or could be used interchangeably with, the glass-plate-holder, and had many advantages, including the convenience of carrying sufficient film for several exposures, making the weight less and eliminating both the danger of glass-plate breakage and the necessity of carrying a burdensome pack of plates in the field. The paper film strip supplied with these roll-holders usually contained twenty-four exposures.

The 'stripping film' which was to be used in this new system of photography comprised a paper base, a layer of collodion, a sensitized gelatine emulsion, and a soluble layer of gelatine between the paper and the collodion, so that, after exposure and development, this soluble layer could be softened by warm water and the paper base separated from the negative and the latter then printed. The broad claims to this stripping film appear in the patent to Eastman numbered 306,594. Thus photographic film in a continuous strip was originated.

It is important to note in this connection that this patent also covered processes and apparatus for making sensitized photographic paper in a continuous web, coated and dried on the run.

Eastman foresaw great commercial possibilities in the film system of photography, and by September, 1884, had about completed plans for the formation of a new company.

[1] Walker was a camera manufacturer who discontinued his own business, which was unsuccessful, to work for Eastman. His employment began in January, 1884.

The first letter outlining his ideas was sent to his brother-in-law, George W. Andrus, of Cleveland: [1]

Sept. 16th, 1884

BRO. A.

We shall probably organize about Oct. 1st, capital $200,000, of which 100,000 will be issued to Strong Eastman & Walker for the American patents, leaving $100,000 working Capital. This half will be placed among our friends.

If you don't want over three thousand I will take it off your hands (at par) at the end of two years if you don't want to keep it.

If you have any friends that want a slice let me know. We don't want to place any lots under 2500 and only with people that will expect to let us manage things, keep their chins quiet and draw their divy when it comes.

We have not tried to place any stock yet, as we only got the Commissioner's decision dissolving the interference with that Attorney I told you about Saturday. But from indications anticipate no difficulty in placing it all as soon as we get ready. . . .

If the thing is a partial success it will be a good thing while if it is a complete success it will dazzle the eyes of the gentle beholder. Still we expect to be given strength to gather in the divvys whatever proportions they reach. . . . Give my love to Ella & the boy.

On October 3, 1884, Eastman sent the first public announcement to Curtis Guild, Jr., publisher of the 'Boston Commercial':

'The Eastman Dry Plate & Film Company of Rochester incorporated Oct. 1st, 1884, paid up capital stock

[1] Andrus married Eastman's sister, Ellen Maria.

of $200,000, has purchased the plant and stock of the Eastman Dry Plate Company, and in addition to carrying on the manufacture of the well known Eastman dry plates will introduce about January 1st a new paper dry plate which it is confidently expected will eventually displace the present glass plates.

'The new process will save Photographers about a quarter of a million dollars yearly on their dry-plate bills.

'The Company has also perfected and patented a roller holder which will reduce the weight of the apparatus required for outdoor photography about one half. The exposures being made upon a continuous strip which is afterwards cut up and developed, the resulting negatives being undistinguishable from those made upon glass.

'The officers of the new Company are:
    'Henry A. Strong, President
    'J. H. Kent, Vice   "
    'George Eastman, Treasurer
    'Wm. H. Walker, Secretary'

When the new company was organized, it purchased the business, real estate, machinery, fixtures, merchandise, patents, etc., of the Eastman Dry Plate Company for $162,000.[1]

The reception accorded the new film system of photography was not one of Disraelian primroses. 'I was unable to see Mr. J. Traill Taylor [2] again before leaving Buffalo,'

---

[1] Strong, Eastman, and Walker received 1620 shares of stock, divided as follows: To Strong, 750 shares; Eastman, 650 shares; Walker, 200; H. W. Gordon, 14; L. L. Stone, 5; and Eliza Tompkins, 1. The balance of 380 shares of the total 2000 shares authorized were sold at par to the following, who, with those mentioned, were the original stockholders: Edwin O. Sage, 100; John H. Kent, 100; Henry L. Achilles, Jr., 35; R. A. Adams, 20; Rollin Steward, 20; Alvah Strong, 5; Brackett H. Clark, 90; and George H. Clark, 10 shares.

[2] For many years editor of the influential *British Journal of Photography*.

Eastman wrote W. Irving Adams, one of the publishers of 'Anthony's Bulletin,' a leading photographic journal, 'but I understand he said in the [Buffalo Professional Photographers'] convention that our Roll Holder is an imitation of Warnerke. Now the so-called Warnerke holder was patented by Melhuish & Spence in England, May 22, 1854, and we are not aware that Warnerke ever made any improvements in it sufficient to give him any claim to the apparatus as an invention. We have a holder [roller] of his make of recent date which we will have our Mr. Cooper show you in New York in a few days. There is about the same similarity between it and our holder as there is between an old flint lock blunderbuss and a Smith & Wesson self acting six shooter. It would not do for your journal to make such a mistake as to say they were the same thing, hence, I would suggest that Mr. Taylor defer any extended description until we can show him both of them and explain the working of ours.[1]

Another letter Eastman sent to a photographer in Boston is evidence of his confidence and earnestness:

'You are one of these men who cry down all improvements never doing anything yourself for the good of the art, you discourage others all you can and when you are finally driven by the energy and ability of others to new methods and processes, you submit with the worst possible grace.

'You have been compelled to accept the dry plate, and when we get ready we will force you to accept films or

---

[1] 'It is perhaps difficult to say why the Warnerke slide did not attain popularity. The drawback which we experienced in using it arose from the trouble in affixing the film or paper to the roller and winding it upon it, operations which had to be conducted in the feeble light of the dark room. It fell into desuetude and became almost forgotten.' (*British Journal of Photography*, 1887.)

you will be driven from your present outdoor business
by those who are willing to progress with their art.'

But despite 'the opposition of all the old fogies' and an
article in the 'Detroit Free Press' ridiculing roll-holders,
Eastman forced his system, by letter, advertisements, and
demonstrations, upon the photographic world. Business
became a battle. He challenged every criticism and met
every attack. He countered the Detroit jeremiad with a
prophecy: 'The camera is getting to be as necessary to
the newspaper correspondent as the pen.' (June 25,
1885.) He had Walker superintend an exhibit he assembled for the International Inventions Exhibition [1] in
London, which was so successful that he was awarded
the highest medals by three British organizations: the
International Exhibition, the Photographic Society of
London, and the Royal Cornwall Polytechnic Society.
The gold medal of the Exposition Universelle in Paris
and similar medals from Florence and Melbourne followed other honors from Moscow and Geneva. The
Prince [2] and the Princess of Wales accepted a camera
with the roll-holder and film as a gift from the inventor
and began to take their own pictures.

On August 11, 1885, the London 'Times' and two
weeks later the 'British Journal of Photography' recognized the advantages of the new system, the 'Journal'
recommending a 'personal examination of the ingenious
mechanism.'

'For general outdoor work, but especially for tourist
use,' read the notice in this influential publication, 'the

---

[1] In his first letter to the managers of the exhibition Eastman wrote: 'We
enclose application for space and would respectfully ask a favorable consideration of same inasmuch as we claim to have perfected the first *practical*
system of Film Photography.'

[2] Later King Edward VII. He and Queen Alexandra were the pioneers
in the royal ranks of amateur photography.

roll-holder will be preferred, at least, when the prejudice existing against such innovations has been removed.'

'All these yield satisfactory prints and there was nothing whatever in their prints to indicate that the negatives had not been taken on glass plates,' concluded the editors of the 'Photographic News.'

The following month two American publications, the 'Philadelphia Photographer' and 'Anthony's Bulletin,' capitulated. But, when the treasurer of the Eastman Dry Plate and Film Company made his first annual report to the stockholders October 1, 1885, the year's profits amounted to only $1807.64, a long way from a 'divvy.'

Walker was the only member of the concern who was worried. Other directors and stockholders in Rochester never wavered, and, although Eastman was confident and absorbed in the experiments which he was conducting, he took a few minutes' respite one day to write Walker, the first managing director of the company in Europe.

'I know that you do not approve of this conservative way of doing things, but I hope you will see the wisdom of it later on. If our business was likely to be temporary and we were obliged to boom it and drop it like a new toy, it would be different, but the business is likely to be a permanent one if built on a sure foundation, which foundation is *good goods*. To make good goods (the goods being entirely new) requires experience and is a slow matter. Perhaps it is a slower matter with me than it might be with some one else, but I do the best I know how. But when we get there, we "get there" to stay.'

From his office in Rochester he directed every detail of the business. 'We shall be able to popularize photography to an extent as yet scarcely dreamed of,' Eastman wrote Vernon Welsh, Esq., of London, when he applied for space in the International Exhibition at Oporto, Portugal, having the Latin-American markets in mind.

Although Eastman has been advertising in a limited way, he began now to take full pages in the leading photographic journals, in the United States and Great Britain. Copy for the first film advertisement was sent direct to the publishers, in his own handwriting:

The Eastman Dry Plate & Film Company
Works 2, 4, 6 & 8 Vought Street
Office & Studio 343, 345 & 347 State St.
Rochester, N.Y.   U. S. A.

Announcement

Shortly after January 1st, 1885
The Eastman Dry Plate & Film Co.
will introduce a new

Sensitive Film

which it is believed will prove an economical and convenient substitute for glass dry plates both for outdoor and studio work.

In connection with this film will be presented new and efficient devices for exposing the same in the single sheet and in the roll.

The whole forming a complete and practical system of

Film Photography

The world was searched for paper and other raw materials. While the best photographic paper came from the mills of Steinbach and Company, Malmedy, Prussia, Eastman was eager to find a supply nearer home. When he found this paper best adapted to his needs, he sent samples to American manufacturers asking them if they could match it.

'It looks as if we should use a lot of paper,' he asserted

in a letter to the Hurlbut Paper Company of Massachusetts April 11, 1885, 'and it will pay you to make it if you can.'

The Eastman Company, even in those early days, was a heavy consumer of silver. Writing to Anthony, from whom he purchased most of his chemicals and silver, he said the present consumption was about forty pounds per week.

The first commercial film was manufactured March 26, 1885, and Walker, who had returned to Rochester, described the eventful day in thirty-two words! 'We started coating yesterday — it would have done your heart good to see the thing work — a prettier sight I never saw and strange to say without a hitch to the end.'

'Without a hitch' is significant. There had been a delay of nearly four months because, as is common knowledge in manufacturing, there are always unforeseen difficulties when a laboratory process is first adapted to large-scale production, but when the Eastman machines operated as a unit for the first time, all the directors must have been thrilled.

When the film business began to make inroads into the glass-plate sales of other companies, one of Eastman's competitors came to Rochester and told him that his firm had been in existence long before Eastman became interested in photography and that in the end the younger man would discover that 'it was always the dog with the longest tail that wagged last.' Eastman wrote Walker about the incident later as the film business expanded, adding with a sense of humor and enjoyment: 'the dog's tail is now shorter than it was then.'

'How is the battle going in Boston?' he asked one of his salesmen. 'Brace yourself for a grand boom,' he wrote another executive, as the growth of the business and the progress of experiments added to his confidence. His capacity for continuous hours of work, his ability to concentrate upon all business details as they came up and arrive at rapid decisions, his inflexible determination and exacting requirements of others made it more and more apparent to his associates that there was no horizon to his vision. Many were the nights he slept in a hammock in the factory and many were the days he cooked his own meals in the plant. And many, too, were the times when Mrs. Eastman came down to take him home to a 'square meal' and a good night's rest. Had it not been for his mother, it is doubtful whether he would have left the business at all.

Being a mechanic he had designed every piece of machinery in the factory. Although he did not possess a scholastic training in chemistry, he had a practical knowledge of many chemicals and chemical reactions gained through years of experimenting with emulsions and paper. He read all the photographic journals, which he received regularly from England, Germany, and Belgium. He studied their pages, translating the formulæ himself, and discovered that no one had made any greater progress than he had.

While he was the first to develop a 'stripping' film, it was not what he wanted, or what he believed the photographic world needed. He had, moreover, carried his experiments far enough to satisfy himself that he was on the right track, but the days and nights were too short for him to experiment and direct the business also.

As the problem was primarily one of chemistry, Eastman turned to Professor Samuel Allan Lattimore, Ph.D., LL.D., head of the department of chemistry at the University of Rochester and one of the leading chemists in the United States. As early as 1872, Dr. Lattimore

was appointed chief chemist of the Board of Commissioners of Rochester, selected to furnish a water supply for the
city. In 1880, when the New York State Board of Health
was established, he was appointed one of six chemists to
ascertain and report on the general subject of the adultera-
tion of food. In 1879, President Rutherford B. Hayes
appointed him to make the annual assay of the gold and
silver coinage of the several mints of the United States
Government. He was a fellow of the American Association for the Advancement of Science and had been a
member of the American Chemical Society since its
foundation.

In 1885, Mortimer F. Reynolds, President of the
Rochester Savings Bank, through his interest in Dr.
Lattimore's work, contributed the funds necessary to
erect and equip a chemical laboratory for the University
of Rochester, which was considered, at the time, one of
the most modern chemical laboratories in the country.

Eastman had known Dr. Lattimore for some time and
had had him test one of the first roll-holders and spools
of film which he made.

'The holder we sent out with Dr. Lattimore,' Eastman
wrote at the time, 'was simply an experiment to find out
how the instrument would work in the hands of an inex-
perienced person. As Dr. L. lives here and would send
his exposures to us to develop, it was a good opportunity
to determine whether any weak points in the apparatus
would be developed.'

Through this association Eastman became acquainted
with an 'ingenious, quick-witted fellow' named Henry M.
Reichenbach, Dr. Lattimore's assistant, and, upon the
professor's recommendation, offered him a position some
time in August, 1886.

Writing Walker, in London, November 7, 1886, Eastman stated that he had employed 'a young chemist who devotes his time entirely to experiments.' About this time he engaged Joseph Thacher Clarke, of Boston, as the 'scientific expert for Europe.' On April 30, the following year, Eastman advised Walker of the progress of the experiments, and, referring to his first chemist again, said: 'He knows nothing about photography. . . . I told him what was wanted and that it might take a day, a week, a month or a year to get it, or perhaps longer, but that it was a dead sure thing in the end.'

This, to our knowledge, is one of the earliest known records of an American manufacturer engaging a trained chemist to devote all his time (at the expense of the business and with no stop-watch on his efforts) to chemical research in industry.

Eastman was still searching for a better substitute for glass, for he considered the stripping film only the beginning. Patiently, he unfolded his ideas to Reichenbach, and the latter began his experiments while Eastman turned his attention to other aspects of the business. While the Patent Office granted all the claims in the original applications, he found that a farmer in Hunter, Dakota, named David H. Houston, had obtained a patent on a visible indicator and a film-puncturing device which indicated when an exposure length of film had reached the required position.

This was recognized immediately as an improvement. Eastman bought a shop right for seven hundred dollars. Then, conscious of the fact that the improvements in photography were apt to be very rapid and possibly revolutionary, he inaugurated a policy of purchasing control of every photographic patent which appeared to him to be necessary in the development of his business. Meeting Houston in St. Paul later, he purchased the patent outright for five thousand dollars and bought another patent from the Dakota inventor. Returning to Rochester, he wrote Walker that they were now 'solid as a rock.'

Another problem was of equal import. Photographers had to be educated to the new system, for letters began to arrive from all parts of the country. Eastman's replies read like prescriptions:

'In reply to your favor of the 13th instant we enclose formula for soda developer,' he wrote J. O. Hebert, Grand Rapids. 'It is quite as likely to be the ammonia that hurts your throat as the pyro and we would advise you to try this formula.'

'We cannot give you the exact temperature that the flat iron should be to get the best results, but if you will ask your wife to heat for you a flat iron just right to iron a shirt, you will have it O.K. Use plenty of oil. Do the blisters on your negatives come while in the developer, or after fixing? If in the first instance, you must use cooler water. Always use fresh hypo. We shall be glad to hear from you again,' he concluded this letter to H. P. Stultz, Sante Fé, New Mexico.

Inquiries were received, also, from France and Austria. To the Paris letter from Professor E. Stebbing, Eastman replied:

'It is the desire of this company to establish an agency in France and to open up trade there, but we understand there are some patent regulations which require investigation before we take any steps in the matter.

'We regard our patents both on the roll-holder and the film as very valuable, and do not wish to do anything to injure them.' [1]

Eastman was also directing the company's sales, had two men on the road, and wrote many sales letters. The

[1] October 5, 1885.

first reference to a complete photographic outfit is in a letter to William R. Miller, Polo, Illinois:

'We shall be glad to furnish you with a complete photographic outfit for your projected trip around the world. We sell all makes of cameras and fit them with our roll-holders.

'Our roll-holders are especially adapted for long tours, not only on account of the saving in weight and transportation but in the readiness with which the negative paper can be passed through the Custom Houses. Parties traveling with glass plates invariably have trouble.'

In these early days F. A. Brownell, who had a small wood-working factory in Rochester, manufactured the roll-holders, but business multiplied so rapidly that by November, 1885, Eastman wrote the Blair Tourograph and Dry Plate Company of Boston:

'Our contractor here has added new machinery and the prospect is that he can turn out all the cases that we shall need this winter. We have been greatly hampered so far by his inability to turn them out fast enough. We have got the metal work department in such shape that we can turn out an unlimited number of movements.'

Business 'boomed.' Chemical and manufacturing difficulties were overcome. The stripping film was improved, and the new product was manufactured and advertised under the trade name of 'American Film.'

Reichenbach, too, was making progress. The success of the roll-holder system of film photography made it necessary that the new film be manufactured and sold in lengths, which could be wound around the spools, or cartridges, and which would not buckle when in the hands of the user. What was needed was something more than a substitute for glass plates. Whatever was produced had to be adaptable to roll-holders and commercially practical or it would not be of any advantage in this system of photography which Eastman had originated and to which the photographic trade was now becoming sympathetic.

Eastman had Reichenbach try varnishes and solutions of various chemical companies, but these were found to be unsuitable, either because they made a film that was too thin and wrinkled, or there were spots, pits, or imperfections, or they were objectionable in color, or too greasy to be coated with a sensitive photographic emulsion.

Experiments continued until December, 1888, when Reichenbach produced a nitro-cellulose solution in wood alcohol, which, on being flowed upon a glass plate, produced a smooth and clear and to this extent satisfactory film. It had, however, very little strength, tearing easily. It had a tendency to peel from the glass plate when drying, making the surface of the film wavy and irregular. Nevertheless, this was recognized as a distinct step in advance, and it began to look as if Reichenbach was approaching something tangible.

One day this young chemist decided to add camphor to the solution, believing it would strengthen and perhaps soften the substance. When he added what he thought was sufficient for this purpose, he found the camphor would crystallize at some portions of the film, making opaque spots. Finally he hit upon a formula, using a sixty per cent solution of camphor, but discovered that it was necessary to use heat in drying the film, but if, for some reason, the heat was not uniformly applied at an exact and even temperature, it would fail to produce a smooth and clear film or would interfere with the coating with emulsion.

Eastman was watching all of these developments and applying his mechanical abilities to the different tests.

He was contemplating the new machinery and apparatus for manufacturing which would be necessary while Reichenbach was pursuing his research.

At last Reichenbach found the 'key.' By adding a solution of fusel oil and amyl acetate, the camphor was retained in the solution during the drying of the film, and the first transparent, flexible film was perfected.

By March 3, 1889, the patent attorneys had completed the first drafts of the applications, which Eastman returned to J. B. Church, of Washington, D.C., with the following letter:

'On reading the claims of the two applications signed and executed yesterday I find that the fusel oil claims Nos. 1 & 2 must come out, as I can lay no claim to the chemical part of the process. The mechanical part only is mine & the chemical part Henry M. Reichenbach.

'You are doubtless aware of this and will readily recognize the oversight.

'As the claims are at present drawn, neither Reichenbach nor myself could father them, as they combine the chemical & mechanical features, which are separate inventions.

'The papers were executed very hurriedly so Fred [Church], who came down after them could take them with him, hence I failed to notice the tangle.

'I should like very much to have Reichenbach's name connected with these applications and think it would please him. Hence I think it would be a good plan to file an application on the exact chemical formula I sent you, whether we can get any allowance or not, and have him execute it. Then why not combine the 3r. 4" & 5" claims of one process application with the one claim of the other in one case.

'This would make four applications necessary.

'1 Chemical formula H. M. R.
'2 Mechanical process   G. E.
'3 Apparatus   G. E.
'4 Article mfg. (if possible to frame a claim) G. E.

'The drawing for the apparatus case can be made when Fred returns to Rochester. We are making some changes in the details of the table.

'Please return the claims incorrectly executed. Address correspondence about the new films to G. E., personally.'

On the same day he wrote Walker:

'In view of the importance the new film will give roll-holder patents, would it not be well for you to secure options on any English patents not owned by us. . . . It will be our endeavor to fortify ourselves as much as possible by controlling all the roll-holder patents that we can.'

A new factory was equipped immediately and a sample of film was rushed over to England. 'It will show you,' he wrote Walker, 'the style of goods proposed. We can make it in any length required. We have overcome all but some minor difficulties in the manufacturing and expect to be running at the Court Street factory by May 1st.'

The experiments of Eastman and Reichenbach solved, for the first time in the art, the problem of making, on a commercial scale, transparent nitro-cellulose photographic rollable film. December 10, 1889, patent No. 417,202 was granted to Reichenbach by the United States Patent Office, while on March 22, 1892, and July 19, 1892, two additional patents were granted to Eastman and Reichenbach.

These patents describe the process and apparatus as actually used by the Eastman Dry Plate and Film Company, to whom all patents were assigned, in the manufacture of this film. They provided that the base of the film was made from their patented solution of nitro-cellulose, which was deposited and spread on glass tables, two hundred feet long and three and one half feet wide, by means of a mechanism suitably timed for the production of a base with a smooth surface and of uniform thinness; this solution being then dried and coated with gelatine emulsion, which was also dried. The web of film was then stripped from the glass tables and slit and cut into strips of the required length and width for the roll-holders.

In July, 1889, Eastman went abroad with Fred Church, one of his patent attorneys, to look after film patents and prospects in England. By September 23, he was in a position to write Strong, who was spending most of his time in Tacoma, Washington, where he and other Rochester men had founded the Traders' Bank: 'We are doing a big business here, $22,500 to date (18 working days) and plenty of orders on hand. We ought to scoop $30,000 for the month and thus end the year in a blaze of glory, enthusiasm, and piety.'

Eastman's confidence in chemical research was justified. Reichenbach had produced the formulæ for the first transparent, flexible film.

'It will not be long before your concern will need a practical chemist,' Eastman confided to Walker: [1] 'The best way to do is to make application to the Prof. of Chemistry in some good technical school and have him recommend two or three first class boys. You can then interview them and take your choice. ... If he is any good he will be the most profitable man you can hire.'

Opening the mail at the office one morning Eastman found the following inquiry from Edison:

[1] October 28, 1890.

EDISON PHONOGRAPH WORKS

ORANGE, N.J. *May* 30, 1889

The Eastman Dry Plate Co.,
   Rochester, N.Y.

GENTLEMEN:

Please quote us discount upon your Kodak camera, your list price, $25.00. Also discount upon reloading camera, list price $10.00.

Yours truly,

EDISON PHONOGRAPH WORKS,

T. A. E.

It was just another order, filled in the routine way, without a discount!

That this first Kodak, purchased by Edison in the summer of 1889, was used by the inventor in making his first motion-picture camera is shown on pages 540 and 541 of 'Edison: His Life and Inventions,' by Dyer, Martin and Meadowcroft.

'Having at last obtained apparently the proper material upon which to secure the photographs [reference is made to the nitro-cellulose film then used in ordinary Kodaks], the problem then remained to devise an apparatus by means of which from twenty to forty pictures per second could be taken; the film being stationary during the exposure and, upon the closing of the shutter, being moved to present a fresh surface. In connection with this problem it is interesting to note that this question of high speed was apparently regarded by all Edison's predecessors as the crucial point. . . .

'After the accomplishment of the fact, it would seem to be the obvious thing to use a single lens and move the sensitized film with respect to it, intermittently bringing the surface to rest, then exposing it, then cutting off the light and moving the surface to a fresh position; but who, other than Edison, would assume that such a device could be made to repeat these movements over and over again at the rate of twenty to forty per second? Users of kodaks and other forms of film cameras will appreciate perhaps better than others the difficulties of the problem, because in their work, after an exposure, they have to advance the film forward painfully to the extent of the next picture before another exposure can take place, these operations permitting of speeds of but a few pictures per minute at least.

'Edison's solution of the problem involved the production of a Kodak in which from twenty to forty pictures should be taken in each second, and with such fineness of adjustment that each should exactly coincide with its predecessors even when subjected to the test of enlargement by projection. This, however, was finally accomplished, and in the summer of 1889 the first modern motion-picture camera was made.'

On September 2, Eastman received another letter from the Edison laboratories:

DEAR SIRS:
Enclosed please find sum of $2.50 P.O.O. due you for one roll Kodak film for which please accept thanks — I shall try same to-day & report — it looks splendid — I never succeeded in getting this substance in such straight & long pieces — Sincerely yrs.

E. K. L. DICKSON

Can you coat me some rolls of your highest sensitometer — please answer.

Dickson was Edison's chief assistant working in the famous Room Number Five in the laboratory at Orange.

When this film reached Edison, he remarked: 'That's it. — Now work like hell!'

On September 7, Dickson was informed: 'We have no film of higher sensitometer now on hand, but occasionally have it considerably quicker. Should we have some of its kind, we will try to bear you in mind.'

In his history of the motion picture, Terry Ramsaye describes the use of this film in Edison's first motion-picture machine, and adds:

'The Edison peep show machine was christened the Kinetoscope, and the camera wherein the pictures were made was the Kinetograph. . . .

'Mark you well this Edison peep show Kinetoscope. Every strand in the thread of motion picture destiny runs through it. It is the inescapable link between the gropings of the past and the attainments of the present. Every motion picture machine, every motion picture enterprise, every motion picture personality, screen star or magnate of the screen theater, can be traced to some connection growing out of the little black box that Edison dubbed the Kinetoscope. This is one of the absolute facts of the history of the motion picture.'

This is the genesis of the motion picture. Edison made the first motion-picture camera and Eastman made his first reel of film. It is a remarkable coincidence that neither of these men knew of the experiments of the other, yet within a few months their contributions had been joined in the production of the first moving picture. Still, this was only a one-man 'peep-show,' and five years more were to elapse before a satisfactory projector was developed and an actual screen performance could be shown to an excited audience in New York City.

In the mean time there were many experiments and improvements, both at Orange, New Jersey, and in Rochester.

MR. EASTMAN IN 1890

On July 23, 1891, Eastman sent the following letter to Reichenbach:

'Enclosed is a small fragment of film furnished Edison for his phonograph arrangement.[1] He perforates it on both edges and delivers it by means of cog wheels. The film has to move 40 times a second and the movement has to be made in 1/10 of that time. It is then quiet for 9/10 of the period, while the picture is being taken. The trouble with the film we have sent him is that the cogs tear the film slightly, as you will see by the enclosed, and gives blurred images. I gave the Edison representative a sample of the double coated film made last August and told him if heavy enough we could furnish him that if he would take a whole table at a time in 41 in. strips. His idea is to have us slit it 8 in. wide and then make a slitter of his own and cut it up narrower. Edison now has an order in for some narrow strips of film of our regular make. Please fill this and use the thickest skin that you can find. Edison's agent will let me know about the *doublecoated film* in a few days.'

On November 3, 1891, we find an order from the laboratory of Thomas A. Edison for twenty-seven rolls fifty feet long and one and one half inches wide, .005 inches thick, coated with the highest sensitometer, and a similar order coated with the lowest sensitometer.[2]

December 8, 1891, Eastman sent another memo to Reichenbach: 'It is quite necessary that we should perfect our method for making double coated film. I think

---

[1] In the days before the words 'motion picture' were used, it was common practice to speak of a 'phonograph arrangement' because this suggested motion.

[2] The 'sensitometer' was an instrument for measuring the speed of plates or film in which they were exposed behind a series of numbered densities, the highest number readable after development being the sensitometer number.

that if you persist in your experiments you can get rid of the electricity.'

Electricity in the film! Another strange anomaly! Edison, the electrical wizard, took the camera and made a motion-picture machine, and now Eastman, a photographer, had a problem in electricity to solve for Edison.

Here was a disturbing puzzle. Something had to be done, for nitro-cellulose film was highly charged with electricity in cold weather. It seriously interfered with Edison's work and was causing markings on Kodak film.

Experiments were carried on in Rochester until April, 1892, when 'an open-and-shut cure' was discovered. On the 18th, Eastman reported the result to Walker:

'One day, reflecting upon the theory that the discharge was caused by two surfaces, one of which was positive and the other negative, it occurred to me that if one of the surfaces was metallic there could be no generation. The idea of making one of the surfaces metallic naturally followed. A little further reflection, however, staggered me, because it seemed that the emulsion must be metallic, but I knew that it would spark as badly almost as the dope. I finally decided that every metallic particle in the emulsion must be insulated by the surrounding gelatine.

'Thinking about this matter convinced me that if the gelatine substratum which we were then experimenting with, could be rendered a conductor at all it would not be by the use of any insoluble matter. I then naturally thought of the soluble salts and knowing that nitrates would not interfere with the emulsion, I decided to try them first. I directed Reichenbach to try the first experiment with Ammonium Nitrate, but he tried it with Potassium Nitrate, and found it worked perfectly. This was immediately before the 1st of January.'

But litigation, the 'loud-speaker' champion of all great discoveries, was lurking in the shadow of Eastman's success. The battle, however, was to come later. Meanwhile, these records are clear:

1. Eastman invented the first film, a coated strip of paper, the coat, or pellicle of which was stripped after exposure and developing, making a transparent photographic negative.
2. Eastman was the first to begin experiments with nitro-cellulose as a possible base for film.
3. Reichenbach obtained the first patent on transparent, flexible, nitro-cellulose film, which he made by discovering the importance of camphor, fusel oil and amyl acetate.
4. Eastman invented the machinery and processes for making film.
5. The Eastman Company was the first to manufacture and sell both kinds of film.
6. This company created the market for film by developing the Kodak which was the first great consumer of film.
7. This company made the first film for Edison's Kinetoscope, the first motion-picture camera.
8. Eastman was the first to eliminate electricity from film, which had caused marking in cold weather.
9. He was the first to produce, manufacture, and market film in continuous strips, or reels.

These facts were firmly established between 1884 and 1891.

Such is the story of the origin of film — the 'magic carpet' of the motion picture and the Kodak. The 'story,' from that day to the present, is as endless as the millions of reels which record the fact and fancy of the world in pictures, sound, and color. It is the basis for the greatest portion of mass entertainments. In medical and dental diagnosis it is indispensable. It is often the key to scientific research and military strategy. In education and many of the arts, it is the medium of an era of new orientation. Perhaps as much as any other single discovery, it has aided in making all the world akin.

CHAPTER III

THE KODAK

WHEN Eastman marketed his first film, two products were necessary for taking pictures: a camera with a lens and shutter and a spool of film coated with a sensitive emulsion. While the inventor had devoted much of his time to plates and film, he worked, as Kreisler plays the violin. 'Technique, to me,' said the famous musician, 'is a mental, not a manual thing.' While film experiments were under way, Eastman was thinking also of a light, portable film camera.

Among the leading camera manufacturers in the United States in 1885 were E. and H. T. Anthony and Company, and the Scovill Manufacturing Company, both in New York City. Business relations between the Eastman Company and the former concern had been so unsatisfactory, however, that the Rochester directors adopted a resolution February 27, 1885, 'that all existing contracts . . . be closed at the earliest possible moment!' Anthony and Company were an old, conservative, autocratic house whose injured pride made the partners fear that film would doom their business, and they acted accordingly.

Scovill, on the other hand, seemed 'very much inclined to boom things if we will give them a show,' Eastman wrote David Cooper, one of his salesmen then in Boston, 'and I think they will begin to do something before long.'

The first reference to a complete camera is in a letter to Scovill.[1] 'Enclosed please find specimen of numberless inquiries that we are getting in regard to complete

[1] October 31, 1885.

photographic outfits. What is wanted is a line of complete outfits fitted with the roll-holder. The concern first in the market will be sure to reap a great advantage.'

'There is always a forked road of policy,' Eastman recalled later, and this was one. Should he or should some other manufacturer make the first complete camera? The problem was one of business strategy rather than production, for Eastman had made a 'model camera' early in September. However, instead of undertaking the manufacture of this product at once, he decided to build up the paper business, so that when the first camera was placed on the market his concern could furnish photographers everything they needed to make, as well as to take, pictures. His goal was a complete system of photography rather than a complete outfit.

In July he had started large-scale production of sensitive-coated photographic paper by machinery, a process which he had invented and patented. No one had coated webs of paper, on the run, with sensitized gelatine, prior to this time. The only known method heretofore was hand-coating,[1] but this new apparatus and process resulted in more economical manufacture and more rapid production. The saving in labor amounted to more than ninety-five per cent, while the saving in coating material ranged between twenty-five and fifty per cent. The product, too, was superior to the hand-coated paper. This invention made it possible, for the first time in the art, to produce coated paper of any desired length, the only limitation being the available length of raw paper.

Here was another blow to Anthony's prestige! As the paper business expanded, Eastman was ready to give

---

[1] Progress in the electric light and glass industries was not as rapid as this. The automatic glass-blowing machine was not invented until 1903. Up to that time all electric light bulbs were blown by hand.

more attention to the camera when the foreman in charge of the paper-making and one of his traveling salesmen left the company, the former without any warning and the latter upon a day's notice. It was a terrifying advent of a new year [1] when Eastman discovered that these two men had disappeared.

For several weeks their whereabouts remained a mystery until Eastman learned that Anthony and Company had hired them and that the foreman was duplicating Eastman's machinery in that plant. March 9, Eastman brought suit for infringement of patents and the first of a long series of legal battles with this concern began. A motion for a preliminary injunction was denied.

'Judge Shipman dissolved the stay, but compelled A. & Co., to sign a stipulation not to use complete or allow our machine to go out of their possession until after final hearing,' Eastman wrote Church.

'Our opponents made the point that they stopped using our machine as soon as they saw our patent and had no intention of infringing. . . . The truth is they beat us by superior generalship. . . . We have got to have new counsel in New York. Who can you recommend? We want a fighter.'

Church recommended M. B. Philipp, whom Eastman retained immediately. 'We propose to show the scoundrels that when it comes to "funny" work the country men from Monroe County are not to be sneezed at,' Eastman wrote Walker. 'It will cost us some money now, but if we beat Anthony we shall have a clear field hereafter and get our money back a hundred times over.'

Although the suit was not brought to a final hearing, it is sufficient to record that Anthony never used the machine and dropped the two employee-conspirators like

[1] They left New Year's Eve, 1887.

hot chestnuts. April 23, Anthony tried to retaliate by bringing suit against Eastman for alleged infringement of a patent granted to Thomas C. Roche, but this suit was not pressed, and was finally discontinued several years later by Anthony paying the costs.

On the heels of this plot came an ultimatum from Walker. First, he demanded an increase in salary; secondly, he desired to be relieved from the contract which he had made to give the company the benefit of his ideas or inventions; thirdly, he demanded that the time of notice required of him for canceling his contract with the company be reduced to three months; and, finally, that the company 'give him a bond of indemnity for any loss that he might sustain in assuming any obligations' abroad.

The Board of Trustees authorized Eastman to 'endeavor to harmonize his [Walker's] views with those of the Board.' Eastman was in a fighting mood, but he became a diplomat, negotiated a new contract with Walker for three years, and authorized him to rent 'a desirable location on Oxford Street' (the first of the company's retail stores). There were too many problems at home to warrant a rift in the ranks abroad.

No sooner was this adjusted than the company experienced a serious fire which destroyed much of the interior of the State Street plant February 10, 1888, and closed the factory for two months! While directing the reconstruction of the plant, Eastman decided the time had come for the company to inaugurate a complete system of photography. Then came a long letter from Strong, who was still in Tacoma. It was addressed 'Dear Skinney,' and after relating the progress of the new bank, concluded with this paragraph:

'You are a queer cuss, Geo., and I know you never want any sympathy or comfort from your friends . . . but

I want you to know that *I*, for one, appreciate the mountains of care and responsibility that you are constantly called upon to overcome (and you "git there," too), and if I never express it in words, it may be a source of comfort to you to know that I am always with you heart and hand. Never take my silence for indifference. I sometimes think that we do not know each other very well, anyhow. We surely are neither of us very demonstrative, and Mrs. S. says the Strongs are so queer and I guess she is right. Well, shake old boy.

'Yours,

'HENRY.'

By May, 1888, Eastman was remaking his model camera. It was the 'box' type of small size, 6¾ inches by 3¾ inches deep and wide. It was light, weighing twenty-two ounces, so that it could be very readily carried and held in the hand during exposure. All other cameras up to this time had to be supported by a tripod or on a table. The picture was circular (2½ inches in diameter) and the camera received a film roll of such length as to provide for one hundred exposures or negatives. The price of the camera, loaded with film and including a shoulder strap and leather case, was twenty-five dollars. This camera had to be sent to Rochester, where the exposed film was removed and developed and a new film inserted at a charge of ten dollars.

In June Eastman placed this, his first, camera on the market. He was again on the offensive!

Eastman was determined that this product should have a name that could not be misspelled or mispronounced or infringed or copied by any one. He wanted a strong word that could be registered as a trade-mark, something that every one would remember and associate only with the product which he proposed to manufacture.

'K' attracted him. It was the first letter of his mother's family name. It was 'firm and unyielding.' It was unlike any other letter and easily pronounced. Two 'K's appealed to him more than one, and by a process of association and elimination he originated 'Kodak,' and gave a new name to a new commercial product. The trade-mark was registered in the United States September 4, 1888, and this particular camera was designated as the 'No. 1 Kodak.' [1]

The next thing needed was a booklet describing the new system of photography. Within five hours he had composed the following text for the first primer:

THE 'KODAK'

'THE MARCH OF IMPROVEMENT in any given field is always marked by periods of inactivity and then by sudden bursts of energy which revolutionize existing methods sometimes in a day.

'*For Twenty Years* the art of photography stood still;

---

[1] Before 'Kodak' could be registered in England, the Comptroller of the British Patent Office required a letter from Eastman explaining the derivation of the word, to which he replied:

'"*Kodak*." This is not a foreign name or word; it was constructed by me to serve a definite purpose. It has the following merits as a trade-mark word:

'*First.* It is short.

'*Second.* It is not capable of mispronunciation.

'*Third.* It does not resemble anything in the art and cannot be associated with anything in the art except the *Kodak*.'

Writing John M. Manley, University of Chicago, December 15, 1906, Eastman stated: 'In regard to the word Kodak I can say that it was a purely arbitrary combination of letters, not derived in whole or part from any existing word, arrived at after considerable search for a word that would answer all requirements for a trade-mark name. The principal of these were that it must be short; incapable of being misspelled so as to destroy its identity; must have a vigorous and distinctive personality; and must meet the requirements of the various foreign trade-mark laws, the English being the one most difficult to satisfy owing to the very narrow interpretation that was being given to their laws at the time.'

then a great discovery opened a new channel for improvement, and now for the last ten years the art has been in a state of rapid evolution.

'*Ten Years Ago* every photographer had to sensitize his own plates and develop and finish his negatives on the spot where the picture was taken. This necessitated the carrying of a dark tent, baths, chemicals, and all the paraphernalia of the studio into the field, and a familiarity with chemicals that could result only from long practice and study. The introduction of the gelatine dry plate made in large quantities in thoroughly equipped factories, relieved the photographer of one of his greatest burdens, and opened the door of the art to thousands of amateurs who had previously been deterred from learning to make pictures by the uncertainties of the 'wet' process, as well as by the smell of ether, the silver stains and the stuffy dark tent.

'*Four Years Ago* the amateur photographer was confined to heavy glass plates for making his negatives, and the number of pictures he could make on a journey was limited by his capacity as a pack horse. Then the invention of the Eastman-Walker roll holder and Eastman's American film rendered it possible to carry in a small compass an indefinite number of films which could be rolled off and exposed one after another simply by turning a key. These improvements added new pleasures to the art of picture making by photography, which have already been appreciated by thousands.

'*Yesterday* the photographer, whether he used glass plates or films, must have a dark room and know all about focusing, relation of lens apertures to light and spend days and weeks learning developing, fixing, intensifying, printing, toning, and mounting before he could show good results from his labors.

'*To-day* photography has been reduced to a cycle of three operations:

1 — Pull the String.   2 — Turn the Key.
3 — Press the Button.

'This is the essence of photography, and the greatest improvement of all; for where the practice of the art was formerly confined to those who could give it study and time and room, it is now feasible for *everybody*.

'THE KODAK CAMERA
'renders possible
'THE KODAK SYSTEM

whereby the mere mechanical act of taking the picture which anybody can perform, is *divorced* from all the chemical manipulations of preparing and finishing pictures which only experts can perform.

'Hence, it is now easy for any person of ordinary intelligence to learn to take good photographs in ten minutes. Not simply to take one picture as an experiment, but to repeat it over and over again with such accuracy as to average over eighty-five per cent good pictures from the start.

'This statement is fully substantiated by the experience of hundreds of purchasers of the Kodak who are already enjoying its use.

'There is no jugglery about it; photography has simply been brought down to a point where the mechanical work can be entirely separated from the chemical work. Besides this, the part of the work left for the novice to do has been greatly simplified. Heretofore the so-called "detective" camera has been the only instrument suitable for wayside photography, and even with this form of camera it has been necessary to perform upwards of ten operations in order to simply make one exposure, as the mere act of "taking" the picture is called. The omission on any one of these consecutive operations entailed a liability of total failure of the picture.

'The Kodak reduces the ten or more operations heretofore necessary to make an exposure with detective cameras to three operations, reduces the weight and bulk in the same proportion, and increases the number of pictures that can conveniently be made on one trip from *six* to *one hundred;* and it makes this very decided advance not by any sacrifice of quality of results, but in a way that guarantees a far better average than ever attained under the old condition.'

When Eastman applied for an American patent, he advised Walker [1] in regard to foreign protection:

'Our application has been filed for an American patent on the Kodak, but the patent will not issue for some months. We, therefore, desire to call your attention to the fact that the filing of applications in some other countries before the issue of the American patent will shorten the life of the latter materially.

'A recent decision against the Edison Company by Judge Wallace decided that an Austrian patent which had been issued before the American but not until after the American application had been filed, limited the life of the latter to one year, because the Austrian patent was issued for only one year; although it was capable of being extended from time to time up to fifteen years.'

By October, Eastman marketed the 'No. 2 Kodak,' a larger camera, containing a film with sixty exposures which made pictures 3½ inches in diameter, and business continued to grow.

Up to this time American film (the 'stripping film') was used exclusively. Meanwhile, Reichenbach had been

[1] June 28, 1888.

making progress with nitro-cellulose film, which was such a vast improvement that Eastman wrote Philipp,[1] 'The new film . . . will, it is absolutely certain, *entirely* replace glass plates at least for amateur work at once, or as fast as the goods can be made.'

This month Eastman became a national advertiser, contracting for full pages 'in all the magazines for November and December to catch the holiday trade,' and again advised Walker: 'We find that it does not pay to advertise the Kodak in anything but the magazines and weeklies of the very choicest circulation. Harper's, Century, Scribner, Outing, and the following weeklies: Scientific American, Harper's Weekly, Frank Leslie, Puck, Judge, Life, Time, Truth.'

'As you are aware,' he answered an inquiry from 'Art in Advertising,' 'there are a great number of ideas sent me for adoption. They all were in effect that the button should be pressed, and that we would do the balance of the work. I finally cut out everything else but:

' "Kodak cameras. You press the button — We do the Rest."

'I can only add that no man was more astonished to find the phrase so universally popular. It has been highly gratifying to me.'

Meanwhile, there were other problems multiplying in number almost as rapidly as his business, which was vastly exceeding all expectations. 'The devil is to pay at Court St. this week,' he confided to Walker. Dust, smoke, lack of capacity, and 'frilling' seriously hampered the manufacture of film. Eastman began to look around for a suitable location where a new film plant could be built, selecting, finally, several farm properties on the

[1] May 26, 1889.

Boulevard, in the town of Greece, near Rochester, upon which he obtained options. Contractors began immediately to drill for water, as an adequate supply of water was, and is to-day, one of the primary requisites in the manufacture of film.

Up to this time he had been conducting practically all the correspondence of the company in his own handwriting, but decided that he needed a private office and stenographer.

In the spring of 1890, Miss Alice K. Whitney came to Rochester for a vacation with relatives. A friend told her that Eastman was looking for a stenographer, but that he was a 'hard man' to work for! Walking over to the unimposing factory on State Street, she was interviewed by Eastman and offered a position at once. Since June 2, 1890, she has been his secretary.

In August, 1890, Brackett H. Clark, one of the directors, began to purchase the Boulevard farms on behalf of the company, and Kodak Park was in the making.

Meanwhile, business was so great that the concern had difficulty developing films as fast as they poured into Rochester. Complaints of delays appeared in letters to the press and in editorials, particularly in New York City, and Eastman attempted to stem the tide by answering some of the attacks:

'The letter published under the heading "A Painful Pleasure" in your paper of August 15 does this company very great injustice, implying as it does that this company requires four weeks to fill its orders for developing Kodak films.[1] At the present writing we have only five orders on our books for developing that are older than August 7 [12 days]. Our orders are usually filled within

[1] Letter to the editor of the *New York Evening Post*, August 19, 1890.

the limit of time mentioned in our advertisements — ten days. Occasionally an order contains some overexposed negatives which have to be intensified and printed two or three times to secure the best results. We never hesitate to do this on account of the work, but it occasions delay in filling that particular order. Your correspondent's order may have been delayed on this account.

'Your correspondent also complains that he cannot obtain transparent film for his Kodak, and instead of giving us credit for filling the gap with stripping film, which is just as good for his purpose and which we are ready to furnish, makes that also a ground of complaint. He takes it for granted apparently that we are making no effort to relieve the shortage. If he had inquired of us he would probably have been informed that new factories are being built with all possible haste in England and this country. Our system of film photography, which is the only one that has ever been brought to a degree of perfection which renders it a commercial success, has been built up within a very few years in the face of grave difficulties. The manufacture of transparent rollable films is only a year old, and the wildest enthusiast would have said when our first factory was built that it would be sufficient to supply the demand for several years to come. It is now being run day and night.

'We think any reasonable man, instead of seeking to discredit our concern, would put up with a little temporary inconvenience, and give us the credit for having accomplished a good deal in simplifying photography so that he can use a camera at all without learning the whole art.'

Still the demand for Kodaks and film increased so

rapidly that, in September, Eastman concluded a letter to Walker by remarking that 'if this thing continues we are afraid we will be mobbed.'

In December, 1891, the A B C series of Kodaks was introduced, embodying a daylight loading feature which made it possible for the amateur to load and unload his camera in daylight. Hereafter it would be unnecessary to ship the Kodak to Rochester to be serviced. Film could be bought and used anywhere, and the avalanche of orders which reached the company again surpassed all calculations.

'The craze,' wrote the 'Chicago Tribune,' 'is spreading fearfully. . . . Chicago has had many fads whose careers have been brilliant but brief. But when amateur photography came, it came to stay.'

The Kodak and Kodak stories began to appear everywhere. It was the big news of the day and the feature in many magazines. Society leaders, scientists, and business men became enthusiasts.

'Prof. S. W. Burnham, now of Lick Observatory, is Chicago's most famous amateur photographer,' the 'Tribune' reported. 'His pictures have taken prizes wherever they have been exhibited. His picture of a cat springing upon a bird captured a prize at the Paris Exposition. His views above the clouds are known among photographers all over the United States.

'Another amateur almost equally well-known is Mrs. N. Gray Bartlett. Professionals and amateurs unite in praising her exquisite work. She has an inexhaustible fund of original ideas in posing. Within the last three months her pictures have been published in Wide Awake, St. Nicholas, Outing and Scribner's.

'Prof. Bartlett . . . took up amateur photography as an aid to his lectures on chemistry at the Chicago Medical College.

'Mrs. Dr. Shears takes interior views of an unusual nature. In order to assist her husband in surgical work she photographs tumors, cancers and other cheerful things of like character. She has "taken" a man before, during and after an epileptic fit. Her views are of great value to the medical profession and are copied widely in their journals.

'James Barker, General Passenger Agent of the Monon Route, takes fine views along his line and uses them on the railroad folders and as advertisements. . . . Leonard Volk, the sculptor, makes an annual trip to Wisconsin. If his rifle does not secure the deer his camera does. . . . Harry B. Stiles, son of Gen. Stiles, took his camera when he made a trip through the South. He now proudly exhibits some characteristic Southern scenes with the pickaninnies as the prominent feature. . . . Mrs. M. S. Avery has made a beautiful series of photographs of her young daughter as Marguerite plucking the petals from a daisy as she repeats: "He loves me; he loves me not." . . . George E. Hale makes use of photography in his study of spectrum analysis. . . . E. Burton Holmes' subjects are well-chosen and unique, many being from places not often visited by tourists.

'Montgomery Ward has taken some excellent Mexican views, full of spirit. Portraiture is the point in which Mrs. D. M. Stevenson excels, though her views of California scenery are admirable. Mesdames C. T. Yerkes, George M. Pullman . . . all "press the button" of the kodak with good results.'

In England the same conditions prevailed. 'I am amazed at the excellence of the little Kodak's work,' wrote Rudyard Kipling in the days before testimonials were articles. of commerce, while Gilbert and Sullivan introduced the Kodak in their comic opera 'Utopia.'

'The ballet girl as a Kodaker, is now delighting the opera-goers of London,' read a London dispatch to the New York newspapers. 'Whether appearing as sailor, soldier, bandit or fairy she has long held an important place in the popular fancy. As Robin Hood's merry men, as the Forty Thieves or as the sweet fairy nymphs the public loves her, collectively, of course. As a Kodaker she must be irresistible. It is in "Utopia," Gilbert and Sullivan's new opera, that she assumes this rôle. Two modest maidens describe themselves in a song in which the following sprightly stanza occurs:

> "Then all the crowd take down our looks
> In pocket memorandum books.
>   To diagnose
>   Our modest pose
>   The Kodaks do their best:
> If evidence you would possess
> Of what is maiden bashfulness,
> You only need a button press —
>   And we will do the rest."

'These two modest maidens and all the girls of the chorus carry Kodaks!

'That the song and chorus is charming goes without saying. The names of Gilbert and Sullivan are a sufficient guarantee of that. But have the managers stopped to consider what the effect is to be on the front rows? There is in this seeming trifle a financial problem beside which the silver question pales into insignificance. Through the innocent kodak the Behring sea troubles are likely to once more agitate the civilized world! Think of a bald-headed man — and most likely married too — looking into a battery of fifty kodaks! The kodak buttons click in unison. Too late, the horrible idea comes to him that fifty witnesses to his frivolity are contained in those fifty little black boxes. His hard old heart beats wildly and a sea of crimson rushes up his massive forehead, across the broad expanse of unadorned cranium, and disappears in the row of fringe on the back of his neck. With a wild rush he leaves the theater, and hastening home, he pens with trembling hand, the check that is to buy for his unsuspecting spouse the sealskin that has long been her earthly ambition.

'If the kodak becomes a stage fixture, will it not be the direct cause of the extermination of the seal? And, will not opera houses be built hereafter without any front rows?'

The Kodak was grist for the jesters' mill. Day after day, for many years, there were new bags of Kodak stories until this variety of fun became a favorite indoor sport in the 'gay nineties.'

The New York 'Sun,' famous under Dana's direction for its anecdotes, reported one day that 'Edison's accomplishments are not all in the electric line. He can tell a good story capitally. He told one the other day about an experience he had recently in an upcountry town in Pennsylvania one Sunday morning. He had been out to see some iron works. A cold rain was falling and he got soaked through. When he reached his hotel, the first thing he did was to order a hot Scotch.

' "Can't give it to you," said the clerk.

' "Eh! Can't give it to me? Why not?"

' "Because it's Sunday. We can't sell anything to drink on Sunday."

' "Well, but I'm wet through," said Edison, "and cold. I want a drink."

' "Well, I'll tell you what we can do," replied the clerk, "we can give you a Kodak."

' "What's a Kodak?" asked Edison.

' "You just go up to your room and press the button. We do the rest."

' Edison got the drink. '

To J. H. Stedman, however, the Kodak was 'dry,' when he wrote his 'Kodaktyl':

'The Kodak lately caught a fish,
And if the truth be told,
It will catch anything you wish,
Except, it won't catch cold.

'It will take everything you see,
Yes! quicker than a wink;
A pretty girl, earth, sky, and sea,
But it won't take a drink.'

The Kodak idea appealed to politicians and reporters too. The 'Sun' referred to 'Hill's Kodak Convention,' and at a Chamber of Commerce dinner in New York City, Chauncey M. Depew concluded one of his famous after-dinner speeches with the sentence: 'As merchants, as bankers and business men, we say to congress, in the language which advertises that most universal and productive of our institutions, the *Kodak*, "*You press the button and we will do the rest.*" '

Eastman showed his appreciation immediately. 'The Eastman Company has taken the liberty of sending you a Kodak for Mrs. Depew,' he wrote. 'I hope that you will accept it as a slight acknowledgment of a high compliment which you recently paid the Kodak. If Mrs. Depew will press the button of the little instrument when she sees anything interesting on her travels, we will try to convince her that the doing of the rest is not a vain promise on our part.'

The reply of the railroad President [1] was characteristic: 'I am in receipt of your letter of the 22d an-

---

[1] December 24, 1890. Depew was president of the New York Central and Hudson River Railroad Company from 1885 to 1899, and United States Senator from 1899 to 1911.

nouncing that you have sent a Kodak to Mrs. Depew. I know that she will be immensely delighted, but that her pleasure can by no means equal that which 'Buster' will have in using the instrument. I have been the victim of your invention about a million times and in all possible situations and conditions, and I knew of no better way of getting even than by giving it the national advertisement which I did in my Chamber of Commerce speech.'

From Washington, Walter Wellman, the leading correspondent of the time, sent a special despatch to his syndicate of newspapers, entitled: 'Caught With a Kodak,' which pictured political Washington as it had never been seen before.

'I bought a kodak last week, and, like any other boy with a new toy, started out bright and early to see what I could do with it. On my way down Connecticut Avenue I passed Sir Julian Pauncefote and a pair of his pretty daughters out for their morning walk. The Pauncefote girls are great pedestrians, and they wear big, thick soled, broad heeled shoes. Sir Julian is one of the nicest men that ever represented a foreign government at this capital.

'In Lafayette square I caught a glimpse of Mr. Blaine, walking about with his head down, evidently in a brown study, and with his derby hat pulled pretty well down over his eyes. This is one of Mr. Blaine's little peculiarities, and it matters not what sort of a hat he is wearing either. With a derby the effect is not so striking, but a high hat does not look well when tilted so far forward, even on such a fine white head as Mr. Blaine's. Have you ever noticed that the thoughtful, sedentary man is prone to shield his eyes with the brim of his hat, while the man of animal spirits and great bodily vigor tilts his hat far back on his head in very love of light and air?

'At the Capitol the industrious little kodak found many scenes meat, and fit for its devouring, but the most of these shall be saved for a future letter. The kodak is no respecter of persons, and in good time it will have some interesting stories to tell of its espionage of the great men who meet every day in the big state house.'

The triumph of the Kodak more than fulfilled the restrained prophecy of 1884, that if the company was "a complete success it would dazzle the eyes of the gentle beholder,' but Walker still remained a pessimist!

'I think you are just now taking too gloomy a view of the prospects in England,' Eastman wrote.

'There is certainly a chance to do a big thing abroad in the next two years if we go in vigorously for it. . . . If we can only make a good showing I think we ought to start companies in France, Austria and Berlin this fall or winter. The business is bound to grow year by year until it becomes an enormous one and if we can maintain our control of it, or even divide it, there is sure to be big fortunes in it. No temporary set-back should be accepted as a knock-down.' [1]

Twelve years had almost passed between the time Eastman took his first lessons in photography and the success of the Kodak system, but while every one else was enjoying the dominant sport of the 'gay nineties,' the inventor discovered Reichenbach and two other employees engaged in a conspiracy to form a rival company and use the secret formulæ and processes which they had been entrusted with.

This, like the previous case of disloyalty, came to Eastman's attention on New Year's Day. He confronted the three men immediately with the evidence. Their

[1] January 19, 1892.

answers revealed their guilt, and they were discharged instantaneously. Upon investigation Eastman discovered that Reichenbach had allowed 1417 gallons of emulsion to spoil and had made 39,400 feet of imperfect film — a financial loss of $47,900.

But this experience did not shake his confidence in trained chemists, for both before and after this incident Eastman was seeking chemical assistance. On November 3, 1891, he had asked Professor Thomas M. Drown,[1] of the Massachusetts Institute of Technology, to select a young chemist from the graduating class 'who can devote some attention from now until graduation to photographic chemistry. I do not want any one who is not painstaking, thorough, and throughly reliable. Harum-scarum youths are not of any account in this business. I have a great deal of confidence in the material you turn out at your institution.'

Dr. Drown made a recommendation and Eastman added in another letter on the 25th: 'The position which will be open in our works is that of assistant manufacturing chemist and the work will be principally in connection with the manufacture of photographic sensitive emulsions.'

Immediately after Reichenbach's [2] discharge, East-

[1] Dr. Drown had studied chemistry and metallurgy at Harvard, Yale, Freiburg, and Heidelberg, and was Professor of Analytical Chemistry 1885–87; Richard Perkin Professor of Analytical Chemistry, 1887–95. In 1889, he was the chemist in charge of the natural waters of the State appointed by the Massachusetts State Board of Health.

[2] Reichenbach and associates formed two companies in later years and engaged in the photographic business. Both failed. April 9, *1909*, Eastman wrote:

'MY DEAR HENRY: On my return home from several weeks' absence I find yours of Mar. 19th. While I do not now cherish any ill feelings towards you on account of the past I think you can see that it would be impossible for me to give you employment in the Company on account of the influence it would have. With best wishes, I remain,

'Yours very truly,

'GEO. EASTMAN.'

man sent letters to Professor Ira Remsen, of Johns Hopkins; Dr. Charles F. Chandler, of Columbia University; and to the Chemistry Laboratory of Cornell University, asking for a young chemist, 'who has recently graduated and who is steady, reliable, and a worker.' And, at the same time, he retained Dr. Leonard Paget to continue the research work of the company in New York City, when another storm broke.

On August 8, 1893, President Grover Cleveland called an extra session of Congress, and in a special message explained that he was 'constrained' to take this step because of 'the existence of an alarming and extraordinary business situation,' which involved 'the welfare and prosperity of all our people.

'With plenteous crops, with abundant promise of remunerative production and manufacture, with unusual invitation to safe investment, and with satisfactory assurance to business enterprise, suddenly financial distrust and fear have sprung up on every side. Numerous moneyed institutions have suspended because abundant assets were not immediately available to meet the demands of frightened depositors. . . . Values supposed to be fixed are fast becoming conjectural and loss and failure have invaded every branch of business.'

This 'extraordinary' situation struck the Eastman Company in two places at the same time, in London and Rochester.

After the International Inventions Exhibition, Canada and other British dominions became interested in the new system which Eastman originated. By 1886, the 'Petit Journal' and the 'Journal Illustré' of Paris were featuring the work of M. Nadar,[1] the company's repre-

---

[1] 'The value of aërial photography was realized long before the [World] War; the first attempts were made as early as 1858, when M. Nadar took

sentative in France, who had been court photographer to Napoleon III. The same year the Eastman Company was awarded a diploma by the Société Genévoise de Photographie. Recognition in Russia, Germany, Austria, Belgium, and the Latin countries soon followed, and by the time the flexible film and the Kodak were marketed, Eastman products were sold by dealers in the Orient as well as in Europe.

This was not spontaneous or accidental. Shortly after Walker went abroad, Eastman outlined the general policy, stating that the development of foreign trade would 'distribute our eggs and pad the basket at the same time.'

From 1886 to 1889 the business both at home and abroad increased faster than the company could multiply its facilities, so that a change in the capital structure was necessary to finance new factory buildings and additional distribution agencies.

There had been but one capital change since the Eastman Dry Plate and Film Company was organized in 1884, an increase from $200,000 to $300,000, primarily to take over all foreign patents and rights retained originally by Strong, Eastman, and Walker. By June, 1889, the company had a surplus of $116,735.77, and no indebtedness. Eastman estimated that the new film would more than double the net earnings, which were then approximately $100,000 annually, about 33⅓ per cent on the capital.

Strong and Eastman exchanged a number of letters with Walker regarding the possibilities of organizing an English company.

'There is one thing which may not have occurred to

some successful photographs of Paris from a balloon.' (*Photography as a Scientific Instrument.*)

you,' Eastman wrote. 'The new film will command the Colonial Trade completely a/c of the ease of transportation & probably a/c of keeping qualities, too.[1]

'The field for it is universal and no estimates so far made are based upon a more exclusive control of it than we have of Bromide paper. If we can fully control it I would not trade it for the telephone. There are more millions in it than anything else because the patents are young and the field won't require 8 or 10 years to develop & introduce it.'

On November 28, 1889, the Eastman Photographic Materials Company, Limited, was incorporated in London with a capital of £150,000, to take over the business, good-will, etc., of the Rochester Company in London, Paris, Berlin, Milan, St. Petersburg, Melbourne, Sydney, Shanghai, Canton, Constantinople, and Japan, and all other countries except the Western Hemisphere.

The following month the Eastman Company was incorporated in Rochester, with an authorized capital of $1,000,000, consisting of ten thousand shares at par, which were distributed on the basis of three and one third shares for each share held by the stockholders, who agreed to contribute to the company ten per cent of their new holdings. This stock was sold publicly in Rochester to increase the working capital, while the parent company retained a majority of the stock of its foreign subsidiary, selling only the preferred shares and a portion of the common for expansion and working capital abroad.

The company was now in a strong financial condition. Contracts were executed immediately for the construction of three buildings at Kodak Park. Under the supervision of Darragh de Lancey, the first manager at the Park and the first graduate of Technology to be

[1] May 5, 1889.

employed by Eastman, duplicates of the machinery were shipped to the new factory which was being constructed at Harrow, England.

Large-scale production of film and printing paper was soon possible in England as well as the United States. Eastman, with the activities of his companies multiplying with great rapidity, assumed such dynamic executive direction of all affairs that Strong, after traveling to Europe with him, wrote the younger partner upon his return to Tacoma: 'It takes a pretty broad-gauged man to keep up with you.' Eastman retained Walter S. Hubbell, of Rochester, to direct the legal battle against Reichenbach and his co-conspirators. Philipp was busy in New York handling a suit against Eastman by the Celluloid Company, which had charged infringement of three Stevens patents covering an alleged process in the manufacture of flexible film.

Eastman was also suing the Blair Camera Company for infringing the Kodak by their manufacture of a 'Kamaret.' By this time he had no 'holy horror' of litigation as some of the English directors had. His confidence in his own rights and faith in the patents of the company were unyielding. Philipp's arguments in court he praised as a 'work of art.' Although he won in the Reichenbach and Blair cases, he compromised in the Celluloid suit by agreeing to purchase material for the film base, or the 'dope,' as the nitro-cellulose mixture was called, from the Celluloid Zapon Company, a licensee of the parent company. But this nearly ruined the business, because the 'dope' of this company was not equal to that purchased from Charles Cooper and Company. Film manufactured from this new supply failed in the hands of Kodak users and the company had to recall thousands of dollars' worth of film from the market.

AIR VIEW OF KODAK PARK

'We cannot be charged with any lack of due care in testing our films,' Eastman wrote John Wanamaker.[1] 'The lot in question, which we have recalled from the market, showed when tested an unusually high speed and fine quality, so good in fact that we took occasion to send out a special circular to the trade calling their attention to it. No change was shown in this film during a period of several months and all exposures made on it were in every way satisfactory; it was not until warm weather set in that we first commenced to notice the change, and after investigation notified the trade of the numbers we had found defective, asking them to return them. These covered but a few emulsions, as we found after going through the stock on hand, which was very large. Later we found that other emulsions were affected and notified the trade to return any they might have in stock of the whole series of film, although we were aware at the time that some had not shown any deterioration. We notified them at the same time that they might replace to their customers any of this film on which claims were made, if the negatives or a good portion of them were returned showing that the film was at fault.

'The failure of the film was a matter entirely without precedent and one that we could not foresee. We have too much at stake in the reputation and sale of our KODAKS and roll-holders to take any chances in sending out film.'

When this occurred, Eastman went back into the laboratory again to experiment. March 31, 1892, he was able to write Strong: 'I have made a new invention which will enable us to sell every bit of our scrap film. At the present time there is about one third of the film which will not cut up into full rolls. It is therefore a total loss

[1] October 1, 1892.

except for the silver and celluloid. I have hit upon a scheme which will enable us to use it all up at good prices. It will be worth from $5000 to $7000 a month to us when running full speed.'

May 23, 1892, the capital of the Eastman Company was increased to $5,000,000 through a stock dividend and the name was changed to the Eastman Kodak Company. This prompted the 'New York Tribune,' in a special edition in June, to include Eastman's name among 'tariff-made American millionaires.' Upon being so advised, he wrote the editor: 'I am in receipt of your favor concerning American millionaires. My name is not rightly in the list and should be omitted from the revised edition. Whatever money I have made in my business has been owing rather to patent than to tariff protection.'

Up to this time, Eastman had taken no interest in a protective tariff.

Having had considerable success at the Paris Exposition with his complete photographic system, he planned as early as 1891 to make the World's Columbian Exposition in Chicago a mecca for amateur photographers from all parts of the earth. While he had been searching for men for some time to take over different departments of his business, he had need, now, for another executive who could assume direction of advertising. A friend in Rochester recommended Lewis B. Jones, of Ilion, New York. Jones had been a reporter in Rochester in the days when Samuel G. Blythe began his newspaper career. Eastman wrote Jones: 'Our mutual friend Mr. W. F. Balkam has had some talk with me about you and says that you would like to get a place with some large concern where you would have a chance for promotion. I am looking for a live young man in our advertising department. There is opportunity enough in the position to give full scope to the abilities of any man. The pay to start with would be ten or twelve hundred dollars. I want a man who can do some writing and would have the ability after a time to take entire charge of the advertising department. If you think that you would like the position, I wish you would write me what your qualifications are and state whether you could come up here and see me.'

Jones was employed in May, just as Walker climbed on his high horse again. This time he sent in his resignation, precipitating a crisis which had been brewing for several years.

Strong was asked to go abroad and investigate. He found that the factory at Harrow and the branch at Nice, France, were operated at considerable loss; that Nadar had won a suit against the company in Paris which cost forty thousand francs. The London corporation had so many variegated obligations that drastic measures were necessary.

Eastman, in the mean time, had selected George Dickman as Walker's successor and dispatched him to London. Writing 'My dear Dickman,' March 18, 1893, he outlined a few basic policies:

'I enclose a letter which I very much wish you would present to your Board of Directors. I do not think that it will embarrass you in any way to do it because they cannot hold you responsible for my utterances. Some policy has got to be adopted that will keep you supplied with goods and the only way to get the cobwebs out of —— and —— [two directors] minds is to have them understand what their actions are going to lead to.

'I believe that it was a great mistake for Walker to call them into consultation on the matter at all but inasmuch as they already had a hand in the matter I do not see but what they have got to settle it. I am a believer in one man management and that a Board of Directors is valuable only as an advisory instrument to a good manager. I would strongly advise you to adopt the same course that I have, viz. to call on your Board for advice only as to general policy and never as to details. If you cannot run the business alone as far as these matters are concerned, you will certainly be no better off by letting four or five others dabble at it. So far as I am concerned I have confidence in you and will back you, mistakes or no mistakes, until you have had a fair chance to show what you can do.'

While these developments were taking place in Europe, Eastman was pushing the construction of new buildings at the Park, including a new experimental laboratory. The new camera works were opened and thousands of new customers were added at the World's Fair. 'We have introduced nothing but radically new things ever since we started, and as every one of them has been a success I do not think that we need reproach ourselves with being in a hurry,' he wrote Dickman.

But Strong was having irrepressible difficulties in London and cabled Eastman that the company could not continue the dividends. 'If so, well and good,' Eastman replied, 'my idea is that if the dividend on the ordinary shares is to be passed, that the preference dividends should be passed, also. That in order to do this every possible thing should be charged up to profit and loss this year so as to have a clean deck for the next year. . . . It will be much better for the Co. to make one very bad year than to make half a dozen poor ones.'

Strong followed this policy, left Dickman in charge, and returned to Rochester, but not until he had suggested to Eastman that he cable Walker to come to Rochester. This spark brought an explosion!

'I hardly think I shall follow your suggestion and wire —— personally to come over. Why should I? I do not want to see him, I even cherish the hope that I may never see him again. He has been a care and a worry to me ever since I knew him, and now when it looks as if I had got rid of him, his infernal swelling, pompous incapacity for anything but making mistakes I don't think I shall ever call him to me. No, indeed. If he has the cheek to come here I won't entertain him in my house or have anything to do with him.

'If any diplomacy is needed, my dear boy, it is looking to you to keep him out of my way for I assure you that if he is allowed to bother me in any way, shape or manner I will give up my job. I have enough to worry me without any of his blankety blank nonsense.

'As far as conciliating him for fear of any harm he can do, I can't do it. It sticks in my crop. Besides that I am not afraid. He never invented anything by himself and he never will. He has not perseverance enough. If it was not so awfully costly the best way to do would be to let him fuss around the Harrow factory until he gets tired. But I advise you that if you want the E.P.M. Co. to earn any money you had better see to it that he is stopped off short from spending any of the company's money.

'I don't want to talk over anything with him or to exchange ideas. I have been perfectly free to tell him my plans while he was in the employ of the company but now he is out of it, it is not business.

'I am getting tired of the company's borrowing money and I don't propose that it shall borrow another cent except what it has to to finish the new building. As long as I could lend it all the money it wanted, well and good, but when it comes to carrying —— —— share, — both, I can't do it. I won't skin around among the banks either. I am not used to it, I don't have to do it, my salary don't cover that kind of financial work, and — I won't do it.' ¹

Then came the panic of 1893!

July 26, while in Chicago with Jones, taking advantage of every trade opportunity at the Fair, Eastman received a smashing cable from Dickman. The foreign subsidiary had borrowed from a London bank and immediate payment was demanded.

'It will be very inconvenient, if not impossible for us to send you this amount,' he replied by letter. 'We have just got through paying for our new buildings and machinery and have not yet accumulated any spare cash. In addition to this our collections are way behind. . . . You probably have some idea of the state of finances in this country through the newspapers. Since then things have gone from bad to worse. I doubt very much whether even this concern could borrow a dollar at any bank in this city. Concerns that have never been refused and about whom there is not the faintest question as to responsibility are being daily refused discounts at the bank. Every bank is holding on to every dollar that it can get in fear that it will suddenly be called upon by its depositors.

'It seems to us, in view of the fact that you have reduced your loan from £10,000 to £3500 and paid £2000 of this since July 1st, that you can stand the bank off for a time. I do not understand why you consider it inadvisable to call in the unpaid subscriptions.² Times are getting worse all the while and if it is hard now to call this in it will be harder bye and bye.'

---

¹ February 22, 1893.

² The capital stock of the E.P.M. Company was increased from £150,000 to £200,000 through the issuance of 5000 ordinary shares at £10 on May 26, 1891, and the subscriptions had not been fully paid.

On the 31st he wrote Dickman again:

'Self-preservation is the first law of nature and the Company must be protected for the sake of its other stockholders. It never will need this money any more than it does now. We cannot say anything more except that we hope vigorous action will be taken.

'We dare not make any promises because the bottom is liable to drop out of everything at a moment's notice.'

'Financial matters are not improving here,' Eastman added ten days later. 'In my judgment this winter is going to be the hardest time this country has seen for very many years. Our business has not been seriously affected yet but no doubt it will be and we shall have all we can do to take care of our own finances. It is extremely unlikely that we shall be able to lend you any ready money.'

While Dickman was pressing the English stockholders for payments under the terms of their subscriptions, Eastman was receiving foreboding letters from Strong, who was back in Tacoma striving to save the Traders' Bank from a catastrophe.

'The situation in Tacoma to-day, and for the future, will be just exactly what the people of Tacoma make it,' wrote the Tacoma Ledger. 'They can continue the present uneasiness if they persist in doing so, or they can go on about their business in the usual way and permit the city to return to its normal condition. There is no doubt in the world that every bank in the city is entirely solvent, and that it can meet all demands likely to be made on it. A vast amount of money has been brought here within the last few days to strengthen their cash reserves, and they are fully resolved to stand together and help each other through if necessary. Those who call upon them for money will get it. If, however, they withdraw it and take it away and deposit it in safety vaults or in some other supposed place of security and compel it to remain idle, they will, by so doing, voluntarily withdraw from the city and the state so much of the means of its prosperity. Certainly all the money we have is needed in circulation. We cannot afford to embarrass business or to close it up by withdrawing from it the means by which it goes on. To do this is simply to reduce the city to its original condition as a wilderness, so far as it is possible to do so.'

On the 4th of June, Strong reported: 'We are still on deck, but the deck is a little slippery yet.' But it was not long until the Traders' Bank closed. In January, Strong came to New York City to arrange a loan to reopen his bank. By March, the situation was critical again. Eastman made repeated efforts to cheer his senior partner. 'It looks very much as if things were fast coming to a focus in Tacoma. If worst comes to worst and they enter up judgment, don't you think you had better come home and try and make some arrangement of your affairs here which will protect your interests? I think things can be fixed so as to give you plenty of leeway. Keep a stiff upper lip and do not lose sight of the fact that if the emulsion goes wrong, plates fog, the Solio turns yellow and the Bromide paper blisters, all of these troubles will disappear after a while.'

Within less than two months, however, Strong had to advise Eastman:

'The indications are favorable for a great upheaval. You know that I have had great hopes and some faith that the Traders' Bank could be pulled through notwithstanding your opinion to the contrary. I am now about ready to acknowledge that your opinion was about correct. Business has not returned but that can be partially accounted for by the fact that there is no business worth mentioning and what there is, is absorbed by the British banks and the Fidelity Trust Company.

'This hanging on the ragged edge of uncertainty is most trying and I cannot flee from the wrath to come. I fear that the news of further trouble here will be disastrous to Mrs. Strong's recovery. You are my only confidant and I want you to know the facts at all times and in all cases. Now you can study over the case. I may be taking a wrong view of the situation and I surely hope that my fears are groundless but I have given you my opinion flat. This is all confidential of course. No use in making other people miserable.'

May 18, Strong telegraphed that a receiver would take over the Traders' Bank. Liquidation was unavoidable.

Afterwards the Colonel returned to Rochester, where he assumed an active interest in the Eastman Kodak Company, of which he was still the President. And, in passing, it might be added that he was able to salvage his fortune and pay his debts through the help of an unnamed friend.

During the peak of the panic, in August, 1893, Eastman was confronted with a new type of competition. Early in 1892, he had introduced, commercially, a new gelatine-coated printing-out paper under the name 'Solio,' which became popular at once.

The sales of 'Solio' were very extensive and profitable, so much so that they began to eat into the business of competitors, one of whom was Charles S. Abbott, of Jamestown, New York. Eastman respected the American Aristotype Company and its head. So he wrote Abbott:

'We are perfectly frank to say that we deprecate any such warfare as threatens our concerns. We have always deemed it best to sell our goods on their own merits and to point out their superiority without attacking the quality of our competitors' goods or misrepresenting them in any way. The following clause, extracted from our instructions to our traveling men, clearly indicates our policy in this respect:

' "Solio is to be sold on its merits. Do not attempt to run down your competitors' goods, but point out Solio's advantages."

'We would much prefer to continue this policy unless forced to change it by the actions of your Company. When, however, our traveling men are met with such statements as those reported to have been made by your demonstrator to Mr. Boyd and we are unable to obtain any satisfactory denial or explanation from you, we feel obliged to defend ourselves, and in defending to assume the offensive.

'We hardly like to construe your letter as a threat, but in case it is we will say that you will find that the financial standing of this Company is beyond the reach of attack, that we are proud of our successes and sorry for our failures, which we have never attempted to cover up, and that we are not afraid of their being contrasted with the record of any other concern.

'If, however, your letter is, as we assume, written in a different spirit you may rest assured that we are not only willing but anxious to dwell in peace and harmony with our business competitors and that we are not even disposed to be critical in regard to the manner in which they conduct their competition provided it does not transgress all bounds of fairness. We fully realize, as doubtless you do, that money spent in the detraction of our rival products will simply tend to discredit them both and can better be used in making converts from our common rival albumen.'

The 'Solio war,' however, could not be averted. It was simply postponed. Then, in the dark days of September came a cable remittance from London.

'If I were subject to heart disease your cable of this date might have been attended with fatal results,' the Treasurer replied. 'To have two thousand pounds dumped in upon us while we thought you were still suffering for money was a great surprise. I am anxious to know how you got it.'

In the mean time rumor-mongers began working overtime in Rochester. Thumbing through the pages of the record, we find a long philippic from Myron G. Peck, a promoter, who said that he was prompted by Eastman's 'curious views' to 'lay before you their [the stockholders] views. There is not so much criticism, or "fault-finding," as blank astonishment at your own showing of the results of your personal management — "one-man management," as it is called.[1]

'It seems well understood your "Board" — to whom you refer, as the responsible parties, in all your transactions, have little, or nothing, to do with the management of the Company's affairs. Some of them deny all responsibility, "you do it all"! and *they* are only asked to assent to what you do, or propose to do.

'Such widely diversified interests as you attempt to manage, require not only great executive ability, but financial experience, time and careful thought, excellent judgment and complete self-control.

'No one possesses all these qualifications, and, if *any* man attempts to exercise them, or to run the business without them, he is sure, sooner or later, to wind up and bring disaster on all connected with it.

'You create $5,000,000 of stock but fail to make pro-

[1] October 12, 1893.

vision for earning the money to pay dividends on it. Holders of the stock never know when, if at all, dividends will be paid, and the stock becomes valueless, in consequence.

'You speak of the "cry by stockholders, for continuous dividends" as if they had no right to expect anything for the use of the money they paid you for your stock.

'You simply kill the hen that lays the golden eggs. . . . A prominent financier and able lawyer, who is a director in four of our local banks, recently gave a review of the Eastman Company from its small beginnings to its last default in its dividends. From personal knowledge the actual assets of the Company, in his opinion, free from all indebtedness, have never been enough to warrant the issue of $25,000 of stock. He declared it was the delusion of a visionary, inexperienced man to suppose a great volume of stock could be issued on a passing fancy, and inflated from $50,000 to $300,000 then $1,000,000 and then $5,000,000, without the bubble bursting.

'In his opinion there had never been a greater swindle perpetrated in this community than selling this Eastman stock, on your representations of its fabulous earnings, at the prices you had sold it for. . . .

'Stockholders think the affairs of the company should be looked into, the books examined by an expert, and a competent lawyer pass upon the transactions of the past three years, to decide if there is legal authority for all that has been done — what sales of stock have been made, and at what prices; the cost of running the business, and the gross income from it.

'I doubt if you see the danger ahead. You may hope to hold matters in their present shape until better times; but when can better times come to the Eastman Company? With the decline in your business and dull times ahead, the net earnings of the company, if there are any, will be absorbed for two or three years to come, to pay the indebtedness. If stockholders have to wait for more experiments, under the present policy, the cry for "continuous dividends" may become a cry for "receivership."'

Peck concluded his letter by asking for an interview, which was declined in the following brief acknowledgment:

'The criticisms, suggestions and threats concerning the management of the Eastman Kodak Company contained therein have been duly noted. In regard to the criticism of people who are not directly interested in Eastman Kodak Company which you propose to repeat to me, I desire to say that I do not take any interest in them. I am doing the best that I know how to put the company on a basis satisfactory to all concerned and am willing to be judged by the results of my work when it is done.'

Here was a business keynote . . . to judge work only 'when it is done.'

For several months Eastman had been searching for a master emulsion maker. His own time was so consumed that he could no longer sleep in a hammock in the laboratory at night, punctuated by alarm-clock signals when it was time to stir an emulsion. In December he heard that a professional photographer in Louisville, Kentucky, owned a half-interest in a new emulsion coating machine made by Dr. J. H. Smith, of Zurich, Switzerland. This, combined with the fact that William G. Stuber had a national reputation in his profession and had made a photographic study of Colonel Henry Watterson, the picturesque editor from the Blue Grass State, which was awarded the coveted medal of the American Society of Photographers, prompted Eastman to communicate with Stuber.

'In regard to the Smith coating machine would ask whether you can give a clear title to it, free from the payment of royalty? Also, please state whether you are prepared to come here for an interview in case we pay your traveling expenses. There is some prospect of the position of foreman of our transparency plate department being open, in which case it may be desirable to have an interview.'

On January 4, Eastman sent another letter:

'I offer you, commencing February 1st, a position as manager of our transparency plate department, salary to be $30.00 per week and 1 per cent on the net receipts for glass dry plates, the arrangement to be continued as long as your services are satisfactory; either party to have the privilege of terminating this contract at any time. You are to have entire charge of the department, under the manager of works at Kodak Park, and you are to conform to the regulations of work at that place; also to sign our printed agreement in regard to patents. It is understood that you are to procure for us the Smith coating machine heretofore used by the Stuber Dry Plate Co. at a price not exceeding $1,200.00, that you are to organize an experimental glass plate department and that as soon as you have satisfied us that you can make plates suitable for the market you are to teach our emulsion maker, who shall be designated by us, how to make your emulsion.'

Stuber accepted these terms, moved his family to Rochester, and began his ascending career with the company.

The panic which had proved so disastrous to many industrial concerns ended for the Eastman Kodak Company without any additional indebtedness. The company was able to take advantage of all cash discounts.

WILLIAM G. STUBER

It succeeded in getting its previous existing debt carried at six per cent. In addition, new construction was completed at the Park, new machinery was paid for out of earnings, and under the exacting directions of the treasurer the company was operated with greater efficiency, effectiveness, and economy than ever before, and the annual report showed a net profit of $87,718.

The policy outlined in 1886 had survived 'extraordinary' business conditions. By distributing 'the eggs' abroad, the 'basket' *was* padded. Dickman had proved his fortitude. By reorganizing the foreign business, collecting subscriptions due on the stock, and by pushing the sales in all Continental cities, the managing director in London was able to advise his chief that the foreign subsidiary could resume dividends.

'If you can,' Eastman replied, 'it will be a good thing, but if you cannot I would strongly advise you to write off everything that is doubtful on your books. . . . I have always made it a practice to charge off everything doubtful here immediately so that we have never had any dead horses around.'

By this time Eastman was in a strategic position to resume an international offensive. To Strong, alone, he confided his objective. 'The manifest destiny of the Eastman Kodak Company is to be the largest manufacturer of photographic materials in the world, or else to go to pot. As long as we can pay for all our improvements and also some dividends I think we can keep on the upper road. We have never yet started a new department that we have not made it pay for itself very quickly.'

This was the new objective — a big international business founded upon the 'Kodak System.'

CHAPTER IV
INTERNATIONAL EXPANSION

IF there are dates in history that cast their shadows like pyramids in the rays of a setting sun, the years 1895 and 1896 loom high. Within this period the following developments greatly accelerated our national progress:

1. The first commercial automobiles were built in the United States.

2. Henry W. Oliver and H. C. Frick, representing Andrew Carnegie, concluded an agreement with the Rockefellers for ore, which stimulated the great expansion in the steel industry.

3. Professor W. K. Roentgen discovered the X-ray at the University of Würzburg, Germany, and made the first 'shadowgrams.'

4. Major Woodville Latham gave the first public showing of motion pictures on the screen.

5. Thomas A. Edison produced the Vitascope, embodying his and Thomas Armat's inventions.

6. Louis and Auguste Lumière obtained a French patent for a camera and projector which they named the 'Cinématographe.'

7. The Eastman Company perfected the first positive motion-picture film.

8. Congressman William McKinley was elected President of the United States on a gold standard platform.

The birth of two new industries — automotive and motion picture, which were to rank, within a quarter of a century, among the largest businesses in the world —

alone would distinguish these years from their immediate neighbors.

The telephone, the electric light, and film photography were already necessary utilities in the life and commerce of the world, although neither the telephone nor the electric light had expanded as rapidly as film photography. While President McKinley had talked from his Ohio home to Mark Hanna, his manager at the St. Louis Convention, and used the long-distance telephone throughout the campaign, it was ten years later before Professor Bell inaugurated service between New York and San Francisco. The electric industry had to wait seven years more (1903) before the automatic glass-blowing machine was invented which inaugurated mass production of incandescent lamps.

In the year 1896, however, Eastman made his one hundred thousandth Kodak and was manufacturing film and photographic paper measured in units of miles — between three and four hundred miles monthly — in Rochester and at Harrow. This was, indeed, large-scale production at low cost for a world market, eight years before mass production started in the automotive industry.[1] This, however, was only a start compared to

[1] One factor common to the automobile, the airplane, and the Kodak is their relationship to the bicycle. Several early manufacturers of gasoline cars were graduates of the 'wheel business,' either as manufacturers or agents, among them Winton, Overman, Pope, and Thomas. Wilbur and Orville Wright began their experiments with lighter-than-air machines in their bicycle shop in Dayton, while Glenn H. Curtiss stepped from the photographic industry into the bicycle business and from that into the hydroplane industry. From June 22, 1895, to October 5, 1895, Curtiss, who was seventeen years of age, was employed in the spooling room at Kodak Park at $3.50 a week. Young Curtiss returned to Hammondsport, New York, after leaving Kodak Park, to work for a local photographer and later became employed by a bicycle merchant.

Two of the pioneers in the automotive industry were friends of Eastman, Selden and Overman; the former was his first patent attorney. On May 8, 1879, Selden applied for a patent on a self-propelled vehicle operated by a

what Eastman had in mind to do. Strong, his staunchest friend, confessed that his projects were 'paralyzing,' but to Eastman they appeared so self-evident as not to excite surprise. 'My desires are limited only by my imagination.' That was Eastman's 'explanation.'

The secret of his actions lay in the infinite care with which he prepared every detail of a project. 'If you see where I have made a mistake, I will be obliged if you will point it out,' he had written ten years before. 'I want practical information — not argument. . . . I am perfectly willing to take your word for a thing if you say you can do it, but I want to know how you do it — so I can do it myself.'

'I know full well his persistence,' Colonel Strong recorded, 'and that his indomitable will must result in success.'

Eastman launched his programme of expansion in 1894 without awaiting the election of a Republican

gasoline engine and letters patent were granted to him on November 15, 1895. In 1882, Otto, a German inventor, patented a gasoline engine, of the so-called Otto cycle type. It was this type that enabled Henry Ford in 1911 to emerge the victor at the end of a long legal battle over the Selden patent.

'Haynes is given credit for priority of his gas car, the Duryeas and Winton were the first manufacturers, but the pioneer who did the most to set the United States upon its career as the world's greatest producer and user of gasoline automobiles was R. E. Olds, for he grasped the magic of mass production. . . . It was the Olds policy of mass production of an inexpensive car that carried Henry Ford to fame and fortune.' (Malcolm Keir, Professor of Economics at Dartmouth College, in *Manufacturing*.)

'In 1904 the Maxwell-Briscoe Company was the first to advertise that every part of their car was manufactured in one plant. The year before the first multiple drill and press was introduced to work cylinder blocks and heads; in the same year a machine to grind cylinders was developed, also the first lathe to turn the cam shaft.

'The Ford Motor Company was incorporated June 16, 1903. That year 11,000 automobiles were made by all companies. By 1908 production of all makers amounted to 60,000 cars. It was 1918 before the day of the purely assembled car had passed.' (From *The Automobile Industry*, by Ralph Epstein.)

President as most corporations did. He had voted against Cleveland, although he respected him, but he was not building his company upon the shifting sands of politics. Patent protection was preferred to political protection, but, above all, he believed that leadership depended 'greatly upon a rapid succession of changes and improvements. . . . If we can get out improved goods every year nobody will be able to follow us and compete with us.'

A succession of new products appeared in 1894, a new Kodak, additional lines of printing paper and film. In 1895, Eastman introduced a revolutionary change in camera construction. He marketed a folding, pocket Kodak, the ancestor of all modern roll-film cameras.

'We are shipping Mr. Dickman some samples this week. . . . We are very proud of the Pocket Kodak and of the rapidity with which the tools have been made,' Eastman wrote Walker. 'The first model was completed on Washington's Birthday. The model was afterward much modified and the tools have been practically completed in two months and a half. Within three months we hope to be turning them out in large quantities, as we have made extensive preparations to sell them.'

By July, the Pocket Kodak was selling so fast that Dickman cabled a standing order for two thousand a month for the European market alone.

'We take it that this indicates that the Pocket Kodak is to be as great a success with you as it is proving with us,' Eastman replied. 'We have not yet been able to average over 150 cameras per day, but we have got help enough already trained to turn out 300 per day. . . . I shall strain every nerve to increase the product up to 600 per day, or more if necessary, and shall not leave for my vacation trip until I am fully satisfied as to the output.

'It is taking a big pile of money to get out the Pocket Kodaks, and that, in addition to the amounts expended in the dry plate and collodion departments, leaves us very short. It is only by putting a large amount into the Pocket Kodak tools and extra machinery that we shall be able to make them at a price that will net us any profit.'

Strong, however, viewed the developments in a slightly different light. 'We have a tremendous capacity for the consumption of money,' he wrote Dickman. This was only natural. He had just returned from Tacoma to work again in Rochester, and dollar bills 'looked as big as the floor plan of a factory.'

This type of camera was not new with the Eastman Kodak Company. The Boston Camera Manufacturing Company, owned by S. N. Turner, and the Blair Camera Company had placed folding cameras on the market in 1890 and 1891, but these attempts had failed because they endeavored to avoid the Houston patent which Eastman controlled.

Eastman had considered a folding camera for several years, and in 1894 concluded the time was opportune for introducing it. Two months afterward, in the midst of its international success, Turner was granted a patent covering a photographic film roll or spool for daylight-loading cameras. Thus Eastman lacked one of the patents necessary in the manufacture of a pocket, folding camera. As soon as Eastman learned of this, he communicated with Philipp. 'I am inclined to think that we could make a good deal with Turner to pay him a royalty on his spools and make his spools for him. It would be better for both parties than having a fight. If you agree with this, you can arrange an interview.'

Returning from a hurried trip to London, Eastman

met Turner in New York City and secured an exclusive license.

By August, Eastman wrote his attorney that 'business is booming. We did the largest month's business on record last month. Turner is going to get a pretty handsome thing out of his royalties. It will certainly be over $5000 a year.' This was more money than Turner had ever made or ever expected to make. Three weeks later, he sold his business and contract to Eastman for $40,000 cash and retired.

In September, Turner made his first visit to Rochester, where Strong showed him how cameras, film, and paper were being made or processed by a continuous line of workmen and machines. 'Prodigious!' Turner exclaimed.[1]

'If the cameras were the only thing that produced a profit, it would be no object to sell double the number and make only the same net profit; but before the camera is dead, we ought to make at least as much from the film used in it as from the camera itself, probably more,' Eastman counseled Dickman. 'I believe that every camera is good for at least twenty spools of film. Besides this, the introduction of these cameras is going

[1] August 8, 1919, Eastman wrote George H. Austin, New York City: 'The facts in regard to Mr. Samuel N. Turner are that we purchased his invention outright and that afterwards in some litigation against us he made an affidavit in which he denied he was the inventor of the invention which had been patented by him and sold to us. The patent was finally declared invalid on the grounds that there was no invention. How much Turner's action had to do with this decision it is impossible to say, but he certainly did all he could to invalidate the patent. I was always of the opinion that he was the real inventor and that he was influenced to do what he did by a stronger man mentally than he was. As we had developed the invention successfully and made money out of it, I felt kindly disposed to him in spite of his action and, therefore, when I found he had lost the money we had paid him and was in straitened circumstances, the Kodak Company put him on a pension and carried him until he died.' ·

to lay the foundation for an enormous business in larger cameras of the same kind. We are getting out a Bull's-Eye camera which is positively the finest thing that was ever made.'

The success of film photography stimulated the inventive genius of the world. Rochester was recognized as the photographic headquarters. Hundreds of devices were examined. 'The trouble with most of these devices,' Eastman wrote, 'is that they will not work every time, and a photographic thing that will not work every time is not worth anything. There are also a great many things in the way of photographic apparatus that would be very good if they could be made cheap enough, but the manufacturing difficulties are so great that the cost is prohibitive.'

The Bull's-Eye camera and Falcon Kodaks were marketed in 1896, selling at twelve dollars and five dollars, respectively, the lowest prices for which cameras had ever been sold. A cartridge of film containing twelve exposures for the former retailed at ninety cents and for the latter at sixty cents. Photography, now, was really within the means of every one for the first time in the history of the art.

The dry-plate and paper business, however, were not going so well. Eastman had tried for several years to maintain prices, but competitors were continually undercutting him. His attitude is clearly stated in a letter to G. Cramer, of St. Louis, one of his chief competitors:

'Since you ask the question, I will frankly state that I did get the impression in Cleveland, and I hope unjustly, that you and Mr. Abbott were endeavoring to force me into a false position. I have no doubt whatever that we are all working for the general good of the trade, and it seems to me that, in the consideration of such a broad object, business rivalries ought to be ignored and any action which gives rise to the feeling that one is attempting to place another in a false light will prevent that harmony of action which is necessary to attain the object in view. I am very glad to see the interest that you are now taking in the movement to maintain prices and that you are now at last adopting the method of doing business which we have pursued for many years.'

But the 'Solio war' could not be settled without an open fight and Eastman was compelled to attack the American Aristo Company in special advertisements:

For some time past the American Aristo Co. has used the following absurd advertisement extensively:

> ' $5/8$ of the entire amount of Paper
> consumed in the United States is
> American Aristo.'

A CHALLENGE

Before SOLIO was introduced there may have been a shadow of truth in the above advertisement, but knowing full well that it is, and for at least a year has been, a ridiculous exaggeration,

We Hereby Challenge

The American Aristo Co. to publish a list of 1000 names which shall include all the photographers in any one section of the country, $5/8$ of whose total consumption is American Aristo or $5/8$ of whom now use American Aristo. Let them prove the claim on either basis — if they can.

WATCH THEM DODGE

Those who are familiar with the awkward manner in which the American Aristo Co. backed down and suddenly decided to 'wash its hands' of the late Chicago controversy — when we published our overwhelming evidence in the shape of testimonial letters from 80 Solio consumers in that city, while they could show but 53 users of 'Aristo' — will watch with interest to see what method of evasion will now be adopted.

NOT THROUGH YET

We propose challenging them to prove some of their other astounding statements next month. We are not through yet.

At the height of this trade battle Eastman received a small package and a letter from Walker. Opening them, he learned that a German university professor had discovered 'a new kind of rays' and that with them it was possible to take 'shadowgrams.' The package contained two glass plates, showing X-ray pictures of a human hand and a frog, the first two photographs to be taken by these rays. Another week passed before there were additional details. Then the February issue of 'The New Light,' a British photographic journal, arrived, containing a translation of Professor Roentgen's article, as it appeared originally in the 'Sitzungsberichte der Würzburger Physik-medic Gesellschaft.' It was illustrated by 'shadowgrams' of a 'living frog through sheet of aluminum,' exposed twenty minutes and a 'living hand through black vulcanized fibre, exposure four minutes.' [1]

'Of special interest in this connection,' Professor Roentgen wrote, 'is the fact that photographic dry plates are sensitive to the X-rays. It is thus possible to exhibit the phenomena so as to exclude the danger of error. I have thus confirmed many observations originally made by eye observation with the fluorescent screen. Here the power of the X-rays to pass through wood or cardboard becomes useful. The photographic plate can be exposed to the action without removal of the shutter of the dark slide or other protecting case, so that the experiment need not be conducted in darkness. Manifestly unexposed plates must not be left in their box near the vacuum tube.

'It seems now questionable whether the impression on the plate is a direct effect of the X-rays, or a secondary

[1] 'You might recall the fact that Roentgen was first put on the track of his discovery of these rays by observing their influence upon a box of unopened photographic plates.' (Letter from Joseph Thacher Clarke to Eastman, January 8, 1911.)

result induced by the fluorescence of the material of the plate. Films can receive the impression as well as ordinary dry plates.'

It was several months before the first X-ray machine was brought to the United States, but a market for X-ray printing paper developed almost immediately in Europe. Dickman ordered one thousand assorted sheets, as this X-ray paper was packed differently from other bromide paper in that each sheet was inserted in a separate envelope. Within a short period a New York house began to manufacture X-ray products, and the Eastman Company made an arrangement whereby it was to furnish plates and paper for X-ray photography. Throughout this time Stuber spent many days at the Dime Museum in Rochester, where the first X-ray machine was exhibited, taking pictures and studying the plates and all the while experimenting with new emulsions at Kodak Park.

This is the origin of X-ray photography in the United States. It required many years of experimenting, however, before the present system of radiography was developed. In the beginning the X-ray was an attraction in Main Street museums. To-day it is one of the chief servants of science, medicine, dentistry, and research.

In the summer of 1896, Eastman went abroad to organize 'the European campaign for the coming year.' Here he was convinced that 1897 would witness a vast increase in business. Strong was informed immediately and asked to expand production at the Camera Works and build an addition to the State Street factory. 'I may be wrong,' the President replied, 'but I am of the opinion that we can make all the cameras that we can possibly market during the coming year without any additional plant. You may take this opinion for what it is worth, and at the same time be assured that I am not setting up my judgment against yours.'

But before an answer was received from London, Eastman had cabled Rochester to expand the film capacity of Kodak Park. This, again was 'paralyzing' to the Colonel.

To Dickman, who had permitted the laboratory at Harrow to conduct film experiments, Eastman expressed again his confidence in research:

'I believe in experiments as much as any one and in fact our entire business has been founded upon them, but there are well-directed experiments and ill-directed ones, and I am firmly of the opinion that the search for a dry stripping film at the present time is ill-directed; and besides that I object to the spirit in which the experiments are being conducted, that is, condemnation of the present film. We are in shape to make the grandest success out of it that we have ever made out of anything if we follow it up and if we do not we are liable to fritter away our opportunities. If you have any doubts about transparent film yourself, I think that we can dispel them when you come over here.'

By February, Eastman's 'paralyzing' plans were justified. Dickman increased the European orders to five thousand Pocket Kodaks and twenty thousand spools of film per month. 'To say that we are delighted and surprised at these big orders is to express our feelings mildly,' Eastman replied. 'I am very glad to know that you are so far ahead on your sales for the first quarter. The increase figures about 71% on the combined sales. We can beat you a little, our increase for the same time being 85%, but you are doing well. . . . I really think that $2,000,000 a year in the near future is not improbable [$850,000 in 1895]. We have not begun to develop the business yet either in this country or in Europe. We are very likely to do $1,500,000 here this year. . . . Our experimental department is in good shape and we have new goods blocked out for a year in advance.' [1]

April 6, Eastman urged Dickman to train men and have them learn languages so that they could take over the management of wholesale depots 'in every large country.'

'We are getting things in shape in the Camera Works so we can certainly beat the world on design, workmanship, and price, and there is no reason why we should not sell cartridge cameras anywhere in large quantities all over the world. If you can get the system introduced as generally in your territory as we have got it here, your two-million limit will be reached, but we do not think that we have begun to develop the trade here. We will get a camera before long that will reach the people . . . and then our organization for selling them will count the way it has in a smaller way on the Pocket Kodak.'

While Eastman was directing the development of his world-wide business, the motion picture, which had been indulging in a Rip Van Winkle dream for nearly six years, awoke with a suddenness that surprised every one, including Edison. Since 1889, Edison's peep-show Kinetoscope had ruled the Penny Arcades, but on May 20, 1895, Major Woodville Latham took the whole city of New York into his confidence by projecting motion pictures on a screen for the first time publicly. 'It was only a ghost of a show,' Ramsaye records, 'but it was first.' Heretofore, motion pictures were presented only in a small box-type machine operated automatically when a coin was dropped into a slot. Latham called his machine the 'Pantopticon.'

[1] April 16, 1896.

The New York 'Sun' sent an enterprising reporter over to Orange to inform Edison.

'That is the Kinetoscope,' retorted the inventor. 'This strip of film with the pictures which you have here is made exactly as the film I use. The holes in it are for the spokes of the sprocket, which I devised. The throwing of the pictures on the screen was the very first thing that I did with the Kinetoscope.'

The Major, however, had presented the first public screen show.

Three months before, February 13, 1895, the Lumière brothers obtained a French patent for their 'cinématographe,' which they demonstrated in their shop at Lyon on March 22. Meanwhile, Robert W. Paul was experimenting in London and Thomas Armat in Washington. February 28, 1896, Paul demonstrated his projector at the Royal Institution in London.[1]

On April 6, 1896, Eastman read an account in the 'New York Herald' of an exhibition in New York City of the Vitascope, which embodied Edison's and Armat's inventions.

'The first picture shown,' the newspaper reported, 'was a colored panorama of a serpentine dance by Annabelle, who went out to West Orange to pose one day last summer. The film roll on which the photographs were attached was arranged over a half-dozen spools and pulleys, and the machine was set in motion.

'Even the inventor himself was surprised at the result, although with his usual critical eye he discovered flaws

---

[1] From *A Million and One Nights*, by Terry Ramsaye.

'. . . It is only an enlarged kinetoscope, the adaptation of a toy to the requirements of actual life, but that is just what was done with the telephone. Once that was a curious toy, now with it you can talk with a man in Chicago and recognize the tones of his voice. It will not be safe to decry the possibilities of the new living panorama.' (The *Brooklyn Daily Eagle*.)

in the film which he declared must be disposed of before the vitascope would come up to his ideal.

'Annabelle danced for five minutes, and then a panorama of the latest English Derby was thrown upon the screen.

'The feature of the new machine which astonished all who saw last night's views was the almost entire absence of vibration in the pictures as they appeared on the screen, and which had been the hardest obstacle to surmount in perfecting the apparatus.'

The general managers of the Kodak companies in Paris and London sensed the commercial possibilities of a new film market simultaneously while Eastman was working on a programme of financial reorganization. In June, the managing director in London arrived in Rochester. His enthusiasm was on fire. Hurrying to the Park, he found Stuber and the other experts engaged in experiments for a more durable and more adaptable film for Edison.

On June 22, 1896, Dickman sent the Paris office 'two samples of the skin made yesterday afternoon in my presence at Kodak Park as an experiment, getting ready for this industry. They made only 19 feet of it but it is perfectly successful.'

This was the first strip of positive motion-picture film ever made for commercial purposes.

Dickman returned to Europe effervescing confidence, while Strong took charge of the Ciné business in Rochester. Strong 'landed' the first big contract with Edison. Dickman followed with a substantial order from Charles Pathé.

'If the disease breaks out seriously,' President Strong concluded one of his letters, 'I think we will have no surplus film, as this trade will keep up, I judge, through the winter.'

The 'disease' was 'serious.' December 31, Strong began a series of letters to Eastman in London which record motion-picture history in the making.

'You may have taken some large orders for Ciné film, but I propose to knock you silly. I spent all of yesterday forenoon negotiating a contract for 300,000 feet of 2½ inch film to be taken within six months. Our price is 5¢ per foot per inch wide. A 10% discount is to be given on the first 100,000 feet, if 200,000 feet are taken the discount is to be 15% and if 300,000 feet are taken within the time specified, 20%. It took considerable assurance to hold the party down to these figures, but I feel comparatively safe for the reason that Blair is doing very little, if anything, at present in the film business, and in addition to this *all the concerns on the face of the earth, outside of ours, could not make this quantity of film and supply it promptly within the time specified.* If we could capture Lumière and supply him with film, we would control the world. Have you made any special effort to supply him? Can we not make a figure low enough to meet his views?'

In some of the early experiments, Lumière had purchased strips of celluloid from the Celluloid Company in New York, and Paul had used similar strips coated by Blair in London, but this method soon proved to be unequal to the Kodak flexible film.

'We have had all the Ciné orders from the United States customers that we could handle this week. [January 28, 1897.] We have just booked a standing order for 20,000 feet every Saturday for five weeks. The large order which I wrote you about some time since which was to be used in the Corbett-Fitzsimmons fight has not yet materialized.'

But within a few days the promoters returned to Rochester, and Dickman was advised:

'The great prize fight is now an assured fact, as near as it can be, and we have commenced shipping on the order for 30,000 feet of negative film to take the pictures. The fight comes off on St. Patrick's Day, March 17th [at Carson City, Nevada], and if the sun shines and there are no mishaps I expect to receive a telegram on the 18th to commence shipping the positive, and I hope they will never stop until the entire 300,000 feet are completed. I was afraid for a time that the scheme would fall through, but it is now beyond a question, I think. They are to use film 2½ inches wide, so you see it walks into money very rapidly.'

The prize-fight pictures were reported to be total failures. When these accounts appeared in the London newspapers, Eastman asked his senior partner for the facts.

'We have evidence from headquarters that such is not the case.' Strong replied.[1] 'There has been great agitation in the legislatures of various states looking toward the passage of laws preventing the exhibition of such pictures, and it is surmised that this report of the failure of the negatives was a dodge of the parties interested, to quiet the minds of our law makers with the hope that the matter would be dropped until they had adjourned. Whether this is so or not is a question. They certainly have some reason for not denying the rumor.'

Thus the prize-fight pictures forecast the first censorship cloud on the horizon of the new industry, but Edison, Paul, Lumière, and Eastman went boldly on with their plans and their new art.

'We have already sold the Edison Mfg. Co. about 300,000 feet of Ciné film and they are about to place an order with us for 35,000 feet per week,' wrote Colonel

[1] April 16, 1897.

Strong. 'Our price to them has been, for 1⅜ inches wide, 6⅞¢ per foot, less 20% and 5%; we are not giving any such discount to any other party. All film that we have sent to the Edison Co. has given perfect satisfaction and we have never had to replace a single inch up to date, which is remarkable.

'You speak as though sharp competition in the manufacture of Ciné film had already appeared. What have you to fear besides Lumière? Are there others? The Blair people seem to have dropped out entirely, but of course they are liable to "bob up serenely" at any moment, and there may be new factories springing up at any time, but up to the present moment we know of none.'

It is important at this time to fix the names Lumière and Blair, as well as that of the Celluloid Company, as among the only other firms which were attempting to manufacture film for motion pictures, because, within a short time, we shall observe the name of another individual, who, up to this date, was long on claims and short on film because he had not produced an inch, a yard, or a reel of it.

Before the first positive film was produced at Kodak Park, all film used by all the inventors of cameras and projectors was negative film.[1] The new positive film, however, had to be perfected. In the first place, it did not have body enough to withstand the hard usage to which film was necessarily subjected in the rapid move-

---

[1] Many problems still had to be solved before the industry finally adopted negative film to photograph the action and positive film to project it in the theaters. Eastman originated the metal containers used in shipping film; the marking of film; and established a company policy of not engaging in marketing photoplays or making prints. He thought this interfered with his customers' business. Lumière originated the .35 millimeter width for film, which has remained the standard for all professional uses.

ment through the machines. It lacked, also, the necessary tenacious adhesion between the gelatine emulsion and the nitro-cellulose base to resist the separation of the former from the latter as a result of continuous usage.

'Film,' said Strong, 'is not like flour that can be turned out under any and all circumstances at a moment's warning and without limit.'

These difficulties were all overcome at the Park, the first by increasing the thickness of the film base and the second by the application of a substratum of gelatine containing a nitro-cellulose solvent which had an affinity for the film base. This was a trade secret, and although it was developed at the Park, the company discovered, in 1904, that Russell S. Penniman, who was employed in a smokeless powder factory at Dover, New Jersey, had been issued letters patent covering it. Eastman immediately purchased the patent, in line with the unbroken precedent which he established in 1889 of controlling every *bona-fide* invention in the art of film photography.

This policy was reiterated in a formal communication to the English subsidiary. 'The patents which cover our present methods of manufacturing film should be kept up. . . . The film business has the greatest possibilities of profit of any branch of photography and we must try to cover every avenue that leads to it.'

In Rochester and at Harrow the factories had to be operated day and night. The motion-picture industry had arrived. Kodak film was giving life to the silver screen in the United States, France, Germany, and England.

Even the Nelson Monument in Trafalgar Square lost the mantle of darkness which it had worn at night during many decades. Atop the surrounding buildings flashed the first four electric signs which the throngs at Charing Cross had ever seen. 'Kodak' was one of these.

Through the streets of Paris sped the somber omnibusses. Dickman foresaw an opportunity to be the first to display advertisements on these conveyances. 'Take all Paris omnibusses three years, privilege to sublet,' Eastman cabled in reply, and since then Paris busses have carried advertisements as well as passengers.

On the Pravda in Moscow, Unter den Linden in Berlin, in Vienna, Copenhagen, Brussels, Milan, Rome, and Madrid appeared the Kodak signs. Eight years after the word was coined, it did not have to be explained or interpreted. It was cosmopolitan, so that by the spring of 1897 Eastman was ready to enter the arena of international finance.

'I have formulated a plan for the consolidation of the English and American companies and have submitted it to the Directors, who have approved it,' he wrote Dickman. 'The affair involves an option to me on all of the stock of both companies and I expect to be in possession of this option, so far as the stock owned in this country is concerned, by the end of next week. If my anticipations are realized, I shall immediately go to England to obtain the options of the English Company. The scheme is to organize a new company which will take over the options. . . . The difference between the total capital stock of the new company and the amount necessary to take up the options will be used in promoting the new company.'

There were five reasons for the merger: 1. The uncertainty in regard to the dividends on the preference shares of the English subsidiary. (Some stockholders, when the dividends were passed in 1892 and only partially paid in 1893 and 1894, held the dividends were

KINGSWAY BUILDING, LONDON

cumulative. Eastman contended otherwise. It was believed that a consolidation on favorable terms would forestall litigation.) 2. Both the English and American companies, to date, had been privately owned by a few stockholders, most of whom were interested in creating a wider market for their securities. 3. Additional capital was needed and by increasing the number of shares and the number of investors, the stockholders would obtain rights or new stock which they could sell or retain. 4. The advertising which would accompany the public offering of securities in England, the United States, Germany, and France had a definite business value. And 5. It gave employees, customers, and concerns supplying the companies with raw materials an opportunity to become stockholders. Incidentally, it offered an opportunity 'for the promoter, who was myself [Eastman], and the underwriter to make some money.' This fact was 'fully disclosed to all interested at the time and consented to.' The directors, 'George Eastman not voting or taking part in the proceedings,' voted unanimously, in fact, enthusiastically, for the proposal.

Eastman had been studying the subject for nearly a year, and had obtained from his solicitors in England an outline of the procedure necessary to comply with the laws of that country. He had examined a number of international stock issues and was thoroughly posted in the law and the financial policies involved. He was cognizant, too, of the existing prejudice in London against foreign concerns because of the failure of several fly-by-night companies whose securities had been unloaded upon British investors.

But business was war, and the 'whole art of war consists in getting at what is on the other side of the hill.' [1]

[1] From a classic remark of the Duke of Wellington.

Eastman was fully prepared to get at the obstacles on the 'other side of the hill' before he started.

As Walker was the third largest stockholder, he had Colonel Strong write him in regard to the directors' agreement with Eastman and then he added the following information:

'Strong wrote you by last mail about the proposed scheme to amalgamate the two Companies. I enclose herewith two copies of each agreement, one for you to sign and the other to keep. We had a meeting of the large stockholders last night and every one present signed.

'I expect to sail with Mr. Hubbell for England on March 6. In the mean time would like to hear from you and if you approve the plan to have you sign the enclosed agreements and send, with your stock, to the Trust Company or to your counsel to deliver them.

'I find I have omitted to give you the results of our last year's business [1896]. I have been so busy and had so many things to think of that it escaped my mind. We made $445,940.00 net, after charging off $30,769.00 on account of bad debts, tools, etc., etc. Of this $201,620.00 went into dividends and $240,320.00 to working capital.

'We expect to do better this year, but doubt whether we can pay more than 6% because we have to build a new camera works and finish the improvements at Kodak Park, which will all together cost a little over $200,-000.00. We let the contract for a new camera works Saturday, to be finished on May 15th, and we expect to have the machinery humming on that date. It will be the finest manufacturing plant in this part of the country. We concluded not to build [a camera factory] at Kodak Park, because we could not get the building ready in time to get any good out of it this summer.'

Obtaining options from practically every stockholder

in the American company, Eastman sailed for London, where he presented his project to the English board and stockholders, securing their options. He was now in possession of options and contracts with the two corporations vesting him with full power to promote the consolidation. Returning to Rochester, he perfected his plans during the summer, sailing again for London August 25.

After submitting the text of the first 'Prospectus of the Eastman Kodak Company, Limited,' to his solicitors, Kerly Son and Verden, he had the first 'private and confidential' proof from the printer and was ready to open negotiations with the bankers and brokers.

In this prospectus, Eastman marshaled these facts:

'The amalgamation of the businesses of the Eastman Kodak Companies has become especially advantageous at the present time, owing to the expiry of a working agreement which until recently has existed between the American and the English companies.

'The favorable position of the New Company to profit by the enormous expansion of the trade in photographic apparatus and materials in every country of the world, may be judged from the following advantages which it possesses:

'(1) The united business which the company will control, and from which it will receive the profits, is the largest of its kind in the world. The EASTMAN Specialties have been brought to such perfection and simplicity, that any person of ordinary intelligence can in a few minutes learn to use a Kodak, and produce pictures that are in no way inferior to those of experts. "You press the button, We do the rest." The demand for photographic materials and apparatus has consequently already increased enormously, and it has a far wider increase before it.

'(2) The large output of Kodaks creates a constantly increasing demand for the FILMS manufactured by the Company.

'(3) It does not rely upon the sale of one article, but supplies almost all requisites for the amateur and the professional photographer.

'(4) It extends to most of the civilized countries of the world, and therefore its profits are not likely to be seriously affected by adverse trade conditions in any one country.

'(5) The Company has the exclusive right to the use of the trade names KODAK and SOLIO, which have been very extensively advertised, and are now well known all over the world as guarantees of first-rate apparatus and workmanship in connection with photographic materials.

'(6) The Company is possessed of valuable patents for Great Britain, America, France, Germany, and Belgium, several of which have been sustained in Courts of Law, and of various secret processes and formulæ, which give it a practical monopoly in various branches of its business.

'Very large sums have been expended upon the erection and equipment of FACTORIES at Rochester, and at Harrow. The plant and the machinery are by far the largest and finest of their kind in the world.

'The premises in Rochester consist of:

'Block of Offices in the center of the city, possessing a floor space of 30,600 feet super.

'Camera works adjoining, possessing a floor space of 142,700 feet super.

'Factory at Kodak Park, near Rochester, of recent construction, with a floor space of upwards of 202,200 feet super, the land covers an area of about 20 acres.

'The factory at Harrow, Middlesex, was erected in

1890. The buildings possess a floor space of 45,800 feet super, the land covers an area of about 7 acres.

'The Factories have been recently greatly enlarged, and are believed to be sufficient for the anticipated increase of business for 1898. When further enlargement becomes necessary, ample land space exists for such enlargement.

'The Company has secured the services of the existing highly experienced staff, and the organization, both in England and America, which has been so successful up to the present, will be retained. The policy of maintaining the excellence of the specialties and the introduction of improvements will be continued.

'For 1898 a new line of KODAKS will be introduced to the public including a FOLDING POCKET KODAK of an entirely NEW TYPE which will make a picture more than twice as large as the famous original Pocket Kodak, and which will be more easily carried either in the pocket or on a bicycle. Experts pronounce this new Kodak to be the greatest advance yet made in cameras and predict for it unexampled success. In addition a new CARTRIDGE ROLL-HOLDER has been constructed which will enable the cartridge system to be applied to EXISTING CAMERAS OF OTHER MAKERS, thus greatly enlarging the market for the Cartridge Film manufactured by the Company.'

Facts, these were! Eastman always believed in the power of facts. Note, however, no references to motion pictures! While audiences were forming in queues everywhere where pictures were shown, while Edison alone had consumed nearly one million feet of Eastman film, the 'promoter' was deliberately understating, not overstating his case or promoting the company as a speculative enterprise. It was a serious undertaking — not a gamble, and motion pictures were considered generally to be in this latter class.

The first obstacles we find reflected in one of Colonel Strong's letters: 'I am surprised that ——, —— & Company should object to the use of their name in connection with the new company. Their opinion of the Eastman Kodak Company will undoubtedly grow as time passes. I suppose [Albert O.] Fenn [cashier of the Alliance Bank] suggested to you a long time ago that it would have been much better to have opened our account with ——, ——, —— & Company and possibly he was correct. [The banks referred to are large international banking houses.]

'I can see that you are going through the same experience that I had and if you do not get wearied before you get through I shall be surprised. Those great capitalists are very tiresome; they make appointment after appointment and always have something new to suggest which requires further consideration and it seems as though the end would never come.

'I think you will find it absolutely necessary to use a promoter. I give you all credit for being able to accomplish wonders and accomplishing what few others could, but I think, as before stated, you will find a first class promoter of great assistance and possibly indispensable.'

Opposition to Eastman's plans became so formidable that the subscription lists which were to have been opened in November were withheld.[1]

---

[1] 'Nowadays one is used to hearing of things that take one's breath away, but the latest prospectus of a proposed company that we have seen is perhaps the most marvelous on record. We refer to a company on the eve of coming out and formed with the object of purchasing the Kodak . . . can anybody in his sane senses look upon "Kodak" as being worth two millions sterling? The idea, alone, shocks one. Truly the promoter of to-day regards the intellect of his fellow man as filmy.' (From the London *Rialto*.)

Meanwhile, the profits continued to multiply, but as Eastman's confidence in the earning power of his companies increased the banks became more and more conservative. It must have been difficult for them to grasp the full significance of the undertaking they were asked to participate in. While Eastman was earnest and convincing, his youth and personal modesty were baffling. He was so youthful in appearance that it was not uncommon for strangers to say when they met him: 'Oh, I must have made a mistake. I wanted to see your father.' They assumed that he was the son of the founder of the concern.

When the Christmas holidays arrived, Eastman made a hurried trip home to be with his mother. While in New York City he called upon Brown Brothers & Co., 59 Wall Street, where he outlined his programme with such conviction that the bank wrote him:

'Referring to our conversation of to-day, and your request that our name should appear as bankers on the prospectus left with us this morning, we beg to say that assuming that you are able to carry out your arrangements as proposed, and that the Board of Directors in London are such as will meet the approval of the London & Westminster Bank and ourselves, we will, with pleasure, allow the use of our name, as bankers, in the United States.'

The two words 'with pleasure' added a touch of Christmas spirit that was welcome after the struggle in London.

Hastening back to England on January 4, he revised the proof-prospectus, fixed the capital at £2,000,000, and decided that the subscription lists could be opened by January 24, 1898. But, although the preliminary annual report increased the estimated profits, he found it necessary to postpone the public offering another month.

The Colonel, in Rochester, was swamped with orders for Ciné film. When cash accompanied orders, he would write Eastman that he enjoyed being 'overstocked ... with that kind of goods,' and he always hoped that his junior partner was 'gaining flesh every moment and enjoying life.'

One would not gather in reading the articles in the British newspapers that Eastman was 'enjoying life.' The press was hostile. 'Photographic cameras especially designed for the dabbler,' 'cheap notoriety,' 'chequered career,' 'Kodak "Kid"' — these 'were some of the editorial phrases that pierced the eyes of the readers.

As usual, Eastman had kept himself and his own personality out of the picture. On February 1, however, he broke the rule and granted his first interview to the 'Westminster Gazette':

'Very shortly, we are able to announce, the public will have in its hands the prospectus of a very interesting undertaking, with a capital of two millions sterling; for the Eastman Photographic Materials Company is to become a public concern. To complete the negotiations for the flotation of the colossal enterprise, which is to include every stick and station connected with the Kodak Companies, both in America and in England, there has recently arrived in London from New York Mr. George Eastman, the inventor of the photographic materials which bear his name. For more than eighteen years the history of photography and the history of the Eastman companies have been identical. It was with the advent of the dry plate, nearly a score of years ago, that the name Eastman first became known in the photographic world.

'Mr. Eastman, with whom a representative of the "Westminster" has had an interview, is an American, only forty-four years old, with the keenest of business heads. Starting life as a bank clerk, he always took an extraordinary interest in photography, and the story runs that while he was yet an amateur, amusing himself here and there by taking uncommon views and faces, with a camera which can only be described as crude, the future millionaire entered a barber shop, one of the assistants of which he was on familiar terms with, and during a shave he unveiled to his friendly operator a scheme for creating a new camera. The two then and there mapped out arrangements for forming a company, and in 1879 appeared "George Eastman." The barber episode reminds one of Sir Richard Arkwright. "The business growing rapidly," said Mr. Eastman, "we took large premises at Rochester, New York, where the camera factory is now stationed, and in 1889, ten years afterward, the Kodak made its appearance in England — to become first a toy, and then a recognized boon." '

After questioning him regarding the origin of 'that awe-inspiring word Kodak,' the article continues:

' "I understand that you have made the cameras only in New York; the films, solio and bromide are prepared in Harrow?" — "Yes, that is so. Our Rochester factory, which is the largest camera factory in the world, and which it would be impossible for fire to so far destroy as to stop the manufacture of Kodaks even for a single day, has an output of film during the busy season of upwards of 150 miles per week, of the Pocket-Kodak width, while figured on a basis of cabinet width, 105 miles of sensitized paper is coated each week. To accomplish this over five acres of floor space are necessary and the power from the great engines is distributed over the plant through the medium of seventy-five electric motors."

' "As an expert would you say that photography as an art is more advanced here than across the ocean?" "Treating the question from an artistic point of view, I should say that the English are better photographers than the Americans, but as regards mechanical ingenuity and workmanship, the latter are streets ahead. You have more skilled amateurs; we have more professional workmen. Material is cheaper in England than in the States." '

Two weeks later, the 'Rochester Herald' published a two-column story, 'A $10,000,000 Scheme Fails at the Finish. Eastman Wires from London, Says that Negotiations cannot be Completed before Options Expire — Outcome is a Surprise.' 'The stock which people were scrambling for last week at $105 can now be bought considerably below par.'

The article was a sensational shock which Hubbell, counsel of the company, resented in a letter to the proprietor of the newspaper: 'Your sneering allusions to the stock seem to show that your only desire in publishing the article was to belittle its value, if possible, without reference to the facts. The business of the company has had a phenomenal growth and is rapidly increasing every month. Its profits make it a large dividend paying concern and if anybody is foolish enough to sell his stock "at considerably below par" (at which you say it can be purchased), he will undoubtedly regret his action before he is a week older.'

What had really happened? Eastman had discovered that the negotiations could not be completed within the time limit in the options, upon the terms he had drawn up. Rather than sacrifice a financial structure which he considered sound, he decided to postpone it.

Returning to Rochester, Eastman wrote Lord Kelvin,[1] whom he had invited to become vice-chairman of the board and who was as interested in film photography now as he had been, in 1876, in Bell's first telephone:

'I arrived at Rochester on Sunday morning, the 27th of February, after a very pleasant passage. I found that my cables announcing the postponement of the issue had been accepted as really meaning that the affair was ended. It has been, therefore, rather more difficult to pick up the strings than I anticipated, and I felt obliged to cable Mr. Verden and Mr. Dickman as follows:

' "Impractical. Many shareholders prefer keeping present shares. Letter."

'I was then called away to New York for two days on a very important matter, which delayed further progress. On my return here again, however, I find a little reaction setting in, and it may be possible to get the options, but not in time to carry the scheme through this spring. If obtained at all, the options will have to run until January 1, 1899, and I shall not be able to get every share as before, but shall have to be satisfied with 85%, or more if possible. While no doubt there will be one advantage which is important; we shall have earnings up to at least July 1, and they will strengthen the statement very materially.

'I hope that the prospect of further delays, over what was expected when I left London, will not lessen your interest in the affair, and that you will be willing to go on with it when the time comes, the same as before. I

[1] The only thing that worried Lord Kelvin, to judge from his letters, was this: 'Do you not think the large advertisement of profits "exceeding £200,000 for 1898" proposed in the draft prospectus might invite injurious competition?' Lord Kelvin subscribed and paid cash for several thousand shares in the new company.

shall take the liberty of advising you from time to time as to the progress of our efforts.'

By March 24, Eastman was in a position to write the chief stockholders here and abroad that it had 'been decided to go on with the new English company on very much the same lines as before.' Business was expanding rapidly. By April, it was 33⅓ per cent ahead of 1897 when the Spanish-American War loomed upon the horizon. 'War with Spain seems to be pretty certain now,' he notified Dickman. 'I do not see that it can affect our trade very much. I expect it will be over before we want to float our company, but even if it is not, I propose to float it.'

'Everybody here is feeling jubilant over the first reports of the Manila victory,' he wrote Walker.[1] 'Up to the present time we have not had any details except those that have leaked out through the Spaniards. Two companies of Rochester boys have been ordered into camp down on Long Island, three of our men were among the number. Others belong to the Naval Reserve and they expect to be called out very shortly. The feeling here is very confident that if Spain sends any of her war vessels over on this side of the Atlantic they will never go back again.

'I am turning my attention to peaceful pursuits; am now engaged in preparing plans for a greenhouse. When I come to England next will have many garden experiences to compare with yours.

'Peace extends only to private life, however. In business it is war all the time. Just now we are beginning suits against the Blair Camera Co. and Reichenbach, Morey & Will. We do not always win but when we lose the victory does not seem to have much attraction for the enemy.'

[1] May 3, 1898.

In July, however, there was a legal victory in England. It was featured by 'The Times' and hailed by the press generally, which 'admired . . . the pluck and persistence with which the Eastman company has pursued its suit.'

'A highly important trade-mark judgment has just been delivered by the House of Lords,' the 'Drapers' Record' reported. '. . . The appellants — the Eastman Photographic Materials Company, Limited — applied to register the word "Solio" . . . but the mark was refused by the Comptroller upon the ground that it was descriptive of the character or quality of the goods. This was sustained by the lower courts. . . . Upon appeal to the House of Lords the Lord Chancellor and Lords Herschell, Macnaughten, Morris, and Shand unanimously reversed this decision, and held that "Solio" is an invented word, and . . . the mark should be registered.'

This '. . . practically upsets the previous practice at the Patent Office, or at least threatens to secure a much more liberal interpretation of the Act.'

Early in October, Eastman returned to London, ready to reënter the arena. Before leaving Rochester, a correspondent of the New York 'Sun' showed him an article from the 'Newark Sunday Call':

'KODAK FILM INVENTED HERE'

'The World Pressed the Button and Newark Does the Rest. A Long Litigation

'The Rev. H. Goodwin's Victory in the Patent Office. He Receives a Patent as the Inventor of Film.' [1]

[1] September 13, 1898, the Reverend Hannibal Goodwin was granted Letters Patent No. 610,861 'for Improvement in Photographic Pellicles and Process of Producing the Same.' The statement that Kodak film was invented in Newark was false, of course.

He notified Philipp that he had asked the 'Sun' to interview him. Later he answered an inquiry from Price, Waterhouse and Company, auditors of all Eastman companies, 'I have not read Mr. Goodwin's patent yet, but I can say this, that we do not anticipate any interference with our business. . . .'

In November, the 'Prospectus' for Kodak, Limited, was in the hands of the public. Six large banking houses, two from the United States, and one each from England, Scotland, France, and Germany, were listed among the bankers. Sir James Pender, M.P., and Lord Kelvin were chairman and vice-chairman of the board, respectively. The new capital structure consisted of 600,000 cumulative preference shares of £1 each and 1,000,000 ordinary shares of £1 [1] each, and in the public notices it was specifically stated that 'Mr. George Eastman who is the vendor and promoter of the Company, and *who is selling it at a profit* . . . will also be entitled to the premium payable on the public issue of the Ordinary Shares.'

When we consider that promoters heretofore and hereafter seldom, if ever, advertised the fact that they were profiting by the sale of stock, we may understand some of the wonderment that this frankness created in the realm of international finance. That any bank or individual should profit by marketing company shares was always implied, and thoroughly understood by insiders, but it was never advertised. But Eastman, who had never speculated in the stock of his companies and who thought that the public was entitled to the real facts as much as any insiders, was either a 'country fellow from Monroe County' or a pioneer. In either case the stock was over-

---

[1] January 7, 1898, Hubbell to Eastman: 'However, as you say, the reduction [in the number of shares from two million to one million six hundred thousand] injures no one but yourself, and if you feel that it is for the best it is all right — but I am awfully sorry to see you let so much good money go.'

subscribed despite the public attacks which the Reverend Mr. Goodwin launched in the New York and London newspapers. Kodak, Limited, was a reality. Twenty years after Eastman had taken his first lessons in the art of photography, Kodak shares were listed on the Exchange in London, the financial capital of the world! [1]

Upon his return to New York, Eastman obtained Philipp's opinion of the Goodwin patent, examined the patent carefully himself for the first time, and on December 15, 1898, wrote George Davison, the new managing director of the company abroad: [2] 'I hope that you will be able to carry your point with the photographic journals, that they should not force us into fighting our patent suits in the newspapers. No good can come from it to us or to him. If anything is said about it by any of our Directors, I authorize you to say that I consider there is absolutely nothing to be feared from Goodwin. If he brings suit against us, it will be greatly to our advantage because it will have a deterrent influence on would-be competitors. I am really very sorry that Mr. Goodwin has not got a good strong patent, because if he had I am pretty sure we could get hold of it and add it to our collection.'

In his annual report for 1898, the Treasurer read a

---

[1] December 17 Eastman wrote Hayden: 'The subscriptions were about 700,000 pounds, or an oversubscription of 70,000 pounds. I met with a great deal of opposition from "the City," the brokers having done all they could to down the scheme. At one time it looked as if we were not going to have much of a subscription, but it finally turned out all right and we got the best lot of subscriptions any company could have, being all investment money and nothing speculative.'

[2] On November 22, Andrew Pringle, Chairman, Eastman Photographic Materials Company, Limited, sent a report to the stockholders and subscribers: 'It is my melancholy duty to inform you that Mr. George Dickman died on the 15th instant, after an illness of only a few days. A more able and genial colleague no Board ever had. . . .' Dickman, who had lived in the Orient, had struggled for many years against an illness contracted in China.

carefully prepared review to the Board and had copies made for the stockholders. It was the first public statement Eastman authorized of the results of the negotiations and the profits of early investors.

'Since our last annual meeting a transaction has been completed which has changed the relations of many of the old stockholders to the Company. . . . In November an English Company was organized, with a capital of £1,600,000, to take over the property under option. The shares of this company had been largely subscribed beforehand by the old shareholders, so that it was necessary to market only 336,846 of the preference and 283,742 of the ordinary shares. These shares were oversubscribed by the public, the ordinary shares being issued at a premium of 25 per cent.

'Those who elected to take preference shares will get equivalent to a little over 7½ per cent on the par value of their old shares, but have converted their holdings into a security nearly as safe as a government bond. . . . Those who elected to take ordinary shares will get equivalent to about 12½ per cent on the par value of their old stock, and probably more at the end of the year. And, finally, those who elected to take cash for their shares received $126 per share for stock that was hard to sell at $50 when the conversion was first talked of.

'In this connection it may be of interest to refer to the past experience of the shareholders in the Company. One, who, with another member of his family, invested $10,000 and kept the shares until now and converted them into ordinary shares, has received in dividends $47,-100 and now holds 33,200 shares, worth at the issue price $201,275, or a total of 25 for 1 in a period of about fourteen years.[1]

[1] In 1909, ten years after the organization of Kodak, Limited, the net

'What the future of the Company will be none can say, but it certainly seems brighter than ever before. In our especial line we are forging ahead faster than any competitor and our position in the trade is being strengthened in many ways which are bound to render the business more permanent and secure than would have been thought possible a few years ago. Our business is rapidly extending over the whole world, and this, together with continued improvements being introduced by us which make the practice of the art easier and cheaper, is likely to lead to a volume of business the extent of which can hardly be estimated now.'

Eastman was thinking, always, in terms of 'continued improvements.' In the early revisions of the 'Prospectus' he had inserted this paragraph:

'Special chemical and mechanical departments with a staff of skilled hands are maintained for *experimental* purposes in order to keep in advance of all demands for improvements in every branch of photography.'

One of the interesting and unexpected results of the merger was the new interest which the British royal family took in photography. Queen Victoria had a 'wet-plate' dark-room, where her pictures were developed at Windsor Palace. King Edward and Queen Alexandra had used one of the first roll-holders and were the first among the royal ranks abroad to adopt film photography. And now their son, Prince George, and Princess Mary (King George V and Queen Mary) were supplied 'with new outfits of our up-to-date cameras,' Eastman wrote Strong.[1]

annual earnings exceeded the total capital £1,600,000 subscribed in 1898. The final prospectus and subscription blanks were mailed from Rochester to all Kodak dealers in the United States. Very few of them subscribed. W. D. Gatchell, of Louisville, returned the blank with this sentence: 'Regarding stock, it is useless to offer Kentuckians anything with water in it.'

[1] March 27, 1899.

'Our Oxford Street manager was called to attend at Marlborough House to explain the working of the special Bull's-Eyes and other Kodaks. They are going to take the new apparatus with them on their proposed journey to Greece and Crete. They have been working with the old model cameras in many instances, and I am very glad that they have now taken to the daylight-loading system.

'Our Oxford Street manager reports that he elicited the fact that no one shares royalty orders with us for cameras, and states that her Royal Highness, the Princess of Wales, thanked us for the trouble we always took with her orders.'

'Man is not the creature of circumstances,' said one of England's great Prime Ministers. 'Circumstances are the creatures of men.' [1] So, too, are America's great industries.

[1] Disraeli.

CHAPTER V

LORD KELVIN'S OBSERVATION

WITHOUT human resources neither art nor industry could exist. Unfortunately not all large employers of labor, after President McKinley's reëlection, cared to admit it, with a result that it became popular to assert that as the rich became richer the poor became poorer, and many were the workbenches polished with grievances.

Every industrial leader had his own policy, while some had principles. Some executives possessed a warmth of human contact that had a medicinal effect upon labor. Others were ruthless. A few were students of human problems. Many gave orders from their pedestals of superiority. Still others philosophized from the safe haven of a resort at the seashore or from the fashionable parade grounds of Europe. Naturally there were many varieties of employers and a like assortment of labor groups. Upton Sinclair had not yet written 'The Jungle,' so the bitterness of later years was not as evident in the late nineties and early nineteen-hundreds. Man power was more plentiful than money. The cleavage was there, but it had not yet become a 'great divide,' although during the first year of President Roosevelt's administration the power of business and the growing strength of labor were headline topics in the press.

Eastman, who employed something like three thousand men and women here and abroad at the turn of the century, was not the type of executive who boasted that his office was always filled with workers who came to him with complaints. This was not his idea of organization. In the first place, he qualified organization. It

should be 'profit-bearing'; otherwise there was no reason
for an organization. Secondly, he held each manager,
superintendent, and foreman responsible for conditions
in his own department. He established a rule that complaints should be straightened out at the 'source of their
birth,' not at the top.

To understand the evolution of human relations in
Eastman's life, we must retrace our steps to revisit the
savings bank where he was employed as the second book-
keeper in the year 1881. His immediate superior resigned. Eastman had been doing much of his work. He
was in line for promotion. His work was satisfactory and
the other employees knew it, but the executives brought
in a relative of one of the influential directors and gave
him the position. This was so 'against every principle of
justice' that it branded a truth in his youthful mind. It
was not a grandiloquent theory, but a simple fact: If he
ever became an employer he would be fair.

This is the key to Eastman's own policy, a sympathetic
determination of what was fair. 'We are slow, but we
follow the path of our destiny as light is given us.' [1] When
he decided what was right, he acted so that when
Colonel Strong wrote that the firm believed 'rather in
works' instead of talk, he voiced a conviction that extended through the ranks. Eastman, however, never
revealed his ideas or activities to groups. Contacts were
always with individuals, with men upon whom he relied
to carry out his purposes. Recognition and reward were
both personal and individual.

Turn back a few pages of the records and we find that
his cash profit as the promoter of Kodak, Limited, was
$969,000. Here was his first fortune not invested in the
business. Besides, he and his mother were, jointly, the

[1] Eastman to Charles S. Abbott, February 13, 1902.

MRS. GEORGE W. EASTMAN

largest stockholder in the company. On January 25, 1899, he cabled this sum to his account in Rochester.

Almost before the ink was dry on the draft, he gave executives in Rochester, London, Paris, and Berlin, trusted employees, his attorneys and personal financial advisor a total of $178,585. In addition, he loaned other executives sufficient funds to enable them to subscribe to substantial blocks of stock in the new company. For the Mechanics Institute of Rochester he agreed to purchase the land and 'build thereon a building suitable for the uses of the Institute, the whole cost to be $200,000; and to turn the property over to the Institute when completed, free from encumbrance.' The final cost, however, exceeded this figure. Besides, personal contributions to hospitals and local charities were increased several fold.

Within a year he had given or obligated himself to give very nearly fifty per cent of this cash profit to individuals and institutions, and, except for the gift to the Mechanics Institute, which became public against his wishes, no one ever knew, until the letters were read thirty years later, that Eastman was building the foundations for philanthropy and wage-dividends, employee stock-ownership and copartnership in industry in the last decade of the nineteenth century.

As cases are always more interesting in the laboratory of human experiments, the early association of Eastman and Harris H. Hayden may be cited. The latter was a partner of Buell's in the insurance firm where Eastman worked as a boy. When Hayden had saved ten thousand dollars, he left what he called a 'one-hoss town' for New York City. Eastman offered him a partnership in his first business, nearly a year before Strong invested his first thousand dollars. Hayden declined. When the first company was organized, he was offered part of the

treasury stock at par, which was not accepted. Still
Eastman enjoyed his companionship, invariably visited
him in New York, and entertained him frequently in
Rochester. Finally, in 1889, Eastman loaned him money
to purchase stock in the business, but Hayden sold parcels
of it from time to time to finance his various undertakings
in the metropolis. In 1898, when De Lancey became ill
and wished an indefinite leave of absence, Eastman offered the managership of Kodak Park to Hayden.

'What is needed there now,' he wrote, 'is business
ability and the ability to keep the heads of the technical
branches pulling in the harness together. I have got to
make a pretty prompt decision in regard to this matter,
and I would be glad if you could make up your mind
what you will do without much delay. It looks to me as
if you were wasting your time in puttering with the
phosphate business under the conditions which you related to me. As far as the copper mine is concerned, it
seems to me that that is a too uncertain and speculative
affair to weigh much in the balance against something
solid like this.'

But the third offer was declined. Hayden was still
hypnotized by the great city. Within a short time, however, he was ready to accept the managership of the
Nepera Chemical Company in Yonkers when Eastman
purchased that company.

Then a few years pass. The Nepera Park plant had to
be moved to Rochester and Eastman was compelled to
write his friend:

'I have for some time been rather worried about the
prospect of your coming here to Rochester and have lately
come to the conclusion that it will be of very doubtful
expediency. I have no doubt you will be surprised at
this, but I feel that I ought to let you know how I feel

about it as soon as possible. The fact of the matter is I know from what you have said to me once or twice that you are dissatisfied with the salary you are getting and that you expect to do better if you come to Rochester. It was certainly my expectation that there would be some opening that would enable me to shove you right along, but our ideas in regard to the conduct of business differ so radically that I do not think that prospect still continues. If you come up here to Rochester, you would get pocketed down at Kodak Park, doing just the same work that you have been doing lately, and it would probably be very difficult for you to get away from it. I am, therefore, firmly of the opinion that the best thing that can be done will be for you not to come here, but to seek some other connection. I know that this cannot be done in a moment and I am perfectly willing that your salary should continue for such a length of time as will enable you to make such connection, even up to one year.

'As far as the personal part of this is concerned, I am mighty sorry, but you know that I have never allowed personal considerations to interfere with the conduct of the business and I am too old to do it now.'

When Hayden first declined the managership of Kodak Park Works, Eastman turned to a young chemical engineer, Frank W. Lovejoy, who came to the plant January 7, 1897, three years after graduating from the Massachusetts Institute of Technology. After consulting other executives at the Park, he learned that two of his responsible men objected to Lovejoy as manager. There had been jealousy and intrigue before, but Eastman had such complete faith in his men that he never took drastic action unless it was vital to the progress of the company. 'These are little matters,' he wrote when two executives clashed at the Park. 'I think I fully appreciate the work that both men are doing and I do not think that they are likely to gain or lose in such matters as these. . . . You may tell Mr. —— that I think he is doing excellent work and as far as I know he has no occasion for anxiety except the anxiety which is inseparable from the manufacture of any delicate article.' Then he wrote the Colonel, who was in Hawaii, where his son-in-law was Governor of the Islands.

'I have made no headway in getting a substitute for De Lancey. Out of about 300 answers to an advertisement I put in the New York Herald I only selected three for further investigation, and only one of them panned out well enough to warrant sending for the man. He proved to be altogether too small for the job. I am very much afraid that I will have to go down and tackle the job myself as soon as you get home. I do not think it would do any harm for me to spend the summer on the plant if we are going to have a new man, because in such a case I ought to be more familiar with it than I am. I am afraid it will be a hard matter to get anybody to fill the bill.

'I am glad to know that you are going on to Japan. Never mind the time it takes. We will stub along the best we can.'

In the mean time, two other executives became ill and Eastman again unburdened his thoughts to his senior partner:

'I have not heard of any more of our principal men that are likely to give out right away, but it does seem as if some kind of a cyclone had struck us. I am sure it would only take the collapse of two or three more to give me paralysis, locomotor ataxia, or some other blooming disease.

'In regard to the son of —— [a director], I told him the

FRANK W. LOVEJOY

other day that I found he could not run the —— ——
—— and asked him what I should do with him. He said
he did not want to lose his job, so I told him he could
come back to State Street. He seemed to take it easily
enough and I truly hope his father will not feel badly
about it. The trouble with the boy is that he lacks horse
sense. It is not lack of experience, but a congenital
disease.'

As De Lancey was ill, Eastman appointed Lovejoy
assistant manager, but kept a rigid control of employee
policies himself, as he studied Lovejoy and weighed the
relationship of educated and self-schooled men. His own
ideas were crystallized. 'I should not be willing to increase the salary of a man who has failed to fill his position satisfactorily,' he wrote. ' —— is certainly not a man
we want in our employ and I do not think that any consideration such as you speak of should operate to keep
him. As far as —— [a chemist] is concerned, if the rest
of the staff cannot recognize the fact that he was inefficient, nothing that we can do with —— would help that.
The technical men at Kodak Park must recognize the
fact that they must make a record in order to hold their
jobs. If they do not, they are not any better than un-
educated men; in fact, not as good because an educated
man who is not efficient is a spoiled man.'

It was evident by this time that there was no panacea
for solving personnel problems, so Eastman decided to
make another search for men, even though he was
rapidly reaching a conclusion, for he wrote the Colonel:
'Mr. Lovejoy is taking hold fully as well as I expected.
He may turn out to be a very valuable manager. . . . I
am on the lookout for two new chemical engineers and
have appointments with four or five recent graduates
who are coming to see me. I intend to keep a good stock
of this material on hand.'

Within a few days he sent the following letter to Sheffield Scientific Institute, Columbia School of Mines,
Massachusetts Institute of Technology, Rose Polytechnic
Institute, and Purdue University: 'We have openings for
several young men who have been educated as chemists
or chemical engineers, preferably the latter, to learn our
business. If there are any among the graduates of your
institution who are looking for engagements and whom
you can recommend, we would be very glad to be put
into communication with them.'

Personnel problems, however, did not divert Eastman
from the minutiæ of manufacturing. 'In going through
the camera works,' he notified Brownell, 'I notice a good
many changes in the layout which have never been communicated to me. A good many of these changes entail
the expenditure of a great deal of the Company's money,
which should have properly had my consent before it was
incurred. Therefore, please take notice that hereafter no
changes, improvements, or alterations are to be made in
the plant, or machinery purchased, without my consent
in writing. If any alterations are now in progress, or have
been ordered, you will please give me a list of them, with
an estimate of the expense.'

His heart, however, was at the Park, where the engineers were working on a new method of making film.
Since 1889, film had been made on long plate-glass
tables. Now a drum system had been devised to make
film continuously twenty-four hours a day, and Eastman
sped the news to his London manager: [1] 'If it proves a
success we shall immediately start the construction of five
more machines, which when finished will give us about
3½ times our present capacity. We do not anticipate,
however, that we shall be able to add much to our sum-

[1] March 27, 1899.

mer's output with this new process because it will take
about a year to get it under control. We expect that the
new process will reduce the cost of manufacture very
materially, as it will wipe out about 4/5 of the labor in
coating the dope and the emulsion. It also will require
very much less power, heat, and light. It is our intention, in case it works satisfactorily, to abandon the glass-
table process and use the present film rooms for the
continuous coating of gelatine paper, freeing our present
coating rooms for other use, and thus avoiding further
extensions to the plant for some time.'

To the English directors he sent a formal notification
of the new process:

'Sometime last year, foreseeing that our present
facilities would be taxed to supply the increased demand
this year, I instituted a series of experiments looking toward the increase of our manufacturing capacity without incurring such a heavy expenditure as has been
necessary heretofore. These experiments contemplated
the casting of the film base, stripping it from its support,
and then coating it with emulsion, the present method
being to complete the operation while the film base is
attached to its support. A similar process has been used
by some of our competitors but not with any great degree
of success. I hoped by the use of better machinery to
obtain results which would not only equal our present
method but perhaps surpass it. I am pleased to be able
to report that these experiments have been nearly completed and that working machines have been finished to
carry out both parts of the process. During the summer
the new process will be used by the Blair Camera Company and the American Camera Mfg. Co.[1] on their
product and while they are using it I propose to con-

[1] Eastman had purchased these concerns.

struct additional machines so that next year we can use it, releasing our present film rooms to take care of extensions in other departments. It is anticipated that an outlay which would be sufficient to only increase our present capacity 50% under the present method will, by the new process, increase it about 250%. At the same time there will be a considerable economy in the labor used in making and packing the film. It is my opinion that when we get into a position to make such a large quantity of film we can devise means for largely increasing the present consumption.'

It 'works like a charm,' he wrote. 'The hopper which deposits the dope works perfectly. The variation in thickness across the web of the completed film is not more than 1/4000 inch. This is greater accuracy than we ever obtained on tables.'

On the heels of this success the first factory was started in Canada [1] with the organization of Canadian Kodak Company, Limited. Early the following year, Eastman went abroad, and, in notifying Lovejoy, wrote that he wanted the 'film experiments' to be 'prosecuted with vigor while I am absent in Europe and would like to have you give me a summary each week of what has been accomplished.'

Always there was the incentive and the order to 'experiment.'

Finding everything progressing satisfactorily abroad, Eastman returned, and left in May for his first long vacation in the West, accompanied by his mother and Mr. and Mrs. Hubbell. Returning to Rochester he wrote Lovejoy: 'This is to confirm my conversation with you just before I left for California in which I stated that your services as assistant manager of the Kodak Park

[1] December, 1899.

works during the past year had been highly satisfactory to the Company and that you could draw salary at the rate of —— per year from April 1st last, with promotion to Manager of Kodak Park Works.'

Then came the first threat of serious labor difficulties. The tool-makers at the Camera Works and the machinists at Kodak Park were on edge and Lovejoy was counseled: 'I herewith enclose a copy of the notice from the Machinists' Union, which I send to you simply that you may understand the situation as between the machinists and employers who belong to the National Metal Trades Association. We propose to keep out of any agreement on the ground that we are not metal workers *per se*, but employ machinists merely as a side issue in our business and that it is not practicable for us to make regulations as to their time which would not apply to the balance of the employees.'

A report as usual was sent to London. 'There has been a strike of six or seven machinists at Kodak Park for about two weeks and day before yesterday the machinists at Brownell's went out in sympathy. . . . We have foreseen this trouble for some time. . . . There does not seem to be any prospect of the union's being able to prevent our getting our work done in other shops and we do not expect any serious interference with our work.'

These strikes were the beginning of a unique employee experiment in Rochester which more than justified Eastman's bold concept of labor strategy.

In the spring of 1901, public attention throughout the country was focussed upon the duel between George F. Baer, president of the Philadelphia and Reading Railway, and John Mitchell, leader of the United Mine Workers of America, with President Roosevelt and J. P. Morgan watching from the side lines. The anthracite operators and miners were rapidly approaching the *impasse* which changed the duel with pens and ink into a devastating strike.

In these days strikes were more or less contagious and were considered the workers' most valuable weapon. While the press naturally featured this spectacular fencing between a Philadelphia aristocrat and a young man who arose from the mines, there was an interesting experiment under way in Rochester which attracted no national notice.

This was not unusual or unnatural. More than one hundred thousand men were involved in the coal controversy, and in addition the public was a vital third party, as Roosevelt maintained. In Rochester less than one half of one per cent of this number was concerned, and the public generally neither knew nor cared what transpired there, although among Genesee Valley industries, the Kodak 'experiment' was not without considerable sociological significance.

In June, 1901, thirty-four of the buffers and polishers in the Camera Works, after repeated solicitation by labor-union organizers, decided to affiliate with the union. Eleven workers in the same department refused, although in Rochester, as elsewhere, it was generally considered the popular and right thing to join a union.

As soon as the men were organized, they were instructed in their duties, not the least important being to compel their employer to recognize the organization and comply with its demands. Brownell, manager of the factory, submitted a detailed report to Eastman. The work in this department was partially on a piece basis and the hours of work and compensation were generally considered better than in other local shops at the time. Their workroom was on the top floor, light, airy, and healthfully ventilated, as exhaust fans were connected with each machine to carry away the dust.

As the Kodak business was running at full capacity and the polishing department was unable to handle all the work which was required, a large amount of the polishing and plating was 'contracted out' in shops about the city.

Eastman had long since established a policy of not permitting anything to interfere with the business.[1] Brownell

[1] Whatever attitude other employers might take, Eastman did not intend to pussy-foot or conceal his opinions in vague phrases. When an inquiry came from Ralph M. Easly, who had recently organized the National Civic Federation in New York, Eastman answered his questionnaire, but declined to send a representative to any general conference. He did not believe in 'outside' direction.

'1. We employ both union and non-union labor.

'2. As we understand your question no restrictions have been imposed by the unions in any of our shops.

'3. The hours of labor are nine.

'4. We consider it practical to gradually reduce hours of labor by voluntary agreement throughout given industries. We ourselves about a year ago voluntarily reduced the labor in our own works from ten to nine hours.

'5. We prefer the piece system of payment wherever practicable. Have had little experience with the premium system, but consider it very promising and theoretically more just to both parties.

'6. We aim to provide healthful workrooms for our help and give them as many conveniences as possible in the way of cloakrooms, washrooms, bicycle sheds, and lunchrooms. We do not go further than this because we are inclined to think that the average self-respecting workman does not care for and sometimes resents attentions which can be construed as patronizing.

'7. We believe that the organization of employers is necessary in order to deal effectually and fairly with the labor question.'

In a memo to Lovejoy, who was asked about labor policy, Eastman wrote: 'Proprietors are friendly to labor organizations up to a point where they attempt to limit product or dictate as to the management of the business.'

It was not until several years later that Eastman was financially able to put the capstone upon the policies affecting personnel which were being formulated in these early days. But at this time it is important to note that the responsible executives were stockholders in his company; several executives were receiving percentages upon the sales of various products and the salaries and wages paid, hours of work and factory conditions were equal or superior to those prevailing elsewhere.

knew also that the place to settle disputes was at the source, but he recognized, above everything, his employer's unrequited urge to try to find new ways to every objective.

When the committee representing the strikers and the union called upon the manager, they presented, according to custom, a list of grievances and an 'agreement,' providing, among other things, that a union representative 'shall have access to the factory during working hours' and that 'there shall be a shop steward in each factory appointed by the organization, whose duty it shall be to see that all men in said factory are in good standing in the organization.'

Brownell not only refused to comply with the proposed agreement, but he announced, after consultation with Eastman, that the department would be discontinued and all the polishing and plating would be 'contracted out.' Then he made this novel proposal to the committee:

That they form a coöperative company, rent a shop near by, buy or lease at a nominal figure the entire equipment of machinery, etc., from the Eastman Company, and take all the polishing and plating that they could handle on contract. While they would be in competition with other outside shops, they were informed that as long as their prices were as low and their work as well done as that of their competitors, they would have the preference. They would be paid weekly for all work, so that lack of capital would not prevent their undertaking the contract.

The Eastman Company had two primary interests, the work had to be done and the men were experienced, therefore any agreement other than union direction of the Camera Works would be acceptable. Besides, Eastman sensed that what the men really wanted was more money, and that if they could earn it by assuming responsibility and doing the work, they were as much entitled to the reward for business ability as was any other concern. The company, after the men decided to accept the proposal, superintended the moving of the machinery and tools to the new factory of the 'Union Polishing and Plating Company,' assisted them in organizing the new corporation, and agreed to keep them supplied with orders!

This appeared to be Utopia made-to-order. Work, good pay, no risk! Naturally the men entered into the scheme with vim. Each stood upon an equal footing in the company. Each was a stockholder, as he had subscribed one hundred dollars for a share of stock. The business was launched with every prospect of success. Nine members were elected to the board of directors. One was chosen president, another general manager, and a third superintendent, and the wheels of a Socialistic enterprise began to run as smoothly as any Capitalistic corporation.

The Eastman Company furnished the work in sufficient quantity to keep the shop running, paid good prices, and, every Saturday, sent a check for all the work done to date, thus assuring them of ready cash for their payroll and other expenses. The bulk of the work was done by the piece, and the men were so compensated until the orders increased so rapidly that outsiders had to be employed. Then the day rate was adopted, shareholders being paid five cents an hour more than outsiders.

For three months everything worked to perfection until the men became dissatisfied or jealous of their president. They demanded his resignation and elected the vice-president as their leader. Two months later, three shareholders were 'discharged.' By Christmas, thirty of the original thirty-four were able to draw a bonus of five dollars each. By March, business continued to improve, two more stockholders were dropped, and another bonus of five dollars each was voted.

As every man was an equal partner with an officer or director, he acted accordingly. When one man became irregular, another adopted a similar policy. If one man could bring in beer while he worked, another could do likewise. If cards could be played in the office, they could be used equally as freely in the boiler room. Finally these conditions became so prevalent that the directors adopted resolutions against beer and cards. Also, as a nine-hour day was being championed by the unions, they voted to abolish piece work and adopt the nine-hour day. After a month's trial, they returned to piece work, and the manager and president were forced to resign.

The twenty-six remaining stockholders elected a new manager, who adopted the Rooseveltian policy of wielding the 'big stick,' but this policy lasted less than a week, for the men circulated a petition, secured a majority vote, and demanded his resignation. Nevertheless, his actions had a salutary effect. Within a short period the new president was able to increase the volume of work. Some of the men took greater interest, devised new methods of handling the orders, and were soon able to speed production to such an extent that between April 24 and May 29 four dividends were paid, making a total during the six weeks of twenty-five dollars each for the twenty-four remaining stockholders.

The company was successful beyond expectations until it was discovered that one of the best wage-earners had been falsifying his records. He was discharged. Another was given five days to account for two thousand small parts which he had had in his possession, but they could not be found, and he was dismissed.

Meanwhile, another inequality developed. Some of the more efficient men could complete a week's work in three or four days, but, as the union rules would not permit them to draw more than the established weekly rate, they would 'lay off' the rest of the week, although they, as stockholders, were still entitled and did share in the company's surplus in dividends.

While this condition of affairs did not tend toward harmony, business was so prosperous that dividends climbed to fifty dollars per month per shareholder. With this feeling of security they became more or less indifferent. It became popular for the more prosperous to 'go fishing' a week or two each month, but the management soon awoke to the belief that the Union Company was paying dividends to men who had not helped to earn them.

This complication, however, was not as serious as another which developed when the manager employed non-union men, because he found them more flexible and easier to deal with. Thereupon the 'business agent' of the local union summoned the manager for an explanation and he was placed on trial. The jury, however, brought in a verdict, 'No cause for action,' after a short but heated deliberation.

Weeks and months passed rapidly until, by the latter part of 1903, less than half of the original stockholders remained and the Union Company was no longer a one-hundred per cent union shop!

By this time the more industrious workers decided that there should be a change in their dividend policy; that instead of allowing each stockholder an equal portion of the surplus whether he worked or not, each one was to receive his share of the surplus in proportion to the number of hours he worked. For two weeks this plan seemed at last to solve all the company's problems. There was a new era of prosperity and no end to their enthusiasm. Some of the men pinned their dividend checks to the lapels of their coats when they played pool, so exalted were they over their success. But this, in turn, brought less attention to work. The shop became short of hands. Jealousy and hard feelings developed more generally than ever before. The directors held a special meeting and decided to return to the piece system. This was promptly done, but the organization lost its 'push.' Interest and ambition waned, and the president and general manager, who had withdrawn from the local union, but retained membership in the International, organized a competitive business, cut prices under those prevailing in all other similar shops in the city, and bid for the Eastman business.

A committee of the Union Company called upon Brownell and asked him to refuse to make any contracts with the new concern. This he declined, because throughout this period he had been contracting with all other shops in Rochester equipped to do the work; the amount of business was increasing, and there was no legitimate reason for debarring any concern. As Brownell actually needed all the help he could obtain, he urged the men to go after the business with their old-time vigor, and promised that the Eastman Company would stand back of its contract until forced to revoke it by their non-performance of the work.

Some of the men labored hard, but the former president and general manager were too able and industrious, and as they had retained their stock in the original company they offered to buy out the remaining fourteen shareholders at twenty-five dollars per share. This offer was accepted, and by June 1, 1904, three years after the union went into business, it was a private 'capitalistic' enterprise.

While there was nothing spectacular about this 'rare practical experiment in coöperative labor,' how many business executives of this period would have encouraged a labor union to go into business? Could there have been a better or more practical device to enable workers to learn that business is a 'battle' and not an imaginary island of 'Utopia,' as described in the inimitable fiction of Sir Thomas More? How Roosevelt might have dramatized this experiment had he known the facts, for the United States, at this time, was a divided economic organism in the hands of unions and trusts!

'Great new problems confront the people in this trust age,' Arthur Brisbane editorialized in the Hearst newspapers. 'Trusts have got to be regulated by public sentiment,' Dr. Arthur T. Hadley told a church audience in Boston. 'Lave us laugh an' sing th' octopus out of existence,' mused 'Mr. Dooley,' commenting upon President Roosevelt's first message to Congress.

However strange it may seem to-day to review the public fear of trusts and labor unions, it was real and vital at the time. By the nineteen-hundreds the word 'trust . . . passed into the common tongue as the familiar name for every sort of combination whatever.[1] . . . Rockefeller was the outstanding exponent of combination, Carnegie of ruthless competition. Rockefeller, thinking in terms similar to European "cartels," would go to other men in the oil business, would talk to them about the desirability of combination, would ask his competitor to unite with him, would offer to give either cash or stock in the Standard Oil Company for his competitor's plant. If the competitor declined, he would be subject to the

[1] *Our Times*, by Mark Sullivan.

Standard's competition, and likely to find himself sooner or later a casualty.

'Carnegie did nothing like that. . . . Carnegie as a rule rarely tried to persuade or force a competitor to sell out to him, rarely entertained any notion of buying him out. Carnegie generally paid no attention to rivals except to gloat when his methods made them squirm, or succumb. . . . By these methods Carnegie had become by 1900 the greatest steel-maker in America.'

But Carnegie was impatient to retire, and Morgan was persuaded by Charles M. Schwab's eloquence to organize and finance the United States Steel Corporation.[1] This focussed attention upon all large aggregations of capital, silhouetting upon the horizon of public imagination the figures of Rockefeller, Carnegie, and Morgan.

Eastman was not in this picture because his policy differed from all three, and even though he did have to work in this atmosphere, the control of his enterprises was largely in his own hands, not in Wall Street. He had no lobbyists in Washington or Albany and was not seeking to influence legislation anywhere, nor was he attempting to evade the law or take advantage of any legal elasticity. His policy of large-scale production, at low costs for a world market, extensive advertising and industrial research, had all been established before the 'trust era.' He believed this policy was fundamentally sound, and being still a pioneer and a young man, he was building for an indefinite future.

Immediately upon his return from London in 1898, he had written:

'The idea that this business is ephemeral has no foundation in facts. If the bulk of the pictures taken by amateurs were taken as a mere pastime, there would be

[1] March 3, 1901.

something in the argument, but such is not the case. Most photographs are made for the purpose of obtaining a record which cannot be had in any other way. When the desire for a pictorial record of daily life disappears, then amateur photography will decrease, and not until then.

'One very important thing connected with our future prosperity was never mentioned in connection with the flotation of the new company, because it was not an accomplished fact until the day I left London.

'We have secured for nine years the monopoly for North America of the products of the only two mills in the world which make photographic paper for gelatine printing-out processes. Only those who are thoroughly acquainted with the photographic trade can understand what this means.'

Before leaving London Eastman had written Philipp: 'The paper deal was successfully put through and we are now the exclusive agents for North America for Rives and Steinbach paper for gelatine printing-out processes.' The 'Solio war,' too, was over. Abbott had accompanied Eastman to England on the last voyage. They had so many interests in common, both personal and business, that by August 10, 1899, they organized the General Aristo Company, capitalized at $5,000,000, 'to purchase each of the following properties, or a controlling interest therein:

'(1) The photographic printing paper business of the Eastman Kodak Company of Rochester, N.Y.;

'(2) The American Aristotype Company of Jamestown, N.Y.;

'(3) The Nepera Chemical Company of Nepera Park, N.Y.; [1]

[1] After inventing 'Velox,' a photographic printing-out paper for use with artificial light, Dr. Leo H. Baekeland manufactured this paper at Nepera Park.

'(4) The New Jersey Aristotype Company of Bloom-
field, N.J.;

'(5) The Photo Materials Company of Rochester,
N.Y.; and

'(6) Kirkland's Lithium Paper Company of Denver,
Colo.

'The purchase does not include the real estate, machinery or merchandise of the Eastman Kodak Company, but an arrangement will be made with them to
operate their photographic printing paper plant on
terms favorable to this company. . . . All of the common
shares (25,000 at par) and 17,750 preferred shares of this
issue have been taken up by private subscription or will
be issued in payment of the properties to be acquired;
the balance, 7270 preferred shares, are offered for public
subscription at par.'

This time the Colonel did not have to congratulate
Eastman 'with all the words applicable that can be
found in the dictionary,' for the subscriptions flowed in
as if a new gold field had been discovered.

'Whenever the photographic art is practiced there
Rochester is known,' proudly boasted the 'Rochester
Democrat and Chronicle,' 'a fact that will be of no little
advantage to the new organization, for as the purchaser
turns to Pittsburgh for steel, to Grand Rapids for furniture and to Chicago for grain, so does he turn to
Rochester for photographic goods.'

The 'San Francisco Call,' however, raised the issue
of 'Imperialism':

'The Eastman Kodak Company has started a rate
war on this coast to force the smaller dealers out of the
business and compel some of the large Eastern manufacturers to enter into a trust. The company has sought
in more ways than one to gain absolute control of the

trade. From time to time it has absorbed smaller concerns that threaten to become competitors for the business of the amateurs. Some of the concerns refused to be absorbed and grew on apace until their proportions began to worry the Eastman people. Some few months ago propositions were made to these institutions to enter into a combine. Negotiations were evidently not satisfactory and a compact was not effected.

'On this coast there are more than 20,000 amateur photographers and they form a very important factor in the business of the competing Eastern companies.

'On October 23 the trade received notice from the Eastman Company that a cut of one third in the price of all the goods sold by the company would be inaugurated on this coast on November 1. The leading dealers got together Wednesday night and after a lengthy discussion decided to abide by the cut and advertised a reduction on the Eastman goods.

' "The result of this is going to be," said a prominent dealer in San Francisco, "that the smaller dealers — especially those in the interior towns who have been handling the goods of other concerns — are going to be frozen out of the business by the Eastman people. This is the greatest rate war in photographic supplies that has ever been inaugurated in this country and there is no telling where it is going to end. There is every indication that it is going to be a fight to a finish. If the smaller concerns are able to hold out against the Eastman people a compromise may be reached after all of them have lost a great deal of money, but if the aggressors win out a trust will undoubtedly be formed that will force the price of amateur photographic supplies up to a figure where the pastime will become one of the greatest luxuries in the country." '

This attack was so far from the mark that Eastman answered it in the 'Kodak Trade Circular':

'The "Call" reporter may not be able to grasp the idea, but for the future growth of our business and profit we do not look for a "forcing up of prices," but rather for such a reduction as shall enable us to make Kodakers of every school boy and girl and every wage-earning man and woman the world over.'

From the standpoint of paper, Eastman's position was now impregnable, and he had fulfilled 'the policy which we represented to the foreign mills that we would pursue; that is, purchase all concerns left out of the deal when they could be obtained at a reasonable price.'

This, too, completed one phase of Eastman's industrial strategy. The second, which was prosecuted simultaneously, was the manufacture of a cheap camera. 'I am working on one which I hope will fill the bill,' he informed Colonel Strong. This was the 'Brownie,' a dollar camera, marketed in 1900. Meanwhile, Eastman had concluded negotiations with D. L. Goff, a wealthy textile manufacturer of Pawtucket, Rhode Island, who had been the financial backer of the Blair Camera Company of Massachusetts and Maine and who had lost upwards of one hundred thousand dollars. He was paid —— shares of Kodak, Limited, for the Blair Company and in later years retrieved his losses through the increase in the value of Kodak stock.

By purchasing the Blair Company and the American Camera Company plant at Northboro, Massachusetts, and by backing the new Brownie with a volume of national advertising,[1] Eastman was the outstanding

[1] The June, 1900, number of the 'Kodak Trade Circular' announced that 'the mediums that we are using have an aggregate circulation of over 6,000,-000 copies per issue and we are not using them once but many, many times — most of them every issue. Here is a list of some of our recent Kodak and

manufacturer of cameras in the United States, although there remained at this time thirteen other competing concerns. The largest of these, E. and H. T. Anthony and Company, offered to sell all their capital stock to Eastman for $268,750, but the offer was not accepted. This resulted in a consolidation of Anthony with the Scovill and Adams Company and the formation of the Anthony and Scovill Company in 1901.

'People who have an itching to manufacture the goods do not understand what they would have to encounter when they come to try to sell them,' Eastman wrote.

Problems of distribution now became so formidable that Eastman's strategy had to include merchandising upon a different and larger scale. As the agencies which he had established abroad had been successful, he decided to open wholesale distributing houses in New York City, Chicago, and San Francisco. His policy was established by the following succinct statements:

'The matter of stock keeping is one of the principal things that you have to control and one of the three principal things upon which your record will be judged, namely: Satisfactory service to customers; Ratio of expenses to sales, and, Accuracy of stock keeping.

'Chicago has been and is likely to remain the hotbed of all opposition and we have felt the necessity of strength-

Brownie Advertising: June magazines: Munsey's, 3 pages; McClure's, 3 pages; Cosmopolitan, 3 pages; Leslie's Monthly, 3 pages; Harper's, 2 pages; Century, 2 pages; Scribner's, 2 pages; Review of Reviews, 2 pages; Outing, 2 pages; Outlook, 2 pages; Ainslee's, 1 page; Pearson's, 1 page; Recreation, 1 page; St. Nicholas, 1 page; Woman's Home Companion, 2¼ pages; Success, 1 page. In the weeklies we have done scarcely less, having used full pages twice in Collier's during May, and full pages in the Saturday Evening Post, the Christian Herald, and Leslie's Weekly, with a half page in the Youth's Companion in May, which is to be followed by a full page June 28th. Among other mediums used extensively are Puck, Judge, Life, Harper's Weekly, Scientific American, Christian Endeavor World, Silver Cross, Sunday School Times, Young People's Weekly and the American Boy.'

ening our hand there. Personally I have been opposed
to having anything to do with the retail trade in this
country but for strategic reasons I have lately modified
these views. . . .

'In working our policy here we have always attempted to lead instead of force the dealer.' [1]

Eastman was now ready to open chain retail stores also
wherever the business here or abroad warranted it. The
first of these was in London. Lyon, France, followed,
but this brought a written protest from twelve photographic dealers in that city.[2] Eastman made a quick but
considered response.

'To begin with,' he replied, 'I will admit that if your
evident assumption is correct that there is only a certain
fixed amount of trade in our goods to be had in your
locality, and that our object is merely to get away from
our already established customers as much of that trade
as possible for our own retail establishment, then our
action would be detrimental to your interests and quite
unwarranted. Experience has shown us, however,
beyond all question that the amount of Kodak goods
that can be sold in any given territory is largely dependent upon the advertising that they receive and the
prominence with which they are presented to the public.
It follows naturally from this that wherever we have
established branch houses the trade in that locality has
grown very materially and the effect has been, not to

[1] From letters to the manager in San Francisco, October 16, 1901, and
to the London manager January 22 and May 25, 1902.

[2] November 21, 1900, Eastman wrote Fred A. Cole, New York City: 'We
have not had any negotiations with the Lumière people and do not know
what they have to sell in this country. They are our principal competitors
in France in several lines of photographic goods but I am not aware that
they have any business in this country unless it be in connection with the
Cinématograph trade, in which we are not interested except as manufacturers of the film.'

decrease the sales of our dealer customers, but, on the contrary, to increase them.

'Our policy all over the world has been, and still is, the protection and encouragement of our dealer customers and I am quite sure that no move has been made in the present instances which will be detrimental to your interests unless you make it so yourselves.'

In the direction of the affairs of an international business there develops a complex interrelationship of problems. Coupled with the labor-capital issues in the United States and sales policies in France was the mounting income-tax question in England. As a result of the South African War, taxes were playing havoc with the company's earnings. Eastman sent a long communication to his solicitor in London:

'The excessive taxation which our concerns are subjected to the present year and the prospect of a large increase when the General Aristo Company is absorbed render it, in my judgment and that of the other large American shareholders with whom I have talked on the subject, necessary to consider what steps can be taken to put the Company in the best possible position against such inroads on its earnings. The amount of taxation which confronts us, aside from real estate taxes which would not be altered in any case, is as follows:

Eastman Kodak Co., City tax on personal property	£ 3,000
Eastman Kodak Co., County tax on personal property	800
English income tax, 5% on entire earnings of £360,000	18,000
General Aristo Co., City tax on personal property	400
General Aristo Co., County tax on personal property	100
British income tax, 5% on entire earnings of £140,000 (when absorbed)	7,000
	£29,300

'The only plan that has presented itself so far is the one which has been mostly followed by the large American corporations, that is to say, to organize under the

laws of the State of New Jersey,[1] which are distinctly
favorable to corporations and the interpretation of which
has been well settled. I am having the exact course of
procedure looked up by our counsel in New York, who
will make a report on it at an early date to accompany
one from Mr. Hubbell giving his opinion as to the
amount of local taxes such a company would have to
pay here. Before submitting or definitely suggesting this
matter to the Board I want to explain it to you and get
your criticism on the plan, which is as follows:

'To organize a company called the Eastman Kodak
Company, which I shall hereafter call the New Jersey
Company, and have it purchase from the shareholders
of Kodak, Limited, the entire business and pay for the
same in the shares of the American company upon a
basis which would enable the shares of the American
company to earn the same amount as the shares of the
English company:

'To obtain a modification of the General Aristo option
which would enable the New Jersey Company to purchase the shares of the General Aristo Company on the
same basis as the English Company would have done:

'To wind up the present Kodak, Limited, and incor-
porate a new Kodak, Limited (British), which I will
hereafter call the British Co., with a moderate capital,
say £200,000.

[1] June 1, 1901, Eastman wrote Lord Kelvin: 'I can only say that the American shareholders would feel very sore if their noses were to be held down on
the English income-tax grindstone, with only the hope that the machinery
might possibly stop before they were injured. They do not feel that they
ought to be made to take the chances when the remedy proposed does not
involve any injury to the English shareholders, but rather a benefit. While
we feel very much disturbed over this tax matter, there is no disposition to
force the decision of it and we have consented, therefore, to Mr. Verden's
suggestion that no attempt should be made to carry out the New Jersey
scheme in July, as was arranged before I left London, but to defer it until the
latter part of September.'

'To wind up the present Eastman Kodak Company (of New York) and the General Aristo Company. The New Jersey Company would then be direct owner of the entire American business and would be the owner of all the capital stock of the British, German, and French Companies. The foreign business would be carried on through the British Company. The New Jersey Company would pay local taxes in New Jersey amounting to not exceeding $5,000.00 per year and local taxes in Rochester of probably not more than that. If the profits of the English business amounted to £20,000 the tax would be £1,000 or a total for all three of the above of say £3,000, as against £29,300, what we are confronted with now. I presume that the sale of the English Company to an American Company outright may meet with opposition, but I see no escape from it, as the American shareholders, who own ¾ of the common and nearly ½ of the preferred shares, will not submit to the payment of the outrageous taxes which are now proposed if they can find any way out of it.

'Of course the real control of the business would not be changed by this operation and the management need not be changed in any way, but the English stockholders would have to take shares in the New Jersey Company or else sell out. I presume the Americans would absorb any shares that would be thrown on the market at a reasonable price. It is within the bounds of possibilities that the Kodak organization will hereafter want to absorb various other branches of the industry, both in this country and abroad, and the plan proposed leaves the way open to do this, whereas the present plan with its burden of taxation would render it impossible. I would like very much to be favored with your criticism on this plan and your views as to its feasibility.

'As I understand it, the way the Memorandum of Association was drawn a majority only of each class of shares would be sufficient at a general meeting to carry a resolution to sell out the business. I do not think that any prospects of a setting aside of the assessment on the American earnings by the English tax assessors would materially affect the desire of the American shareholders to effect this change, because there will always be the fear that some other decision might be made, and the certainty that the taxation here of a New York Company is sure to increase beyond what it already is.'

In August, while plans were maturing for the reorganization of the companies and the formation of this American corporation, Eastman 'had a call from Mr. F. A. Anthony,' and he dictated a report immediately to Philipp:

'He opened the conversation by stating that he had seen an account in the papers of the proposed dry plate combine and it occurred to him that we might want to acquire control of the Goodwin Co. I asked him what the Goodwin Company represented and he said they had a small factory down in Newark, where they were making film from their own dope, and that they owned the Goodwin patent, with which no doubt I was familiar. I said yes I was. In reply to a question as to why he thought the proposed combination afforded any better time for acquiring it, he said he thought we could acquire it at less expense. I told him I did not follow his idea, and asked him whether he would sell it for less money to such a combination than he would to us. He said no, but it might be easier to raise the money. I then asked him what he wanted, assuming that such a combination was going to be made. He said he wanted half cash and half stock. I asked him what amount, and he said the capital stock of the Goodwin Co. is one million dollars and that is the amount he had in mind.

'I said that seemed to be a large valuation and asked him why he considered the Goodwin patent so valuable. He said, first, that he had been advised that we infringed it and that there was a prospect of a large recovery from us; secondly, the right to work a valuable process. I told him I could not see how the Goodwin patent could protect anybody in the manufacture of any kind of film that would be salable at the present time; and that as far as the claim against us was concerned, we were only looking for somebody to sue us under that patent: That we had been hoping for years that somebody would muster up enough courage to do it, and that now that he and Richard Anthony and Mr. Adams had acquired control we had renewed hopes. I told him that I had not consulted you on the point, but that I thought we would be even willing to aid him to such an extent as to admit exactly what we were using and thus relieve him from the necessity of proving something that might be difficult. He said Mr. Philips Abbot had been investigating the patent lately and had advised him that we infringed. I said so much the better; that if he would only sue us there would be no hard feelings, it would be regarded as a friendly act.

'He then asked if the patent would not be valuable to us as an article of manufacture. I said I thought not; that there were some objectionable claims in that patent which we had decided to get canceled if we could and that papers had already been drawn in a suit to be instituted for that purpose. I told him that I did not know of a more flagrant attempt to get something that did not belong to him than the one by the Rev. Goodwin: That he had been fumbling away with his application with no prospect of getting anywhere with it, when we came out with something definite; that he then attempted to grab it by importing claims into his specification that would cover us. He said, well, the Reichenbach patent necessitated the use of camphor. I said that Goodwin certainly did not invent the combination of camphor and cotton. He said no, but as he understood it Goodwin showed how not to use camphor and that he understood we did not use it. I told him we did, and that I thought the camphor could easily be extracted from any of our film.

'He then said something about Goodwin's having beaten us in a former suit, and I told him he must have been misinformed, that we had certainly beaten him in the interference; that he could easily satisfy himself if he would examine the records. He said he had not been advised to that effect by Mr. Abbot; in fact he did not know that Abbot had examined that record, but he had always understood that that was the outcome of the case. We shook hands and parted on the best of terms. I am thankful that we do not want to buy the Goodwin patent.'

There was one business principle that Eastman's caller did not have any knowledge of. In 1896, upon a similar occasion, but involving another concern, Eastman wrote Walker: 'We will not pay him any backsheesh to keep still.' This principle was still in force!

On October 24, 1901, the Eastman Kodak Company of New Jersey was incorporated 'to acquire the stock of or absorb the various manufacturing and selling corporations known as Kodak, Limited, London; Eastman Kodak Company, Rochester, New York; and the General Aristo Company, Rochester, New York; having factories at Rochester, New York, Jamestown, New

York, and Harrow, England; also the Eastman Kodak Société Anonyme Française, of France, and Kodak Gesellschaft m.b.H., of Berlin; the above Companies having headquarters in Rochester, London, Paris and Berlin, and Branches in New York City, Chicago, San Francisco, Liverpool, Glasgow, Brussels, Lyons, Milan, Vienna, Moscow, St. Petersburg, and Melbourne.'

The authorized capital was $10,000,000 six per cent cumulative preferred and $25,000,000 common stock, all of which was quickly oversubscribed.[1]

There was a 'terrible struggle to satisfy all the people who wanted a slice, and even now there are many left out entirely,' Eastman wrote George Davison, London manager, when the new company was organized. To care for some of the many requests from friends, lawyers, bankers, business associates, and others, Eastman personally sold the company 170,000 ordinary shares and Strong added 80,000, making a total of 250,000 shares. 'When we came to figure up the underwriting, we found there were so many that had to be given some kind of a show, we had to cut everybody down a little to make room.'

In a series of letters to executives at home and in London, Eastman outlined his future policy. First he noted the possibility of German competition and then discovered a 'spy' from Germany in Kodak Park, who took 'French-leave' in the midst of the investigation.

'I enclose herewith copy of a letter received from

[1] The officers and directors of the first New Jersey corporation were: George Eastman, President; Henry A. Strong, 1st Vice-President and Treasurer; Charles S. Abbott, 2nd Vice-President; Walter S. Hubbell, Secretary; A. K. Whitney, Assistant Secretary. Directors: George Eastman, Henry A. Strong, Sir James Pender, The Right Hon. Lord Kelvin, Charles S. Abbott, Edwin O. Sage, George Ellwanger, Walter S. Hubbell, and William H. Corbin.

the American Consul at Heidelberg,' Eastman notified
Brownell. 'I send this to you because it bears upon the
point that I have been trying to impress upon you lately;
that is, that we have great reason to fear that the Germans will make very serious inroads upon our business
if we conduct it as we have been conducting it the past
year or two. It appears from this letter that they are
not only copying us but that they are proposing to lead us
in styles of our own cameras. When this thing occurs your
shop will be very much in need of work. The situation is
wholly inexcusable because we have, and have had for
years, better facilities than any of the Germans and the
only reason that we have not kept a long way in advance
of them is the lack of energy in your experimental department. If the Germans get out a 4×5 folding
pocket camera before we get out the $3\frac{1}{2} \times 5\frac{1}{2}$, which
we have been working on so long, it would be simply a
disgrace to us.'

Writing Davison he outlined the 'campaign for
1902':

'Greater efficiency and economy in the establishments
that we have can only be attained by close supervision on
the part of yourself and Mr. [F. C.] Mattison [assistant
manager in London] and I would submit for your consideration the suggestion that greater results can be obtained during this present year in this direction than in
any other.

'On this side of the water I propose to make a great
effort to get costs down again in the camera works to
where they belong, and to make further improvements
in manufacture at Kodak Park.

'The general policy in purchasing these established
businesses is to exploit both the wholesale and retail
business. The retail business can be very materially

stimulated by our example, as it has been in Europe. If the policy proves successful there is no doubt but what we can purchase almost any of the concerns that we want throughout the country.'

The final phase of Eastman's business strategy included the dry-plate business. Writing his solicitors in London he stated:

'The Seed concern [dry-plate manufacturers] makes from 40% to 50% of all the dry plates manufactured in this country. Their reputation as a businesss concern is of the very best. The only reason for their wanting to consolidate is that Mr. Henry C. Huskamp, the principal owner, is getting to be a pretty old man and wants to put his property in a more secure position. He fully realizes the overpowering influence of the Kodak Company and knows that as an isolated concern his Company is not as strong as it would be if allied with the Kodak Company. If the Seed Company agrees to come in I shall propose the same kind of a deal to the three other large concerns. They will comprise all of the American concerns desirable to include.'

In May, 1902, Eastman acquired control of the M. A. Seed Dry Plate Company of St. Louis, the Standard Dry Plate Company of Lewiston, Maine; in June he purchased the card-mount business of Taprell, Loomis and Company of Chicago. During the year he acquired, by purchase, the control of the following retail stores: Sweet, Wallach and Company of Chicago; O. H. Peck and John H. Fouch of Minneapolis; Zimmerman Brothers, St. Paul; Minneapolis Photo Materials Company, Edward M. Katz and C. T. Shape and Company of Milwaukee; Kortwright and Kline, Sioux City, Iowa; Horgan, Robey and Company, and the Benjamin French and Company, of Boston.

Thus the foundations were laid for the chain-store system of retail selling, which within less than a score of years was to be considered universally in American business as the keystone of efficient and economical distribution of manufactured goods.

This aggressive policy brought forth anew the cry of 'trust,' whereupon a letter was sent to the trade reporting that 'a number of concerns who want the photographic paper trade very badly are trying to gain it by an appeal to prejudice — are trying to gain it by shouting "anti-trust." Inasmuch as we have the trade that they want, the presumption is that we are the people designated as the trust.

'Having failed to make any inroads upon our business by cutting below our prices, they are now endeavoring to prejudice you against us on the ground that ours is a large concern. It is. Ours is the largest photographic business in the world. We have made it so — not by appeals to prejudice, but by steadily furnishing our customers with goods of the highest quality at a consistent price. For 22 years we have adhered strictly to this policy and it has won out to the advantage of ourselves and to the advantage of the American photographer.'

Eastman was so convinced 'that our policy, if properly put before the dealers and the consuming public, will be accepted' that he wrote Davison:[1] 'A year ago at the convention, before our policy had been thoroughly tried out, there was a good deal of talk on all sides against the "trust." Of course, the outside dealers and manufacturers helped it along all they could but at the Buffalo convention last week there was none of this talk that cut any figure whatever. The photographers are satisfied

[1] August 11, 1902.

and the dealers are satisfied, all except the very few that are not handling our goods. The point that we endeavor to satisfy them on is that we are working for the interest of the photographer and also for the interest of the dealer. We do not make any blow about taking care of our own rights. Neither the photographers nor the dealers care anything about this whatever. They would just as soon see us imposed upon as not and under no circumstances can we work up any sympathy for ourselves. The tocsins, "What have they done for the dealer?" and, "What have they done for the photographer?" are the ones that are going to carry us to victory.'

Before Eastman originated film photography, photographers were called 'Knights of the Black Art.' This was prior to the advent of the daylight-loading cameras. By the beginning of the twentieth century, the Eastman system was the world standard, but it was still necessary to develop all films in a dark-room. This phase of the art was not given much attention in Rochester or London, and one may imagine Eastman's surprise when he received a letter late in 1901 from A. W. McCurdy, private secretary to Professor Alexander Graham Bell, stating that he had invented a machine to develop negatives which any amateur could use, and asking Eastman to permit him to make a demonstration.

Following a consistent policy of examining everything new pertaining to film photography, Eastman invited McCurdy to Rochester.

The inventor arrived carrying a small, oblong, metal-lined wooden box. With the enthusiasm characteristic of craftsmen he related how a roll of film, after exposure, could be unwound into the box by means of a celluloid apron attached to a spool revolved by a crank on the outside. He stated that the developing, fixing, and washing of film, three successive operations, could be performed in this enclosed tank.

McCurdy demonstrated and Eastman studied the process and the results. 'It is a complete failure,' he declared. 'What we have been striving for all along has been greater latitude for the amateur. You destroy that latitude. For a picture that had been perfectly exposed your developer is all right, but for the average amateur it will never work.'

McCurdy was dumbfounded. 'I have spent everything I have saved and every cent I have earned,' he said finally, 'and I haven't either the money or the courage to go on. You take it and make it right. You can do it and I can't.'

'No, I won't take it,' Eastman replied. 'It is your invention and you will have to work it out.'

The two men discussed the possibilities and McCurdy left. Within a day or two he was back at the State Street headquarters.

'I've got it!' he shouted triumphantly, and made another demonstration. He had done what every photographer would have told him he could not do. He had developed and fixed the film in the same tank, something that had never been done before, because it was vital to both the developing and fixing of a negative that all traces of 'hypo' be thoroughly washed away before the film was immersed in fixing fluids; otherwise it was streaked. McCurdy demonstrated that by quickly swashing the film in water after developing, using the same tank, there was no trace of streaking.

McCurdy wanted to sell the invention outright, for whatever Eastman would pay.

'It is worth more than we can afford to pay you in one

lump,' Eastman answered. A royalty was thereupon agreed to, which McCurdy invested in Kodak stock, and as this climbed in value he had a rich reward for abolishing the photographic dark-room.

After all patents here and abroad were transferred to the company, the engineers redesigned and perfected the model and in August, 1902, the company announced: 'The final triumph has come. . . . Cameras will be improved . . . photographic processes will be still further simplified, and the lens manufacturers will make marvelous strides towards perfection, but nothing that remains to be accomplished in the simplifying of picture-making can equal in importance or interest the simple device by means of which the gloom of the dark-room has been dispelled. . . . Now amateurs may themselves accomplish every step of picture-making . . . without once straining their eyes beneath the feeble rays of a ruby lamp.

'This stage in the development of photography has been reached by a natural evolution, an evolution culminating, it is true, with a stroke of genius which adds the final triumph to the growth of the Kodak idea — Simplicity.

'The Kodak Developing Machine not only develops film without a dark-room, but does it better than it is done in a dark-room. It widens the photographic field and gives the amateur better results than he obtained before. There are many things that may be done more perfectly by machine than by hand — developing negatives is one of them.

'From a physical standpoint the machine gives better results than can be obtained by hand, because it does away with the possibility of foreign substances in the developer settling on the negative and making spots; it does away with the possibility of defacing the negative with finger marks, and it prevents the corners of one negative from scratching the face of another.

'Chemically the advantages are boundless. In abolishing the dark-room, it also abolishes the dark-room lamp. Every experienced photographer knows that in cases of prolonged development the fog from this lamp often becomes serious. The beginner is especially prone to fogging his negatives by examining them too close to the ruby lamp. . . . In the machine, the negative being in absolute darkness, there is nothing to fog it.'

'I have just had the opportunity of seeing one of the Kodak developing machines which you are about to place on the market, and have witnessed its operation,' Dr. Bell wrote. 'Surely this invention marks a distinct step in advance. It is simple, ingenious, practical.'

This formal statement was obviously written for publication, and did not reflect Professor Bell's enthusiasm, for he had McCurdy demonstrate the invention in his home in Washington to several groups of scientists, and in April came to Rochester to visit Eastman. A few months later, Eastman welcomed another scientist, Lord Kelvin, the first man to befriend the telephone, but who was now one of the English directors of the Kodak Company. The visit of the distinguished British scientist not only symbolized half a century of industrial and scientific progress, but it marked the culmination of Eastman's business strategy which made his company one of the young industrial giants of the world.

Before his elevation to the peerage, Lord Kelvin was William Thomson, son of Dr. James Thomson, Professor of Mathematics at Glasgow University. After graduating from this institution, his first position of importance was that of electrician for the Atlantic cables in 1857–58 and again in 1865 and the following year, when he invented the mirror-galvanometer and siphon recorder, in connection with submarine telegraphy. In 1869, he acted as electrical engineer for the French Atlantic cable; in 1873, for the Brazilian cable; in 1875, for the West Indian cables; and in 1879, for the Mackay-Bennett Atlantic cable. In 1876, he perfected an electrical improvement in the mariner's compass, and by the time he revisited this country, as Eastman's guest, he had been Professor of Natural Philosophy at Glasgow University forty-six years!

Although Marconi had invented high frequency wireless communication in 1896, it was still a novelty in 1902, so much so that the 'New York World' featured the invitation which the trustees of Columbia University sent to Lord Kelvin by wireless to attend the installation of Dr. Nicholas Murray Butler, as president of that institution.

'Now there is an invention of some commercial use,' Lord Kelvin told the 'New York Tribune.' 'The workings of wireless telegraphy are marvelous. I spent several hours in the Marconi room on the ship on the voyage, where the workings of this wonderful invention were demonstrated to me. . . . There is no limit to the scope of wireless telegraphy, and you can rest assured that it is not fully developed yet.'

'In the long procession of men of science and letters that marched across the Columbia campus to the gymnasium, where President Butler was installed,' reported the 'Sun,' 'Lord Kelvin was one of the most noticeable, as he was the most renowned. The first man of science of Great Britain, as he is often called, is nearly 78 years old. His ruddy face is fringed with a snow-white beard and his hair is white. His step is halting and his slight figure is bent.'

Eastman and Abbott had met Lord Kelvin at the dock, and from that time until his departure, three weeks later, he was honored at Columbia, Yale, Rochester, and Cornell Universities, by George Westinghouse, inventor of the airbrake, members of the Cabinet and Supreme Court, the American Institute of Electrical Engineers, the press and the public. Traveling in the private car 'Grassmere,' the Kodak party visited Niagara Falls because of Lord Kelvin's interest in hydroelectric developments. Then the photographic plants at Rochester and Jamestown were inspected. Here it was that the 'prince of science' [1] made a memorable public address, stating that the developments in photography had been one of the largest contributions to progress in scientific research.

Another strange anomaly! The man who was one of the pioneers in chemical research in the United States had achieved, by creating and perfecting film photography, a place in science which neither he nor any other American had recognized. Lord Kelvin had made another discovery, the important relationship of photography to all scientific research.

Before Lord Kelvin revealed his ideas in regard to photography and science, he recalled the part which he had taken as a member of the advisory board which had charge of the construction of the Niagara Power Plant. At this time he was particularly interested in the electrochemical industries, and learned, for the first time, of the manufacture of nitric acid from air by means of a direct current of sixteen thousand volts. The idea of utilizing

[1] 'This is a year of royal visits. We have welcomed Prince Henry, we may welcome the Prince of Wales, but we have now with us one greater than either, a prince of science by his own right, William Thomson, Lord Kelvin, mathematician, physicist, electrician, leader of thought in a century of marvels. . . . Lord Kelvin's presence does honor to the United States. We welcome him heartily.' (Editorial in the *Sun*, New York, April 20, 1902.)

LORD AND LADY KELVIN, CAPTAIN HENRY LOMB, AND
MR. EASTMAN AT THE MECHANICS INSTITUTE

the energy of the Niagara River, in the form of electricity, was first conceived by a European scientist, Sir William Siemens, who visited the Falls in 1876. While crossing the Atlantic upon his return, he occupied himself with a series of calculations, arriving at the conclusion that the energy of the river at the cataract alone equaled over sixteen million theoretical electrical horse-power.

Continuing his studies, he arrived at the definite conclusion that the energy at Niagara Falls could be utilized commercially. In presenting his ideas to European scientists, he ventured the opinion that by erecting very powerful dynamos in series, one thousand horse-power of energy could be transmitted thirty miles through a three-inch copper wire. After Edison invented the incandescent electric lamp, Siemens predicted that this current could be utilized 'in burning the carbons in electric lamps, and in improved processes of separating metals.'

When the international commission was appointed to construct the first power plant at the Falls, Lord Kelvin was chosen as chairman.

'I hope to live to see the day when one of my dreams will come true,' the British scientist said in Rochester, April 28, 1902, 'when we shall transmit electrical power over three hundred miles, with a voltage of forty thousand. Fifteen years ago when I said that I was laughed at, but with the wonderful transmission of power at Niagara Falls, my dream will be realized in the near future. Power is already sent from Niagara Falls to Buffalo and will soon be sent to Toronto. I believe the time will come when it will be sent for hundreds of miles in all directions. I regard Niagara Falls as the greatest problem in America for scientists to solve. The time is coming when coal and oil will be too scarce and too expensive to be used for the manufacture of power. There is at

Niagara Falls an inexhaustible supply of power that in fifty or a hundred years is bound to be utilized to the fullest extent. This world must depend on its water for power in the future.'

After visiting the paper plants at Jamestown, the camera works and Kodak Park in Rochester, Lord Kelvin delved into the possibilities of wireless telegraphy, predicting that as the system was developed 'it would be possible to send messages around the world.

'That is no more wonderful, is it, than the telephone seemed twenty-five years ago? I witnessed at Philadelphia in 1876 the first test of the telephone and with all its original imperfections, I predicted at that time the practical and commercial value of the new invention. I believe Marconi is on the right line and that his invention will become as important in the commercial world as the telephone has proved.'

At Jamestown Lord Kelvin focussed his great mind upon photography, and in a public address, said: [1] 'I have seen applications of science of the most interesting kind, not merely the rough and ready applications of science which we see every day, which do not reach the depth and the subtleties of science. But in the factory which I visited to-day there are applications to real scientific problems, which I have considered with great interest. I received a real scientific welcome there. I knew a little of those works before, I know more about them now, and I hope to know still more hereafter.

'I feel that my association with Mr. Eastman in the great company which he has created has been a continued pleasure to me and has given me more enjoyment in the application of science to the uses of mankind than almost anything I have ever been associated with. In

[1] *Rochester Democrat and Chronicle*, April 27, 1902.

Mr. Eastman's work science is applied with marvelous results and wherever you go through the civilized world, the results of Mr. Eastman's labors add to the enjoyment of life.

'The success of the photographic work here depends upon knowledge, invention and science, and because the founders of this industry were not satisfied with imperfect results, it has become one of the most interesting and valuable applications of science that is known. The great success of the work speaks for itself.

'Photography as developed by these allied companies, is not only an amateur pleasure, but in art it has become an institution of great value. Mechanics, engineering, scientific research of all kinds, are applied by the photographic process.[1] The properties of the stars and their characteristics are discovered to us by photography. The latest advances in astronomy are founded on photography.

[1] 'Astronomical photography began July 17, 1850, when W. C. Bond, of Cambridge, Massachusetts, obtained pictures of some bright double stars. In 1864, Rutherford photographed the Pleiades. The introduction of dry plates stimulated astrography, and in 1882 a great comet appearing in southern skies was photographed at the Cape of Good Hope Observatory. April 16, 1887, an international congress met in Paris to discuss a general photographic survey of the heavens. The problem was to develop an astrographic telescope mounted so as to allow for the movement of the stars. A standard was adopted at the Paris Conference. . . . The apparent brightness of a star is the first indication we have as to its size, or, conversely, to its distance. . . . A floating zenith telescope was constructed in 1901 by Bryan Cookson. . . . The instrument is used for photographing the trails of stars across the meridian.' (From 'Astronomical Photography,' by Charles Rundle Davidson, Royal Observatory, Greenwich, in *Photography as a Scientific Instrument*.) The origin of photography in the engineering and metallurgical industries is estimated at about 1900 by John Henry G. Monypenny, Chief of the Research Laboratory, Brown, Bayley's Steel Works, Limited, of Sheffield. Writing in 1923, he observed that 'The value of the camera has been increasingly recognized year by year in the metallurgical and engineering industries during the last quarter of a century. Probably one of the earliest uses of photography in these industries was in connection with the microscope. . . . There are now few laboratories in metallurgical or engineering works which are not equipped with a photomicroscope.'

'I mention this to show the grandeur and dignity of the work of photography, as exemplified in these factories at Jamestown and Rochester. My close association with Mr. Eastman is a great gratification to me, and my connection with the Eastman Kodak Company as a director is a pleasure. I am proud to be a representative of my English colleagues here.'

This 'leader in modern thinking,' as he was characterized by Dr. Rush Rhees, president of the University of Rochester, stimulated the interest of universities and industries in electrical and chemical research, in hydroelectrical power transmission and wireless telegraphy. He had been identified with the telephone, electric power transmission and film photography — three great American discoveries which were destined to combine human resources, large capital reservoirs, and scientific research in a vast vinculum of progress, despite the critical decade that preceded the World War.

CHAPTER VI

THE MOTION PICTURE PAYS TRIBUTE TO EDISON

'THE ideal large corporation,' Eastman wrote, 'is one that makes the best use of the brains within it'; and in the evolution of his policies it is evident that he was not over-looking the intangible assets of initiative, vision, and direction. He had stressed the importance of 'the company' for many years, and was determined to make the organization rather than one individual supreme. The transfer of responsibilities, however, was not a task that could be accomplished by punching a time clock. It was destined to cover a period of many years and was one of the most difficult jobs he ever undertook.

In 1901 and again in 1904, the Anthony and Scovill Company made repeated efforts to sell out to Eastman and settle the Goodwin case. Although this would have given the Eastman Company a monopoly of the American photographic market, Eastman refused all offers. In 1901, he could have bought his competitor's business for less than a million dollars. Three years later the price was jacked up, and Eastman recorded the facts in a letter to one of his associates. A representative of Anthony and Scovill came to Rochester. 'He unfolded the modest proposition that we could get control of their company for the sum of $1,500,000; or buy them outright for $2,-750,000. Later, he lopped off $250,000 to make it nice, even money. He said that would be a mere bagatelle for us and we could get our money back in sixty days. When I tried to pin him down as to how we were going to get it back, he said "by raising prices"; that if we bought them we would have absolute control and that we could raise prices and discharge our traveling men. When I told him that I would be afraid to do this, he seemed to think I was a pretty weak specimen. He talked for an hour and a half, trying to make me think as he did, and at the end of that time I told him he would have to bring up some new argument before I could consider it; that we were perfectly satisfied that we could not maintain a monopoly of anything; but there would always be a full line of outside goods and that it would be simply throwing away money to invest it in their stock.'

But the New York crowd were anxious to sell. Their attorney called the following day with a new proposition, lowering the price to $2,000,000. 'I pointed out that this still included $800,000 for good-will and that I did not see any prospect for dealing on any such figure,' Eastman wrote Philipp. 'He then wanted to know what I would do and I told him that if we bought his business, we should have to see our way clear to earning at least 14 or 15% on the investment; not by throttling competition, but by continuing their business. He kept insisting upon the importance of compromising the patent suits between us, and I finally told him that I would not pay anything for this purpose; that I did not see how the Goodwin patent could possibly be sustained broadly enough to interfere with our manufacture of film.'

It was not by settling a lawsuit or by monopoly that Eastman aimed to achieve further progress. 'Go out and hustle for the trade,' he wrote Davison. That combined with research, the development of personnel, and the quality of merchandise offered the public were his 'fighting arguments.' Furthermore, the trade knew he was not afraid to fight!

'I propose to fight until there is at least a quarter of an inch of ice on the surface of the hottest place that has ever been mentioned in sacred history,' he wrote Strong when another competitor tried the hold-up method of settling patent litigation.

Writing to Philipp, who was in complete charge of the Goodwin case, Eastman declined to enter into any further conferences: 'As to the Turner patent, I cannot see that anything would be gained by any compromise. If the patent is declared good, we own it. If it is not, the invention is open to everybody and we do not consider the Anthony outfit any more formidable than plenty of others who would rise up to succeed them if we should buy them out. In regard to the Goodwin patent, I have stated my views very fully. The only desire I have in connection with it is that the owners will press their suit to a conclusion. If they continue their dawdling tactics I hope that you will force them to an issue.'

More than a decade had passed since the Goodwin patent was issued and still the new owners were unable to make a commercially practical film according to his formulæ. Although litigation was expensive, Eastman had complete confidence in Philipp and had no intention of compromising. Finally, December 15, 1908, the New York owners filed suit, which they did not bring to a hearing, however, until May, 1913.

During 1906, Eastman kept in close communication with Philipp in regard to anti-trust laws.

'Since I talked with you I have been considering what would happen to our business in case anti-trust laws should go into force that would be so rigid as to prevent our offering inducement to dealers for selling our goods exclusively. In the first place, our terms were not instituted with the idea of obtaining or maintaining a monopoly. The real object of our system is the *prevention of substitution* and that is just as important to the public as it is to us. The crime of substitution has become such a general one that in some countries a regular crusade has been attempted by associations of manufacturers, with a view to educating the public against it but that is beginning at the wrong end of the problem and is a very long and tedious proceeding. The quickest way to attack the problem is through the dealer. We accomplish it by putting him in a position where there is no temptation, viz: by restricting him to our goods. Under such a restriction we can spend our money for advertising with a reasonable certainty that we will get the benefit of it. Without that restriction unprincipled dealers will take any article that they can make more money on and force it on their customers, saying that "it is better" or "just as good" for less money. As I look at it, it is very important to us that we should be able to continue this restriction and I think we should immediately begin to lay our plans so as to meet such legislation as that proposed in Massachusetts, and which will doubtless be copied elsewhere. I wish you would give your serious consideration to the proposition which I advanced in New York, namely; that we give our agents territorial rights, and let me have an opinion as to whether the scheme is a good one. What I would propose to do would be to give each agent certain territory, well defined on the map. Where the city is large enough to require more than one dealer I would define his territory by street limits and agree not to put another dealer in such limits.'

In the mean time Eastman himself was thinking in terms of human resources. He had long since reached the decision that brains were more important than patents, machines, money, monopolies, or processes. His paramount interest was in men, in the welding of human beings into an organization that would pioneer as a unit, progress as a unit, lead as a unit. Considering the organization as a whole, he decided that two executives appeared determined to throttle his efforts and they were promptly eliminated.

Informing Philipp of one of the changes, Eastman declared: ' —— is leaving us owing to dissatisfaction with what he calls his "position at court." He got an idea sometime ago that he was to be my successor, and as things are not working out in that direction lately, he threatened several times to resign and finally carried out the threat and I have accepted the situation. I am sorry to lose him, but am satisfied his efforts to build up a machine of his own so antagonize him with the rest of the organization that it is of no use for him to go on.'

To another executive who complained of cliques, Eastman responded by offering him another position, and then admonishing him that 'the only clique that is recognized in this business is one whose chief object is to get the best results for the company by efficient coöperation and no man who does not show the very best result in his own line will ever be a member of that clique.'

From 1882 to 1908, the organization had grown from five employees to 6130. Eastman's system of organization was built upon the selection of 22 managers, 43 assistant managers, 47 superintendents, 10 assistant superintendents, 229 foremen, and 24 assistant foremen, who were entrusted with the details of every phase of the business.

'With possibly half a dozen exceptions all the above have risen from lower positions,' he replied to a questionnaire from 'Harper's Magazine.' [1] 'It is rarely the case that any position in the company is filled other than by promotion. The consolidations as effected by this com-

---

[1] Letter to John K. Mumford, April, 1908, on condition that no reference would be made to Eastman or the company.

pany have resulted in almost every case in the retirement of the owners and the promotion of employees to managing positions at higher salaries than they have ever received before.

'If anybody *alone* decides whether a man is to be promoted it is the man himself. Men who are capable of promotion are conspicuous and as a rule attract the attention of others beside their immediate superiors. A foreman might in individual cases possibly hamper a man's progress but in a well-organized concern such an occurrence would be very apt to be noted by the foreman's superior.

'It does not require any separate system to show a man's competence and eligibility for promotion. The ordinary records ought to show it as far as it can be shown by any written records.

'The same brains and ability can get greater results in a large corporation on account of the better coördination of the organization mechanism.

'One of the first qualifications for a manager, superintendent or foreman is ability to recognize ability in those under him and to stimulate their initiative. Any concern where this is overlooked will be full of dry rot. The ideal large corporation is one that makes the best use of the brains within it.[1]

'The only sound reason for the combination of many companies under one management is to obtain greater efficiency. Where different plants under the same management are turning out the same kind of goods the tendency is constantly to raise the standard and to do this the workers must be given an incentive.

[1] Writing Mattison, September 19, 1912, when he was recovering from a serious illness, Eastman said: 'Take all the time you want to get well and make a thorough job of it. Good men are scarce in this world.'

'Consolidation has greatly increased the opportunity for a good worker to secure recognition. In small plants it often happens that personal favorites or relatives are promoted over deserving employees. Favoritism in a large corporation is so destructive to all organization that it has to be eliminated. Large corporations pay higher salaries than small ones. Opportunities of men increase with the size of the corporation just as they do with the size of the community in which they work. Men are continually leaving small towns to go to large ones for the sake of greater opportunities afforded and there is a tendency of able men to seek, or to remain with big corporations for the same reason.'

Eastman never believed in coddling men. His standard always was their value to the company. Even when the personality of a manager made it difficult for others to work with him, Eastman would decline to take any action as long as he felt that individual eccentricities were not injurious to group effort.

'The company has always tried to show its appreciation of competent men,' he informed one of his managers who reported that, in his opinion, another executive was indulging in rather unguarded comments about what he might do if he resigned. Threats of resignation never caused Eastman any loss of sleep. 'There are so many things required in order to make a success in this day in the photographic manufacturing business that the company is not greatly alarmed at what any man can do. All of our big competitors to-day can make good emulsions, some of them can make mighty good film; lots of them good plates and paper; some of them have been in business longer than the Kodak Company and people have left the Kodak Company to go into business, but with very few successes even when they started with

conditions much more favorable than they are now.
Although Mr. —— has been indiscreet in his talk, this
can be said of him, that up to the present time he has
never endeavored to evade his obligations to the company.'

During the financial panic of 1907, Eastman's chief
concern was the weekly payroll of Rochester employees
and he solved the stringency by importing gold from the
English company, proving again the wisdom of distributing the eggs 'and padding the basket at the same time.'
Upon this occasion the policy was of distinct advantage
to the employees.

'The situation here is very uncertain about currency,'
he wrote the London manager. 'We cannot tell which
way the cat will jump. We had no difficulty in getting it
for this week's payroll and I am promised it for next week.
Your shipment ought to be available for the following
week in case it is impossible to get it here. So many cities
are going on a clearing-house certificate basis, it is possible that Rochester will have to do it. I want to save our
hands any possible inconvenience caused by having to
accept such scrip in place of cash. It is quite likely that
you may have to make only this one shipment, but I shall
cable you next week whether or not to make another.
There is not a bank in Rochester that has currency
enough to cover more than a two or three days' run and
it has been impossible to get any from outside the city.
At one bank to-day seventy people drew all their money,
presumably to hide it away until the scare is over, and it
was a short day, too. It is hoped, however, that the scare
has reached its height and that next week people will be
in a calmer mood.'

Ten days later he cabled London to repeat the gold
shipment. 'The financial situation is improving some-

what all over the country and it looks as if I might have to call on you for only one or two more shipments of gold before we can get plenty of currency. On Saturday we put the enclosed circular in our pay envelopes and it has been very favorably commented on.'

'Keep This Money Circulating' was the title of the anti-panic leaflet:

'All rumors about shutting down and laying off help are absolutely without foundation. Currency is becoming more plentiful and all danger of a necessity of paying by check has passed.

'Conditions in Rochester are not bad. The wage earners are the only ones who can make them bad. Take, for instance, our own case, and we are no exception: We sell our goods out of town and are paid for them by checks or drafts. These are deposited in the banks for collection and some time must elapse before these banks can realize on them. We put no currency into the banks because we do not receive payment for our goods in currency, but we do pull $50,000.00 in currency out of the Rochester banks every week for our pay roll. What becomes of this fifty thousand? When conditions are normal, you pay out the bulk of it to the grocer, the butcher, the dry-goods house and to the other retail merchants, and those of you who are putting aside for a rainy day, place your surplus in the bank. The merchants in their turn deposit the money so that by the time another week has gone around, the money which we drew out to pay you with has been re-turned to the banks. It is evident, therefore, that when we go to the bank for the next week's pay roll we draw out the same money that we paid you with the previous week. Money is only a medium of exchange anyway, and to be useful must be kept moving. It doesn't earn anything or help anybody when hidden in the teapot.

Pay your bills, spend as before or put your money in the bank and there can be no necessity for paying by check or for laying off help. You are sure of your cash; help the other fellow.

'You have no more reason for hoarding your cash now than you had a year ago. Steady work and steady cash pay are assured. Save money if you wish, that is always wise, but don't take it out of circulation. Put it in the bank where it will earn for you and will help everybody do business.

'Full time, a full force and real money on Saturday — there's nothing else in sight in our factories.'

This action was a decided advantage to Rochester banks, as the Kodak Company was the largest industry in the city. Its payroll constituted one fourth of the city's total weekly wage payments, and at the height of the financial storm, when New York bankers decided to stop shipping gold outside that city as a protective measure, Eastman's importations helped to stabilize the local situation.

By December, Eastman was able to write his counsel in New York that the company was 'closing a year of extraordinary prosperity as far as total results are concerned. This comes in a considerable measure from the increase in the Ciné film business, but every other department in America has been doing well except the American Aristotype Company. They made some bad paper about a year ago that gave them an awful blow and which was the cause of gaslight papers taking the place of collodion papers to a large extent. Our sales up to November have not been affected in any way by the financial depression, but November has shown a general falling off in the increase of about everything except Ciné film. . . . For the first nine months of 1907 our silver cost us between 68 and 69 cents. The last few weeks we have bought it as low as 54 cents. If this price holds, of course it will make a tremendous difference to us, as we are using between four and five tons a month.'

By this time the company was, and still remains, the largest consumer of silver in the United States next to the United States Mint. This tremendous increase in the use of silver in emulsions was an excellent barometer of the growth in photography. But Eastman was no longer interested in remaining the largest manufacturer in this industry. He realized that an industry might be large and still not be the leader, and it was leadership, continuous leadership, the subtlest factor in business, that fascinated him. And leadership in an age of progress he believed would rest with those companies which achieved and maintained group pioneering and never closed their eyes to opportunities for expansion.

For years he had been interested in a 'house in Asia.' Early in January, 1908, he concluded an agreement with Thomas Baker, 'a thoroughly practical man,' senior partner of Baker & Rouse, of Australia, by which the company obtained a majority interest in the business in the Antipodes and made possible not only expansion in the Orient, but team-work in that part of the world with the leading photographic concern. Also it brought to the company J. J. Rouse, whom Eastman considered the best merchandiser in the industry.

In the mean time James H. Haste had a corps of research men at the Park engaged in experiments to produce non-inflammable (N.I.) film. By April, 1908, Eastman was in a position to write W. S. Gifford, the new managing director in London, 'it looks very much as if we had got the right thing.'

'I think,' he wrote Haste, that 'the outcome of our

experiments warrants our going on with the installation for making cellulose acetate. You may therefore order the tanks, and so forth, and push the installation to completion as rapidly as possible.'

In 1911, in an account tracing the growth of photography from a manufacturing point of view, Eastman recounted the history of acetate film.

'There was a substitute already known for the nitrocellulose, namely cellulose acetate, which had many of the properties of nitrate, but sheets formed from it lacked the tenacity of nitro-cellulose sheets; in fact if they were not positively brittle the sheets became so after the lapse of a comparatively short time. As you perhaps know, the strips of moving picture film, one and three eighths inches wide, are provided with a series of small perforations near each edge, which engage with the spurs of the sprocket wheels in the taking and exhibiting apparatus, whereby the film is progressed through the machine with a series of jerks. This entails considerable strain on the film which being only five thousandths of an inch thick, has to be of great toughness in order to stand the wear and tear of repeated use by the exhibitor, amounting on the average to at least one thousand exhibitions for each film.

'When the photographic manufacturer took it in hand he had first to overcome the objections referred to before he could use it. By this time a dozen or more concerns in America, England, France, and Germany had had their attention attracted to the problem, some of them with very large staffs of chemical experts, especially in Germany, and it may interest you to know that it was an American chemist who first solved the problem of toughening the material.'

This was the kind of business leadership Eastman was proud of. His company was the first to produce a non-curling film for 'still' pictures. Now it was the first to produce a commercially practical safety film. In this it was many years ahead of the market, for it was some time before industrial, medical, and educational motion pictures assumed large enough proportions to utilize non-inflammable film.

While Eastman was engaged in welding his forces into an organization, he received a criticism from a London broker that English shareholders were being discouraged from retaining their stock. Eastman nailed this immediately as 'absolutely untrue. If there is not any demand for Kodak shares on the London Exchange, it would appear to be owing to lack of interest on the part of the brokers themselves, who prefer to deal in more speculative industrials,' he wrote; and then he answered the suggestion of a 'catastrophe' that was in the minds of others besides the Londoner: What would happen to the company without Eastman's personal leadership?

'There may be something in the suggestion, "People will not invest in Kodak because they fear that should a large holder die and the shares be put on the market there might be a terrible slump." That, of course, refers to me. The "catastrophe," however, would not consist of the shares being put on the market, but in leaving the business without a head. As you yourself know, the organization of the business has been conducted on lines that would minimize this danger. While there is not now and never has been a surplus of good men in the concern, there has never been a vacancy in any important position where some man in the ranks has not been found to fill it, as a rule better than before.'

Eastman himself did not fear such an eventuality. By developing group responsibility, group initiative, and unity of action within the organization, he was endeavoring to provide continuity of leadership. That was his aim rather than the temporary protection of the company in the case of the loss of any one individual.

Naturally, however, he could not give his undivided attention to this policy even if his ideal could have been realized within a measurable length of time. While he might 'go through every department with a fine-tooth comb' to 'eliminate or alter every operation that can be improved upon . . . to reach a state of perfection that will be satisfactory commercially,' men and women were not machines. They were entitled to the same consideration as any executive or director. Their health was as much of a concern to him as his own. He engaged specialists to examine the eyes of the workers in the photographic dark-rooms at the Park; had health conditions in all factories studied by experts and compared conditions with those in other industries in Rochester, England, and Germany. In no single instance did these investigators find that conditions elsewhere were equal to those within the East-man factories. This fact may be of more than passing interest to those who thought, before the outbreak of the European war, that German industries were so far in advance of the world in safeguarding the health of employees.

As time and patience were essential in dealing with the psychological factors constituting personnel relations, and as Eastman's reservoir of patience in dealing with individuals always seemed inexhaustible, he was able to concentrate upon the chemical and technical problems which confronted the scientists at the Park and at Harrow in their experiments to develop safety film. In the fall of 1908, most of the difficulties appeared to center in the complexity of the patents, two of which appeared to be controlled by a German company. In October, three

representatives of this concern came to Rochester for a
conference and after extended consideration of the German claims, Eastman wrote his London manager:
'Philipp, [Joseph Thacher] Clarke, and I have been over
all the matter which has been accumulated . . . and we
have come to the conclusion that we can drive a four-
horse stage through anything that exists; that is to say, the
film that we propose to make will not infringe any existing
patents when interpreted according to the state of the art
at the time they were taken out.'

But by December the 'four-horse stage' had lost a
wheel. Acetic anhydride was essential in the manufacture of the new product according to the new formulæ.
Germany controlled the world market and no American
chemical concern could produce the quantities necessary
to supply the Rochester factories. Then, equally suddenly, but soon after Eastman was assured of a continuous
and adequate supply from Germany, he learned that
Congress was considering what appeared to be a prohibitive duty on this chemical.

Up to this time Eastman's interest in the tariff was
limited. 'Our concern is a little bashful about taking
a prominent part in these attempts to regulate the tariff,'
he had written W. A. Taprell, but now there was no alternative, and he had Hubbell telegraph Chairman Sereno
E. Payne, of the House Ways and Means Committee, in
Washington:

'Have just learned that hearing will be given to-morrow
on revision phraseology Schedule A relating to chemicals
paints and oils Section one. This Schedule includes
acetic anhydride which if duty is made twenty five per
cent ad valorem will be liable to duty of five cents per
pound at present. By ruling of court it is classified as
acetic acid anhydrous at two cents per pound. Eastman

Kodak Company has recently discovered and perfected process for manufacturing non-inflammable film for moving pictures which will be of tremendous importance by reason of its safety. I used every effort to purchase anhydride in this country but none of the big chemical companies would undertake to make it and leading chemists say it cannot be made here. Kodak Company was therefore forced to purchase abroad as no substitute can be used. It therefore made contract with German concern to furnish a quantity monthly about as large as total yearly imports into this country heretofore. This contract extends over two years duty to be paid by us. Cost of manufacturing new film will be greater than cost of manufacturing present film even if duty is not raised because the acetic anhydride, which costs twenty cents per pound takes the place of mixture of nitric and sulphuric acid used in present inflammable film costing less than two cents pound. Anhydride cannot be made in this country because of patents held by foreign manu- facturers and because the process requires use of large quantities of liquid chlorine which is not made in this country. All our calculations and estimates to customers for new film have been made on the assumption that the duty would not be increased. At least ninety per cent of all moving-picture films used throughout the world are now made in America. Unless we can make the non- inflammable film, this country may lose all or greater part of this trade. Acetic anhydride should be on free list not only for above reasons but because one of the principal materials used in its manufacture, acetate of lime, is all obtained from this country. We ask therefore that it be put upon free list or if that cannot be done then that it be made subject to a specific duty not to exceed two cents per pound which is present rate. This matter is of tremendous importance to Kodak Company.'

Hubbell tackled this task with enthusiasm, made contacts with members of the Senate Finance and House Ways and Means Committee, and eventually received a letter from Chairman Payne: 'There is no question that the duty should be reduced. It [acetic anhydride] cannot be made in this country and is the basis for a large manufacturing industry, and it would seem that there is no argument for increasing the duty to 25 per cent.'

The immediate result of this direct action was to clear the way for the commercial production of non-inflammable film, the foundation for industrial, medical, educational, and amateur motion pictures. This was a great forward step in film photography.

In the mean time the organization had developed new X-ray plates, plates for astronomical photography, new Kodak models, and scientists at the Park and at Harrow were experimenting with color photography. Eastman was happy. These developments were chiefly the work of the organization. They were evidences of group pioneering, not of individual effort. Brains were being coördinated. Men and women were becoming more and more company conscious. All that was needed now, was Time and Patience. He had the Patience and hoped for the Time.

'I am glad to hear that you are enjoying better health,' he wrote Baker in Melbourne. 'I have sent for a copy of Metchnikoff's book,[1] as I do not want to miss anything in the way of prolongation of life.'

Seventeen years after the experiments of Edison and Eastman made the motion picture possible and practical, the two men met for the first time. The event is recorded in an amusing, matter-of-fact letter to the Paris manager:[2]

[1] *The Prolongation of Life*, published 1908.
[2] May 3, 1907.

'I had a conversation at Orange on Wednesday with Thomas A. Edison and he told me the Pathé Company had mentioned in one of their letters that they were using 45 miles of film a day. This would equal, they figure, about 75,000,000 feet a year. Mr. Edison wanted to know if that was so. I laughed and said they did not buy that last year.'

Seventeen years later, the two inventors were 'introduced' to each other at a luncheon in Edison's honor given by the motion-picture industry in New York. Both men had forgotten this early meeting, although it was the beginning of the Motion Picture Patents Company, which marked the end of a ten-year war between Edison and the producers and distributors of photoplays. Incidentally, the organization of this company enabled the Eastman Company to collect the first substantial royalties which Edison received for this creation of his marvelous mind.

'I am glad to hear that M. [Charles] Pathé and Edison are coming to an agreement,' Eastman wrote. 'I proposed this to Mr. Moore, the manager of the Edison Kinetoscope Department, several months ago in New York. At that time Mr. Edison was in the South and he told me that as soon as Mr. Edison got back he would ask me to come down to Orange and state my views. This I afterward did. I told Mr. Edison I did not believe it would be a good thing for him to try to monopolize the whole ciné business (producing, distributing, and exhibiting); that in order to give it its full development it needed several minds to originate the great variety of subjects required. He and his general manager, Mr. Gilmore, seemed to agree with this proposition, and I understood that shortly afterward Mr. Gilmore went abroad. I shall be very much pleased if they make a

GUESTS AT THE LUNCHEON OF THE MOTION-PICTURE INDUSTRY TO MR. EDISON

Left to right: Robert L. Owen, Will H. Hays, Mr. Edison, Mr. Eastman, Edward I. Edwards
Lee de Forest, Adolph S. Ochs

connection with Pathé Frères, because up to the present time they have not been getting their share of business, and I believe it is because they have lacked enterprise in getting up their films.'

Early in June, Eastman entertained Charles Pathé in Rochester, and the latter part of the month he sent word to Philipp that 'the Edison people want to have a conference in regard to their scheme for forming an association to work under their motion-picture patent.'

The seed was sown now for action. Edison and Eastman, the two dominant figures in the motion-picture industry, had met and exchanged ideas. The keys to the situation were in Edison's and in Eastman's hands, not by election or selection, but because Edison controlled certain basic patents, excluding film, while all the producers and distributors of motion pictures were Eastman's customers. While the latter had competitors in the film business, none of them were producing or could produce either the quality or the quantity of film which his company manufactured. Even Pathé, the outstanding figure in Europe, was Eastman's largest customer.

In October, Edison was nearer to harvest time than he had ever been before, when, on the 24th, Judge Christian Kohlsaat, in the United States Court at Chicago, held that the cameras used by William M. Selig infringed the Edison patent. This brought the leading producers and exchange men into a series of conferences with Edison's counsel and with Eastman and Philipp.

The ten-year war in the United States and Europe over motion-picture patents had involved every one but Eastman, who recognized, as did most of the others, that a peaceful solution of the issues was imperative before there could be either progress or prosperity for the industry or any individuals engaged in the various phases of the business.

December 2, Eastman notified his counsel of interviews in Rochester with Alexander T. Moore and William Pelzer, representing Edison. 'They informed me,' Eastman wrote, 'that they had about concluded an arrangement with other moving picture makers, including Messrs. Pathé, on the line which I had suggested, viz: That they should all come in and take licenses under the Edison patent, pay a royalty of one half cent a foot and submit to the terms of sale of the Edison Company which would put the business on a more firm foundation. For instance, establish uniform prices and provide an allowance for the return of worn-out film, which would insure its being taken out of the renter's hands when it ought to be.

'There are three elements in this affair, ourselves, the makers of the pictures, and the renters [exhibitors]. The renters have already formed an association, with a view to controlling their business and preventing price cutting, and they are in favor of the picture makers regulating the sale of the film. The picture makers, as licensees under the Edison patent, will increase their prices so that they will, on an average, make one cent a foot more, after paying royalty, and *the Edison Company will get the benefit of large royalties.*

'At the present time outside of Pathé there are about 20,000,000 feet of film a year being consumed in this country. As for us, we are to be the sole licensees of Edison and we are to sell the film at one-half a cent a foot more to the picture makers; or, in other words, collect the royalty and turn it over to Edison. I have agreed to all this, providing they can draw a contract that will meet with your approval. What I propose is that the license shall be drawn in such a way that we can cancel it at any time, on reasonable notice, and put ourselves back in the place that we now occupy. The scheme looks like a good one to me, providing Edison, and this is also a condition, gets all of the legitimate picture makers into the thing to start with. Pathé, when he was here, indicated to me that he would not go into it but Moore reported that he has agreed to it. We do not know yet how much film Pathé is selling in this country but I would not be at all surprised if he is selling at the rate of 30,000,000 or 40,000,000 feet a year. Our total shipments to him now amount to something like twice that. We are furnishing him some film here in America but he is evidently not running to his full capacity in his new factory.'

Before the negotiations had progressed very far, Eastman discovered that the New York agent of Pathé was 'trying to use us to help freeze out his foreign competitors,' and he immediately telegraphed Philipp, 'I informed Mr. [George] Kleine [then the principal dealer in motion pictures in the West], when he was here Friday, that we would not under any circumstances allow ourselves to be used to freeze out anybody who was legitimately in the business, and that if we sent any of the N.I. [non-inflammable] film to Europe, we would send it to all of our customers alike.'

Eastman dealt with all parties on the same exacting lines. On December 6, when he received the first draft of a contract from the Edison Company, he suggested to Philipp and Moore that they come to Rochester for a conference. 'I am willing to go into the deal,' he recorded, 'providing the customers he [Moore] mentions in his letter agree to take licenses, and provisions are made in our own license that we can, on reasonable notice, cancel the license. The license should also permit us to make films in this country for shipment abroad without payment of any royalty. The licensees that Edison has selected use about 9/10 of all the film used in this country, not including Pathé. We should also have the right to sell film in strips for moving pictures, in narrower width than the standard, without the payment of any royalty, in order to provide for concerns like the Iconoscope Company, which is making a small house apparatus which is liable to require a good deal of the narrow film. This business, as I understand it, will not interfere with the one that Edison is trying to protect.

'On hastily reading over the proposed license to us I note that it is not an exclusive license as was talked by the Edison people. This was a fundamental condition and I would not consider it in any other way.

'Unless the Edison Company will agree to these provisions beforehand it will hardly be worth while for us to make an appointment.'

While these discussions were taking place, the Edison and Biograph officials, Kleine and representatives of Vitagraph, Lubin, Selig, Essanay, Pathé, Kalem, and Melies met in New York City, 'pooled their patents and claimed special rights,' and the proposed Motion Picture Patents Company advanced another step.

A few days later Eastman learned that the American Mutoscope and Biograph Company had been left out and he notified his counsel:

'On Wednesday I had a long call from Mr. [H. N.] Marvin of the Mutoscope Co. He said that rumors were floating about that a deal was being engineered by the Eastman Kodak Co. and the Edison Co. to form a combine and that a contract was now being drawn by the counsel for the Eastman Co. that would freeze out the Mutoscope Co. He claimed that as one of the oldest customers of our company he was entitled to consideration. He said he had tried to find out from the Edison Co. what was going on but without success. I told him that it had been proposed to us that we should take a license under the Edison patents and agree to furnish film only to Edison licensees: that a list of the licensees had been submitted to us and that it contained the name of his concern; that a license contract had been drawn by the Edison Co. and submitted to us, which was not satisfactory, and that it was now being revised by our counsel, in consultation with the Edison representatives; that the whole thing was being pushed along on the assumption that every one of our customers who was entitled to it would be taken in; and that when we decided on the form of contract that would be acceptable to us we would then ascertain who would agree to take out licenses and if any who were on the list did not come in we would decide whether we would or would not cut them off.

'He was very anxious to have some assurances from me that we would not in any case cut them off but I told him that all he needed was the assurance that I gave him, viz: that we would not sign any contract until we had communicated with him and ascertained whether or not he was to have a license. Marvin stated that his camera, which has been declared not to infringe the Edison patent, makes negatives that are superior to those made by the Edison camera and that he can print positives from such negatives on film perforated for the regular Edison exhibiting machine which register more accurately than if made from sprocket fed negatives. He flouts the proposition that Edison can control positives perforated for sprocket feeding. He says that he would take a license under the Edison patents providing the royalty on the film was divided to give half to Edison and the other half either to Edison or to the Mutoscope Co. according to the style of camera used in making the negatives. He intimated that he would fight any other proposition even if we did cut him off. He was quite positive, in view of the fact that they had not been approached by the Edison Co., that they were to be frozen out.

'I did not say anything that would lessen Mr. Marvin's uncertainty as to whether we would cut him off because I should not want to put him in a position where he could increase his demands on that account. Nevertheless I cannot see how we could cut him off unless he refuses to accept some reasonable proposition. I am inclined to think that he is entitled to consideration on the lines that he mentioned.'

Throughout the month of January there were daily conferences either in Rochester, New York, or Orange, and, on the 29th, Philipp advised Eastman of the status of the legal negotiations:

'The Eastman Company can terminate its agreement by giving 60 days notice in writing. The licenses to Pathé and the others run for at least two years. Mr. Edison suggested that if the Eastman Company license was terminated during such two years, or at any time while there were any licensees obtaining film, there would be no way of collecting the royalty. He, therefore, thinks that there should be some clause covering this, and suggests at the end of the 19th clause, or somewhere in the agreement there should be the following provision:

'It is, however, mutually covenanted and agreed by and between the parties hereto that should this agreement be cancelled by the Eastman Company by giving 60 days' notice as above provided, the Eastman Company will nevertheless continue to act on behalf of the Edison Company to collect and turn over to the Edison

Company all royalties from licensees of the Edison Company under said reissued letters of patents, and shall continue to do so so long as there are any existing licenses under said reissued letters patent, the licensees of which shall continue to purchase the licensed film from the Eastman Company.'

Edison's complete confidence in Eastman was evident throughout the negotiations. Convinced that the conferences were headed in the right direction, Eastman departed for Europe to direct the diplomatic negotiations with all the foreign interests.

An international congress of the manufacturers of film had been scheduled for early January but was postponed a month to await Eastman's arrival, 'his presence, as is known, being necessary to the success of the syndical undertaking.'

'Let us note simply,' wrote the editor of the Paris 'Ciné Journal,' 'that the members of the Congress will appear at the meetings with a variety of interests. They all wish a perfect understanding; in this they are agreed. But the disparity in the interests of each: the rivalry of exasperated competition, the personal temperaments, and the fight for the first place are factors which one cannot neglect, and we have every reason to believe that they will come passionately into evidence in the discussion. Further, two preponderating houses in the cinematograph industry hold more than one of the threads which will make the figures dance. If their influence is not directly exercised on the Congress it will weigh none the less with considerable force on the whole and the result of the propositions. We mean the powerful factory of raw films, Eastman Kodak, and the firm Pathé Frères. Their double force will rule the meeting.

'Everyone knows that the Eastman Kodak Co. is

ready to place a non-inflammable film on the market, which will doubtless upset for some time the very varied transactions of renters and showmen. We hope that on this point the Congress, enlightened by information given by Mr. Eastman — whose presence is announced — will be able to speak with reassuring certainty to the trade. Everyone expects it.

'Is this non-inflammable film of such a quality that it will cut out every other mark? It is said so. But it is also stated that the firm Lumière is ready, and that two other manufacturers, one in Germany and the other in France, are doing their best to deliver an equally good film. It would be interesting to have some reliable information on this subject.

'And here at the last hour one of the most important agents on the Paris market brings us a grave piece of news, of a nature to throw trouble into the Congress, on the threshold even of the first discussions. A special understanding is said to have been arrived at between the Edison trust and some European houses which up to the present have not belonged to the United States market: The Company Gaumont and Eclipse-Radios are alone to be admitted, together with Pathé Frères and Melies, to participate in the lucrative joys of the famous American syndicate.

'All the other European marks, English, German, Italian, Russian and French, would thus ipso facto be deprived from exporting to North America, inasmuch as the greater part of the clientele belongs to the union of renters dominated by Edison. One can judge of the blow!

'But all this is only talk. These are the rumors which precede this sitting. Attention! The Congress is about to commence.

'The word is to Mr. Charles Pathé. He belongs to those who can deceive all expectation: he belongs also to those who may find themselves set back for the time being.'

When Eastman reached Paris, it was evident that he was in the vortex of an international motion-picture war and not on the outskirts of the domestic war in the United States. It was clear, too, that the chief thing his European competitors and all foreign motion-picture interests wanted to know was what use he intended to make of the new non-inflammable film which the company had perfected.

Obviously, the English, German, Italian, and French objectives were not the same. It was apparent also that Pathé could certainly 'deceive all expectations.' But Eastman was in a strategic position, because no other film manufacturer could begin to supply the industry with its needs. Therefore, if Eastman insisted upon peace, there was no alternative except fighting Eastman, and this no foreign individual producer could afford to do, for film was his daily bread.

When the convention met, the delegates voted to enter into an agreement similar to that being negotiated in the United States, and Eastman submitted the text to M. Raymond Poincaré,[1] the recognized leader of the French bar, whom he retained as his chief counsel.

Pathé, however, was obdurate. Eastman recorded the developments in a series of letters to Philipp:

'I had a long interview with Mr. Pathé, Mr. Izatts

---

[1] M. Poincaré first made his appearance as a Cabinet Minister in 1893, as Minister of Education, a post he held until 1895. He was Minister of Finance from 1904 until 1906, and the Premier from 1911 to 1913. He was also the War President of France, 1913 to 1920. In 1922, he was Premier and Minister of Foreign Affairs until 1924; and again Premier, and Minister of Finance from September, 1926, until 1929.

and Mr. Prevost, all of the Pathé Company. At first they insisted that the principal reason for taking another license was the opportunity they thought it would afford to shut off the European competitors, but after a somewhat animated argument, I finally succeeded in convincing them that they could not do it, even if we agreed to their demands.

'My main argument was that the Edison Film Patent would not enable the Edison people to get injunctions against the importers of film, and therefore the people shut out would combine and make an opposition, which would probably break down or make serious inroads into their combination. Therefore, it would be much better to get these people into an arrangement, where they could be controlled, and where they would have a chance according to their merits. I pointed out to the Pathé Company that the chief advantage in my opinion was to be found in the regulation of prices, and the control of the renters, and the suppression of the dupers.[1] They finally recognized the force of my argument and Mr. Pathé agreed to write to Mr. Berst at once and authorize him to accept the conditions provided for and already inserted in our license for Edison.'

By March the excitement 'had quieted down to such an extent that the European manufacturers have cancelled the called-for meeting which was to have been held this week,' Eastman informed Philipp. 'I have seen everybody of importance exept the Italian Ciné manager, and he is coming over here on the 18th or 19th. A letter just received from him indicates that he would rather come in under a license than join in a combine to

---

[1] These men were the "bootleggers" of the film industry. They would rent or pirate a picture, make duplicates and rent these duplicates to exhibitors, thereby cheating the producers of revenue which they were entitled to.

fight the Edison Patent. Unless the Pathé people mis-led me, I certainly convinced them that the scheme to keep their European competitors out of the States would be unwise and ineffective, and I have not the slightest doubt that Mr. Berst [Pathé's New York agent], when he cools down, will come to the same conclusion.'

Just as Eastman had everything in order, Poincaré submitted an opinion holding that the proposed agree-ment 'might be characterized as excessive' under the French law and advised Eastman not to participate in a European cartel.

While Eastman was 'much concerned and disap-pointed,' according to F. C. Mattison, assistant manager of Kodak, Limited, he had an alternative which *he* con-trolled. He had persuaded, already, all the leading men in the foreign motion-picture business of the value of recognizing the validity of the Edison patents and had actually achieved his objective without entering into a formal contract. In the public statement withdrawing from the convention, Mattison stated:

'We shall, therefore, in the future conduct our business individually with our respective customers and in so do-ing we shall use every endeavor to carry out the intention of Mr. Eastman, which is to prevent by all honorable means, any attempt to further disorganize the industry in which we are all so vitally interested in whatever way it may be threatened.'

Upon his return to New York, Eastman carried with him the promises of all of his customers, representing ninety-five per cent of the foreign motion-picture in-dustry, to recognize the Edison patents through the Mo-tion Picture Patents Company. On May 18, 1908, the final chapter in the peace negotiations was written when Eastman, and Frank L. Dyer, president of the Patents

Company and vice-president of the Edison Manufacturing Company, signed the contract, which insured a steady stream of royalty to Edison and a continuous stream of business to Eastman.

In order to carry out the arrangement, at least ten different parties had to be satisfied. First, Edison and Eastman, so far as the furnishing of the film and collection of royalty were concerned; then the seven proposed licensees under the Edison Company patent, so far as their relations with the Edison Company and between themselves were concerned and the relations between the Edison Company and Eastman were concerned; and then the renters, so far as their relations to the seven licensees and the Edison Company were concerned. In addition, the whole matter had to be planned so that all of the agreements would be legal, as well as what the renters were to do, and so as to remove it, as far as possible, from any attack on the ground of being an attempt to create a monopoly or in restraint of trade.

Under the terms of the Edison contract, Eastman agreed to sell film only to the Edison licensees and to collect royalty, based upon footage purchased, and pay the same to Edison.

While the signing of this agreement meant peace for Edison and the producers, distributors, and exhibitors of the world, it did not register peace for Eastman as a film manufacturer. Pathé was soon on the warpath again, and Eastman wrote Thomas Baker, apprising him of the facts: 'At the time I went to Arizona in July, we were expecting to put the N.I. [non-inflammable] film on the market in Europe the 1st of September, and as a preliminary to that we had been for some weeks trying to get our European customers to sign a three-year contract agreeing not to use any other N.I. film during that period. There was a certain coterie of them who wanted us to include in that contract price restrictions for the printed films. Our position was that we were willing to do it if all of our customers requested it. The principal ones, with the exception of Pathé, were in favor of it, but he finally refused to sign any contract that prevented him from making film himself; and he suddenly announced his intention of regenerating film and said he had already made his preparations to perform this operation on the nitrate base. We pointed out that that was a violation of our understanding, and as he would not retire from his position his supplies were cut off. He had, however, a stock of film in his warehouse which would last him until some time in November.

'When I got home I sent for Mr. Gifford to talk the matter over, but in the mean time Pathé had begun to issue his regenerated film and had even gone so far as to send some of it out in our boxes. I found on consultation with Mr. Gifford that Pathé's European competitors and even our own people were very much afraid of the effect of the regenerated film, it being certain that Pathé had a stock of unsold remnants of releases on hand which would supply him for a considerable time. I, however, concluded that the best way to handle it was to fight the product and not to depend on our refusal to furnish Pathé stock to make him quit. So I cabled him that after talking with Mr. Gifford I had made up my mind that regeneration was not sufficient to warrant cutting him off and that if he was being put to any inconvenience on account of the lack of supplies, we would let him have film until I could get over there, probably in December. Immediately we received a cable order for about 2,250,-000 feet of film, and since then we have received another order, which indicates that Pathé has not been able to secure a base of supply.

'The reason I was anxious to reëstablish relations with him is that I was afraid that, being driven into a corner, he would make some foolish contract which would prevent our dealing with him again. The next step was to fight regeneration. You have very likely seen in the Ciné journals the steps that were taken to discredit the product. In two or three weeks Pathé begged for an armistice, and I agreed to stop our advertisements if he would promise not to either put it out as new film or put it out in our boxes. This he has agreed to, so the situation stands that he is buying film from us and the regenerated film is so discredited that he cannot sell it for enough to make it pay to regenerate.'

Peace and Pathé, however, were incompatible and by June 22, 1910, Eastman wrote Baker again:

'We have lost Pathé's business since he commenced using the celluloid support and sensitizing it himself, but increases in orders from other customers have enabled us to hold our own so far. Recent reports indicate that Pathé is having some trouble with his film and his ultimate success is by no means assured. In Europe everybody seems to be sticking to our film pretty closely, but in this country, of course, we are confined to the Edison licensees and the Independents simply have to use other film. They have been dividing their orders between Lumière and Ensign. Now, however, the Agfa people are beginning to exploit their product. We have not been able to get any of it yet for trial, but hear it well spoken of.

'Our acetate film is running regular and is much stronger than when first put out, but notwithstanding that the trade does not like it as well as the nitrate film. Since April we have been offering it on trial in England at the same price as nitrate, but the users object to it so

strongly that its introduction, unless the authorities intervene, will be a failure. I cannot see that it makes any
difference to us which way the cat jumps. We are prepared to make either kind.'

Meanwhile, competition from Germany became threatening. 'As to the method of handling this competition,
we will have to determine that from time to time as the
situation changes,' Eastman wrote Clarke. 'I must say
that I do not think much of your proposition to cut prices
because it would not deter them at this stage of the
game from going on with their enterprise. The best thing
for us to do is to bring our products up to the very highest
state of perfection, and reduce our price when we have to.
The trouble with the European administration the last
eight or ten years has been that they consider price-
cutting a panacea for all difficulties. My experience has
been different from this. The money that we would lose
by cutting prices between now and the time the concern
gets going would keep us from starvation during a good
long fight.'

There appeared to be no doubt but that the international film war — the United States *versus* French and
German competition — would continue for some time,
and Eastman decided to direct his attention to new
buildings in this country and England, to the establishment of a color research laboratory at the Park (with a
few weeks' vacation off the coast of Labrador to fish for
salmon), when there was another unexpected development. The 'Independents' arrived!

Up to this time, the summer of 1910, practically every
concern engaged in making and exhibiting motion pictures was a party to the Edison agreement, but the Independents were growing in number and importance. The
first signal came from a visit to Rochester of Louis

Lumière and Jules Brulatour. Eastman listened to their statements, entertained them at the Park, and left for his vacation.

A few days before Christmas, 1910, he met Brulatour in Philipp's office and wrote Gifford that Brulatour sought the interview 'for two reasons: The first was to know whether we could in any way supply him with film; that he was actually furnishing the Independents now 600,-000 ft. of film a week and that they were picking up about 100,000 or 150,000 ft. that he could not furnish; that his contracts with them were exclusive and that as President of their Association he was in a position to enforce them so long as they could not get our film. He thought, perhaps, that it might be open to us to furnish him through a third party. I showed him that we could not do this. He then said that the second thing he wanted to see about was our intentions regarding the renewal of our contract with the Motion Picture Patents Co. He had offers from Wall Street men to furnish all the money needed to put up a factory in the U.S. to make film, on the condition that he would put in $100,000 of his own money, but said he knew perfectly well that if we should throw our supply of film open to the Independents at the expiration of our contract, they might find themselves unable to sell their product and with a big investment on their hands. I showed him that it would be very difficult to get started before our contract expires.

'Brulatour frankly stated that none of the film was equal to ours, and that the minute the Independents could get our film, they would break away from the contracts which he has with them individually, which are yearly contracts. He knew about our new contracts, of course, and stated that they are in the same line that he has been working here. The film that he supplies is mostly Lumière and Ensign.

'I questioned him particularly about the amount of Lumière and other film he supplied, and he repeated that he is now furnishing 600,000 ft. per week himself, so I think this can be relied on.'

Eastman and Philipp soon arranged a new agreement with the Motion Picture Patents Company, to include the Independents, represented by Brulatour. 'The new deal permits us to sell the "Independents" and it also results in our getting individual contracts with the Motion Picture licensees, under which they will use our film exclusively until July 1, 1912,' Colonel Strong was informed.

With peace established within the industry, it grew, and continued to grow until international trade followed the film.[1] The motion-picture industry became one of the largest businesses in the United States, ranking with the railroads, the steel, the building, the electrical, and the automotive industries — the propellants of prosperity.[2]

[1] 'Trade Follows the Film,' title of an article in *The Saturday Evening Post*, by Edward G. Lowry (1925). Credit for the quotation is given to the Prince of Wales from an address printed originally in the London *Morning Post*.

[2] 'It has been proved beyond question that our motion pictures, bringing to other peoples an idea of the comforts and conveniences of American life, help to sell countless other kinds of American merchandise. When the ladies of Buenos Aires or Rio, of Budapest or Belfast, glimpse a Hollywood star flashing across the screen in some especially fetching bit of feminine finery, or using an ingenious kitchen utensil or a handsome piece of furniture, they are very apt to decide that they need something "just like that" — and as a rule they will manage to get it. That means business for our manufacturers. In fact, it can be definitely established that our exports in many lines — shoes, automobiles, office equipment, clothing, hardware — have been directly, though unconsciously, stimulated by the films.

'But their influence is far broader than mere sales influence. As Herbert Hoover recently declared, "if we search into the channels through which acquaintance and appreciation may flow over our borders we discover that a vast new current has been added by the motion picture. It is the most penetrating and persuasive of all methods of world communication!"' (Dr. Julius Klein, in *Frontiers of Trade*.)

CHAPTER VII

AN AVALANCHE OF ATTACKS

INDUSTRIAL progress in the United States has not been a continuous chariot race. The prodigious results have followed rather the continuous application of human effort and human ingenuity in the factory, the laboratory, and the market-places of the world; to the dissemination of economic information and the wide distribution of industrial profits.

Progress in the photographic industry, which may have appeared as spectacular as a gala day in the arena was, in fact, the result of an unending struggle. 'To rest content with results achieved is the first sign of decay,' read the motto in the Kodak Park 'Suggestion Bulletin,' and Eastman, as he said in one of his early letters, never liked to have 'any dead horses around.'

The success of the company naturally brought opposition as well as competition, which became more and more formidable. This did not deter Eastman, Stuber, and Lovejoy or the organization in their efforts to achieve leadership both in the development and perfection of products and in human relations.

The price which the company paid in the expenditure of human effort and research to achieve a measure of industrial progress is indicated by the records of experiments in color photography, the enlargement of the research laboratory,[1] wage dividends, accident prevention,

---

[1] The Research Laboratory was enlarged in 1910 and again in 1912. 'In this year [1912] this building [No. 3] was practically rebuilt to make it more serviceable for a research laboratory — a laboratory equipped with the conveniences necessary to carry on experiments of all kinds, physical and chemical. It was a very complete equipment for experiments of all kinds —

medical supervision, social welfare, the development of new markets for non-inflammable film, new construction in London, Rochester, and Toronto, and the advent of the Autographic Kodak.

An account of some of the world-wide experiments in color photography which Eastman wrote in 1911 is typical of the history of the industry in its universal quest for improvements. Eastman had been invited to talk on the growth of photography from a manufacturing point of view, but consigned the manuscript to the files before the day arrived for his prospective public debut.

'Photographs in color have been the dream of inventors for many years,' he recorded, 'and ever since the publication of the patent of Ducos du Hauron in 1868 the making of pictures in color, of one class, has been purely a manufacturing problem, and apparently a very simple one, namely: the application of three transparent colors in minutely divided particles upon a glass or other transparent support. What seemed at first to be a very easy problem, however, proved for nearly forty years unsolvable. During this period there was probably no time when enthusiasts were not working upon it, and it is well known that fortunes have been spent in the search for a practical process.

'The problem was both chemical and mechanical. It was necessary to put at least one hundred thousand bits of color within the area of each square inch; the particles must not overlap or have any unfilled spaces; and if the colors were not arranged in symmetrical relation they must at least be in certain definite proportions, and must

experiments in regard to photographic matters, and other matters, too — scientific matters that are thought to have a bearing on the photographic industry. There were forty men employed in that laboratory.' (James H. Haste, page 793, *Record of Appeal*, United States *vs.* Eastman Kodak Company.)

be of a given standard of intensity and hue, within the most minute limits of variation. This is a rough statement of the requirements to prepare a support for color pictures which would be commercially acceptable.

'Prominent among those who worked on the problem were James W. McDonough, of Chicago, and Professor John Joly, of Dublin, who finally in 1905 or 1906 became involved in an interference in the United States Patent Office over details of their inventions, the basic process being that of du Hauron. Du Hauron in his patent showed that a plate ruled with three colors in juxtaposition could be used for making color photographs but he did not show any practical way of applying the colors. McDonough in 1892 patented a method which consisted in dusting finely ground particles of shellac, which had been dyed with the three primary colors and then mixed, upon a tacky plate and then by the aid of heat causing the particles to melt and run into contact, so as to leave no clear spaces. The results obtained by McDonough, and by any of his contemporaries, were in no sense commercial and so far as I am aware even the best examples produced by them were crude and did not reproduce color with a sufficient degree of exactness to be satisfactory.

'In June, 1907, the Messrs. Lumière, a well-known French firm of photographic manufacturers, announced that they had solved the problem by a process which involved the dyeing, in three separate lots, of starch grains with the three primary colors, mixing them in the proper proportions, sifting them on to glass plates prepared with a tacky coating, pressing the starch grains flat, and then filling the interstices between the disks with lamp black. It is to be noted that this process was almost exactly the same as that patented by McDonough fifteen years before, but the results were so superior as to virtually make it a new achievement. In fact without making any basic discovery or invention but by close scientific work in the regulating of their manufacturing processes and selection of their dyes they had done for trichromatic photography what Daguerre did for monochromatic photography — produced results. Their process, while difficult to work and very expensive, has shown to color enthusiasts that their dreams can be realized.

'Since the achievements of Lumière, other processes have been perfected and, while the product does not perhaps as yet equal the accurate adjustment as to color, the results produced can be said to be commercial. It is interesting to note that one of these has been worked out by the original inventor, Ducos du Hauron, in connection with his nephew, M. Bercegol, and consists in first coating a plate with gelatine; then with a varnish containing one of the primary colors; parallel lines are then cut through the varnish with a ruling machine; the plate is then dipped in an aqueous solution of a second dye, which attacks the gelatine; a second varnish, impermeable to water, is then spread over the whole and new lines are cut at right angles to the first, deep enough to remove both the previous colors, and a third dye is then applied to the exposed gelatine.

'These two processes of Lumière and du Hauron are the furthest advances, up to the present date [1911], in this department of the art and both are capable of producing results which, as intimated before, are practically perfect. They are both delicate processes to work from a manufacturing point of view, however. As far as the production of a material suited to the use of ordinary hand camera users they are totally inadequate and the problem remains much as before, except as far as the application of the color to the support is concerned. All of the collateral problems have, however, been solved: The sensitizing of the emulsion to the three colors, the selection of the dyes, and the limits of the fineness of the lines or particles, have all been thoroughly worked out. The problem is narrowed down to one which is largely, if not wholly, mechanical. It takes no great prophet to predict that the task, in view of this state of affairs, will be accomplished before very long.

'What I have said in regard to color photography has related wholly to a product to be viewed by transmitted light. The problem of making pictures to be viewed by reflected light is different in many respects, owing to the fact that we have to deal in the one case with colored pigment. Du Hauron showed in 1868 how to make pictures of this class also by taking three negatives, through three colored screens, and from them making colored transparencies by the carbon process, and then superposing them. Results have been produced by this process which are highly satisfactory as far as quality is concerned, but it is obvious that the difficulties of registration in superposing the images alone would prevent the process from being what is called a commercially practicable one. At the present time this branch of color photography does not seem as far advanced as the other, and from a manufacturing point of view it appears to belong to a somewhat distant future.'

While experiments in color photography were continued in the Park laboratory, Clarke studied the developments in Germany and France, and Eastman concentrated upon various financial plans for employees.

'In conversation with our mutual friend, Frank L. Babbott,' [1] Eastman wrote Edgar A. Bancroft, of Chi-

[1] In the intervening years, between the days when Babbott and Eastman

cago, general counsel of the International Harvester Company and president of the Illinois State Bar Association, 'he mentioned you as having given considerable attention to matters relating to old age pensions and employees' accident insurance, and suggested that I write you to inquire whether your concern had issued any printed matter concerning the plans which they have adopted . . . as I am taking some personal interest in such subjects, with a view of working out a scheme for our own employees. . . . I hope before the year passes to get a plan worked out which will deal with the pension part of our programme. It is only recently that I have waked up to the realization that men are growing old in the service of the company and that the business is not so young as I have been wont to consider it.'

With this modest inquiry, Eastman began the expansion of his efforts in behalf of employees and associates, some phases of which were in succeeding years considered unprecedented in American industry.

The next reference to the pension scheme occurs in a long, personal letter to Colonel Strong.

'I am sorry we had to declare the extra dividend. It seems to be necessary on account of the accumulation of ready money. Inasmuch as we have upwards of $1,000,-000 worth of additions to buildings and improvements in sight this year, we may be able to get rid of some of it in more satisfactory channels. January was simply a rotten

were boy neighbors in Waterville and the year 1910, the former had graduated from Amherst College and become a successful manufacturer and banker in Brooklyn and New York City. He had been a member and an official of the Boards of Education in both communities, was president of the Packer Collegiate Institute and the Brooklyn Institute of Arts and Sciences. After Babbott's marriage, Eastman and he renewed their boyhood acquaintance and for many years there were frequent communications and many visits together, as will appear throughout the remainder of the book.

month. Seed plates fell off nearly 25%. We moved that concern just in time to save the business. It would have gone to the dogs like the Aristo business if we had not.

'You may be startled to observe in the notice for the annual meeting that a resolution is to be acted upon setting aside a fund of $500,000 as a benefit, accident, and pension fund for the employees. No plan has yet been perfected as to how this is to be used, but I feel that now while we are making so much money is the time to provide such a fund. It will be set aside out of surplus, so it will not affect the earnings. It will probably be taken out of the bonds which we have on hand. As the company accumulates age, we have got to be prepared to do something for men who have grown old in our service.'

On June 14, 1911, Eastman notified Haste, manager at Kodak Park, that, 'beginning the 1st of July, 1911, I should like to have you make special requisitions on our "Welfare Fund" for all expenditures in the way of payments to employees that are not strictly chargeable to cost of operation. For instance, all salaries and wages paid to employes where on the strictest interpretation of their contract of employment deductions could have been made from their pay. Also all payments, if any, to employee, or on account of employee, in case of accident or injury (outside of their pay). Also please render me a statement of all such payments made during the year 1910, and the first six months of 1911, giving the employee's name, occupation, amount paid, and cause for payment.

'You will see from the above that after July 1st no one is to be carried on the *payroll* except for the services which they actually render. If you have any one on your payroll that is getting pay in excess of his earnings on account of long service or former injury, please bring the case to my attention in order that the matter may be considered in connection with this fund.'

During the hours of reflection at home, Eastman had been giving much consideration to a wage dividend and to employees' stock ownership. 'I should like very much to meet you sometime,' he wrote George W. Perkins, of J. P. Morgan & Company, 'and discuss the matter of stock ownership by employees, as the experience and information that I have been able to gather on the subject does not incline me to favor it on any general scale.'[1]

However, February 25, 1912, he informed Gifford that he was 'considering the advisability of the company's declaring a "dividend on wages," the proposition being to give all employees on the payroll of the company on the 1st of April, 1912, 2% on all the wages received by them during the five years ending December 31, 1911. This will amount in the case of an employee who has worked five years for the company to a dividend of 10% on his average yearly earnings, and it gives each employee an advantage in proportion to the time he has been in the employ of the company, up to five years. Beyond five-year service every employee will fare alike. The payment of the dividend will be accompanied by a note pointing out that it is not to be considered as committing the company to any regular dividends, but that it has only been thought best to do it in view of the company's having had an exceptionally prosperous

---

[1] March 13, 1912, Eastman wrote Babbott: 'I have examined all of the propositions in this line that I could find and made up my mind that I would devise one that was as simple as possible. I do not believe in putting any string on the money. The employee is either entitled to it or he is not. . . . Perkins has written me that he does not approve of paying such dividends in cash. On the other hand, I do not agree with his idea of trying to drive employees in the fold to buy shares in the company. . . . Very few of them are capitalists, and if they have any extra money what they should do with it first is to buy a place to live in.'

year. In case it is decided to do it in other years, it can be modified according to the increase or decrease in the common stock dividends, the present proposition being 5% of the common stock dividend. In case of 30% common stock dividends being paid, the wage dividend would be 1½%, always on five years' earnings. I should be glad to hear what you think about this proposition.'

To Alexander M. Lindsay, who had been elected a director, Eastman wrote, after citing an example of a typical 'dividend on wages':

'I do not suppose that you want to be troubled with business while you are away any more than I do, but I thought you ought to know about it before the notices are sent out. I have talked the matter over with quite a number of our principal men and they think it will be a good thing in every way, such as allaying the unrest caused by the Socialistic propaganda,[1] the discouragement of strikes, etc. If it is found to work well, the company can continue it and allow it to be known that it will be the policy of the company to declare similar dividends on wages, based upon the dividends declared on the common stock. The company could probably always be able to do this. For instance, if the common stock dividend should shrink to 20%, the wage dividend would be 1%, and if it should shrink to 10%, the wage dividend would be taken off altogether, on the theory that a 10% dividend on common stock is equivalent to the fixed wage of the employee.'

[1] John Spargo, one of the leading Socialists of this period, stated in a public address in Massachusetts in 1928: 'Capitalist industrialism, as it exists in America to-day, needs no apologists or defenders. The advantages and opportunities derivable from the tremendous advancement in productive capacity are more generally distributed than ever before. It is equally true that with every advance in production under the impetus of private initiative and enterprise our nation advances towards the only communism that can ever benefit mankind, communism of opportunity. That will in turn give us perfect individualism, which is our goal.'

The seriousness of the anti-capitalist propaganda was emphasized by the activities of one of the English directors, George Davison, whom Eastman had asked to resign as managing director of the foreign business. Although Davison accepted reëlection to the Board of Kodak, Limited, he financed a publication called 'The Anarchist,' until Eastman learned the facts and wrote him:

'While I should not feel at liberty to volunteer any criticism of your attitude on any social question, I do feel that if you are lending aid to an advocate of anarchy you are not a useful or suitable member of our board of directors, and I think you ought to resign. Certainly if it had been known previous to the last election of Kodak, Ltd., you would not have been reëlected. In saying this, of course, you quite understand that there is no personal feeling involved in this matter. If I had other than a friendly feeling, it would have been apparent heretofore. I am not too intolerant to view with great interest the tendency of a man of your stamp toward anarchy and would not have a word to say against it if I did not think it was inconsistent with your holding the position of director in our companies.'

The next step in the evolution of employees' relations was taken March 31, 1913, when Eastman wrote Lindsay: 'At the monthly meeting on the 9th of April, the question will probably come up of shortening our working hours from fifty-four per week to forty-nine and a half. I have had a conference with our factory managers and it has been pretty well agreed that the time has come for some action of this kind.' The Board of Directors naturally followed Eastman's lead, and on May 12, notices were posted in all the factories.

In the mean time the company had adopted a 'Suggestion Scheme' for employees, who were paid from one dollar to one thousand dollars for practical ideas which the company adopted. The results and awards were published every month and ranged from improvements in manufacturing and machine methods to building construction and safety appliances. Employees were prolific in their recommendations and the company was equally alert in adopting them. Over a period of several years the number of individual awards averaged approximately one hundred and fifty per month in the six Rochester plants. Through the coöperation of the employees, the number of accidents per one thousand workers was reduced from 109.72 in 1910 to 22.87 in 1913, with the result that the company, in the latter year, held the record for accident prevention among all the industries in the United States represented at the National Safety Congress held in Chicago.

The establishment of First Aid, a Medical Department, a Savings System for employees' wages, and social activities on a large scale, including lunchrooms for executives and employees and night classes at the Mechanics Institute, followed in rapid succession, attracting the attention of visitors from every State in the United States, from England, Australia, South America, Mexico, China, and Japan.

One problem of personnel which arose from time to time was that of the church affiliations of employees. The first time this was brought to Eastman's attention, he proceeded with his usual exactness to get the facts and had a poll taken of a department where it was alleged that partiality was being shown. This revealed that the number of Protestants and Catholics was almost equally divided, although this was entirely accidental. May 20, 1914, the Reverend John Francis O'Hern [1] wrote East-

---

[1] In 1929 he was ordained Bishop of Rochester.

man that a young girl from his church had charged that three employees in the department where she worked were attempting to poison her mind against the Catholic Church.

'It has always been the policy of this company not to allow the matter of religious faith to interfere in any way with the hiring or discharging of employees, nor with their treatment while in our employ,' Eastman replied. 'I had always supposed, and I am still of the opinion that every superintendent and foreman in our organization understands that he is to absolutely ignore religious opinions among employees and to treat them all the same, without respect to their convictions in regard to matters of religion.

'A man of your intelligence will readily understand, however, that with over six thousand employees in our Rochester factories, it would be impossible for us to prevent employees from occasionally expressing their opinions among themselves on religious or political matters, especially in view of the fact that it is well understood that the company is entirely indifferent as to the political or religious affiliations of the employees. However, we do not countenance their taking time which belongs to the company for discussing matters of the kind. You may rest assured as to this the management will be both impartial and firm.'

Eastman himself had been exacting in his own relations and had only the pleasantest contacts with the various churches.

While abroad in 1912, Eastman made preliminary arrangements for the realization of one of his early ideals — an adequate 'home' for the company in the heart of London. Leasing, for a period of ninety-nine years, a site on Kingsway, he retained Sir John J. Burnet, R.A., an architect who had distinguished himself for his additions to the British Museum, to design and supervise the building, which set the architectural standard of the whole Kingsway development. Also on this trip he purchased the capital stock of Wratten and Wainwright, Limited, of Croydon, and engaged Dr. C. E. Kenneth Mees to direct the company's research work.

To Philipp's inquiry in regard to the facts of the Wratten and Wainwright acquisition, Eastman wrote that, in looking about for a head for the Company's research laboratory [1] at Kodak Park, 'I decided that Dr. Mees was peculiarly fitted for the position, both on account of his education and his practical experience, he being a chemist, a physicist, a practical manufacturer of color sensitive dry plates and of color screens for use in photography, and one of the best known authorities on color photography. On approaching him, he informed me that he would be willing to come to Rochester, but only on condition that we purchased the capital stock of his company. As his concern was a small affair, I told him that would be no obstacle. He then informed me that there was another complication and that was a contract which they entered into to build a plate factory in Budapest. I told him I knew all about that proposition, for it had been presented to and declined by me several years ago. He explained just what the contract was, and I told him that we would accept it as a part of the obligations of the Wratten & Wainwright Co.

'On investigation we found that the Wratten & Wain-

----

[1] This is about the time industrial research began in the automotive industry. Epstein records in his book, *The Automobile Industry*, that Henry M. Leland 'encouraged a young engineer, Charles S. Kettering, to develop an electric starting system,' and in 1912 Cadillac 'came out with complete electrical equipment.' Here was 'a deliberate, calculated attempt to bring forth a definite device.'

wright Co. was doing a business of about $60,000 a year, $40,000 of which was in regular dry plates and the balance, $20,000, in specialties, such as color screens, etc. We paid for the business, including good-will, about $100,000. As soon as the contract was signed, Dr. Mees and the Assistant Managing Director of Kodak, Limited, went to Budapest and negotiated for a cancellation of the contract to build a dry-plate factory there. The Bank, however, interested with Wratten & Wainwright in the project, declined to consider any proposition, stating that they were committed to the Government to have a dry-plate factory started. We therefore made arrangements to go on with the contract, although we would have much preferred to drop it for the reason that we find it difficult to arrange for a competent operating staff.

'The business likely to be done in that country is not very great. The staff required to operate the factory could just as well operate one for a business much larger. The business that we already do in our Harrow dry-plate factory amounts to nearly $400,000 a year, or ten times as much as the Wratten & Wainwright plate business. Their costs of manufacture are very much larger than ours, and unless we can greatly increase their business in color specialties, it is not likely to be a money-making enterprise. Even if it is not, we shall be satisfied, because it is very important that we should have the best man available at the head of our research laboratory, and there is probably not another man in the world having the same qualifications as Dr. Mees.' [1]

Meanwhile, Edison had been making progress with a household motion-picture machine, but before putting it on the market submitted two questions to Eastman:

[1] In his conferences with Mees the only comment Eastman made about the American company was: 'You will like Lovejoy!'

(1) Does the Eastman Company desire to make non-inflammable (N.I.) film for it, and (2) Would the Eastman Company be inclined to encourage or oppose the sale of the Edison machine through Eastman dealers?

To these inquiries Eastman replied:

'To the first we answer yes. In our opinion the N.I. [non-inflammable] film is the only material that can be used for the purpose, the regular film being so dangerous as to render its use out of the question. In regard to the strength of the N.I. film, we are very sure that our present film is just as strong as the nitrate film and will give satisfaction as far as that is concerned.

'To the second we would answer unqualifiedly that we would encourage the sale of such a machine through Eastman dealers. We, as you know, have been experimenting in this line and have had the intention of putting out such a machine. Our interests, however, lie with the film, which is paramount, and all we want is to see the field occupied by some one who will exploit it vigorously and successfully. If the Edison Co. has such a machine and a feasible scheme for exploiting the field thoroughly, all we ask is to supply the film. With that understanding we will be glad to give you all the assistance possible.'

This appeared to open a new market for non-inflammable film, which had not been a success with the motion picture industry, due to the universal preference of the trade for nitro-cellulose film.

Then came another surprising invention. H. J. Gaisman, inventor of the Auto-Strop razor, submitted to Eastman a device for autographing Kodak pictures. 'This invention,' Eastman wrote Clarke,[1] 'has for its object the autographic marking of the films as the exposures are made. It is a very simple device, but not by any means

[1] February 16, 1913.

MR. EASTMAN AND MR. EDISON

an obvious one, the proof of which is the action of the Examiner of Patents, who, in acting upon Mr. Gaisman's application, said the subject matter was entirely new, but his application would be refused because it was obviously inoperative. Mr. Gaisman replaces our duplex black paper with a thinner red paper and inserts between the film and this red paper a strip of ordinary thin carbon paper, such as used in typewriter work, with the face *toward the red paper*. This is all there is to the invention so far as it relates to the film spool. As to the Kodak, he simply makes a door in the back of the Kodak which opens a slot directly over the bar of the exposing mat which goes next to the guide-roll, at the key end of the Kodak. The opening of this door presses down a frame around the opening so as to press the red paper down on to the film to make contact and also to shut out the light from entering around the edges of the slot. Then with a stylus or ordinary pencil, preferably anything harder than a No. 2, the operator writes a title upon the red paper, exposes through the slot, shuts up the door, and proceeds with the next exposure. A facsimile of the writing is found on the film upon development. This invention has commercial advantages of a high order.'

It captivated Eastman, and soon became the leading factor in the camera trade of the world. Gaisman was offered liberal royalties, a percentage which would have netted him considerably more than a million dollars, but he preferred a cash payment, accepting a check for $300,000, the largest sum ever paid up to this time for a patent by any industrial concern.

Eastman's policy of paying liberally for all patents had been established in the early days of the business, and was emphasized strongly in May, 1912, when he protested and fought the Oldfield Bill (H.R. 23417). Writing

to Congressman H. G. Danforth in Washington at the
time, Eastman declared: 'My objection to this bill is
fundamental. I believe it is against public policy. In
effect the author of the bill takes the position that the
United States has been paying too much for its inventions
and proposes to curtail the reward that is now offered to
inventors. This in face of the fact that under the operation of the present laws this country has emerged from a
producer solely of raw materials to the greatest manufacturing country on the face of the earth. I know that
many people, perhaps the majority, think that we are a
nation of inventors by virtue of birth. This theory does
not account for the fact that foreigners, from countries
where inventions have never been as abundant as they
are in the United States, become prolific inventors on
coming to this country. Unless this sudden development
can be attributed to the food, or climate, it must be on
account of the reward that is offered them. I am one of
those who believe that it is solely owing to the latter.

'An English, German, or French workman who patents
an invention in his own country by that act mortgages his
future to the amount of the taxes which become payable
after the lapse of a few years. He is very likely poor and
unable to exploit the invention himself; perhaps the invention is a little ahead of the time and he is unable to
get capital; but, being an inventor, he is naturally opti-
mistic and goes on paying the increasing taxes until his
means are exhausted and he has to drop his patent. In
this country he pays a small fee for his patent, whereupon
the invention becomes his sole property for seventeen
years; no taxes to pay; no obligations of any kind; and no
restrictions. If he is unable to introduce it himself, he can
lay the patent away until somebody else wants to make
use of it, when he is in a position to claim his reward.

'It is undoubtedly a fact that this privilege has been abused, but it is also undoubtedly true that the abuse is a mere incident to the great benefit that it has been to the inventor, and through him to the country. Likewise, when it comes to marketing the invention, he has been able to adopt means which have proved most effective in getting a profit out of it. He has been able to elicit the coöperation of distributors by securing to them a proper reward through and by means of protecting the retail selling price. In my opinion it is not a question with this country whether it can get its inventions cheaper, but whether it can get them at all without giving an adequate and liberal reward. The age of invention is by no means past and the progress of this country is just as much dependent as ever upon the stimulation of inventors.

'Therefore, any attempt to lessen the reward to inventors should be carefully scrutinized and nothing of the kind should be undertaken until it has been passed upon by a competent commission which has carefully weighed all considerations which apply to the subject. I am of the opinion that the suggestion of President Taft, that the matter of amendment of the patent laws should be left first to a commission, is a wise one, and I earnestly urge upon you the importance of doing everything in your power to secure this action.' [1]

The versatility of Eastman's grasp of industrial problems is no more strikingly illustrated than in the contrast between these opinions in regard to patents and the correspondence which he had with Senator Robert F. Wagner, Chairman of the New York State Factory In-

---

[1] Congressman Danforth read this letter to the Committee, and wrote Eastman: 'It seemed to make an impression upon them, but I doubt very much if it will change their mad attack upon the existing laws, which, as you justly say, are doubtless defective in spots, but that does not justify the wholesale revision upon which the Committee is entering.'

vestigating Commission. Replying to a questionnaire prompted by the nation-wide agitation for a minimum wage, Eastman added, again emphatically, his own convictions: 'I am wholly opposed to the establishment of a minimum wage because I believe that, if such wages are fixed by governmental edict, the result will be to increase prices in the same proportion, thereby leaving the worker with only the same purchasing power that he now possesses.

'The effect of the establishment of a minimum wage on the employer or industry would not be detrimental unless there was some discrimination which put one employer or industry at a disadvantage with another.

'As to the workers, the immediate effect would only be upon those who would obtain increased wages. I cannot see that it would affect the liberty of action of the workers. There might be some effect on the average worker caused by employers using the agreement that the minimum was enough. This I consider remote. The workers, however, who proved unable to really earn the wage would be discriminated against by employers. The regularity of employment of inefficient workers would be lessened and any increase in cost would eventually find its way into the price of the product.

'I am unreservedly of the opinion that the only way to increase wages, or the purchasing power of wages, which is practically the same thing, is to increase the efficiency of the worker. This can be done through education, the better organization of industries, a better distribution of labor, and the further introduction of machinery. This latter has been carried so far, however, in many industries that little further advance can be expected. What little advance is made in the future in this direction is likely to be largely offset by the present tendency to inefficiency in the individual, unless it can be checked by education.

'The establishment of a minimum wage would not affect the industry with which I am connected, because we have few, if any, employees to whom it would apply.'

The progress of 'the company' was attested to upon many occasions. Theodore Roosevelt's letter to H. G. Ponting, official photographer of the Scott Antarctic Expedition, was one of many. Captain R. F. Scott and two of his associates had lost their lives near the South Pole. When Ponting returned, he showed his pictures in London, where Roosevelt saw them.

'I came within an ace of asking my host to bring me behind the scenes and present me to you yesterday,' wrote the former President, 'but I thought you would probably be so busy that it would be an unwarranted waste of your time. I do not know when I have seen an expedition which impressed me more than yours did. *The pictures were wonderful*, and I would not on any account have missed seeing them.'

Ponting sent Eastman some 'samples from the negatives . . . of the famous enterprise. To understand fully what your films went through,' Ponting wrote, 'you must know that there was not sufficient room in our hut to store them. They had to be left outside, where they were subjected to temperatures that fell far below zero for many months together. They took over seven months on the voyage to the far South and, of course, passed through the tropics. They have, therefore, been subjected to the extremes of heat and cold.

'I must further tell you, that as we kept our hut at a temperature of about 50 degrees Fahrenheit, there was often a difference of more than 100 degrees between the interior and the exterior. This necessitated the very greatest care in the handling of photographic films and plates.

'These films were bought in England in 1910 [May]. They arrived in the Antarctic in January, 1911. Some of them were taken to the South Pole, and were there exposed on January 17, 1912. These exposed films were brought back by Captain Scott to the last camping place where my late chief and his two remaining comrades of the Polar party lost their lives in a terrible blizzard which raged for nine days.

'These films lay beside their dead bodies for eight months before the search party, on account of the months of darkness, were able to reach the spot. They were then discovered and brought back to the winter quarters hut, where they were developed in January, 1913. The films have therefore passed through the tropics, through one Antarctic winter buried in the snow, and have lain through another winter in the temperature which must have fallen 80 degrees below zero, before development and after exposure; and they were two and one half years old. I have these negatives now and enclose a print from one of them. They must beyond all question be the most remarkable negatives in the world. Without them we should never have actually seen how Captain Scott and his companions looked when at the uttermost extremity of the earth nor what they found there, the tent of the Norwegian Amundsen, who reached this goal just a month earlier.'

Beginning in 1911, and extending over a period of nearly ten years, Eastman was the storm center of a series of legal and political attacks, from those of President Wilson and Attorney-General McReynolds to others engineered by competitors who owned the Goodwin patent, and a nation-wide propaganda against fixed prices.

In 1911, while the Eastman Company did a large percentage of the photographic business in the United States, it did not have a monopoly in any one field. The records of that year reveal the following competing manufacturers, all doing business in this country:

Cameras:
    Ansco (Anthony and Scovill) Company, Binghamton, New York.
    Seneca Camera Manufacturing Company, Rochester.
    Gundlach Manhattan Optical Company, Rochester.
    The Hall Camera Company, Brooklyn.
    The Conley Camera Company, Rochester, Minnesota.
    C. P. Goerz American Optical Company, New York.
    Reflex Camera Company, Newark, New Jersey.
    Expo Watch Company, New York.

Film:
    Ansco Company.
    Lumière North American Company, Burlington, Vermont.
    Houghton, Limited, or Austin Edwards, London, England.
    Defender Photo Supply Company, Rochester.

Paper:
    Defender Photo Supply Company.
    Multiscope and Film Company, Burlington, Wisconsin.
    Kilborn Photo Paper Company, Cedar Rapids, Iowa.
    Rochester Photo Works, Rochester.
    Mirmont Photo Paper Company, Brooklyn.
    Ansco Company.
    Willis and Clements, Philadelphia.
    United States Aristotype Company, Bloomfield, New Jersey.
    The Haloid Company, Rochester.
    Sussex Photo Paper Company, Newton, New Jersey.
    Cramer Photo Paper Company, Chicago.
    The Artex Photo Paper Company, Columbus, Ohio.
    The Pifer Positype Company, Cleveland.
    Letol Post Card Company, San Francisco.
    Wellington and Ward, London.
    Ilford Company, London.
    Wallace Chemical Company, New York.
    Sears, Roebuck and Company, Chicago.
    Burke and James, Chicago.
    The Photo Products Company, Chicago.

Photographic plate manufacturers:
G. Cramer Dry Plate Company, St. Louis.
Hammer Dry Plate Company, St. Louis.
Central Dry Plate Company, St. Louis.
Lumière North American Company.
American Dry Plate Company, Worcester, Massachusetts.
Defender Photo Supply Company.
Magnet Photo Materials Company, Boston, Massachusetts.
Forbes Plate Company, Rochester.

Chemical manufacturers:
Ansco Company.
Bayer, New York.
Berlin Aniline Works, New York.
Bostwick, Brooklyn.
Burrows, Wellcome and Company, New York.
Burke and James, Chicago.
Chicago Chemical Company, Chicago.
Charles Cooper and Company, Newark, New Jersey.
Cramer Dry Plate Company.
Defender Photo Supply Company.
G. Gennert, New York.
Hammer Dry Plate Company.
Lumière North American Company.
Mallinckrodt Chemical Works, St. Louis.
Merck and Company, St. Louis.
Charles L. Mitchell, M.D., Philadelphia.
George Murphy, Inc., New York.
Schering and Glatz, New York.

Professional sundries manufacturers:
Burke and James.
James H. Smith and Sons Company, Chicago.
G. Gennert.
Ansco Company.
Seneca Camera Manufacturing Company.

Shutter manufacturers:
The Multi-Speed Shutter Company, New York.
Wollensak Optical Company, Rochester.
Bausch and Lomb Optical Company, Rochester.
C. P. Goerz American Optical Company.
Michigan Photographic Shutter Company, Kalamazoo, Michigan.

The spectacular success of the motion-picture industry was probably one reason for directing attention to the business of the Kodak Company. The volume of the company's film business on February 20, 1911, is recorded in a letter to the London manager:

'The capacity of the machinery which we have at present installed and in running order, not including machinery used for making Cartridge film, if kept running constantly is 34,500 two hundred ft. rolls per week. This does not mean that this is our theoretical capacity if the film was every inch of it good, but it is based on the actual shipping output per machine which we are able to average month after month. The above is equal to 1,894,000 rolls per year, fifty-two weeks, or 378,800,000 ft. of film. Our total output last year was about 185,000,-000 ft. . . . allowing liberally for shut-downs for repairs to machines, there is no doubt but what we could, as at present equipped, turn out, if required, somewhere about 340,000,000 ft.'

On October 30, Eastman sent another letter to Gifford recording the beginning of the Government's activities.

'About the time I wrote you in regard to changes in our sales policy, Mr. Philipp received notice from the U. S. Attorney-General's office that the Government was about to take up an investigation of our business, to determine whether or not we were violating the Sherman Law. On Thursday and Friday last I was in New York with Mr. Hubbell and had an interview with Mr. Clark McKercher, who is Assistant U. S. Attorney-General and who has been detailed to conduct this investigation. During the interview Mr. Philipp explained to Mr. McKercher as fully as possible what our situation is and told him what action we had in mind to put ourselves in conformity with the Supreme Court decision in the Parks

Medicine case. Whether or not this action will satisfy the Government will depend on the result of the investigation which Mr. McKercher is about to undertake. The impression that I gained from the conversations with Mr. McKercher is that the Government is endeavoring to have the courts declare that even the patentees shall not be allowed the privilege of dictating the retail prices at which their goods shall be sold. There have been no decisions in the lower courts sustaining this position, and there is, of course, some doubt as to whether the Supreme Court will go that far. Until it does, we do not feel that we ought to disrupt our long-established sales policy. I will keep you acquainted with the progress of the investigation as far as possible. Some fears that I had that the investigation would be undertaken in a captious spirit were allayed by the interview. Mr. McKercher appears to be a man of unusual ability, with a personality which does not create friction.'

On November 17, Eastman wrote Sidney M. Colgate that: 'The decision of the Supreme Court controlling the situation as to the restriction of prices in what is known as the Miles Medicine case made it necessary for the Company to amend its terms of sale. If, in view of this decision, your counsel advises you that any goods outside of patented goods can be legally restricted, we would be very much interested in knowing the grounds upon which such advice is given.

'We feel that it will do the industries of this country which are exploiting proprietary articles great injury to take away from them the right to prescribe the retail selling prices of their goods, as it enables unprincipled price-cutters to wantonly injure the businesses which are dependent upon the sale of such articles.'

To Paul Fahle, of St. Louis, Eastman declared that: 'It

scarcely seems possible that the people of this country will consent to a condition of affairs under which it will be illegal for capital to combine in any way, because that would mean retrogression, many failures in business, stagnation and possible panic. If this country cannot have large aggregations of capital, it certainly cannot compete with large aggregations of capital in foreign countries.'

In England the right of a manufacturer to enforce his restrictions against even a third party, who had purchased them with notice of such restrictions, was sustained. The first case in this country that really established the new theory was known as the Miles Medicine case, where a manufacturer of so-called 'patent medicines' sought to restrain a violation of a contract by a jobber who sold his goods at cut prices. The Supreme Court decided that such a contract was in restraint of trade and a violation of the Sherman Act. The article in question was not a patented article and the Court intimated that the decision would not apply to patented articles. Afterwards a number of bills were introduced into Congress with a view of taking away the right of the patentee to make such restrictions. None of these bills had passed at the time Eastman was writing, 'but, owing to the ignorance of the public on the subject and the clamor for any kind of legislation which it is hoped will help to reduce prices, there is grave danger that some such bill will be passed before very long. When I allude to the ignorance of the public on the subject, I refer to the almost universal impression that fixed prices interfere with competition. Cutting prices is generally looked upon as competition. If one should admit that it is competition, which I do not, it is perfectly apparent that the scope of the competition is limited by the margin of net profit that the dealer makes. It can be easily demonstrated that this margin is too small to affect prices in any marked degree, especially upon articles known as fixed-price articles.

'The reason I use the word "especially" in connection with these articles is that when a manufacturer adopts the fixed-price method of selling his goods, he has to fix the margin which the dealer shall have. He invariably fixes it at the lowest possible figure that he thinks will induce the dealer to handle and push his goods. Anything more than this he regards as money thrown away. This figure, or amount, varies according to the class of goods, the expense of handling, and the loss caused by deterioration of stock. The expense of handling varies according to the space required to stock and show the goods, the amount of time taken by salesmen to sell them, etc., but whatever the conditions are, the manufacturer has to be careful not to go beyond the amount that is necessary to pay the dealer his actual cost and a net profit sufficient to induce him to push the goods, for the reason that his cut-price competitor will take advantage of it.

'As an illustration: The ordinary average expense of selling small articles in retail stores is about 20%, without including interest on capital invested. The average discount on proprietary articles that are sold over the counter is, we will say, 33⅓%. The margin of net profit after taking out interest on capital, is, we will say, 10% or 12%. This 10% or 12% then is the absolute limit of any economy to be gained for the public by the open-price method, that is, assuming that you could drive merchants to sell goods without any profit. Whether or not this would be possible, or desirable if possible, is scarcely worth discussing any more than the desirability of reducing cost through the lowering of wages.

'If one denies that mere price-cutting is true competition, the question then arises, What is competition? Real competition that benefits the public consists in lowering costs and giving the public the benefit of it. It has already been shown that one cannot reduce the percentage cost of distributing goods to any great extent, but the possibilities of reducing costs in manufacture are almost unlimited. You will pardon me for taking as an example the articles which I am most familiar with, cameras. The cost of such articles depends almost entirely upon the way you, to use a shop expression, fit up to make them. If you are going to make 1000, you make certain small tools, and the cost will, we will say, be represented by $10.00 each. If you are going to make 10,000, you make more elaborate tools, and the cost will perhaps be reduced to $7.50. But if you expect to make 100,000, or 200,000, or half a million, you would spend money for automatic machinery which would cut out more and more labor until possibly the cost would be reduced to $5.00. Now we will say that the article that costs $10.00 would market at $20.00 list, one third of which, or $6.66, is given to the dealer, leaving $3.34 gross profit for the manufacturer and $10.00 for shop cost. If you can fit up to make the same article for $5.00 and give everybody the same percentage of profit, the list price would be $10.00. In this case the dealer gets the same percentage of profit, but only half the actual money for handling the article. Thus it will be seen that reducing the cost of manufacture has not only benefited the ultimate purchaser to the extent of that reduction of cost, but also the same proportion of the manufacturer's profit and also of the expenses of handling it through the dealer. The dealer benefits by selling more cameras. Instead of selling one at $20.00, he will probably sell three or four at $10.00, hence his profit will be really increased. It will thus be seen that while a dealer's percentage of discount cannot be materially reduced, his actual amount of profit on a given article can be reduced 50% or more by the reduction of the manufacturing cost.

'The next thought that arises, perhaps, assuming that the manufacturer, for his own advantage, is striving to reduce the cost, is what is there to induce him to give the benefit of it to the public. The answer to this is: Competition by other fixed-price articles of the same kind; or competition by cut-rate articles; or, in most instances, both of these influences; and here I want to make the statement that fixed prices have nothing whatever to do with competition. They do not relate to competition. They only have to do with distribution. Most proprietary articles have to have their merits urged upon the public, by advertising and by personal solicitation of salesmen in stores. Unless retail dealers can be assured of a profit they will not handle articles the price of which is known to the public, but will devote themselves to articles upon which the price is not known and upon which their profits cannot be gauged by the public.

'To return to competition: In the first place, fixed-price articles always have the name or trade-mark of the manufacturer behind them, and it is for the interest of the owner of the name, or trade-mark, to maintain the quality of the article. Among manufacturers there is no form of property that is considered more desirable than the good-will of a business. Contrary, perhaps, to general opinion, it ranks with real estate in stability. Good-will is reputation, a reputation for something good. When a manufacturer fixes a price on a trade-marked article, he tries to put into that article the best possible value for the money. If his competitor is a manufacturer who has also adopted the fixed-price method of distribution, he also strives to put into his article the greatest possible value, and the struggle between them is conducted on a quality basis. If, however, his competitor is a manufacturer of a cut-price article, the struggle of the competitor is to produce something that will pass as a substitute for the other and always better known article, upon which a greater discount can be given to the dealer.

'The argument for a cut-price article is never that it is better than the fixed-price article, but only that it is just as good, or nearly as good, for less money. If it really is just as good and is sold for less money, the maker of the fixed-price article can do nothing to prevent the purchaser from buying it. The purchaser has a perfect right to exercise his discretion in the matter. Why, then, discourage or try to hamper the man who is making an article upon which he is willing to stake his reputation? It is simply interfering with the mode of distribution which has been found to be the most advantageous by a majority of the most reputable manufacturers and which, as before stated, has received the most hearty acquiescence by the public. The whole tendency of the method is toward the improvement of the goods; whereas the whole tendency of the other method is toward the depreciation of the goods. There is always some one to make cut-price goods, and why deprive the public of the privilege of exercising its choice? Price-cutting, if not based upon reduction of costs, has only one tendency — monopoly. In price-cutting wars it is invariably the small manufacturer who goes to the wall. The ultimate result is always a rise in prices because the strong are left in possession of the field and the natural tendency is to make up for losses.

'I have stated that fixed prices have to do with distribution, and this is where the ethical claims of the manufacturer come in. Why should a man, perhaps an inventor, who has an article which the public needs be deprived of the best method of introducing it? It very often happens that the public does not know that it needs the article; is not conscious of wanting it. As a rule the public has to be educated to its own needs. It does not see the merits in an article until it has been, so to speak, thrust down its throat and held there by some enthusiastic, imaginative person whose object is, of course, to make money, but knows he can only make it through giving the public something that he thinks the public ought to think it needs. In order to make the article at a price where any one will buy it, he may have to invest a large sum of money in an installation for manufacturing it. If when it is ready for sale he is debarred from employing the necessary agency for introducing it, he will be forced to offer it to the few large stores who are willing to take it, advertise it as a novelty, and drop it when its novelty is gone. Of course a man in the face of such a proposition will not engage in the enterprise.

'On the other hand, why subject men who have spent years in developing and introducing articles to the onslaught of cut prices, engineered by the big department stores who have only two desires: one to lessen the number of their competitors and the other to attract people to their stores by cutting prices on prominent articles? It is not alone the big man who is going to be hurt in such a transaction. There are hundreds and thousands of small manufacturers of proprietary articles who will be put at the mercy of pirates if such a policy is carried out unless they adopt the uneconomical method of consigning their goods. Consignment of goods means furnishing the capital for the dealer. Small manufacturers as a rule are not overburdened with money and many will be unable to adopt that method of distribution.'

Two of Eastman's competitors were quick to take advantage of the Government's investigation, and Eastman dealt with both attacks with characteristic candor:

'I have read the letters of —— of the —— Camera Co.,' Eastman wrote S. P. Burrill, of Rochester,[1] who forwarded them. These letters asserted that:

' "The Eastman Company has purchased practically all its competitors that have not been obliged to go out of business, owing to their unfair and non-American competition.

' "Notice: They bought the American Aristo Company; The Angelo Paper Company; The Artura Photo Paper Company, their most powerful rivals in the sensitized paper business; they bought the Seed, Stanley and Standard Dry Plate Companies, their most powerful rivals in the dry plate business; they bought the Blair Camera Company, the Century Camera Company, the Photographic Materials Company and the Rochester Optical and Camera Company, the latter a three and a half million dollar corporation, all their most powerful rivals in the Camera business; they have bought scores of other Companies that they were unable to sandbag."

'These statements are unqualifiedly false, aside from the fact that the Eastman Company did, from time to time, during a period of years, purchase most of the Companies named. For instance, the Eastman Company has not purchased the Ansco Company, which undoubtedly does a larger business than any other concern in the photographic trade outside of the Eastman Company. The Ansco Company makes a larger line of photographic materials and apparatus than any other competitor, in-

[1] December 13, 1912.

cluding cameras, films, and sensitized papers. The Eastman Company has not purchased the Cramer Dry Plate
Company, nor the Hammer Dry Plate Company (both
large concerns), which were the principal competitors
of the Seed Company.

'All of these Companies, according to the best information which I can obtain, were never so prosperous as
they are at the present moment. These and many other
so-called "Independent" companies do an increasing
proportion of the trade. The Eastman Company has
been solicited to buy out the business of a number of large
concerns during the last few years but has declined so to
do. The "three and a half million dollar corporation"
referred to by ——, the Rochester Optical & Camera
Company, was a Rochester concern largely overcapital-
ized, and which, as I was informed at the time, was ruined
by internal dissensions and mismanagement. This company finally sent for Mr. Louis Kirstein to take control of
its business in the hope that it might be saved from ruin.
But even his ability and untiring effort were not able to
put it upon its feet and it went into voluntary liquidation.
After disposing of its more salable assets, our company
purchased, in 1903, its remaining assets, consisting of real
estate, machinery, patents, some of its contracts, etc., for
a sum which, after paying their debts, left only about
$130,000 for their shareholders. We made this purchase
at the urgent request of a committee of the shareholders,
who felt that it was the only way to save something from
the general wreck. If —— refers to that company as
having been driven out of business by us, we have only to
say that at that time we did not manufacture glass-plate
cameras (except a trivial amount), nor film packs, which
were the principal products of that company; hence such
a charge would be absurd; as is the statement that we

have bought "scores of other Companies that they were unable to sandbag."

'It is perfectly true, as before stated, that this company has absorbed a number of companies. Some of these companies have been purchased to avoid or settle patent litigation and as investments, but the most important ones have been purchased in pursuance of a definite line of policy which this company has now followed for many years. That is, to enable it to make a complete line of the very best photographic materials and apparatus. This policy grew out of the field which it has created by the introduction and exploitation of film photography. The invention of the Kodak and the transparent film, both of which inventions were made inside the Eastman Kodak Company, created a vast and new demand for photographic materials. To further the sale of film, it was of the utmost importance that Kodak dealers be furnished with the best of everything in order that Kodak users may get the best results, thereby creating a wider interest in photography and a greater sale of Kodaks and film. With this policy in view, the Kodak Company purchased the Seed Dry Plate Company, which owned the best formula for the preparation of sensitive gelatine emulsions that the world has ever known. This emulsion was applied to film, and Kodak users the world over were given the benefit of it without any extra cost. The American Aristotype Company manufactured collodion printing-out paper, the best in the world. It was largely superseded by the Artura paper, which obtained a vogue in spite of the most strenuous opposition on our part. The Artura paper is a gelatine developing paper and after two or three years of experimenting, during which we failed to make a paper equal to it, we concluded to buy it, and paid over one million dollars for it. Mind you, this was paid to men who entered the business during the period that —— claims we have been "sandbagging" our competitors. The Angelo paper was an entirely different paper from either the American Aristo or the Artura paper, being what is known as platinum paper, used only by a certain restricted group of high-class photographers and not competitive in a general way with either of the other papers.

'We are quite at a loss to account for ——'s rabid attitude in regard to the Kodak Company. He was a salesman in the employ of the wrecked Rochester Optical & Camera Company. *After* it was sold out to the Kodak Company, he started in business for himself and we understand that he has been very successful. It is not strange that he has been successful, because the methods of the Eastman Kodak Company in handling its business do not prevent competitors from entering into the business and succeeding in it. As far as I know none of our competitors who has made good goods has been unsuccessful in the last ten or twelve years, and none has been obliged to go out of business through the Eastman Kodak Company's methods of doing business. The enormous growth of the business caused by the broadening of the art by the inventions introduced by the Kodak Company has fed all of its competitors.

'Finally, the Eastman Company has for a number of years pursued the policy of reducing the prices of its products and also of adding valuable improvements to them without raising their prices.

'In these days, when it is so popular to attack concerns simply because they are large, one has to stand a good deal, but such reckless statements as those made by —— deserve the severest rebuke.'

Within a week another competitor, Thomas Wallace,

of the Expo Camera Company, of New York City, launched an attack.

'I am in receipt of your letter, undated,' Eastman replied, 'threatening attack upon the writer and the Kodak Company unless certain things are done which you demand. You call attention to certain previous letters of yours which have not been answered, with respect to which we have to say that they were unanswered because they called for merely a reiteration by us of what we had already sufficiently made clear to you — that we were not prepared to modify our terms of sale to suit your especial wishes. Now as to your statement of the grounds upon which you say you propose to attack us, if the premises upon which you propose to base the attack were sound, we have no hesitation in saying that you would be justified in your criticisms. These premises are: That we, by unfair means, have created a monopoly in the photographic trade, and that we are preventing you arbitrarily from marketing a meritorious article. This is wholly false. We have used no unfair means in getting the trade we have, and we have no monopoly in either the manufacture or the distribution of photographic goods, even in lines which we originated. There is not a single branch of the art in which we do not encounter the fiercest competition, both as to the manufacture and as to distribution. It is perfectly true that we have a large list of dealers who handle our goods, under our terms of sale, which are perfectly well known to everybody. Every one, or any one of these dealers is at liberty at any time to take up the goods of our competitors, but as a rule they stick to ours for the simple reason that we make the most complete line of the very best and most reliable products. There are several thousand dealers in photographic goods, however, who do not sell our products, and there is probably not a town of any considerable size in the United States which does not contain one or more of such dealers.

'There has never been any time up to and including the present when the manufacturer of any meritorious article could not find a ready sale through these dealers. There are many examples showing the success of such articles, but, mind you, in all cases success has depended upon merit. You have not, in our opinion, a meritorious article, and it would not make any substantial difference in your sales whether our terms of sale were modified in your particular favor or not. I do not suppose you will agree with this opinion, but it was with the view of enabling you to satisfy yourself on this point that we agreed to sell you film. We had a perfect right to decline to sell you film, but even in that case you would not have been barred out of the photographic market, because there are plenty of other films which you can buy. Assuming, however, that our film is necessary because it is the best, our agreeing to sell you put you in the best possible position with the public. You could say: "Here is a camera which I can sell you with the very best film." If the camera had any merit whatever there would be no trouble in selling it in large quantities just as the Ensign Vest Pocket camera was sold until we put a better one on the market.

'The trouble with you is that, being unsuccessful in marketing a commercially worthless article, you want to find somebody besides yourself to fix the blame upon, and you come to us complaining about our policy, which policy we maintain is based upon ethical principles from beginning to end and acts as much in the interest of the dealer and the public as it does in our own. You write to us just as if we had gone out into an old established trade and by some chicanery had induced the existing dealers to throw out other competing goods and give us a monopoly. The fact is that we absolutely created the art of film photography and that we started from 80% to 90% of the customers on our books in the business of selling photographic goods. Now you come to us and say: "Having organized this great force for distributing your goods, I am entitled to share it and you are ethically bound to help me share it." Why in the world don't you ask us to have our traveling men carry your samples? You have not asked us to do that, but you do ask us to give you the benefit of another part of our distributing facilities which we have built up with great labor and expense.

'When I started in the photographic business, it was wholly in the hands of three houses, who were in turn manufacturers, importers, and jobbers. Practically all the trade passed through their hands, and they were understood to have secret trade agreements which gave them actual monopoly of the trade. They sold to only about seventy-five dealers in photographic goods, no one of whom could have carried on his business except in connection with these three houses. My attempts to do business through them were unsatisfactory and my concern started out to interest other people. Since then there has been scarcely any increase in dealers who handle photographic goods exclusively, but we have induced several thousands of druggists, stationers, and jewelers to carry our goods as a side line. We only sell a small percentage of this class of merchants. The great majority are still outside the trade. Instead of whining at our success and showering abuse and threats upon us, why don't you start out as we did and try to establish a selling system for yourself? Conditions are much more favorable now than then, and I can say to you with confidence that if you had an article with one half the advantages over the Kodak that the Kodak had over its predecessors, you could go out and supersede us. It would probably take you twenty-five or thirty years to do it, but it has taken us that time to attain our position.

'Rather than adopt such a course you threaten us with newspaper attacks of the Ida Tarbell-Rockefeller type if we refuse to be intimidated. Such a threat, in view of the present state of public opinion in regard to successful corporations, is a serious one, but we have no hesitation whatever in repeating what we have already said, that we will not, under any such threats, change our policy simply to suit you. It may be that, before the public can be thoroughly educated in regard to the advantages to them of such trade restrictions, they will be done away with by law. When that time comes, we will comply with the law, notwithstanding our belief that such laws would deprive manufacturers of proprietary articles of a large part of their incentive for improving their goods and selling them on the merit system and also make the crime of substituting well-nigh universal.

'This letter is intended for you personally, although I have not the slightest objection to your showing it to any one, provided you show the whole of it.'

As the sun was setting on the Taft administration, Eastman was extremely uncertain of the future.[1] He had declined to become one of the chief financial backers of the 'Bull Moose Party,' despite the earnest solicitation of

[1] Although he subscribed $1000 to the Taft campaign fund, Eastman wrote Frank L. Babbott, October 31, 1912: 'I do not know how you feel about the election, but I never felt so indifferent in my life. As for the "Trust" proposition, it has got to work itself out. The only question is, who are going to serve as victims for experimenting. Of course, none of us want to be rabbits, but some have been and more will undoubtedly be used.'

Perkins and others, preferring political party regularity even though the Taft administration appeared to be determined to force him to agree to a settlement which he felt was economically unsound.

Writing Baker, the day before New Year's, he unburdened his anxious mind.

'As far as the general business for the new year [1913] is concerned, it does not look unpromising, although there is some uncertainty as to what the effect of the change to a Democratic administration is going to be. There is some prospect of Wilson's going on with the campaign against the trusts. I do not know that I have mentioned it to you, but this company has not escaped investigation. During the past six months it has been very thoroughly overhauled by representatives of the Government. I had an interview with the Assistant Attorney-General in Washington on the 26th. They think they have a pretty weak case against the company, but as near as I could judge from what was said they do not like to whitewash any concern that is making so much money as we are. They are going to let us know within a week or ten days whether they will give us a bill of health if we will change our terms of sale, or whether they will insist on entering a suit against us. I dread a suit, but after a number of conferences with our experts have not yet determined whether we will fight or do what they want us to. In the mean time there is a very determined effort to amend the patent laws in a manner which would render our terms of sale illegal outside of the Sherman Law. In case the pending bill, known as the Oldfield Bill, which has already been reported favorably by the Committee, is passed, we will have to capitulate anyway.

'The situation in regard to the trade in motion-picture

film is rather ominous. Our competitors are getting more business all the time and probably improving their product. Changes in the method of distribution through the Exchanges are being made which eventually may throw the purchase of film into two or three hands in each country, and that, I am afraid, will not be very favorable to us. As far as excellence in production is concerned, however, we ought to be able to keep the lead. We are improving our processes and methods in every direction, and I can truly say that at the present time we are making more satisfactory goods than ever before in every department. We have recently put an improved emulsion on our Ciné negative which brings it up to the very highest plate speed and quality, a thing that has never been accomplished before by anybody. Plates, with which we had trouble a year ago, have been running beautifully for six months, and we are now getting back trade that we lost at that time. All kinds of paper are running satisfactorily. In fact the manufacturing department is in such good shape that I feel nervous because it looks too good to be true.'

The tension was broken temporarily by a long sea voyage. Returning on the 26th of March, Eastman collected the threads of business together and again wrote Baker, giving him the latest news.

'We went on board the yacht at Charleston so as to avoid the disagreeable passage around Cape Hatteras, and then struck out for Nassau, San Domingo, Porto Rico, down the Windward Islands to Barbados, La Guayra, Puerto Cabello and Colon, and back by way of Jamaica and Cuba to Charleston. We had a little rough weather, but no bad storms, and on the whole we were very fortunate in this respect. I was much impressed by the work at Panama, and think that alone would be worth a long uncomfortable trip if it were necessary to undergo it. Some of the tourists who go down there complain of the heat and food on the tourist ships, but we, of course, were free from that. We had a good refrigerating machine on the yacht and all of our supplies kept perfectly. If we had not been able to take our supplies on the yacht, we would have fared rather poorly, because the markets in pretty much all of the West Indies are rotten bad.

'You ask about the effect of the slides on the Canal and the prospect as to when it will be opened. I do not think any one can prophesy very closely as to this latter. The locks, the big dam, and the spillway are very nearly completed and there is no question but what they will be finished this summer, but where the slides will stop is beyond the power of anybody to state. I have never seen dry earth slide at such a slight angle anywhere. The earth moves just like a glacier. Since we were there, I have seen in the newspapers accounts of another movement which tore up all the tracks but one and filled the prism of the canal 20 ft. deep. All the engineers can do is to keep digging it out as fast as it slides in until it stops. There is one big hill, the bank of which is more nearly vertical than most places where the slides have taken place, that has not begun to move yet. If that begins to go, it will mean some big digging.

'You will have received our statement ere this. I think very likely it marks high-water mark in our profits. The changes in the tariff, encroachment on our Ciné business by our foreign competitors, changing of our terms under pressure of the Government, and all that sort of thing is bound to tell in the near future, although up to date this year the increase in our sales has been nearly 30% in America, and nothing in Europe.

'As far as the Government situation is concerned, we hope to clear it up this week through a conference with the Assistant U.S. District Attorney, who is coming here with Mr. Philipp. They will file a complaint and we will submit to a decree ordering us to change our terms of sale by admitting the goods of our competitors to the counters of Kodak dealers, and a few other minor things that they insist upon.

'Next month the long-drawn-out Goodwin suit is to be argued. This suit you will perhaps remember is the one brought by the Ansco people under a patent to the Rev. Hannibal Goodwin. If it were not for the influences of the socialistic and anti-trust agitation upon the minds of Judges, we would feel no uncertainty as to the outcome of this suit. If it should happen that we lose in the lower courts, we will, of course, appeal. We think we are in a position to go on without using anything that can be claimed under the patent.'

The New York owners of the Goodwin patent, taking advantage of the avalanche of attacks upon Eastman and the general hostility of the public toward all large corporations, brought suit against the company before Federal Judge John R. Hazel in Buffalo. Eastman naturally entrusted the defense to Philipp, who had received, prior to this, in addition to all fees, retainers, and expenses, a gift of one million dollars from his confident client.

While the case was under way there came another attack from an unexpected quarter. The June, 1913, number of the 'World's Work' appeared with an installment of President Wilson's book 'The New Freedom,' which showed very clearly that Eastman's leading opponent was in the White House.

'Take such an everyday thing as a useful invention and the putting of it at the service of men,' the President wrote. 'You know how prolific the American mind has been in invention; how much civilization has been advanced by the steamboat, the cotton-gin, the sewing machine, the reaping machine, the typewriter, the electric light, the telephone, the phonograph. Do you know, have you had occasion to learn, that there is no hospitality for invention nowadays? There is no encouragement for you to set your wits at work to improve the telephone, or the camera, or some piece of machinery, or some mechanical process; you are not invited to find a shorter and cheaper way to make things or to perfect them, or to invent better things to take their place. There is too much money invested in old machinery; too much money has been spent advertising the old camera; the telephone plants, as they are, cost too much to permit their being superseded by something better.[1] Wherever there is monopoly, not only is there no incentive to improve, but, improvement being costly in that it "scraps" old machinery and destroys the value of old products, there is a positive motive against improvement. The instinct of monopoly is against novelty, the tendency of monopoly is to keep in use the old things, made in the old way; its disposition is to standardize everything. Standardization may be all very well —

[1] These statements show an amazing lack of information on the part of President Wilson. In both film photography and the telephone many millions of dollars had been spent on experiments, new inventions, and the replacement of old machinery by new processes of manufacturing. What disappointed Eastman was that a man occupying the positions President Wilson had occupied, at Princeton University and as Governor of New Jersey, should not have informed himself more fully before writing this article. Nevertheless, Eastman did not let his personal feeling prejudice him against all of President Wilson's policies. Writing Congressman Thomas B. Dunn, March 31, 1914, he stated: 'I believe you can do Rochester and the country a big service by standing by the President in his attempt to straighten out the Panama toll situation. America cannot afford to take a purely technical view of its treaty obligations.'

but suppose everything had been standardized thirty years ago, we should still be writing by hand, by gaslight, we should be without the inestimable aid of the telephone (sometimes, I admit, it is a nuisance), without the automobile, without wireless telegraphy. Personally, I could have managed to plod along without the aeroplane, and I could have been happy even without moving pictures.'

Developments in Washington, however, convinced Eastman that attacks from the Department of Justice and the Executive were not to be the only ones from there. 'It seems to me,' he wrote Hubbell, 'the point I called your attention to yesterday afternoon should be urged if possible in fighting the tariff reduction on film. The point is that the only excuse for taking the tariff off is to slug the Kodak Company, thereby benefiting foreign competition. If it does this, the Government will lose the revenue from the film that is just coming into the market in competition with ours. It has not been the tariff that has kept out foreign film, but simply the fact that the foreigners could not make the film. Now that they are succeeding, their imports are sure to grow because the present tariff is no barrier. I am leaving the need of fighting the tariff battle to you. Please see that everything possible is done.' [1]

While all these developments were under way, the French and German film manufacturers launched an offensive against Kodak in Europe, and Eastman went abroad to meet the attacks and aid Gifford and Mattison in their strategy. Returning in the middle of August, 'Mr. Colfax met me at the dock with the cheerful news

[1] 'After elaborate hearings before Congress in 1913, the session of that year put this raw stock [film] on the free list.' (*Boston American,* June 10. 1921.)

that the Goodwin suit had been decided against us,' Eastman informed his London manager. 'I saw Kennedy, Philipp being still away, and he says that the decision shows that Judge Hazel did not understand the case. Of course it will be appealed. There was a sensational article in the "Sun" yesterday stating that we were liable to be called upon to pay somewhere between five and twenty-five million dollars. If this should prove to be the case and the Government should succeed in their suit to dissolve us, what will be left of the Kodak Company?'

An appeal was filed immediately in the United States Circuit Court of Appeals, while Eastman now assumed personal direction of all questions of policy and procedure in the face of the impending Government suit. An article by Louis D. Brandeis, of Boston, in 'Harper's Weekly' (November 15, 1913), he found 'very interesting,' and wrote the famous jurist whom President Wilson later appointed to the United States Supreme Court:

'I have read pretty much everything that has been published on the subject and yours is the most convincing presentation of it that has appeared up to the present time. In writing you I have two objects in view: One is to express my appreciation of the fine work you are doing in helping to correct one of the greatest economic mistakes of our time; and the other to call your attention to one side of the argument which I think has heretofore been somewhat neglected. You touch lightly upon it in the remark near the end of your article, that "such competition (between dealers) is superficial merely." I do not think the public appreciates that this is not only a fact, but must be a fact because the margin that a dealer has to play upon is very small. It can safely be said that in the selling of proprietary articles there is not more than a margin of 10% between a dealer and bankruptcy after he has paid his running expenses. While pirates may cut to the extent of their whole discount temporarily, any permanent lowering of the price by dealers must be confined well within this limit of 10%. The public, therefore, has to look for the cheapening of goods to the manufacturer instead of to the dealer. To give some illustrations, with which you are no doubt perfectly familiar: Competition between dealers could only have lowered the price of the Gillette safety razor say 50¢, but competition between manufacturers has furnished other safety razors for $1.00 and for even 25¢. In the case of cameras, the first Kodak was sold for $25.00. The limit of competition between dealers would have made the minimum price $22.50. At the present time a camera much better in every respect except the covering of the case is sold for $2.00. Any piratical competition between dealers which interferes with distribution only hampers the manufacturer in reducing his costs. I do not for a moment think I am presenting any new ideas in what I have said, but I am quite sure that the public does not realize that there can be no substantial competition between dealers in proprietary articles.'

In December, Z. M. Larwill, a Cleveland book merchant, sent a circular of the Pan-American Union, which added irony to the policy of the Wilson administration. 'It seems very amusing,' Eastman replied, 'that the Secretary of State of the United States should be responsible for a circular offering a book carrying a discount to the dealer of 45% and forbidding him from cutting the price, when another branch of the Government of the United States condemns that practice as reprehensible.'

The attitude of the Wilson administration was perplexing. By January, 1914, several of Eastman's business friends submitted suggestions in regard to procedure. These were entirely voluntary, as Eastman refused to follow the customary practice of mobilizing 'influences' to bring them to bear upon the Government, squelching, among other things, an attempt to arouse the company's employees to action and protest.

In a letter to L. M. Antisdale, editor of the 'Rochester Herald,' Eastman stated that all the facts relating to the origin, development, and commercial operations of the company were placed in the possession of the Department of Justice more than a year ago.

'That was during the previous administration. While I have no knowledge that Mr. McReynolds, the present Attorney-General, or his subordinates, have ever examined the record of the investigation instituted by Mr. Wickersham into the history and methods of our organization, I think it reasonable to assume that they have done so. The Wickersham investigation was most searching, and was entered upon in a spirit which was anything but friendly to us. Being based, in the main, upon a grave misconception of the spirit and conduct of our company, it was begun in the quite evident belief that it would uncover some very damaging facts as to our suppression of competition and mistreatment of competitors. The only way to meet such an inquiry and to correct these false notions was by giving free access to all the books, records, and other historical data of our business. This we did, not only willingly, but, to a large extent, voluntarily. We gave the investigator all that he could think of as being worth while, and, in order to save future trouble to either the Government or ourselves, gave him many things that he did not ask for. The report of this investigator covered all of these data, and is, I assume, now on file with the Attorney-General.

'I cannot think of any material fact bearing upon the character of our company and its business methods which was not included in the scope of the Wickersham investigation. If there be any such omitted fact, and I can learn what it is, it will be a pleasure to submit it. Not only have we nothing to conceal, but it is now, as it was a year ago under the former administration, most desirable that the Government should know the facts, in order that we may not suffer by its misinformation.

'At the conclusion of the Wickersham investigation, the Government submitted to us several propositions for the rearrangement of our terms of sale. This was done, not because it was alleged that we had actually violated the law, but because it was deemed by the Attorney-General advisable that we modify the terms in the interest of freer trade relations. We did not agree with the Department that the changes proposed would produce the effect sought for, nor did we regard them as just to our company and its shareholders. Yet, rather than to prolong the argument or to put ourselves into collision with the Government, in turn, we agreed to accept.

'It seems to us only fair that the Government should specify the particular points in which our conduct of our business does not conform to the law or to business ethics. It has been our desire, and is still, as evinced in the history of the investigation, to meet all requirements of the law and of fair dealing. I think we have done so. But if the Government thinks we have not, it ought to tell us so, and in what particulars we have erred and continued to err. No such intimation has been made to us.

'You can see from this statement of facts how difficult our position is. We want to comply with the law and have always wanted to. We believe we have done so and more.'

In March, the United States Circuit Court of Appeals sustained the decision of the lower court in the Goodwin case. Eastman hurried to New York to consult Philipp. Philipp was crushed by the decision, and Eastman was left with no alternative except to enter at once into negotiations for a settlement, paying the Ansco Company five million dollars in cash. At last the New York owners of the Goodwin patent received their 'pound of flesh.' Eastman had lost the lawsuit, but he had not compromised his principles. Returning to Rochester he was met by a reporter from the 'Post-Express.'

'There are a lot of fairy tales going the rounds about the Goodwin patent, but it can be stated that the Eastman Company will continue to manufacture and to sell films. It can, furthermore, be stated that the Eastman Kodak Company has not made "large sums of money" out of the Goodwin patent. As to our present and future output of films, it may be well to say that the Eastman Company is now manufacturing a film which cannot in any way infringe upon the Goodwin patent.

'Cutting out a lot of extraneous matters,' said Eastman, 'the story of the Goodwin patent is this: Away back in May, 1887, Rev. Hannibal Goodwin applied for a patent on a nitro-cellulose film for photographic purposes. The patent was refused on the ground that no invention was shown.

'Before Mr. Goodwin made his application for a patent, the Eastman Company had marketed a roll-holder and a paper-backed film; the company knowing full well, at the time, that the film-roll system, if it became successful, would mean that the film of the future would be a film with a transparent base. In 1888, the Kodak was placed upon the market. A film-roll was used in this camera. The system became a success, and the following spring, April, 1889, the Eastman Company made two applications for photographic films, with nitro-cellulose base; in other words, transparent films.

'One application was denied by the Patent Office at Washington, while the other was granted, the patent being issued on December 10, 1889, and numbered 417,202. This Eastman Company patent described in detail how a commercially practicable film could be made. The Goodwin claim rested on a suggestion for film-making without any practicable details as to the method of operating it. Please note that the Eastman patent was basic in its character and under it were manufactured all the films used in photography for many years.

'As was the case in another famous patent wrangle, which has engrossed the attention of the courts for years, nine days after the issue of the Eastman patent, the Rev. Mr. Goodwin, in a new application, wrote into his application the word "camphor" which did not appear in the original application and which he learned about only through the Eastman patent.

'I forget many of the details, but it is safe to say that during the many years that the Eastman Company was engaged in manufacturing photographic films and constantly improving its processes, Mr. Goodwin was engaged in radically altering his papers in an effort to keep pace with the commercial developments of the art by the Eastman Company. During all this time, remember, Mr. Goodwin never made a roll of film. In fact, if we take up the film story in its order, it readily will be seen that Mr. Goodwin filed his application for a patent in 1887.

'In 1889, the Eastman Company patent was filed and granted and the Eastman film was successfully placed on the market. In 1898, the Goodwin patent was issued, and in 1902 suit for damages was started under the Goodwin patent. It is well worth notice that the suit for damages was started after the death of Mr. Goodwin, who, up to the time of his death, had failed to take any action against the Eastman Company. This is true also of the heirs of Mr. Goodwin.

'Kindly remember this: The Eastman Company had been making and marketing films for nine years before the Goodwin patent was issued. And thirteen years had elapsed after the Eastman Company first marketed films before the Goodwin suit was started.

'The Eastman Company film was the first practicable film for cameras put on the market and it has been manufactured and sold, with improvements, for the last twenty-five years.

'Another thing you want to remember is that Goodwin never made a foot of salable film. There has never been any film made and sold according to the process set forth in the Goodwin patent, although over $15,000 was sunk by Mr. Goodwin himself in 1900 in an effort to make the Goodwin film practicable for use in cameras.

'Still one other conclusive argument: The present owners of the Goodwin patent do not make film according to the process described in their patent, but by a modification of the Eastman process.'[1]

[1] In the case of the Chicago Film Exchange vs. Motion Picture Patents Company, the Court of Appeals of the District of Columbia said, December 2, 1912: 'The flexible, transparent or translucent tape-like film prepared for taking photographs, was neither discovered nor produced by Edison. It was improved and brought to its present state of perfection by Eastman. When exhibited to Edison, he seized upon it as the thing needed to make his [moving-picture] camera apparatus a complete commercial success. . . . The invention of Edison was exhausted in the construction of the camera, which enabled the photographs of moving objects to be taken upon the Eastman film in the distinct, uniform and satisfactory manner justly claimed for them. The pictures are the direct result of the mechanism of the camera with the Eastman film mechanically adapted to and applied therein.'

To E. T. Bonsfield, of Nottingham, England, Eastman replied that the litigation was ended, 'having been settled with money the employees helped to earn. In recognition of this, and in the expectation that they will help to earn more, we are proposing to continue the wage dividend.'

By this time President Wilson's Attorney-General was determined to destroy the Company and Eastman prepared personally for action.

'Thank you for the clipping from the Wall Street Journal,' he wrote Dr. Rhees. 'The position of the Government in regard to our case is . . . in effect. "If you have been built up in violation of the law, it is not sufficient to reform your evil practices. You must be dissolved. If you cannot be dissolved, you must be destroyed; and we hope we can prove that you have been built up in violation of the law." This in spite of the fact that the experts who have investigated the case say that there is no cause for the dissolution of the Company.'

And to his friend in Australia, Eastman added: [1] 'It

[1] This was an era of persecution as well as prosecution of 'Big Business.' Eastman always felt that the Rockefellers were unjustly persecuted, and upon one occasion wrote John D. Rockefeller, Jr., the following self-explanatory letter:

'Happening to be in Washington at the time you testified before the House Committee, I read your testimony with great interest. I read also your subsequent published statement in regard to your connection with the Colorado strike and have observed generally the newspaper and Administration attitude in regard to the matter, and I write this to express my admiration of the stand you have taken in maintaining a principle which is of the greatest public importance. I believe you have the right-thinking people of the country with you and have no doubt that the outcome will be a satisfaction to you.' (May 7, 1914.)

Throughout the Government suit against the Kodak Company, which attracted wide attention, Eastman received many letters. 'I have been much interested in your case and in the defense which you are making for the benefit of all business,' wrote George K. Birge, president of the Pierce-Arrow Motor Car Company, May 5, 1914. 'This litigation appears to me as the most unjust persecution of a great industry.'

looks now as if the Government suit would be tried out in court. There has already been one hearing at Buffalo and the next hearing is set down for May 25th [1914] in Rochester. The court can sit in either place and has announced its intention of sitting in Rochester whenever it is convenient for witnesses. We have tried every means for compromising this suit short of agreeing to the dissolution of the company. The Attorney-General is insistent upon this point and we therefore propose to fight to the bitter end.'

CHAPTER VIII

THE WORLD WAR

'I REACHED there [London] just a few days before the war was declared,' Eastman wrote Baker, August 26, 1914, and as there was no use trying to do any business, I turned around and came back home again. . . . When I left London communication with all of our Continental branches, except the one at Paris, had been shut off. Business in England, while not at a standstill, had slackened very much. We had to lay off about 2/3 of our Harrow force and were preparing to put the remainder on short time. Here in Rochester we have just decided to cut down the time in most departments 1/3, which is about equal to the proportion of the European business. Our stock of manufactured goods is about normal, but with the decreased consumption, of course, it will be rather heavy in spite of everything we can do. As for raw materials, we have abundant stocks of everything except metol and hydro-quinone. We have nearly a year's supply of metol, normal consumption; hydro-quinone, two or three months' supply, and believe we can get more; hypo, there is abundant supply, without much increase in price. Of gelatine, glass, and paper we have about a year's supply.

'It looks to us as if business might be pretty dull this winter even in America, and we are furling our sails accordingly, keeping a sharp lookout for any business there is to do. We are well fixed as to money, having on hand nearly $4,000,000 in this country, after paying the dividends. Of course we have a lot of money tied up on the Continent.'

Eastman, like other Americans, read the war reports with amazement. 'It is impossible to realize here what is taking place on the Continent,' he observed in a letter to Joseph Thacher Clarke. To Dr. Leon Lilienfeld, an Austrian scientist, Eastman expressed the hope that the 'hostilities will not be prolonged and that we will see you in Rochester within a few months. In the mean time we will go on industriously with our experiments, with the help of Dr. Hans Clarke,[1] who has now accepted a position on our laboratory staff.'

'I am glad to receive your letter of August 25 and to know how you are getting along,' he wrote the Berlin manager of Kodak, g.m.b.h. 'In regard to future supplies of goods, you may order them direct from Rochester. We rely upon you to manage the affairs of the German Company with the same care and interest that you would if you owned the whole thing yourself. As it may be impossible for you to consult with us here, you will have to rely upon your own judgment, in which we have much confidence.

'Of course our business has been much interfered with by the war and we have been obliged to shorten our working hours in many departments. We are, however, doing the best we can to give all of our employees something to do and hope that if things do not get any worse, we will get through the winter without great distress. We feel great sympathy with the people of all the countries which have been drawn into this terrible war and can only hope it will come to a speedy end so that they can take up their accustomed occupations.'

In these early days of the conflict, Eastman was

[1] Son of J. T. Clarke; Director of the Department of Synthetic Chemistry, Kodak Research Laboratories, 1918–28; Professor of Biological Chemistry, Columbia University, 1928.

strictly impartial in his business relations with the belligerents. 'The company' was represented in every country at war and in all the neutral nations. Most of the foreign branches and stores he had opened personally. Since 1879, for thirty-five years, he had been crossing and recrossing the Atlantic, building an international business, which was now in the whirlpool of a devastating war. 'Our European business in every country except Russia either shows a heavy falling off or has been entirely extinguished,' he advised the Chamber of Commerce of the United States, October 6, and two days later informed a representative in Gothenburg, Sweden, that 'our trade in the United States has not yet been greatly affected by the war. Owing to general commercial depression, it was dull both here and in Canada at the time war was declared. This condition has not changed much yet, but we hope with the big crops that have been successfully harvested the times will grow better rather than worse.'

As the Wilson administration was prosecuting its suit for the dissolution of the company, counsel advised Eastman, when the Clayton Act was signed by the President,[1] to terminate the agreement with Edison and the licensees of the Motion Picture Patents Company, and letters were sent out immediately giving the required sixty-day notice, even though the Federal Government was not having a clear track in its anti-trust peregrinations. 'Now comes the Shoe Machinery decision,' Eastman wrote Isaac F. Marcosson, 'which makes four straight against the Government. It certainly does look as if big business was going to have a show in the future.' Only recently Eastman had put in four and one half days on the witness stand in an attempt to explain his connection with the

[1] October 14, 1914.

development of the company to Judge Hazel, while scores of other officials and employees were called also. As far as the Kodak business was concerned, there were wars on two fronts, one in Europe and one at home, but neither wars nor panics were permitted to interrupt scientific experiments. Ever since the advent of the Kodak system, Eastman had dreamed of photographs in natural colors and the research workers at the Park had just succeeded in a color process for portraiture, which was called Kodachrome.

'We have sent an exhibition to London,' Eastman wrote Baker, 'one to San Francisco for the Panama Exposition, and are preparing one for the New York State Convention which will be held here next week. Mr. Mock is making some very beautiful things for the convention and the process is going to be the feature of the occasion. Mr. Hutchison is in New York installing the apparatus in the studio of Mr. Hoyt, one of the leading photographers, and we have a dozen or more applications from the principal men in the country, which we will fill as fast as possible. At the same time we are beginning to equip some of the big hospitals with the process for pathological work. The doctors are very eager for it. Dr. [N. T.] Beers, a specialist in New York and the head of a big laboratory [Brooklyn Hospital], in order to induce us to let him have the process right away, offered us the privilege of using his laboratory for demonstrating to other physicians. It will be interesting to hear what the English color workers think of the process. I am quite sure they have never seen any work equal to that we sent over. I am sending you a copy of the first booklet of instructions. We find that the best practice is to keep the original negatives uncolored; to do what retouching is necessary on them; then make positives, and from them make reproductions. These reproductions can be made by contact, or if made in the camera can be enlarged or reduced. There is scarcely anything in the way of retouching, etching, or auxiliary coloring with the air brush that cannot be done on these plates.

'Dr. Mees has been working for months on a similar process applied to motion pictures, and has it nearly worked out. The result will be a color film which can be exhibited in the standard machine, without variation of speed or light.' [1]

While these experiments continued, Eastman found that he had to devote most of his attention to complications abroad, because the Central Powers appeared determined to confiscate the business within their jurisdiction. Writing the State Department, Eastman forwarded a cable from London:

'Request Department State to cable Vienna Ambassador that Kodak Company in Austria-Hungary, although an Austrian Company, belongs to American Kodak Company and that Gifford Clarke directors Austrian Company are American citizens.'

'If you can do anything for us in seeing that this is attended to,' Eastman advised the Department, 'we will very much appreciate it, as the matter appears to be urgent. When I was in London early in August, Ambassador [Walter Hines] Page sent in a request of practically the same nature in regard to our German company, and we are advised that it aided materially in saving our establishments there from disaster.'

In the wake of this letter came a cablegram from Copenhagen that the German military authorities had sequestered the business in Belgium. Eastman tele-

[1] This process was developed, but not used at the time because the motion-picture industry was not interested then in colored pictures.

graphed the State Department, asking that the Government 'advise the German authorities that our Belgian business . . . is owned entirely by the American company.' Shortly thereafter a remarkable 'grapevine' communication came from Brussels. When the German army entered that city, two loyal women employees in the store there, at great personal risk, took all the books and money (amounting to several hundred thousand francs) belonging to the concern and placed them in 'safekeeping.' They were certain the German officials would not discover their secret cache, and events proved they were right. This little game of outwitting the invaders appealed to Eastman's sporting nature, and at the next meeting of the directors he recommended that the two women be rewarded with shares of common stock. Notifying them of this action, Eastman added, 'The Management is very proud to know that its representatives are acquitting themselves so well in these troublous times.'

Despite these provocations, Eastman approved the policy of the Berlin manager paying four hundred marks each month to the German Red Cross, although he contributed personally to British, French, and Belgian Relief funds, and informed the London and French managers that 'it is our intention to pay wage dividends to the men who have joined the colors on the same basis as if they had been on the payroll for the full amount of their wages.' Almost simultaneously he authorized the Petrograd manager to invest twenty thousand pounds on deposit there in Russian war bonds. Eastman's interest in the Allied cause was mounting. By June, 1915, he was eager to have the United States declare war. 'Very likely,' he said in a bulletin to Baker, 'by the time you get this, the United States will have severed relations with

Germany. The country is very much wrought up over her submarine exploits and is united in the feeling that either she has got to change her tactics or we have got to quit recognizing her. I believe the country is gradually waking up to the fact that this war is just as important to us as it is to England. I hope we will not wake up too late to be of any help.' [1]

'I wonder if the English or French Governments would be interested in this process [medical photographs in color by Dr. Beers] for any of their medical departments. We can send you some pathological specimens if you desire,' he suggested to his London manager.

'The feeling that it is up to the United States to declare its sympathy with the Allies is growing fast. Articles such as the one by Owen Wister in The Saturday Evening Post are helping to crystallize public opinion to the effect that this war means just as much to us as it does to England.'

Funds of the company were now beginning to accumulate rapidly in the belligerent countries (a million marks in Germany and half a million rubles in Petrograd), while Mattison was having difficulties in London. Writing Eastman, he said the British were 'still severely handicapped with difficulties of transport, and you may have gathered from what you read in "The Times" of what an unprecedented state of things prevails in Liverpool. Unfortunately we are beset with labor troubles to the extent that the conduct of the war is imperiled. Lake has been down to Liverpool several times, and it is only by the most desperate efforts that we are able to wrest our goods from docks and get

[1] The Lusitania was sunk by a German submarine, May 7, 1915. The United States sent a protest to Germany on May 13, and on June 2, Ambassador von Bernstorff called upon President Wilson to explain.

them down to London. We are now trying the experiment of motor transport, having sent a motor lorry and trailer down to Liverpool. A terrible lot of drinking is going on among the stevedores. Lord Kitchener went down there the other day and addressed a very grave warning to them. The shortage of staff on the railways hampers things, of course, very much — the North-western, for instance, having lost 20 per cent of their staff serving in the army.

'The military and naval authorities are taking a considerable interest in photography for aërial observation. The admiralty took from us yesterday 20,000 feet of negative which they sent out on a torpedo boat last night to the Dardanelles, together with 20 aëroscope cameras. Apparently they want more definite information as to the damage they do to the forts. Experiments have been going on lately at the military flying grounds in the use of automatic photography on airplanes.'

By July, Eastman was determined to withdraw all company funds from Germany. Ambassador James W. Gerard was instructed by the State Department to protest to the German Foreign Office for hindering the manager from transferring the funds. On the 24th, Zimmermann officially capitulated, replying that the company would have 'unhindered disposition' of the money held in Berlin, but the Under-Secretary of State had his fingers crossed!

Returning to Rochester from a five weeks' camp in the Rockies and visits to the San Diego and San Francisco Expositions, Eastman resumed direction of the business on October 9, writing first to London, Berlin, and Melbourne.

'Yours of the 24th of September at hand with the cheerful news that the British Government is going to take half of our war profits,' he wrote London. 'As a matter of fact I do not object to this. As I understand it the new tax will be as follows: If our profits in 1914 were £100,000 and in 1915 £200,000, the income tax for 1914 was at the rate of 216, £13,000, and will be in 1915 at the rate of 316, £36,000, in addition to which we will have to turn over £50,000, making the total taxation £86,000, instead of £26,000, what it would have been under the old rate. I do not know of any taxes that I should be willing to pay more cheerfully, and I like to think that some of the money is going to be spent for submarine nets.'

The same day he wrote Berlin:

'I am in receipt of your letter of September 16th in regard to buying German War Loan securities with the funds held back against goods manufactured in Harrow. We do not think the German Government is treating us fairly in continuing a supervision of our business and do not think we ought to be asked to buy any of their War Bonds. We appreciate, of course, the fact that they are conducting the supervision in a courteous manner, but all the same we think they have taken an unwarranted stand in view of the proofs that have been submitted.'

To his friend and associate in Australia he added that he had 'no objection' to Baker's subscription of $100,000 of Kodak funds to the British loan. 'We have already taken $250,000 of the British War Loan and $100,000 of the Russian Loan; and have authorized the purchase of $500,000 each of the French and Russian short term Treasury Bills. Last week I personally took $200,000 of the Anglo-French Loan. I believe it is our duty to help in such matters. You ask what rate of interest we are drawing on our investments. Our deposits in banks are at 3, 3½, and a small proportion 4%. We are not making any loans, but the securities that we already have average about 4%.

'I feel the same way about the income tax that I do about the Government bonds. As long as the taxes are the same for everybody, I cannot say that I object to contributing money to help the British Government make its fight, which I fully realize is for all mankind. The recent enactment by the British Government providing for the taking of half of the war profits of business concerns is a most excellent and fair scheme for raising money, and although it will hit us for several hundred thousand dollars the money will be cheerfully paid as far as I am concerned.

By the middle of January, 1916, the company and Eastman personally had $4,000,000 invested in British, French, Russian, and Italian war loans or treasury bills.

The following month he wrote the manager of the Canadian business that he had noticed there would be an income tax 'amounting to 25% on the profits of all business companies in Canada over 7% on the capital. Perhaps it would be well to consult our attorneys to ascertain whether the 7% allowed is to be on the issued capital stock or on the real capital invested in the business. If the former, it might be advisable and necessary to increase the capital stock of the Canadian Kodak Co. to cover the actual investment. I do not wish to evade any taxation, but only wish to secure equality with other Canadian companies. As you know, I am thoroughly in sympathy with the Allies, and if it becomes necessary for the Canadian Government to take more than 25% of the profits of the Canadian manufacturing companies, we will cheerfully pay our share.'

In the mean time Judge Hazel rendered a decision

against the company in the Government suit,[1] and Eastman outlined his policy and feelings in a long communication to the counsel of the company in Australia.

'We are appealing our Government case to the
Supreme Court and have some hope of relief from that
direction. Contrary to your perfectly natural assumption, the fact is that our competitors do not desire the
dissolution of this company, as they know very well that
any dissolution would make things much more difficult
for them. Public opinion in regard to trust prosecutions
in this country is rapidly changing, and it is only our mis-
fortune that we seem to have got into the flood at its apex.

'We are on the eve now of a Presidential campaign in
which the Republican Party has strong hopes of regain-
ing ascendancy. If it does, our weak and vacillating
course in international affairs will be remedied. The
failure of President Wilson to gauge the significance of
the great conflict is simply amazing. He has succeeded
in anæsthetizing a large body of our citizens, but they
are beginning to recover, and the pending campaign

---

[1] The Government suit was filed June 9, 1913. Judge John R. Hazel's
decision was rendered August 24, 1915. The decree of the Court was filed
January 20, 1916, and the appeal of the company to the United States
Supreme Court was filed March 8, 1916. 'Judge Hazel found for the Government that the defendants had acquired a monopoly in photographic
goods by means of (1) contracts with regard to raw paper stock preventing
the trade from obtaining such stock; (2) by acquiring competing plants,
businesses, and wholesale house (or stock houses); and (3) by the imposition
on retail dealers of arbitrary terms of sale which suppressed competition.
The Court found that to satisfy the law there would have to be some division
of the business of the defendant corporation among two or more competing
companies, but what division should be made was left for future decision.
The Government suit did not involve in any way the manufacture of photographic film. In fact those products of the company in which the Court
found that a monopoly had been acquired by illegal combination, involve
altogether not more than one sixth of its business done in the United States.'
(James S. Havens, counsel of the company to Dudley Field Malone, January,
1917.)

will, I believe, wake them up pretty thoroughly, and the fact that the great war is simply and solely a conflict between democracy and military world despotism will be made plain.'

'I am greatly surprised that the British Government seriously considers the prohibition of [the import of] ciné film in Great Britain,' Eastman observed in a letter to Gifford. 'I should think the psychological effect on the masses would be bad if their cheapest and best amusement is interfered with, as it would be. It would be difficult to produce the film in England on account of the raw materials, gelatine, bromide of potassium, acids, and raw cotton. If they struck out the acids and raw cotton and imported instead the finished raw basic celluloid, there would be still a large amount of money going out of the country. I should think the Government would do everything it could to keep the business as it is intact and put a tax on admissions. They would then get back some of the inflated wages that they are paying to the munitions workers.'

The reëlection of President Wilson on the campaign slogan, 'He kept us out of war,' only added to Eastman's belligerency. Then when the United States War College requested that the company equip that institution with processes employing color filters and red sensitive materials, used by the leading Allied military authorities, Eastman was astonished. Perhaps the President would not be able to 'keep us out of war' much longer! One American business man certainly had no intention of keeping out of it, even if President Wilson's new Attorney-General was as determined to destroy the company, as was his predecessor.[1]

[1] After Mr. McReynolds's appointment to the United States Supreme Court, Thomas W. Gregory became Attorney-General.

'I cannot see how we would object to having the future conduct of our business placed, as far as violations of the Sherman Act are concerned, under the Federal Trade Commission,' Eastman wrote another correspondent; 'in fact it is just the kind of work that I understand the Commission was created for . . . it would not require any considerable amount of time for an expert to ascertain from time to time whether or not we had violated the Sherman Act. Certainly we are keeping as far away from it as we know how.'

Although President Wilson was adopting the policy of 'watchful waiting,' Eastman was for preparedness. 'This company is in accord with the Plattsburg movement,' he informed the Rochester National Defense Contingent, 'and is prepared to allow a reasonable number of its employees who can be spared from their duties, without detriment to the business, to attend the Plattsburg camp up to four weeks, without deduction from pay other than an amount equal to the sum received by them for military services.'

In June, Eastman engaged a band to play in the Preparedness Day Parade, while the new plant at Kodak Heights, Toronto, which the company had constructed, but was not ready to occupy, was turned over to the Canadian Government 'for military purposes.'

By Christmas, 1916, Eastman received many greetings from all parts of the world. 'My best wishes for your health on the occasion of Christmas,' Gaumont wrote from Paris, 'and may 1917 give victory to the Allies and the peace which will suppress war for evermore.'

Eastman himself, despite his strong sympathy and efforts for the Allies, did not forget 'the company' in Germany. Four of the oldest employees had been killed in action, and he wrote the manager: 'You may continue paying their wives what is necessary up to one half of their salaries. In regard to your personal affairs, I shall be glad to know how you are fixed and whether you need additional money. . . . In the mean time if you do you are authorized to draw as needed, in addition to your salary, up to the sum of twenty thousand marks.'

'I was very glad the other day to receive a letter from Raymond [Gaumont] and to know that he is in the Aviation Corps,' Eastman wrote the boy's father after the United States severed diplomatic relations with the Central Powers. 'The son of a friend of mine, named Dugan, who is a shoe manufacturer here, is in the French Aviation Corps, and every once in a while his father sends me one of his letters to read. He was in the Foreign Legion until wounded. He got the Cross and then was transferred to the Aviation Corps. Three young friends of mine from Rochester, Taylor, Buell, and Curtis, landed at Bordeaux on the Chicago last week, to take positions as ambulance drivers in the American Legion. Our peace-at-any-price citizens are fast losing their influence, thanks to the activities of Herr Zimmermann, and I reckon we are about ready to line up on the side of the Allies, a united country. The foolishness of a few members of the Senate does not mean anything.'

Before the Congress declared war early in April, 1917, the company and its president had backed the Allied cause with $8,500,000, in addition to heavy war taxes paid in England, France, Italy, Russia, Canada, and Australia, while Eastman made personal contributions to Allied Relief funds and the American Hospital in France.

Eastman made an immediate survey of the field to determine what the photographic industry could contribute toward victory. Within a few days after war was declared, he notified both the Secretary of War and the

Secretary of the Navy that the company was prepared to supply the Government with cellulose acetate for weather-proofing airplane wings and make unbreakable lenses for gas masks. Shortly thereafter, Eastman received information from the War Department that the company could assist in the development of aërial photography, and he wrote Secretary Baker:

'We offer use of any of our experts in an advisory capacity as outlined by Mr. William Folmer and Dr. Mees. We shall be glad to provide school accommodations and instructors for training men for the photographic work of the Aviation Section here in Rochester. Dr. Mees has been instructed to proceed to Garden City, L.I., at Captain Culver's desire, to consult with him as to personnel, and then to take charge of this work as far as you require his services. We will also select some of our younger specialists and recommend them to you for service with the photographic division of the Aviation Section here and abroad.

'We are anxious to make it clear that our motive in this action is only to be of assistance to the United States Government at the present time.

'Mr. Folmer will at once proceed with the construction of experimental models of cameras to be submitted to you, and we will place blueprints of the drawings of these models at your disposal to enable you to obtain tenders for their construction from other firms as well as ourselves.

'Our special emulsion experts will proceed to Langley Field to experiment on different types of sensitive material and we will advise you as to their conclusions and as to the type which we consider desirable for aviation photography.

'Our tenders for all special apparatus and materials required for the Section will be based strictly on their cost to us, plus ten per cent to cover contingencies. It is not our intention to make any profit whatever out of these materials.'

While the company was being mobilized, Eastman wrote the Alliance Bank in Rochester: 'Put me down as one of the early subscribers [to the First Liberty Loan before it was announced] to the extent of two million five hundred thousand dollars.'

'I am glad to know that you are an investor in the War Loans of the Allies,' he wrote Colonel Strong, who was staying at Santa Barbara, California.[1] 'All through the time when the Administration was so backward about assuming its proper attitude toward the war, I felt that individual citizens ought to do what they could to help finance the Allies. . . . I should like to see this war loan oversubscribed heavily enough to give the Germans a good jolt.'

The Allies were in such dire need of financial assistance that even the American Government was 'appalled by the magnitude of the financial task,' one of the Allied War Missions cabled its Ministry. But the public everywhere responded generously to the appeal. Company employees in Rochester, the company officially, and Eastman personally subscribed $4,289,300, and Rochester, like thousands of other communities, went 'over the top' in the first practical effort which the American people were called upon to make.

'Before the American soldier, the American dollar turned the tide,' said André Tardieu, but before the summer of 1917 the tide was far from being turned as far as the determination of one hundred millions of Americans on the home fronts was concerned.

---

[1] Prior to the war, Eastman's letters were always addressed: 'Dear Heinrich.' Now he wrote: 'Dear Heinrich.' Three strokes of the pen changed the name from German to French.

After the first Allied War Missions returned, 'Lord Northcliffe arrived early in June and remained in the United States until November, perhaps the darkest period of the war and certainly the most confused and discouraging from the standpoint of America's war effort,' Professor Charles Seymour noted in 'The Intimate Papers of Colonel House.'

'A nation like the United States, unaccustomed to centralized control and unprepared for war contingencies, could not in the nature of things suddenly attempt to place itself upon a belligerent footing without producing confusion.'

The confusion was not only discouraging; it was exasperating. Officers and technicians were placed in charge of photographic mobilization when their practical knowledge was very limited. Upon one occasion a clerk from a Detroit automobile factory was given the rank of Captain and sent to Rochester to supervise the photographic work for the army. He was such a pompous patriot that Eastman was one of the few men who could listen to him talk without batting an eyelid. Repeated changes in governmental personnel was one of the causes of frequent misunderstandings.

The greatest disappointment, however, came when the War Department declined the company's initial offer to establish a school of aërial photography in Rochester.

'Our company seems to have been more unsuccessful in dealing with the Government than the Institute,' Eastman wrote Dr. Richard C. Maclaurin, president of the Massachusetts Institute of Technology. 'We offered to establish a photographic school for aviators here and furnish the equipment and materials. The reason the Government gave for turning down our offer was that it could not send men away from camps for instruction. Of course, we have facilities here that could not be obtained elsewhere, and we believe that we could teach the men much more effectively than could be done anywhere else, as we would have a staff of instructors such as they could not possibly get together in any other place. It may be that the Government is afraid to accept any favors from one of the so-called "trusts." Of course we are not paying any attention to such discrimination, but are trying to help wherever we can.

'We are especially devoting ourselves to aërial photographic work, and have already devised special emulsions and apparatus for the purpose, some of which are very promising. Among other things we have an automatic film camera which will make fifty exposures, six inches square, in succession, which are equal to anything that can be taken singly with glass plates. This instrument is going to Langley Field early next week for trial, and it is expected that it will be carried by the big Caproni machine in its flight from Washington to New York, which it is anticipated will take place very shortly. The camera has already been tried out at the Curtiss Field in Buffalo. The Allies are using plates almost exclusively, because they have been unable to get the photographic results required on films. This is partly because they have been trying to use the ordinary camera films, which are quite unsuitable for the work. They also have been unable to handle the films mechanically.' [1]

[1] 'That peaceful-looking camera, which we use on Sundays for snapping pictures of our friends and of pretty views, becomes a deadly instrument when it is brought into the military world. . . . The camera in the war zone is no longer a peaceful instrument; it is many times deadlier than its equivalent weight in high explosives.

'Why the camera should be so deadly in the war zone is due to the ease with which any object can be accurately described by means of a photograph. . . . To-day aërial reconnaissance is carried out largely with the aid of photography.' (*Scientific American*, November 24, 1917.)

Although directing the company's war work, Eastman spent most of his time at the local Red Cross headquarters, following appointment as chairman of the first war fund campaign and as chairman of the Rochester Home Defense Committee. After consultation with Henry P. Davison, national chairman, he promised to raise one million of the one hundred millions needed nationally, in Rochester. With a personal subscription of $250,000 and $50,000 each from his oldest partners, Strong and Walker, the campaign opened 'with streets ablaze with Red Cross electric signs and hangers on trolley guide wires, with Red Cross decorations in every show window on the main streets, with every clerk in the city wearing a white arm band with the slogan, "If you can't go, Give!" and with every newspaper carrying seven-column slogans on page one.' [1]

Rochester oversubscribed again. 'War fund at close of campaign one million five hundred thirty-one thousand,' he telegraphed Walker. 'These are days when one is gladder than ever to be an American,' he wrote Gifford, and in a personal letter to executives of the company in Copenhagen, Bombay, Capetown, Madrid, Cairo, Lausanne, Sydney, Petrograd, Milan, The Hague, London, Toronto, and Paris, he added that every director, stockholder, and employee 'would have subscribed to this fund even if we had not been in the war ourselves.'

From the Liberty Loan and Red Cross, public attention was directed to the slogan of the Food Administration. Placards soon appeared everywhere: 'Food Will Win the War,' and Rochester, like other cities, was more intensively cultivated than it had ever been, even when it was one of the most prosperous agricultural communities along the Erie Canal.

[1] Telegram to Seward Prosser, New York City.

'Almost everybody seems to think there will be a general shortage of food this year,' Eastman wrote the superintendent of 'Oak Lodge,' his farm and game preserve in North Carolina. 'In any case it will not be amiss to grow plenty of corn and beans, chickens, hogs, and turkeys.'

'I am plowing up my lawn [around the residence at 900 East Avenue] and planting all of the open spaces . . . in potatoes and onions,' he informed Colonel 'Henri.' 'I made up my mind that this year my gardeners could be better employed in hoeing potatoes than in cutting grass.' Thousands of citizens here and elsewhere did likewise.

In August came a letter from Herbert Hoover, asking Eastman to 'forego all profit on the raw stock [motion-picture film] which we shall require during the progress of our activities.' After Hubbell's conference with the Food Administrator, the request was granted.

In the wake of this came a request from the National Association of the Motion Picture Industry for the company's assistance in the distribution of motion pictures to American military camps in France. 'I told you that we would be pleased to furnish our facilities for handling these films in Paris without profit to ourselves,' he wrote Brulatour; 'in fact without charge except where extra expense is actually incurred. I believe that supplying the camps with motion pictures is a highly important feature in maintaining the morale of the troops and am anxious to see the enterprise conducted in as economical a manner as possible. It is with only this idea that we offer our services.

'We have also establishments in Petrograd, Moscow, and Milan, the facilities of which we are pleased to offer to the Government on the same terms, and you are authorized to make any use of this letter which seems to you advisable.'

Meanwhile, experiments were progressing in the development of an automatic film camera for aërial photography, despite the procrastination of the Signal Corps, which was having another siege of indecision in regard to aërial schools. This, however, did not interfere with the development of the automatic film camera for aërial reconnaissance.

'We have tried the camera out twice in the air at the field of the Curtiss Company near Buffalo,' Clarke was informed, 'and it worked perfectly from the start, and the second trial was made only for the purpose of correcting the focus of the lens. It operates very simply, using the air pressure generated by the plane itself. The pictures are sharp and in every way satisfactory. The speed at which the exposures can be made is variable and the starting and stopping of the camera and the speed regulation is done with one lever so that the instrument is a one-man affair, to be operated by the aviator, which is a very important thing considering the lives it will save.

'The film has a special emulsion which overcomes all the objections which you have noted. The reloading of the camera can be very easily done in the air, but in that case it would probably have to be done by an observer. We expect to send the camera for final army test at Langley Field next week, and immediately after to Pensacola [1] to let the navy test it.

'Lord Northcliffe was here day before yesterday. He was invited here to speak at the dedication of the new Chamber of Commerce building, but he did us the honor to say that he came to see the Kodak Works. I took him

[1] One of the company's experts in Washington wrote Eastman: 'Rear Admiral Howard informed me that the 20 cameras we had recently shipped from Rochester had not been distributed to the various fields, but they were entirely satisfied with the results obtained by the experimental cameras sent to Pensacola early in the year.'

to Kodak Park to luncheon with the staff, and he showed great interest in going about the place. He and his Military Secretary, Colonel Campbell Stuart, saw the new camera in operation on the floor and appeared to be much pleased. It is a very simple thing, there being no complicated mechanism to get out of order.'

On January 2 (1918), John W. Davis, Solicitor-General of the Department of Justice, appeared before the United States Supreme Court and asked that the federal suits against seven so-called 'trusts' be postponed, 'in order that the Government in this time of stress may not meet with competition from private enterprises in its financial operations and the flotations of its loans. . . . The Government must, if necessary, absorb the supply of new capital available for investment in the United States during the period of the war. This, in turn, makes it essential that unnecessary capital expenditures should be avoided in public and private enterprises.

'It is quite clear that the dissolutions which are sought in the pending cases *versus* the United Shoe Machinery Company, the International Harvester Company, the United States Steel Corporation, the Eastman Kodak Company, the American Can Company, the Quaker Oats Company, and the Corn Products Refining Company will require financial operations on a large scale if they are to be genuine and effective. Important as the remedy sought in these cases is believed to be, it must give place for the moment to the paramount needs of the hour.'

'I do not see how putting over the case can hurt us any with the Supreme Court,' Eastman wrote John G. Milburn, eminent New York counsel whom he had retained. 'Perhaps by the time the war is over, the people at large will be educated enough to modify the Sherman Law.

At any rate, I am not going to worry about it. In the mean time our Hawk-Eye factory has taken an order for 5000 gun sights . . . and is considering a project to make range-finders which will run into millions. Another of our factories, the Premo, is making tripods for the Ordnance Department; so it looks as if our factories will all have Government work to do in the very near future.'

On January 10, nearly seven months after Eastman first offered to assist the Signal Corps in the establishment of their school of aërial photography, word was received from Washington that the Government was ready to reconsider its decision and asked Eastman to restate his proposal, which he did in the following explicit detail to the War Department:

'1. We offer, without rental, for a period not exceeding six months from the 1st of February, 1918, the use of the third story of our restaurant building No. 28, known as the Assembly Hall (see photograph herewith), for barracks. This floor contains 13,450 sq. ft. and it is estimated that there is room for bunks for one thousand men and for suitable toilet rooms. The Government would have to install the bunks and the necessary toilet appliances; remove same within thirty days of the end of their occupancy and leave the building in as good condition as at present, ordinary wear and tear excepted. We feel that this work should be done under the supervision of our own engineering department and that all the fittings and plumbing fixtures should be installed under the supervision of our engineering force, to prevent permanent injury to the building and insure no interference with the use of the restaurants underneath. We would be willing to purchase these fixtures when removed, either at an agreed price or on appraisal.

'2. The Government will have to feed its force of men

but we offer the use of our kitchen, which has a capacity for feeding two thousand people at a time, and also our men's dining room on the ground floor of this same building (see photographs herewith) at all hours not interfering with the feeding of our factory force. The Government force could have the use of the restaurant in the evening as a clubroom. They would after each meal be expected to leave the room in clean condition for the next meal.

'We offer, without charge, the services of our engineering force to design, or help design, and supervise all of the work to be done, the Government to pay only the wages of the draftsmen actually employed on the job. The Government to pay all costs of construction work and equipment.

'It is expected that most of the work of construction and installation will be done by outside contractors but any work that our construction department could do to advantage we will be glad to do and charge for it at the same rate as if done for one of our own departments, that is on a basis of cost plus overhead.

'We are prepared to draw on our staff for any assistance you may need. We can loan you a certain number of specialists to assist in the instruction and to give lectures, etc., both from our scientific staff and from those sections of our employees who have to deal with the teaching of photography, a considerable number of our men being engaged on the instruction of photographers throughout the country. We would be glad to loan without charge the services of such of these men as you may require until you can replace them by men trained in the school.'

While this letter was being considered, Hiram H. Edgerton, Mayor of Rochester, offered the Government its choice of three potential flying fields, and on the 30th of January, Eastman received a telegram from General Squier: 'Your kind offer approved by Secretary of War.' This information, however, did not reach the press until spring.

'Plans have been completed for the great enlargement of facilities for training and equipping the aërial photographic force for photographing the German trenches from the skies and keeping up to the last minute the large composite picture of the whole German front,' the 'Scientific Monthly' reported in April, 1918. 'The three schools now operating at Langley Field, Fort Sill, and Cornell will be consolidated into one large school of aërial photography at Rochester, N.Y., where all the primary training will be done. Special equipment has been provided, with over one hundred instructors.

'Aërial photography has greatly developed during the war. During the single month of September, British official reports stated that 15,837 aërial photographs were taken by the British alone. No new trench can be dug, no new communication system opened up, no new batteries placed but the ever-present and infallible camera above records it for the examination of the staff below. So piercing has been the work that camouflage has been developed as a protection, thus forcing aërial photography to even greater ingenuity.

'Every sector of the front is divided into plots about half a mile square, each one numbered and entrusted to a squad of photographers, who become fully familiar with it. As fast as the photographs are made, they are developed, printed, reduced, or enlarged to a standard scale, and then fitted into their place on the large composite photograph of the sector.'

'Tuesday afternoon I received a telegram from Assistant

Secretary of the Navy [Franklin D.] Roosevelt, asking me to come down there right away, so I went that night,' Eastman informed Strong. 'It appears that the Navy Department has had trouble with ——. This concern has had some large contracts for field glasses for both the British and the American Governments, 20,000 glasses for the British and 60,000 for the U. S. They have fallen down in deliveries and quality, and the Navy Department finally decided to take them over and make the shop a branch of the Washington Navy Yard. The outfit has been put in charge of a Navy officer who does not know anything about the business, and Roosevelt wanted the Kodak Co. to take hold and reorganize it; so it has been arranged that Barnes will take the job.'

Negotiations with the Government, even as late as February, 1918, were difficult and delicate.

'It has been very slow work,' Eastman informed Alexander M. Lindsay, 'but gradually we are getting into the game, not with the expectation of making any money, but just to help along.

'As long ago as last June, we offered to do development work for the Government on a cost plus 10% basis, giving the Government the privilege of having any apparatus invented by us manufactured elsewhere if they chose. We did this in the hope that they would feel they could use us without any feeling that we were profiteering. Prejudice against big concerns seems to have had quite a foothold in the Signal Corps, and it is only recently that they have seemed to be willing to take much advantage of our offer.

'We are now very well started, however, in several directions. There have been at least four complete overturns in the division handling photographic matters, and even now the chief of the development division is a college professor who knows nothing about photography. It is our policy, of course, to give anybody who for the time being is in authority the benefit of our loyal coöperation. Seven or eight months ago, realizing that they would have to teach a lot of photographers, we offered to establish a school, at our own expense, and teach about 1000 men, in batches of 200, so they could have them for teachers when they needed them. This offer was turned down on the excuse that they could not send men away from their camps for instruction. This of course was rubbish, but nevertheless the offer was turned down and forgotten. They attempted to start a school at Langley Field, and a few weeks ago discovered that they were up against it and turned to us for help. We reminded them of our previous offer, but the officers then in charge had never heard of it. There was no time left to teach teachers, so we made them an offer to take 1000 men at a time and lend them about 50 of our experts to help do the teaching. They jumped at this offer, and have shown the greatest activity in preparations for establishing the school. You very likely saw the description of it in the Rochester papers last week, but if not I will say that they are going to have the fourth floor of our new building No. 50 for barracks and dark-rooms, and use our restaurant building for mess purposes, indoor recreation and club-rooms, at hours not interfering with our own use. Building No. 50 stands on the Hanford Landing Road, parallel with Lake Avenue, and just back of our athletic field. An entrance will be made admitting the soldiers from Lake Avenue and they will walk around outside the plant, along Lake Avenue and the Ridge Road, to the restaurant building, so they will not have to go through the plant. The half-mile walk will be part of their exercise. We give the space free of charge and the Government is letting the contract for the work of fitting up the barracks, mostly carpenter and plumbing work, to Hopeman & Sons. We will feed the men on a cost basis. It is expected that the first batch of men, about 800, will be at Kodak Park by the 15th of March, and that the fourth batch will be finished by the middle of July. After that probably the school will be moved to one of the big flying fields.

'We had a great deal of difficulty in finding out what the Signal Corps wanted in the way of cameras, but we have carried along development of the work on our own hook and are now pretty well fixed to turn out everything that is wanted, from tripods to lenses. We have a contract for $600,000 or $700,000 worth of cellulose acetate and are expecting another order shortly for a slightly larger amount. At the Hawk-Eye Works we are starting on an order for 5000 gun sights, which will amount to between $300,000 and $400,000. These are all comparatively small items, but they have started pretty nearly all of our factories on some war work.

'One of the rows in the Signal Corps recently involved the name of the Kodak Company, and I have seen some newspaper items which were very offensive. If you have seen them, pay no attention to them. To show the way we now stand with the Corps, I quote from a letter just received from Lieutenant-Colonel Horner: "The management of the Equipment Division of the Signal Corps is more than satisfied with the broad-gauged American way which you and your Company have offered to assist us and are assisting us."

'Frank S. Noble has just accepted an appointment from the Ordnance Department, Production Division, to have charge of speeding up the production [in Northern New York] on all Government contracts. Lewis B. Jones is in the Publicity Division [of the Committee on Public Information] and spends three days a week in New York.[1] Schuyler Colfax is wearing a Major's uniform and spends about all his time in the service. Our Research Laboratory has lost quite a number of men and is devoting most of its time to Government work.'

For some time scientists engaged by the Submarine Defense Association, under the direction of Lindon W. Bates, had been conducting experiments to determine the best methods of camouflaging all types of ships. At the beginning of the war this subject had been studied by artists, but, as it was primarily a question of optics and physics, Eastman had lent Loyd A. Jones, of the research forces, to that Association. One of his early contributions was the invention of a visibility meter, which measured scientifically the visibility of any object on the ocean.

Sufficient progress had been made through these studies in New York City and down the bay to determine that it was impossible to make any vessel absolutely invisible under all conditions of weather and light on the high seas. For this reason an intensive study of the deceptive type of protective coloration was undertaken.

Eastman recorded the formal proposal in a letter to Captain W. R. Du Bose, of the Navy Department:

'We desire to inform you that we shall be glad to place at the disposal of the Navy Department for use in research on camouflage work certain sections of the Physics Department of our Research Laboratory as follows:

[1] Jones was advertising manager before being advanced to the position of vice-president in charge of sales policies. March 3, 1919, Eastman wrote the Advertising Bureau, Liberty Loan Committee, New York City: 'We did, during the stress of war, give $30,000 worth of magazine space in one lump to the Government, through the Division of Advertising, and also made some smaller donations . . . but it is our feeling that the Government should buy its advertising space just as it buys any other commodity.'

'1. The large physical laboratory at present used for spectroscopic work.

'2. The dark-room attached to this used for visibility work.

'3. In addition to these specific rooms the use of the photometer room as it may be required, and of such other instruments in the laboratory as are needed for the work.'

To this letter Secretary Daniels replied on the 25th:

'The Department notes from your letter of February 18th that you offer the Navy Department in research on camouflage work use of certain sections of the Physics Department of your Research Laboratory under the following conditions:

'1. The work to be under the direction of Mr. L. A. Jones.

'2. Naval men working in the laboratory must conform to the general regulations of the laboratory and of Kodak Park Works.

'The Department appreciates highly your patriotic offer of your Research Laboratory and accepts the offer under the conditions above named.

'Mr. L. A. Jones has been offered a commission as a Naval Constructor with the rank of Lieutenant in the Reserve Force, and will, on acceptance thereof, be detailed for duty in Rochester for Camouflage Experimental Work. The Department also desires to detail such other assistants as may be considered necessary.

'Within the next week or ten days the Department intends sending an Officer from the Bureau of Construction and Repair, Naval Constructor W. R. Du Bose, to confer with your company relative to details of use of the laboratory for this Naval work.'

Jones and his staff constructed at the Park a complete

'experimental ocean,' reproducing, by means of a large tank, a movable sky, miniature ships, and artificial lights, a working model, where the various types of deceptive coloration of ships could be studied through a submarine periscope. These observations and studies evolved eventually a scientific scheme of camouflage which was placed at the service of the United States and Allied authorities.

In the mean time the Hawk-Eye Works 'succeeded in producing the best lens for aërial photography that was ever tested by the Signal Corps. Folmer has just completed a camera for photographing soldiers and workmen in munition plants' (for identification purposes), Eastman informed Strong. 'The picture is taken on a spool of motion-picture film and afterwards printed on a card. . . . The work can be done as fast as the men can step into place and step out again . . .' and when Secretary of the Treasury William G. McAdoo was in Rochester, 'we had him down to Kodak Park in the morning. As we went through one of the rooms, they were using the new identification camera and we had the party photographed. . . . I enclose one of the pictures. McAdoo was very much impressed. He told Harry Brewster that the Kodak plant was one of the most important that the Government had. He made an excellent speech at the Chamber of Commerce, which I heard, and I am told that he made an equally good one at Convention Hall, where there was an enormous crowd to greet him.'

Preliminary preparations were soon under way again for the second appeal of the American Red Cross, but Eastman was disturbed when he received the February (1918) number of the 'Red Cross Magazine,' and wrote Chairman Davison:

'Bishop Hickey showed me this morning the February

Red Cross Magazine and called my attention to Rudyard
Kipling's poem "The Holy War" and the stanza on the
49th page, as follows:

> ' "Emanuel's vanguard dying
> For right and not for rights;
> My Lord Apollyon lying
> To the stall-fed Stockholmites;
> The Pope, the swithering Neutrals,
> The Kaiser and his Gott —
> Their rôles, their goals, their naked souls —
> He knew and drew the lot!"

'He says that his people resent and that he resents the
reference to the Pope, and while the publication will not
interfere with his interest in the Red Cross, he thinks it
will tend to antagonize Catholics. The matter has already been noticed in some of the Catholic publications
and was brought to his attention through a Buffalo paper
having quite a large circulation. He feels sure that there
was no intention on the part of the Red Cross Management to allow anything offensive to be published and
hopes that something can be said in the next issue to
make that plain to the rank and file. I fully concur, as
I have no doubt that you will, in the opinion that it is
unwise to allow anything in the Red Cross Magazine that
will needlessly antagonize any of the elements upon
which the Red Cross is depending for support. The
Catholics here, headed by Bishop Hickey, have given the
Red Cross their whole-hearted coöperation, and while
the Bishop is broad-minded enough not to be affected by
any such incident, it certainly will make it harder for him
to work up enthusiasm among his people during the next
drive.'

Although the days were getting longer they were becoming dark and murky from a military standpoint. The
enemy had launched its great offensive on the Western

Front in France in March, 1918, before the American troops were ready to take over their sector of the battle line. When the crisis was reached, General Pershing made his memorable call upon Marshal Foch and placed at his disposal the first unit of three hundred thousand young Americans. When Clemenceau, Lloyd George, and Orlando cabled Washington in June, 'there is great danger of the war being lost unless the numerical inferiority of the Allies can be remedied as rapidly as possible by the advent of American troops,' the United States Government was, for the first time, exceeding its promised quota of 120,000 soldiers each month. During May, June, and July the Navy transported safely 949,601 men, and among them were the first 'graduates' of the Rochester School of Aërial Photography.

While the military and naval forces were forging ahead, the Government was calling upon the public for greater help and larger sacrifices. The third Liberty Loan was launched and oversubscribed and the Nation was on the eve of another campaign, that of the United War Fund, for the Red Cross, Salvation Army, Knights of Columbus, Y.M.C.A., Y.W.C.A., the Young Men's Hebrew Association, and other societies engaged in war work.

By May, the War Chest Drive was consuming most of Eastman's attention, as he concentrated again upon measures to insure a large total from Rochester. Although his previous efforts had attracted national attention, and although asked by Governor Charles S. Whitman, John D. Rockefeller, Jr., Judge E. H. Gary, of the United States Steel Corporation, Dr. John R. Mott, of the Young Men's Christian Association, and many other persons to serve on national committees and direct national or state-wide efforts of various organizations, he declined them all. The Home Front was his particular sector.

In the raising of large sums for war philanthropy, Eastman insisted publicly upon the wealthy citizens of the
city assuming the leadership. He opposed the policy of
various large corporations of declaring special dividends
for Red Cross, on the ground that it enabled 'slackers' to
escape giving as much as they should, when their incomes
were based only partially upon corporate dividends.

On May 28, 1918, Rochester newspapers announced
108,927 individual gifts totaling $4,815,502.97 to the War
Chest. Eastman had contributed $100,000 for the ex-
penses and $500,000 to the fund. 'The assemblage went
fairly wild when the announcement was made,' reported
the 'Post-Express,' 'and it was some time before Mr.
Eastman, who had arisen, could make himself heard.

' "In the first place, my friends," he said, "you all know
just as well as I know that the real giver is that poor
woman who took over the family washing and thereby
saved an additional fifty cents a week in order that she
might put it in this fund. That is the real giver.

' "This is a wonderful organization [there were 5000
workers under the general direction of Harry P. Ware-
heim], and I want to thank you all for the work that you
have done to make this campaign a success.

' "I just want to make a little confession," he added.
"Some people have said they did not want to give because the campaigners were all paid [laughter], and I'll
admit here and now that I have been paid, and paid
in full — with the satisfaction of feeling that I've been
allowed to be a leader in this great organization. And
sometimes it seemed as if I was not much of a leader, but
just a little boy being pulled along by all the rest of you." '

'The campaign ended in a blaze of glory,' Eastman
wrote his cousin Almon Eastman in Waterville. 'A few
of the ultra-conservatives go so far as to say that we

raised too much money, but I reckon it will all be needed before the year is ended. The prod the slackers got was hard, as you perhaps noticed, but there are still some left. Their hides have not been pierced yet, but we hope to get them next year. I never had more fun in working out anything in my life.'

The American Red Cross received two million dollars of this sum, which was nearly three times Rochester's quota.

'Rochester seems to hold the record,' read a postscript on a letter from Benjamin Strong, Jr., Governor of the Federal Reserve Bank in New York City.

By the spring of 1918, chemical research in the United States was in difficulties owing to the control which Germany had of the fine chemicals used for experimental purposes in the university and industrial laboratories in this country. Ever since Eastman's public gift of $300,-000 in June, 1916, to the chemical engineering department of the Massachusetts Institute of Technology, he had received numerous inquiries in regard to chemical research in the United States, chiefly from the National Research Council and the American Chemical Society, so that he was prepared to act favorably upon Dr. Mees's recommendations of June 28:

'With regard to our proposal that we should establish a department in the Laboratory for the preparation of synthetic organic reagents and should place these reagents on the market in order to supply the needs of research workers in organic chemistry. The situation in this country is that the only source of supply of such chemicals, all of which were previously obtained from Germany, lies in the work done at the University of Illinois which was initiated by Dr. [C. G.] Derick, now of the National Aniline Company at Buffalo, and carried on by Dr. [Roger] Adams, now doing research on gas warfare at the American University, Washington.

'In order to find out how our proposals would be received, Dr. Clarke has interviewed Dr. Derick, Dr. Adams and Colonel Bogert, who is the head of the Chemical Research Section of the Army, and who would represent the Government in relation to the supply of organic chemicals.

'Colonel Bogert was extremely sympathetic to the proposal that we should go into the preparation and supply of these chemicals, he said that he considered that it would be a most useful and patriotic service at the present time, and that the government would regard it as an essential war industry and would grant all facilities for its prosecution, even to the point of releasing men from the army if that were found to be necessary. As will be seen later this will not be necessary. Dr. Derick was also anxious to see us take the matter up and regarded it as a valuable service. He will do all that he can to assist us.

'Dr. Adams was most favorably impressed with the idea and has promised to place at our disposal the valuable methods of preparation for over sixty different substances which they have worked out at Illinois, and to refer to us orders for these materials coming from firms requiring them for analytical work. He would much prefer that the supply of such chemicals should be in the hands of a commercial undertaking. He had already approached the National Aniline and Du Pont Companies in the matter without success.

'Dr. Clarke has discussed the matter with some other chemists, notably those of the Du Pont Company and the Hercules Powder Company, who have promised their coöperation and supply of intermediate compounds.

'The conclusions that we have reached as to the present conditions may be summarized as follows:

'(1) The continuance of effective research in pure organic chemistry in this country is largely dependent upon the establishment of a satisfactory source of synthetic reagents.

'(2) No such source is at present in sight. It is unlikely that coöperation between the universities will provide a satisfactory supply and the large dye producing companies, who might possibly be expected to take the matter up, are so busy that it will be quite impossible for them to do anything in the matter for some years.

'(3) Unless something is done immediately organic research will languish and after the war we shall again be dependent upon the German houses for a supply of organic reagents.

'(4) While the business cannot be considered as likely to be profitable the probability is that after it is established it will pay for its own cost.

'(5) Owing to the presence with us of Dr. Clarke and to the high reputation which the Company's products bear, we are in a very favorable condition to develop the production and supply of these chemicals as a branch of the work of the Laboratory.'

In this manner Eastman supported another contribution to the progress of national war work by establishing the first adequate synthetic organic chemical laboratory in the United States. In 1886, he was one of the first manufacturers in this country to employ a chemist to devote his time entirely to research. To-day, thirty-two years later, he is still in the vanguard of industrial research and in a position to assist all university and industrial laboratories to overcome the loss of fine chemicals previously imported from Germany.[1]

In July, Eastman was invited by the British War Mission to 'take a flight in the Handley-Page bomber which is being manufactured in Elizabeth,' he wrote Babbott. 'When I got there I found that they were making some repairs. These took longer than was expected, and it was not until six o'clock that we were ready to fly. It was a wonderful experience and I felt repaid. . . . The flight was almost a chance of a lifetime, because I was allowed to stand in the prow where the two machine guns usually are, and directly in front of the pilot and the observer. The machine carried five men, including myself. It sure seemed to me as if I could run it myself with a little instruction.'

[1] In September, 1921, at the international meeting of the Society of Chemical Industries in Montreal, the members passed a vote of thanks to the Eastman Kodak Company for rendering available synthetic organic chemicals to the Western Hemisphere. At this time the laboratory furnished more than one thousand different chemicals to the American and Canadian markets. To-day more than two thousand are produced.

February 10, 1926, Francis P. Garvin, president of the American Chemical Foundation, speaking at the Rochester Chamber of Commerce, said:

'Although Germany made its great industrial progress from 1870 to the beginning of the World War mainly upon the services of the chemists, and although it had become proverbial throughout the world that the German chemist was the superior of the chemists of all other countries, it was not so. The only difference between the progress of Germany and what might have been the progress of this country was the superiority of the boards of directors of German business concerns over the boards of American concerns; the superiority of German Chambers of Commerce over ours; of German bankers over controlled industries here; and that superiority consisted first in the knowledge of the importance of the relation of chemistry to industrial and national life and in the confidence which that knowledge gave them to spend money upon research.

'In Rochester the neglect of the past has been realized to a greater extent than in any city in America.

'All of our laboratories were dependent for all their fine or experimental chemicals upon Germany. Now, to the number of more than 2000, they are made of better and purer quality and cheaper price through the unselfish, patriotic services of your first and greatest citizen, George Eastman.'

By the time the American Expeditionary Force, united under General Pershing, launched its attack upon the 'Hindenburg Line,' one sector of the Home Front in Rochester, under Lovejoy's direction as general manager, were producing 3600 pounds of cellulose acetate per day for airplanes and gas masks. It was manufacturing all types of aeroplane cameras and film, both for motion pictures and 'still' exposures. It was making aeroplane gun sights and trench periscopes, a new X-ray film for medical diagnosis, approved by the chief medical officers of the army and navy. Its scientists had invented a new liquid fuel for the navy. One thousand men each month were being trained in the aërial photographic school with such conspicuous success that the army engineers asked the company to establish a photographic school near Washington where photographers, other than those engaged in aërial observation and study, could be trained for the A.E.F.

By summer, America's vast resources of men and materials were crossing the Atlantic in endless streams. Eastman and his associates were making frequent trips to Washington in their endeavor to find other tasks. 'I have an appointment with the War Industries Board and hope to find something additional . . . that we can handle to good advantage for the Government,' he reported to Baker. 'Of course the profits will be very small, but that does not cut any figure these days. If we can do anything to help knock out the . . . that ought to satisfy us'; and when Baker's letter from Australia, passing his *en route* to the Antipodes, informed him that there was a prospect of double income taxes in that country for 'every taxpayer' who did not make adequate contributions to war loans, Eastman replied:

'In discussing with the authorities any proportion

which we ought to subscribe to any of these loans, you should bear in mind that we shall have to pay this year to the United States Government probably over 50% of our net earnings (including dividends from Australian Co.). Basing their estimates on the House Bill which is now before the Senate for confirmation, Price, Waterhouse have figured that our taxes this year will amount to $10,500,000; hence it seems to me it would be fairer if the subscription were made by Kodak Australasia than by us as shareholders, providing that could be taken into consideration in figuring your and Rouse's personal subscriptions. Of course you understand that we are not pikers in this war proposition. This company probably holds one of the largest proportions of war securities of any big corporation in this country. We have at the present moment $7,900,000 of the Allied war loans and $9,500,000 of Treasury Certificates, making about $17,-400,000 total war securities. We are putting every cent of cash not needed for current use into Treasury Certificates.'[1]

'I do not think the Senate Finance Committee is really antagonistic to this company,' he answered a letter from Brulatour on taxes. 'It simply wants to get all our money that it can. I cannot see that they need worry, because under the proposed Excess Profits tax they would get about half of it and on the Excess Income tax they would get about 70 or 80% of what I get out of it. I figure that these two taxes superimposed, as far as I am concerned personally, would leave only about 15%. I cannot say that I object.'

During October, 1918, when peace discussions and

---

[1] The final recapitulation in 1921 showed that Eastman personally backed the American and Allied Governments with $27,412,900 and the company with $19,816,300, a total of $47,229,200.

rumors were rife, Eastman's friends besieged him with their opinions. His attitude was the same to all correspondents, and is forcefully put in a few lines to Dr. W. T. Hornaday, of the New York Zoölogical Park (the famous Bronx Zoo), whom Eastman had been helping for many years in his campaign to conserve America's wild game. 'I have always agreed with you,' he replied to Dr. Hornaday, 'but as to advocating now a twenty-five-year boycott of the Germans, I teetotally disagree with you, for the very simple reason that I do not think anybody knows at the present time just what ought to be done with them. The only thing I am anxious about now is that they should be compelled to surrender unconditionally. When they do that, I think the situation ought to be handled scientifically rather than emotionally.'

Through the persuasion of George W. Perkins, Cleveland H. Dodge, and John D. Rockefeller, Jr., at a luncheon in New York City, Eastman accepted the chairmanship for the State for the $170,000,000 drive of the United War Work Campaign.

Eastman himself was still willing to go on until the first reports of the Armistice were received from the United Press Association three days before the peace was formally concluded, when he rejoiced with every one else.

'At this moment of writing we are waiting eagerly for the peace terms of the Allies,' he wrote a friend in Paris. 'I cannot believe that any influence from this side will be allowed to lessen their stringency. The American public is demanding unconditional surrender, not from any bloodthirstiness, but from a belated understanding that the Germans must be convinced that their scheme cannot be put over the world.'

'Rochester was certainly an excited place from the

time the whistles began to blow until late in the evening,' Eastman wrote Albert B. Eastwood, who was serving the Red Cross in Washington, D.C. 'The populace would not pay any attention to denials, I suppose because they knew in their hearts that the report must be more than half true, anyway. When the armistice is signed, we probably will not be able to have another such an exuberant manifestation of joy, but satisfaction will be there just the same. Speaking of exuberance, Miss Whitney was in the elevator going down to lunch just after we received the report over the telephone, but before the whistles began to blow. She announced it to a group of girls who were on the car. One of them threw up her hands and yelled, "Ain't it swell?"'

The end of the war, however, did not bring tranquillity to either business or Government, and one would hardly classify conditions as 'swell.' There was soon to be a trying period of reconstruction and new orientation, of Bolshevist agitation and 'normalcy' before the Nation was to experience a bounteous era of prosperity.[1]

[1] The following citation was received in July, 1920:

THE WAR DEPARTMENT OF THE
UNITED STATES OF AMERICA

Recognizes in this award for distinguished service the loyalty energy and efficiency in the performance

of the War Work by which
Eastman Kodak Company

aided materially in obtaining victory for the arms of the United States of America in the war with the Imperial German Government and the Imperial and Royal Austro-Hungarian Government

NEWTON D. BAKER   B. CROWELL
Secretary of War   *Assistant Secretary of War*
                                    Director of Munitions

CHAPTER IX

THE MASSACHUSETTS INSTITUTE OF TECHNOLOGY

THROUGHOUT these active years, both before and during the World War, Eastman's interest in education and community life broadened with the expansion of his business and the compass of his imagination.

The first contribution to education was made in 1887, when he sent fifty dollars to the Mechanics Institute of Rochester. It was a modest sum, but it was the genesis of his giving. His salary as treasurer of the company at the time was under sixty dollars a week.

Even at this early period in his career, he had strong convictions in regard to the relationship of the individual to the community. In three early letters he laid the foundation stones for his life-work in philanthropy. The first was sent to Mrs. Strong, wife of the genial Colonel and a devout Presbyterian.

'Your letter is received, and I thank you for it,' Eastman wrote, March 19, 1886. 'It caused no surprise, for I know and appreciate the good motives that prompted it. When I went to Sunday School two things were taught, man's duty toward God and man's duty toward man. It is in the performance of this latter duty, as interpreted through the Christian religion, that the human character shows its most charming qualities and causes its motives to be respected even when its aims do not entirely meet the views of the observer.

'I am afraid it would pain you and I am sure it would do no good for me to try to answer your questions. As to the obstacles existing against embracing the faith, they are strong, but I am conscious that they may be removed by circumstances at some future time, but it is not probable that any further investigation or reasoning on my part could remove them at the present time.'

The second and third letters related to the Mechanics Institute. This trade school was founded in 1885 by a group of Rochester citizens under the leadership of Captain Henry Lomb, one of the founders of the Bausch and Lomb Optical Company. In 1891, when the school was merged with the Rochester Athenæum (founded in 1829), Captain Lomb invited Eastman to attend a meeting of business men to discuss the future of the Institute. Afterward, Eastman wrote his two partners, Strong and Walker, identical letters:

'The Mechanics Institute has decided to buy the entire block of ground extending from Spring Street to the canal and from Washington St. to the alley. . . . The whole cost of the property will be $40,000 or $42,000. They will want to raise $50,000 or $75,000 more for the first lot of buildings. Wm. S. Kimball at the meeting this week offered to double his subscription of $5000 if some other subscriber would do the same. I think I will call him. I would like very much to see you put your name down for $5000. You have made a good deal of money in Rochester, and it would not do you any harm in the eyes of the people to let go of a little of it in the interests of an institution which will surely be a benefit to your property here. Looking at it from a cold business standpoint, I think it would be a good investment.'"

Eastman had, as usual, made up his own mind, and in making his first substantial contribution, in view of his own income at the time, he wrote the Trustees:

'I agree with you that the time has come to make a determined effort to put the Mechanics Institute on a solid foundation.

'The results already shown, although obtained under unfavorable conditions, demonstrate the practicability of the scheme and afford a good indication of what could be accomplished by the Institute if it had the means at its command to broaden its scope to the lines of similar institutions in other places.

'I believe that the best investment the manufacturers, merchants, and property owners of this city can make is to liberally endow the Institute and enable it to carry out the plans of its founders to provide technical instruction at home for our young men and women who have to earn their own living, and who, if shown how to use their hands and brains together, can do better work and get more money for it than they otherwise could.

'If given its full scope there is hardly an industry in this city that would not soon feel the effects of the benefit conferred by the Institute, and Rochester would become wider known than ever for the excellence of its manufactures and the skill of its workmen.

'With a view to seconding your efforts I propose to be one of ten persons who will subscribe *at once* five thousand dollars each to the permanent or building fund of the Institute.

'My friend, Mr. William Hall Walker, formerly of this city, but now residing in London, has authorized me to subscribe in his name five thousand dollars for the same purpose and under the same conditions. Mr. Walker writes me that he has been very much interested in the Institute project through talks with Mr. Lomb, and that both as a practical mechanic and as a manufacturer he foresees the vast benefit such an institution will prove to Rochester and he hopes to see it succeed.'

It was during this same period that Eastman became

interested in the Massachusetts Institute of Technology. While formulating plans for a new plant outside the city of Rochester, he communicated with Technology and employed Darragh de Lancey, of the class of 1890, placing him in charge of the first construction work at Kodak Park.

In 1891, searching for another research chemist, Eastman asked Dr. Drown, the distinguished Professor of Analytical Chemistry at the Boston institution, for recommendations, adding that he had 'a great deal of confidence in the material you turn out at your institution.' During the next few years Eastman engaged Lovejoy, Haste, and other 'Tech men.' Enthusiasm for this 'material' increased to such an extent that he began to read the annual reports of President Richard C. Maclaurin and study that system of technical education. This continued for nearly two decades, while he observed the industrial asset value of technically trained men and posted himself in the history of that institution.

The foundation of the Massachusetts Institute of Technology was laid by Professor William Barton Rogers, who, in 1860, presented to the Legislature of the Commonwealth of Massachusetts a memorial suggesting the early establishment of 'a comprehensive Polytechnic College, furnishing a complete system of industrial education supplementary to the general training of other institutions and fitted to equip its students with every scientific and technical principle applicable to the industrial pursuits of the age.'

On April 10, 1861, the Institute was incorporated under an Act passed by the General Court of the State, 'for the purpose of instituting and maintaining a society of arts, a museum of arts, and a school of industrial science, and aiding generally by suitable means the advancement, development and practical application of science in connection with arts, agriculture, manufactures and commerce.'

Although the first organization meeting was held the following year, the Civil War led to the postponement of the School of Industrial Science until February 20, 1865, when fifteen students were registered.

'The most striking thing about Rogers,' according to Dr. Richard C. Maclaurin, president of the Institute, 'was the breadth of his vision and the large view that he had of the Institute's place in the industrial development of America. It was, of course, a very small thing in his day, but he looked forward with clear vision to its future growth. Observe that he saw the Massachusetts Institute of Technology as much more than a school of industrial science, and that he had incorporated in its charter a statement that it was founded for the purpose of instituting and maintaining a school of industrial science, and "aiding generally by suitable means the advancement, development and practical application of science in connection with the arts, manufactures and commerce." The Technology plan enables the Institute to do this by setting up the right kind of an organization to give industrial corporations the information that they want regarding men and scientific processes that are applicable to their industry. A mere school might not be able to do this, but an institution conceived so broadly as Technology is well adapted for this great end.'

After following closely Dr. Maclaurin's administration and reports for many years, Eastman told Lovejoy one day that he would like to meet the President of his *alma mater*. Lovejoy knew this was more than a fortuitous remark and communicated at once with President Maclaurin. Within a few days 'Mr. Eastman' received the following letter. As he was, at the time, a complete stranger to the educational world, it is not surprising if Dr. Maclaurin addressed him without indicating whether or not he knew his first name. Succeeding letters, obviously, were not addressed so generally. However, it made not the slightest difference, for, as it developed, it was not 'Mr. Eastman,' anyway, but 'Mr. Smith.'

The morning of March 1, 1912, Eastman opened the following four-page communication:

MASSACHUSETTS INSTITUTE OF TECHNOLOGY
OFFICE OF THE PRESIDENT

DEAR SIR:

A few weeks ago I had the pleasure of spending a morning on a visit to your Works at Kodak Park, and was so much impressed by what I saw that in public addresses and private discussions ever since, I have referred to these Works as a striking illustration of how a great modern industry has been built up by the application of scientific methods to manufacturing, business and the arrangement of buildings. My experience in Rochester was incidental to a visit to Alumni Associations of Technology in various states — a visit projected with the object of interesting the alumni of this Institute in the great problems of development with which it is now confronted.

The Institute was founded fifty years ago for the purpose of training men to apply modern science to industry in all its phases. It began in a modest way and has steadily grown in size and influence until to-day its power is felt all over the land, and its graduates are found everywhere contributing to the national wealth by their trained intelligence and skill. It began as a local institution, but is now a national one, with students in large numbers from every state in the Union, and over a hundred from foreign countries. The alumni, who know it best, are enthusiastic as to its accomplishments, but they may perhaps be too near to take a proper perspective of its real importance. However, there is no lack of testimony ·from unprejudiced sources as to the value of the Institute's training. Thus, Sir William Mather, a prominent business man in England, reported to a Royal Commission in London with reference to this Institute, as follows:

'The spirit and energy of the students, their conspicuous practical knowledge, the thoroughness with which their scientific knowledge is tested in the course of instruction, and the power of adaptation and resource they possess on entering workshops and manufactories, railroads, or mines, public works and constructive engineering — all these fruits of the training of this Institute are, so far as I have seen, not equalled on the Continent. I think these are the qualities we need in England.'

A few months ago, Dr. Bryce, a distinguished educator from Canada, stated that after visiting all the leading technical institutions in the world, he could say unhesitatingly that no technological school was to be found anywhere ahead of the Massachusetts Institute of Technology. And Mr. Edison has very recently said: 'For forty years I have been employing young men. I have taken them immediately upon graduation from technical schools and set them to work in my mills and I have found that the graduates of the Boston Tech have a better, more practical, more useful, knowledge as a class than graduates of any other school in the country. If every state in the Union had such a technical school, it would be a great thing for this country. It would bring our national problems far nearer to solution, it would improve our business conditions, and it would teach us how to grapple with the evils of the day in a competent and sane manner. There is no question but that the Massachusetts Institute of Technology is the best technical school in the country.'

The steady growth of the prestige of the Institute has had the natural effect of increasing its numbers beyond the limits of its capacity, in spite of its high fees, until to-day its present equipment is inadequate for the demands that are made upon it. It has therefore been deemed expedient to provide adequately for future expansion by removing the Institute to a new site, where it can grow freely. A site of fifty acres has been purchased in the very center of greater Boston — a tract of land with a frontage of a third of a mile on the Charles River Basin. This site is ideal for the Institute's purposes — near to the heart of things, wonderfully accessible from all points of the city and surrounding country, and occupying a position that commands the public view and must command it for all time. Having purchased this site, we are now making a careful study of the problem of re-building, and have been fortunate in securing the services of one of the most prominent engineers of the country — Mr. John R. Freeman — to assist us with the engineering phases of that problem. We realize that we can learn much from commercial buildings of the better type, in the erection of buildings that are carefully planned so as to meet the actual needs of the Institute. These buildings must be worthy of a great institution of learning, but, though dignified, they must be simple, and they must be arranged so as to give the maximum of convenience for the minimum of cost, due attention being given to fundamental problems of lighting, heating, ventilation and the like. In carrying out this work of re-building, we shall have the assistance of an enthusiastic body of alumni, but the growth of the Institute has been so marked in recent years that considerably more than half its graduates have gone forth within the last decade. This means that they are a very young body of men, and consequently that few are in a position to help in any very large way financially. Fortunately, there are in the country men of large vision who appreciate the national importance of such institutions, and are ready to help where they are convinced that encouragement is deserved. A recent communication from Mr. Frank W. Lovejoy suggests that you may be ready to lend a helping hand, and I am writing to say that I should welcome an opportunity of placing our plans before you. I should gladly visit Rochester, if a time could be arranged that would be mutually convenient.

> Yours sincerely
> RICHARD C. MACLAURIN

February 29, 1912.
MR. EASTMAN,
  Eastman Kodak Company,
    Rochester, N.Y.

Eastman replied, suggesting a meeting at the Hotel Belmont in New York City. Here the distinguished educator and the self-educated business man met for the first time, Eastman with his Oriental capacity to conceal his thoughts, and Maclaurin with his Occidental enthusiasm and confidence. The latter related the story of Technology's half-century of educational effort, cramped now by a lack of adequate facilities and funds. He painted his picture on such a vast canvas that it appealed to Eastman's imagination, so much so that he almost missed the midnight express back to Rochester.

If Dr. Maclaurin failed to sleep at all that night, it would not be surprising, for he had found 'Tech's Santa Claus,' [1] a man who wanted to help, and asked nothing in return, not even public or private recognition.

'When I first came to Technology,' Dr. Maclaurin recalled later, 'and had time to take observations, I found that the Institute was in the doldrums. It wanted to move, but couldn't get a move on. It was clear that some one was needed to give a real push; and so, after consultation with my colleagues, I went to describe the situation to [T.] Coleman du Pont [then President of the Alumni Association]. I described the broad features of our condition and said that we must move to a new site. He asked what sites were under consideration and wanted a brief description of each.

'The first one I mentioned was twenty-five acres in area. He said: "Can't you double it?" and I said: "Not this particular site." "Well," he said, "I don't like the look of twenty-five acres. It seems to me too small. Almost invariably when a man comes to me to approve plans for a new factory [du Pont was then President of the du Pont Company], I tell him to double the size of everything, and almost invariably I wish afterward that I had used a larger factor of safety. Technology will occupy a great position in the future and must have room to grow. I don't feel much attracted by twenty-five acres, but I should be interested in fifty."

'I agreed with his policy, but told him, of course, that the main obstacle was cost. "What would fifty acres cost?" he asked. I told him, "Three quarters of a million," and he said he would contribute half a million.'

The second man Dr. Maclaurin interviewed, he added, was Eastman. 'He replied, suggesting a date

[1] *Boston Sunday Post*, January 11, 1920.

for our meeting, and we dined and spent an evening together in New York, going over the whole matter carefully and making the best estimates that were possible at that early stage as to the probable cost of the various portions of our undertaking. At this meeting, as at many others since, I could not fail to be impressed with his capacity to go to the heart of a problem quickly and see immediately what the main points are and to keep to those points in later discussion. He was interested in Technology's problems, but made it clear that his continued interest would depend upon its problems being tackled in a bold way and in a liberal spirit. . . . He likes things done well, but does not think they are well done unless they are done economically.'

Eastman's first commitment, recorded in a formal letter March 6, 1912, was accompanied by a personal note that his name was not to be made public or mentioned to any one.

'In confirmation of our conversation in New York yesterday, this is to say that I am prepared to give the Institute, as a building fund, the sum of two and one half millions of dollars; the money to be used exclusively in building suitable buildings for the Institute on the new property which has been acquired by the Institute on Massachusetts Avenue, fronting on the Charles River Basin.

'By "buildings" I mean not only the structure, but the necessary heating, lighting, and plumbing, but expenditures for items outside of buildings, such as grading, roadways, drainage, water mains, conduits, and subways, and for furniture, etc., not to be included.

'No conditions are made as to the architecture of the buildings to be constructed, but this subscription has been made after listening to your expressions as to the inappropriateness of the Institute indulging in any extravagant architectural features and the desirability of getting breadth of effect, more by the proper grouping and general design of the buildings than by elaborate details. One of the objects of this subscription is to enable the Institute to lay out and treat the undertaking as a whole, thereby possibly getting better results than if the buildings were erected at widely different dates.'

When Dr. Maclaurin informed the Executive Committee of the gift, the largest in the history of the institution, he added that the man's name was 'Smith,' just 'Smith,' he said, with scarcely a twinkle in his eyes, and then he hastened to write Eastman that there would be no clues as to his identity in Boston.

'What I desire to avoid as far as possible,' 'Smith' replied, 'is the notoriety which oftentimes accompanies such gifts.'

Of course the gift itself was not a secret. It was too valuable as a campaign wedge to justify concealment, and as soon as it was announced a 'great guessing competition' started and 'ran the rounds of the newspapers of the country.' The competition was revived as a popular pastime on every occasion when another substantial contribution by 'Smith' was announced. 'At the time of the dedication of our new buildings,' Dr. Maclaurin recalled later, 'suspicion centered on two New York millionaires, each of whom strongly suspected the other. It is said that they dined together to have it out, but separated without having discovered any secrets and with enlarged respect for the bluffing power of the other. As a matter of fact neither was "Mr. Smith." In another center a man, not "Mr. Smith," claimed to be he, and in still another a woman made it known to her friends that she was certain that "Mr. Smith" was her husband, although here she was in error.'

'I have seen some of the clippings from the Boston papers containing accounts of the attempts to locate the donor and have found them very amusing,' Eastman wrote Dr. Maclaurin. 'The matter has quieted down now so that it looks as if the secret might be kept for some time yet, perhaps indefinitely. I am sure it would cause me considerable annoyance if my connection with the affair were made known, and as I cannot see any particular advantage to be gained by so doing I shall be happy to let the matter stand as it now is.

'I do not see why you should not take all the time necessary to perfect your plans before building, particularly as I have fixed it so that in case of my death you will get the money just the same. It is not often that an old institution has a chance to plan an entirely new outfit, and it is evident that there is an opportunity to obtain a very high degree of efficiency in the layout, which, with all the talent at your command, you will no doubt succeed in doing.'

Ever since the foundation of the American Government, industry and education have been closely linked, not only through the industrial acquisition of college and university graduates, but in a greater degree to the scientific contributions which the university laboratories have made to industry. Long before there was research in industry and many years prior to chemical and electrical research in the governmental departments and bureaus in Washington, college professors, as Professor Michael Pupin recently emphasized,[1] made their contributions to industrial progress. The universities were the real research pioneers.

While Edison and Eastman are two outstanding examples of men whose genius was not nurtured in educa-

[1] *Scribner's Magazine*, February, 1929.

tional institutions, both have been foremost in recognizing the undisseverable relationship between industry and the university. As early as 1886, Eastman began to draw trained men from university laboratories. In succeeding years men and women came to his factories in this country and England from the leading technical schools and colleges in the United States and Europe. These men and women brought assets to the photographic industry and to the chemical research laboratory which could not be measured by any known financial or service yardstick.

Throughout the years, as his business grew, Eastman recognized, not only individual contributions, but the larger indebtedness of industry to education. He believed that, in the future, the relationship between the two would be even more important; that the welfare and prosperity of the Nation would depend upon the coördination of industry and education to encourage extensive and intensive original thinking. To foster this ideal was his fixed decision.

After exchanging letters in regard to the architecture of the new buildings, Dr. Maclaurin came to Rochester again in June, 1913.

'In confirmation of our conversation of yesterday,' Eastman wrote on the 9th, 'I agree to increase my subscription to the Institute building fund five hundred thousand dollars, making it three million dollars total. The object of this is to secure the completion of the whole main building as contemplated by the latest plan which you have shown me, these plans having developed a necessity for about 12,000,000 cubic feet capacity instead of 10,000,000 as originally talked, and also providing for the use of Indiana limestone as a facing material on all outside walls except those which are intended to be masked by the School of Naval Architecture and by future extensions. It is understood that if the total expense runs over the amount of my subscriptions, the Institute will supply whatever funds are lacking and apply them on the foundations and the interior fittings, such as electrical wiring, plumbing, or heating, as the case may be; thus leaving my subscription to cover the building first and those other items afterwards as far as the fund of three million dollars will go. I am arranging to transfer to the Institute another million dollars before I go abroad, it being understood that the interest on this and the former remittance received by the Institute will be credited on my subscription at the time of the final settlement.'

With this sum assured, the fifty-acre plot on the Cambridge side of the Charles River Basin, adjacent to Harvard Bridge, soon hummed with activity as the steel skeletons of the low majestic buildings were silhouetted against the sky, making a new view of Cambridge for the old residents of Back Bay.

In the mean time, the European War broke out and communications between Eastman and Dr. Maclaurin were more or less infrequent, until in February, 1916, when the President penned a hastily written note to Eastman:

'I have just heard by accident that Mr. A. D. Little, a member of the corporation of this Institute, is going to Rochester to-day in the hope of seeing you and interesting you in a project for the strengthening of our Department of Chemistry. His cause is a most laudable one, but of course he would not venture to [illegible] you in the matter, if he had any inkling of what you had already done. I could not dissuade him from his project without revealing your identity as a benefactor. I do not feel free to do anything that would even point the way in that direction.'

The President of Technology was much more worried than Eastman, who received Dr. Little and listened patiently to the fullest exposition of the plans of the Visiting Committee for the Department of Chemistry and Chemical Engineering. Although Dr. Maclaurin had forwarded Eastman also a confidential copy of the committee's recommendations, Rochester's silent citizen listened as if he was totally unacquainted with the developments along the Charles River. During the previous summer he had visited Mrs. Dickman in Boston to hear the presentation of 'Siegfried' in the Harvard Stadium, and had slipped away from the other guests for a drive along the Charles River and an unannounced visit with Dr. Maclaurin to the new Technology buildings without any one knowing who the unostentatious visitor was or what he was doing.

Eastman was interested in Dr. Little's proposal, as it involved 'the extension by the Institute of its facilities for industrial research.'

'The last few years have been prolific in discussion of how the chemical engineer should be trained,' the committee reported. 'There seems to be a general agreement that this training must provide some actual close contact with large scale operations. This contact is not furnished by more or less perfunctory visits to a few plants. The chemical engineer must not only be well versed in chemistry and its laboratory methods and possess practical first-hand knowledge of the means and methods of handling and reacting upon materials in the large way. . . . He must be familiar with the equipment and materials of construction adapted to any particular set of these and many other conditions and know the design, capacity,

agitators, evaporators, stills, absorption apparatus, compressors, pumps and many other forms of apparatus, all of many types. Mass action must be considered and the dollar sign to which pure chemistry pays no heed becomes the determining factor in all his chemical equations.

'At no time within the history of our country has public attention been so focused upon the development of our chemical industries as it is to-day. Never has the demand been so insistent for chemical engineers competent to develop and direct these industries. Our present prosperity and future industrial development will be determined largely by the ability of American chemical engineers to cope effectively with these industrial problems.'

Dr. Little could not have selected a theme that was closer to Eastman's ideal, or one that would have expanded his interest in the Institute more than that of research. Eastman listened and questioned his caller without indicating that he had ever previously given a copper to education. When he wrote Dr. Little within a few days agreeing to furnish the total sum of three hundred thousand dollars which the committee required, the head of the Little Laboratories was so overwhelmed that he wrote Eastman he was 'quite unable to express' his 'deep sense of appreciation of your splendid generosity toward the Institute of Technology.'

There appears to be little doubt but that Dr. Maclaurin, too, was surprised, but Eastman enjoyed the game so much that he permitted the Institute to make a public announcement of his name in connection with this gift. This was a fine stroke of strategy, for no one thought that the anonymous 'Mr. Smith' would make a public contribution.

It appears from the letters, however, as if Dr. Maclaurin still did not understand the motives of his chief supporter. When the Little proposal could not be carried out in detail, as outlined, Eastman was ready to modify the conditions:

'The money shall be used, interest and principal as far as necessary, in equipping and conducting the various stations, not less than five to begin with, and also strengthening your laboratories for physical chemical research. In case for any reason it is found inadvisable or impracticable to maintain the stations contemplated, the money is to be used at the discretion of your Board in strengthening your chemical department. I enclose my check for the amount, three hundred thousand dollars.'

This incident caused Dr. Maclaurin to change his method of approach. One might infer from the previous letters that the President of Technology, not understanding fully Eastman's motives, had concluded that he was dealing with a rich man who disposed of his millions as casually as he smoked cigarettes. Dr. Maclaurin, at the time, did not realize, perhaps, that Eastman never did anything impulsively; that his casual manner was only a cloak to conceal the intense study and thought which he had given to the problems and possibilities of the Institute. So, for the first time, President Maclaurin wrote that he would like to discuss 'the larger problems of the Institute's future policy. Your interest,' he added, 'and readiness to help have been so remarkable that I should naturally seek to profit by your judgment and business experience in dealing with the larger problems with which we are confronted.'

After another long conference together, Eastman left on a motor trip to the Adirondacks with the Mulligans and Eastwoods. Returning on the 3d of June, he wrote Dr. Maclaurin:

'On my return home I find your letter of May 27th and thank you for complying with my request to outline the programme you would like the Institute to follow, providing it could raise some more money; also for the statement in regard to interest on my payments.

'In order to close up my previous subscription of $3,500,000, I have requested the Bankers' Trust Company to forward you a check for $21,886.15, which with interest credited $178,113.25 and cash $3,300,000, previously paid, makes a total of $3,500,000.

'In order to help you carry out your programme for further equipment, increase in salaries, etc., I make you the following proposition: If the Institute will raise $1,500,000 additional for its endowment fund between now and the 1st of January, 1917, I will contribute a further sum of $2,500,000, the principal of which is to be used only for extending the main educational building when and as required. The income from any unexpended balance of this sum may be used for current expenses. Payment of the amount to be made in sums of $500,000 as fast as you complete the collections of the sum of $300,000 on the fund of $1,500,000 above referred to. In case the Institute is unable to raise the full sum of $1,500,000 before the 1st of January, 1917, I shall be obligated only for a total sum in proportion of five to three upon what it has raised toward said fund of $1,500,000.

'I make the same request in regard to not disclosing the source of this offer that I made in regard to the $3,500,000 contribution.'

This was another surprise for Dr. Maclaurin which he naturally acknowledged immediately. On the 15th, he described the reception of the announcement to the alumni:

'We have just completed a three-day celebration of the opening of our new buildings. I am told that between forty and fifty thousand people were present and the utmost enthusiasm prevailed. For the first three days of the week admission was confined to invited guests, but for the rest of the week the buildings are to be open to the public. I shall have forwarded to you some newspaper accounts of the proceedings.

'Since I wrote you last, a special meeting of the Corporation of the Institute has been held to accept the extremely generous offer contained in your letter of June 3d. The Corporation appointed a committee to draw up a statement expressing the thanks of the Institute for your continued liberality and its appreciation of the splendid opportunity that is thus presented to Technology to become the greatest school of applied science in the world. . . .

'The public announcement of your great gift was made by me at the banquet held in Symphony Hall last evening. The banquet was in itself a notable affair, especially as we had the opportunity of speaking to thirty-six different groups of alumni scattered throughout the length and breadth of the country.

'The announcement of your gift was received with the greatest enthusiasm everywhere, and I think you would have been interested in hearing the cheers that were given simultaneously from the thirty-six cities that were on the lines [long-distance telephone lines]. During the evening the President of the Alumni Association, Mr. Stone [of Stone and Webster, and also President of the American International Corporation], presented a volume of original drawings representing different aspects of the new buildings and charged me with the pleasant duty of transmitting this to you with the compliments and the most hearty appreciation of the Alumni Association. I hope that I may have the pleasure of conveying this to you in person at any time that suits your convenience.

'The announcement of this great gift so stirred the enthusiasm of the alumni present that a million dollars was subscribed during the evening . . . it has made such an impression on every one who has heard of it that the lasting benefit to the Institute must be great indeed.'

Again the national 'guessing contest' was renewed. Who was 'Mr. Smith'? Only nine persons knew, Dr. and Mrs. Maclaurin; Miss Miller, his secretary; Benjamin Strong, Jr., Governor of the Federal Reserve Bank; Seward Prosser, of the Bankers' Trust Company; Mr. Lovejoy; Mrs. Dickman; Miss Whitney, and 'Mr. Smith'; but they all kept the secret and enjoyed the speculation, for the clues reached many cities, but not Rochester. Although approaching his sixty-second birthday, Eastman was unknown nationally as a philanthropist.

One of the cities linked with Boston by telephone that evening was Rochester. Eastman was a guest of the local club because of his public gift of three hundred thousand dollars, but no one else at the dinner knew that Eastman was 'Mr. Smith.' 'As a guest of the Rochester Technology Club,' Eastman wrote Dr. Maclaurin, 'I was privileged to hear all the proceedings that came over the telephone, and of course I was very much interested. I much appreciate the gift of the volume of drawings from the Alumni and would ask you to keep it for me until a favorable opportunity arises for delivering it. Perhaps I shall be in Boston before long. I am much pleased at the progress already made in raising the $1,500,000 and hope you will be able to get the money collected soon, so that I can relieve myself of my part of the obligation.'

Before the time limit expired, the Institute succeeded in raising the sum, and everything was quiet along the Charles and Genesee Rivers until 'Mr. Smith' sent the following brief note to Dr. Maclaurin, May 23, 1918: 'I shall have on my hands four hundred thousand dollars 4½% bonds of the Third Liberty Loan issue when they are delivered. They are not much good to me because my surtax the coming year will cut out about sixty per cent of the income. I am somewhat inclined to turn them over to the Institute, and this is to ask what you need money the most for at this time.'

Five days later, Eastman replied to Dr. Maclaurin's prompt acknowledgment that the bonds might be added to the endowment as a special fund to be used for the general purposes of the Institute during the war, 'and thereafter the income is to be used for the development of courses in chemistry, chemical engineering, and physics; the principal to be available at any time for adding to the main building after the funds which I have already contributed for that purpose are exhausted . . . my intention being that the main building shall continue to represent the funds furnished by me. . . .'

Dr. Maclaurin by this time was thoroughly imbued with Eastman's interest in research. Both were guests of Dr. George E. Hale, Director of Mount Wilson Observatory, at a dinner at the University Club in New York City, when the National Research Fellowships in Physics and Chemistry, supported by the Rockefeller Foundation, were initiated. Immediately after the Fellowships were announced, March 29, 1919, Dr. Maclaurin wrote:

'Two of the leading alumni of the Institute — Doctors Hale and Noyes [Dr. Arthur A. Noyes, Director of the Research Laboratory of Physical Chemistry, Massachusetts Institute of Technology] [1] — have taken the leading part in bringing about this arrangement and I have been in frequent consultation with them regarding the matter. The plan originally suggested was that the Rockefeller Foundation should assist a small number, three or four, perhaps, of institutions that would be specially selected to develop research in Physics and Chemistry. I was never favorable to this suggestion, deeming it better from the point of view of the national interest to give the affair a broader scope and permit participation in the benefits of the scheme of any educational institution that could satisfy the National Research Council that it was properly equipped with men and materials to carry on research.

'I think the action of the Rockefeller Foundation is an extremely important one for the future of science in this country. Clearly we cannot build a superstructure without laying the foundations adequately, and there is consequently great need for the development of the fundamentals of science on which the industrial applications depend. This Institute will, of course, participate in the scheme to the fullest extent of its capacity.'

In June, 1919, Dr. Maclaurin came to Rochester for another secret visit. While at breakfast with Eastman, he outlined his plans for raising an additional fund for the endowment. Eastman, as usual, was vitally interested, and on the 18th he wrote: 'Just to have the matter on record, I repeat my oral offer as follows: That I will give

[1] Members of the First Research Fellowship Board of the National Research Council were: Henry A. Bumstead, Professor of Physics, Yale University; Simon Flexner, Director of Laboratories, Rockefeller Institute for Medical Research; Dr. Hale; Elmer P. Kohler, Professor of Chemistry, Harvard University; Robert A. Millikan, Professor of Physics, University of Chicago; Dr. Noyes; Wilder D. Bancroft, Professor of Physical Chemistry, Cornell University, and ex-officio the Chairman of the Division of Physical Science of the Council.

AIR VIEW OF THE MASSACHUSETTS INSTITUTE OF TECHNOLOGY

the Institute, for endowment purposes, five thousand (5000) shares of Kodak common stock, providing the Institute will raise an additional sum of three or four million dollars. I prefer to set the sum at four million, but I leave that to you. The time limit is December 31, 1919. In case the Institute is not able to raise the sum I will donate a lesser number of shares, in proportion to the amount raised.'

There was no stipulation this time as to secrecy, but now it was in the interest of the Institute to utilize the pulling power of the mysterious 'Mr. Smith.'

October 15, 1919, Eastman wrote thanking Dr. Maclaurin for the aeroplane pictures of the Institute, received at a time when the newspapers had, for the first time, located 'Mr. Smith,' although neither Dr. Maclaurin nor Eastman would satisfy public curiosity.

'Enclosed is a clipping from a local paper,' Eastman reported. 'I conclude that you were pestered yesterday by a flock of telegrams from this town inquiring about the Boston rumor. The only reason I ever had for withholding my name from connection with my original gifts to the Institute was to avoid the nuisance of the notoriety of big giving. My connection with several transactions lately has by force of circumstances done away with this reason, and in any event the transfer of stock involved in my last offer would make my name public, so this is to let you know that you are now at liberty to make any announcement you choose in regard to my share in the whole affair. I consider that I have saved myself annoyance somewhat at your expense heretofore, and it will no doubt be a relief to you to get the matter off your mind.'

The Institute launched a successful nation-wide drive to raise four million dollars to equal the approximate market value of the Kodak shares. Sunday morning,

January 11, 1920, newspapers throughout the country broadcast the announcement made by General du Pont: 'Mr. Smith is George Eastman.'

'General Coleman du Pont, President of the Alumni Association of Massachusetts Institute of Technology, had the honor of officially ending nearly eight years of suspense,' read the news account in the 'Boston Sunday Post,' 'for graduates and undergraduates of the famous technical college last night when he raised a bedlam of cheering among 1100 women and men who attended the jubilee dinner, by announcing that the Rochester, N.Y., camera man is the one who — except for one contribution of $300,000 under his own name — has given, anonymously, $11,000,000 to the Institute.' [1]

To the tune of 'Marching Through Georgia' the students sang their favorite jingle:

Bring the good old bugle, boys, we'll sing another song
Of 'Mr. Smith' and Dupy [du Pont] and the Corporation throng,
Of loyal Tech alumni, almost ten thousand strong,
Who give — what we want — when we want it.

Chorus

Hurrah! Hurrah! for Tech and Boston beans,
Hurrah! Hurrah! for 'Smith,' whoe'er that means;
May he always have a hundred million in his jeans,
So we'll get — what we want — when we want it.

'But not only to Mr. Eastman did Technology do honor last night,' said the 'Post.' 'To President Richard ("Dick" the old graduates called him, every one) Maclaurin went more than a bit of the praise that was heaped by speakers galore on "Mr. Smith" and the new and greater Tech.

' "Technology's Christopher Columbus," President Maclaurin was dubbed by Charles A. Stone, one of the

[1] The total amounts of all of Eastman's gifts to Technology, the University of Rochester, and Hampton and Tuskegee Institutes are purposely eliminated from this volume, although in each case they exceed the figures given.

speakers. "The Man who discovered 'Mr. Smith,' " he termed the President, whom illness deprived of the pleasure of being present when the ambitions of his leadership for Technology were realized, and each and every time during the evening -- and there were many, many of them — that President Maclaurin's name was mentioned, the sons and daughters of the Institute rose to pay tribute, or filled the hall with their cheers and hand-clapping.'

Not even the echoes, however, ever reached Dr. Maclaurin, for his life-work reached a tragic end four days later.

'The shocking news of Dr. Maclaurin's illness and death has kept me from acknowledging your courteous letter of January 15th,' Eastman wrote du Pont. 'I feel that the loss of such a man is almost irreparable, not only to Technology, but to our country as well. As I have talked to him and learned of the scope of his plans and ambitions for Tech. and its place in the development of this country, I can estimate in a measure the tragedy of losing him at this time. You who have been in closer relation to him are able to realize this more keenly. Helping to make those plans possible — which, by the way, I first learned of by studying his yearly reports — has appealed to me as an opportunity to get considerable sums of money into effective action for the benefit of the whole country better than any other way.'

'Of all the honors he received,' Welles Bosworth, architect of the new buildings, wrote Eastman, 'it was you who did him the greatest honor, in your generous confidence in him, and how beautifully your judgment was justified by his accomplishments. It seems inevitable that the great work that he has so substantially developed must go forward.'

For more than a quarter of a century, Eastman had

contended that 'this country cannot progress industrially without plenty of highly trained technical men.' Massachusetts Institute of Technology was the embodiment of this educational ideal, for here the interests of education and industry were welded.

'I would like to convey an idea to you of my personal appreciation of your services to the Massachusetts Institute of Technology,' read a personal letter from Dr. Willis R. Whitney, Director of Research of the General Electric Company. 'I have tried to think of some adequate way of expressing it, but failed. In fact, I felt as though I could not dictate, or have typewritten, any letter at all. So many ordinary letters are made that way. Your actions will probably help direct for all time an enormous number of young and ambitious Americans. I spent yesterday afternoon at the Institute. I felt, myself, a whole lot of satisfaction and pride in the lot of good, healthy-looking young men I saw there. If I can do this, just because I was once one of them, how much greater should be the satisfaction and pride allowed you who have made its continuation in a healthy state possible. I know of thousands of men, alumni and others, who certainly feel as I do. The country owes you a great debt, which it can never pay. It must be a fine feeling to be the right man in such a right place.'

Within a few days came another letter, this time from a spokesman for higher education:

HARVARD UNIVERSITY
CAMBRIDGE

PRESIDENT'S OFFICE   *February 3, 1920*

DEAR MR. EASTMAN:

Bishop Lawrence [1] has shown me your letter to him in reply to his, which emboldens me to add my word of con-

[1] January 11, 1920, the Right Reverend William Lawrence penned the

gratulation to you for your great gift to the Institute of Technology. I have been a trustee of the Institute for over thirty years; and labored hard to bring it and the Harvard Engineering School together; but unfortunately the difficulties were too great to be overcome.

The Institute has done and, with your assistance, is doing and will do a very great work. I have seen it built up from a small beginning, for my interest in it is hereditary, my father and grandfather having been among its trustees; and, indeed, one of the courts in the new building is named after my father. I suppose few institutions in the world have contributed more to advance industry and the practical arts; and I do not know that any man in the world has done so much to help an institution of engineering as you have done for this.

Very truly yours
A. LAWRENCE LOWELL

Meanwhile, the Eastman Theater and School of Music were under way in Rochester, and Frank L. Babbott had written his friend that he should have his portrait painted 'by the best artist we can find. You have done too much for education in this country to neglect this important obligation any longer. There are two or three institutions that ought to have a good portrait of you, so that their patrons might know to whom they are indebted for their training for their life-work. You have dodged this suggestion a number of times, but I shall pull Mc-Kim, Mead, and White away from your building [the theater] if you try to do it again.'

following note: 'Allow me as a citizen of Boston and a fellow of Harvard University to express to you my gratification at your great gifts to the Institute of Technology: made, too, with such wisdom and modesty.' Eastman did not keep a copy of his reply.

But Eastman checkmated him. 'Would it not suit your portrait aspirations if I should be "sculped" heroic size for one of the figures on the roof with a camera in one hand and a horn in the other?'

CHAPTER X

THE TRANSITION OF EXECUTIVE RESPONSIBILITIES

IN 1919, in addition to his interest in Technology, Eastman had a number of civic enterprises under way in Rochester and was engaged in rounding out his programme for the company's future. Each of these required many months of concentrated reflection and involved detailed attention to such widely diversified subjects as music, preventive dentistry, medical education, industrial relations, the distribution of common stock to employees, the Community Chest, the construction of a theater and School of Music, a new addition to the Chamber of Commerce Building, the manufacture of photographic paper in Rochester to compete with the product of the great Steinbach and Rives mills in Germany and France, the possibilities of recapitalization, and, above all, the responsibilities of management.

Eastman was sixty-five years of age and 'the oldest employee of the company.' [1] Retirement was unthinkable. There were too many things to be done. Too many responsibilities; innumerable obligations crowded his mind. Life was serious, all except the steady stream of stories about the 'Kodak King' in the magazines and newspapers. Some of the sensational ones amused him as much as the comic strips in the daily papers entice their millions of followers. One series was so glaring, he sent photostats to Mrs. George B. Dryden, his niece, with a

---

[1] While approaching his eighty-first birthday, Colonel Strong died at his home in Rochester, July 26, 1919. He was Eastman's first associate in the business; the first President of the Eastman Kodak Company of New York, the operating company, and vice-president, treasurer, and director of the New Jersey company.

note saying, 'You will learn something about your uncle that "ain't so," as Nell would say. The flood of letters from people all over the country, wanting something for nothing, that I am getting in connection with this M.I.T. notoriety makes me thankful that it has been possible to stave it off for seven years.'

'Obligations and responsibilities' at home made it necessary for Eastman to decline an appointment to the New York State Reconstruction Commission. In his first annual message to the Legislature, Governor Alfred E. Smith recommended the appointment of a commission to revamp the State Government. Eastman was one of the first men invited by the Governor to serve as a member of the commission. 'It will be a small body and there will be given to you an opportunity to do a great work for the State,' the Governor urged.

After studying the Governor's message and reflecting upon the invitation for two days, Eastman felt obliged to decline and telegraphed the Executive: 'I am interested in your plan for the appointment of a Reconstruction Commission. The subject is one of the most important among very many important matters now pressing upon the country for solution. It is with regret that I am compelled to say that obligations and responsibilities already assumed render it impossible for me to give that time to the matter without which I would be unwilling to serve. I trust that you will understand my position, for you have my cordial best wishes in working out a solution of this momentous problem.' [1]

One of the primary obligations which Eastman had in mind was that to the employees. It was another contribution by him to the era of distribution. This time the distribution was common stock in the company. On

[1] January 17, 1919.

April 4, 1919, he made public the letter which he submitted to the board of directors recommending that they duplicate his offer so as to provide, eventually, for the distribution of stock having a market value at the expiry of the terms of approximately $20,000,000, thus making the employees, as a group, the largest stockholders of the company.

'For some time I have had in contemplation a plan for recognizing my personal obligation to the loyal wage-earning and salaried employees of this company and its allied companies who have helped to make our business a success. This plan, briefly stated, involves a contribution by me of a substantial amount of common stock to be sold at par to such of the employees above referred to as have shown their loyalty to the company by length of service, the money derived from the sale of these shares to the employees to become a part of a welfare fund to be created for the benefit of all the employees and administered under rules and regulations to be mutually agreed upon by the directors and myself.

'It is my desire to extend the right to participate in the purchase of this stock to those employees still in the service who completed two years or more of continuous service on January 1, 1918, the amount of stock which such employees may purchase to be an amount equal to 2 per cent. of their total wages earned during the entire period of their continuous service before that date.

'The company's records of wages paid to such employees prior to January 1, 1918, indicate that it will require approximately ten thousand shares of common stock to carry out this plan. I wish to donate that stock, but the plan should not end there. It has advantages which are valuable to the company and the present stockholders, and I feel very strongly that the company should make it possible to continue the plan and enable future employees and such of the present employees as cannot participate now, or can participate only partially in the purchase of the above stock, to look forward to the enjoyment of a similar privilege upon a common basis when their loyalty has been shown. This can be done if the company will set aside a portion of its unissued common stock for sale at par to these latter employees, giving to each of them a maximum participation equal to two per cent. of wages earned during five years of continuous service.

'Therefore, I make the following offer, viz: I will donate sufficient common stock, estimated at ten thousand shares, to enable wage-earning and salaried employees of this company and its allied companies still in the service, who completed two years or more of continuous employment on January 1, 1918, to purchase at par an amount of such stock equal to 2 per cent. of their wages earned while continuously employed prior to that date.

'The above offer is, however, made on condition that this company set aside ten thousand shares of its unissued common stock to be issued for cash at par and made available for sale at par from time to time only to wage-earning and salaried employees of this company and its allied companies, as they attain two years of continuous service, the maximum amount purchasable by any employee to be an amount at par equal to 2 per cent. of the total wages paid such employee during five years of continuous employment; with the proviso that an employee entitled to participate on the basis of five years or more continuous service in the purchase of shares contributed by me shall not be entitled to participate in the purchase of the shares set aside by the company, but an employee entitled to participate to a less extent in the purchase of shares furnished by me may share in the purchase of stock set aside by the company as far as may be necessary to bring his total purchases up to the maximum above stated.

'The stock set aside by the company will enable existing employees who on January 1, 1918, had served continuously two years or more, but not five years, to continue from year to year if they remain with the company their purchase of common shares at par until they have acquired the maximum amount above stated, and will enable existing employees who on January 1, 1918, had not served continuously two years to begin their purchases when they have completed that service and if they remain with the company to continue such purchases from year to year until they have acquired the maximum amount above stated. It will also for many years to come enable new employees after they have attained two years of continuous service to participate in the purchase from year to year of common stock at par on the same basis and to the same extent.

'The company should establish a plan to assist employees, whenever necessary, to take up their allotment of certificates and pay therefor in installments.

'Certificates should be made non-transferable before the date of their maturity, and to avoid having too large a number of certificates mature on the same date they may be issued in two or more series, with different maturity dates for each series, the average maturity period of all certificates being five years from date to issue. As fast as certificates mature they may be exchanged for shares of common stock.

'An owner of certificates who leaves the employ of the company for any reason should receive for his unmatured certificates their par value with any unpaid dividends apportionable to them, but in the case of certificates not fully paid for the holder should receive the amount standing to his credit upon his account for the purchase thereof, and in the event of the death or permanent disability of an employee holding unmatured certificates, such certificates should on full payment being made therefor, be exchanged for stock to be issued to such disabled employee or to the estate of the deceased.

'The interests of the employees in the foregoing respects must be safeguarded by equal representation upon committees formed to deal with all such matters impartially.

'The proceeds of the sale of the shares contributed by me may be used, if necessary, to pay for the shares to be issued by the company for sale to employees: but in that case the money so used must be replaced out of the proceeds of the latter sale, in order that the company's welfare fund may receive ultimately the full par value of the common shares contributed by myself.

'Accompanying this are some papers relating to our new plan for selling stock to employees,' he explained to a large stockholder. 'There are a number of things that I want to call your attention to that perhaps are not specifically covered in these papers: The million dollars that will eventually be received from the sale of the stock can be advantageously used in extending our various plants. In fact, we have plans already in consideration that will absorb several times this amount. There is over $5,000,000 (par value) of unissued common stock, hence there will be no action required to increase the capital of the company. Yesterday afternoon the plan was presented and explained to a group of the largest shareholders that we were able to get together on short notice and they approved the plan unanimously, their holdings representing in all about half of the outstanding shares.

'The success of the Wage Dividend encourages us to think that this will be actually a money-making operation for the company. . . . Our labor turnover has been less than in any other concern here in Rochester, and lower than almost any of the big companies. The Wage Dividend will, of course, be continued, but it does not go quite far enough, because it does not give the employees a real proprietary interest in the company. I feel as labor conditions grow more difficult that it will be greatly to the advantage of the company to be a leader, not a follower. One of the great advantages of bringing this to a head now is that it is not done under force of any circumstances. Our employees are well satisfied and loyal, and this can only act to make them more so. We are running a very complicated and difficult business. I do not know any that depends more upon the good feeling and faithfulness of its employees.

'I am only giving you these points so that you will understand the whole situation. It does not seem to me that it will need any argument to convince every shareholder as to the desirability of the scheme.

'You will be interested to learn that the company has been able to earn about the same amount that it did in 1917, notwithstanding that it had to provide for war taxes amounting to about $8,000,000, which is fully double the amount for the previous year. This in spite of the fact that we have not increased the prices on our principal products, film and paper, and only slightly on plates. Business is very heavy and the prospect for this year is correspondingly good.'

From employees and stockholders working or residing in nearly every country in the world, Eastman received enthusiastic letters. Among them was one from Mrs. Alexander Graham Bell, who had been a stockholder since the days of McCurdy's invention. Coming from the wife of the inventor of the telephone, Eastman felt honored and answered, 'We are greatly pleased to have your approval of the proposition and also to advise you that it has been carried out, as there has been no opposition from any of our stockholders.' [1]

By May, 1919, however, it was increasingly evident that labor conditions throughout the country were becoming critical. Eastman's ideas and judgment were solicited from all directions. W. B. Wilson, Secretary of Labor under President Wilson, submitted a brief statement of facts and the department's views, and asked Eastman for his opinion.

'I believe that the continuance of good wages depends entirely upon the productivity of labor,' Eastman telegraphed in reply, while in a letter to B. C. Forbes he added in greater detail that, in his opinion:

'Daily hours of labor, weekly rest periods, and annual vacations are undoubtedly vital factors in the maintenance of healthy and contented people. To-day, as never before, the supreme duty of industry is to give the world more production. Industry must strike a balance between its social duty not to shorten or make unhappy the lives of its workers and its duty to provide for the physical wants of the public. The selling prices of goods are dependent upon production cost, and the cost of vacations would eventually be passed on to the public. A shorter working day and an annual vacation may become standards in industry, but we cannot maintain high standards of living and grant these privileges without a high standard of production.' [2]

[1] July 17, 1919.

[2] A study of wholesale prices in 1914 and 1927 discloses that in the postwar boom, the peak of Eastman prices was 16 per cent above the 1914 level,

Throughout the spring and early summer the fear of Bolshevism, definitely recognized as a destructive force in industry by this time, spread throughout the country. On August 15, Eastman wrote a letter to Kodak employees in which he declared:

'These are days for plain speaking. One of the reasons why, in some countries and in some localities, the poison of anarchy has gained a foothold . . . is because it was not crushed. . . . In such communities the citizens have refused to admit that there was a lurking danger until that danger had become a menace. . . . Don't let us make that mistake here in Rochester. . . . Right now there are those who are trying to poison the minds of the people of this community and of this company. . . . Such propaganda and such propagandists cannot easily be reached by the management. But you men at the bench, you know! And you have the remedy in your own hands. . . .

'It is by no means wholly the affairs of the company and the business that I have in mind in putting this matter before you. Your comfort and prosperity and the growth and prosperity of the company are interdependent. The management and the employees have always gotten along together wonderfully well. There is probably no concern of equal size in the country that has had less of internal friction. . . .

'We, of the management, are anxious not merely that you take pride in your work and in the excellence of the goods that the company produces, but that there shall be opportunity for every one of you. We want you to have comfortable homes and healthy surroundings. We want your children to have good schools and want them

whereas the index of all commodities (U.S. Bureau of Labor statistics) rose 131 per cent. In 1927, Eastman prices were slightly below those of 1914, while all commodities prices were 48 per cent above those of 1914.

to be enveloped in an atmosphere that will make of them good citizens of whom you and the whole community will have reason to be proud.

'None of these things are attainable where anarchy reigns. . . .

'Fortunately, there has been little of this spirit of destruction within our organization. We have been builders, not destroyers. We have seen working conditions improve, with better, cleaner surroundings and more of opportunity for recreation and with greater comforts and advantages for our families. These conditions are not yet ideal, but they can only continue to improve under those conditions of mutual confidence and coöperation that bring loyalty and prosperity.'

Spontaneously, resolutions containing the signatures of thousands of employees came in. Acknowledging the pledge from the employees of the Camera Works, Eastman said:

'Your promptness in placing yourselves on record in opposition to the dangerous elements which then threatened and I believe still threaten the peace and prosperity of our Country, and menace its free institutions, was exceedingly gratifying. Your resolutions display that true American spirit which must be relied upon to work out better conditions in an orderly manner and to stamp out revolutionary tendencies which seek to destroy free conditions which are of the greatest value to every citizen whatever his calling.'

While the Bolshevist agitation was short-lived, it aroused national interest in economic questions. Facing these problems at home, Eastman attended public meetings where economic subjects were discussed, solicited information from authorities in New York and Washington, and invited leading bankers, public speakers, and officials from other cities to his home for conferences. Although he received many requests to join leading national banks and corporations in fighting revolutionary propaganda, he declined all of them because he believed so firmly that his 'obligations and responsibilities' centered in Rochester, and here he applied himself. To strengthen the organization of his own company, Eastman's suggestion of the appointment of new vice-presidents was approved by the directors.[1] Lovejoy was placed in charge of manufacturing; Stuber in charge of photographic quality; Noble in charge of extension of sales; and Havens of the legal department.

'You made the statement last night,' Eastman wrote Allan Walker of the Guaranty Trust Company, 'that if all the incomes over $10,000 in this country were distributed *pro rata* over all those under $10,000, it would only increase the latter 10%. I have been trying for two or three years to get some facts to base such a statement upon, but have been unable to do it, so I should be very much obliged if you would tell me how you arrived at the figures: that is to say, how you obtained the amount of surplus income, how you obtained the amount of the incomes under $10,000, and whether they included farmers' incomes and all classes of non-income reporting individuals. The only figures that I have bearing on this general subject of the division of the surplus incomes were those from an investigation made by Magnus W. Alexander, of the National Industrial Conference Board, who obtained reports from sixty-nine industrials which employed something over 900,000 people. These figures showed that if all the salaries paid in excess of $5000 were distributed among the workmen, it would amount to 25 cents a week. Our own establishment was included,

[1] October 8, 1919.

but it was one of the high ones owing to the large proportion of technical men to whom we pay high salaries.
. . . I quite agree with you that the lack of production is
the root of all our troubles.' [1]

Eastman took advantage of every opportunity to emphasize the importance of production.

'One marked result of the war has been to bring American goods and resources to the attention of the world,
and this gives to America at this time an opportunity such
as it has never had before to secure its share of international trade and commerce. [2] This is, however, only an
opportunity and must be taken advantage of if it is to
become a reality. Aside from the necessity of increased
production, without which nothing can be accomplished, two other requisites of this understanding stand
out prominently. The first is the matter of sound finance.
The method by which foreign purchasers are to pay for
our goods must be carefully worked out. The second is
facilities for transportation of goods.

'The visit of the Allied Trade Commission of Great
Britain, France, Italy, and Belgium to this country is
undertaken for that very purpose, and gives us the
chance to discuss with these commissioners all these matters, to learn from them their views and to obtain from
them their help in this undertaking, which is of such
great importance to all the people of the United States.

   [1] March 2, 1920, Walker replied: 'The figures included in my statement
before the Rochester Clearing House . . . were given to me by Mr. Otto H.
Kahn and confirmed by Mr. M. C. Rorty, statistician for the American
Telephone Company. Mr. Rorty is secretary of the Bureau of Economic
Research, of which Dean Gay, late of Harvard, is chairman, and of which
Messrs. W. T. Hill, W. I. King, and J. J. McAuley, of the University of
California, are members. These economists are so well known as to give
considerable authority to their findings.'

   [2] Eastman to Roland B. Woodward, Secretary of the Rochester Chamber
of Commerce.

As a result of their visit and the careful attention and consideration which American bankers and American exporters and importers are prepared to give this matter, I believe that this country will take the place in international trade which its great resources and the spirit of its people entitle it to hold.'

During the summer of 1920, when the political conventions of the two dominant parties were in session, Eastman watched the proceedings with intense interest. After the nominations of Senator Warren G. Harding, of Ohio, and Governor Calvin Coolidge, of Massachusetts, he received a personal letter from the presidential candidate in Marion, which he promptly acknowledged. Concluding the letter he added: 'It is hardly necessary for me to say that you have my heartiest good wishes for a successful campaign. That we must have a Republican administration to straighten out the tangles resulting from the war is my earnest conviction.'

And as the sun was setting on the administration of President Wilson, a telegram appeared in the newspapers, February 1, 1921, of the settlement of the Government suit against the company. Following negotiations between representatives of Attorney-General A. Mitchell Palmer and James S. Havens, chief counsel of the company, the latter agreed to offer for public sale the Premo, the Century-Folmer, and Schwing factories in Rochester; the Artura brand of photographic paper, and the Seed, Stanley, and Standard brands of dry plates.

By this time, six years after the suit was instituted, the attitude of the country toward 'big business' had undergone a revolutionary change. It was no longer a crime to be 'the largest manufacturer of photographic materials in the world.' Perhaps it never was criminal to have business ambition and vision. 'The Eastman Company,' observed the 'Democrat and Chronicle,' 'was attacked under the Sherman Law at a time when business success was looked upon in Washington as a suspicious circumstance and it might almost be said was regarded as presumptive evidence that a concern was a law-breaker. . . . This hysteria over, the achievements of what was familiarly called "big business" makes, on the whole, one of the strangest chapters in the history of our government.'

'Thus does circumstance mould opinion and career far more than abstract thinking; and emotion quite as much as reason shape systems of government.' [1]

By this time, too, Eastman was not as interested in the substantial vindication of his general business policy as he was in the fate of the employees of the severed factories, who were receiving wage dividends and their share of the stock distribution. Under the terms of the settlement all employees, of the companies offered for sale, were enabled to subscribe to their portion of Eastman's stock.

'Obligations and responsibilities,' as usual, were uppermost in his mind, for in the summer of 1921, when business depression was general throughout the country and the Kodak Works was operated on a three-day week schedule, the company was able to pay a wage dividend of $1,250,000.

At the time, opinion generally attributed the national epidemic of depression to overproduction of goods with high-priced raw materials and labor. While the Harding

---

[1] Although this observation by Albert J. Beveridge in *The Life of John Marshall* (vol. II, page 165) was made to apply to the influence of personalities and politics upon governmental policies in 1780, it is so fundamental that it applies with equal force to the influence of politics upon industry and national industrial policies to-day.

administration and the new Republican Congress were struggling with this problem and the drafting of a protective tariff, Eastman became convinced that it was not overproduction at high prices as much as a lack of synchronization of production and distribution which was at fault.

He became a champion of the protective tariff, arousing the Hearst newspapers thereby to a series of editorial attacks from Boston to Los Angeles and San Francisco. Eastman's interest at the time was not personal, for he was engaged in distributing, not accumulating wealth. He believed that prosperity and protection were synonymous, and shared the views of Charles M. Schwab that a prosperous America could help the whole world, while a prostrate nation could not.

But, wrote the 'New York American,' 'No man is fit to be made Czar over Motion Pictures.' [1]

'The Fordney Bill, as reported, takes from the free list and puts a duty of 30 per cent ad valorem upon raw film, the basis of moving pictures. . . . The motion picture has become a social force of the first importance. Only by keeping open its door of opportunity for all can it be secured against the abuses which autocratic control always develops.

'But if the monopoly of raw film production is confirmed by a 30 per cent ad valorem tariff, a single company will have the motion-picture industry by the throat.

'The head of this one company is an able business man who has been well rewarded for his valuable contributions to society. He does not need, and it would be unwise to put in his hands, absolute power over American motion pictures.'

[1] July 22, 1921.

'Power,' however, was not what Eastman sought. He had assiduously avoided it. His aim was the protection of labor. In the future he foresaw executives and labor sharing, perhaps controlling, industry by ownership of securities, and believed that the basic principle of prosperity was tariff protection, which came, a year later, with the passage of the Fordney-McCumber Tariff Act of 1922. This was the cornerstone of the Coolidge era of prosperity.[1]

In January, 1921, the Eastman Savings and Loan Association began business as a means of providing for regular and persistent saving, and arranging with local builders to erect suitable, modern houses for employees at a minimum cost. At the end of the first year, 5929 employees had purchased $4,552,000 par value of shares in the Association in face of a business depression, which Rochester as other industrial communities encountered, and in spite of a wage reduction which the company was forced to put into effect October 3, 1921.

Thrift was an Eastman habit, and through this Association several thousand employees were enabled to build or finance the purchase of homes. By March 10, 1929, 6889 employees had subscribed $9,373,800 for 93,738 shares of stock in the Association. Moreover, through the Kodak Employees' Association, 1403 employees were assisted financially, through second mortgages, in building their own homes.

'In considering a man for employment the question whether he is thrifty is almost always an important one, no matter what the job is.[2] If he cannot take care of his

---

[1] During the eight years of the Wilson administration the wage dividends of the company, July 1, 1914, to July 1, 1921, amounted to $6,034,770.83, while during the eight years of the Harding-Coolidge administrations, from July 1, 1922, to July 1, 1929, the total wage dividends was $19,436,223.46.

[2] Eastman to B. C. Forbes, October 14, 1919.

own affairs, it is presumptive evidence that he will be weak in the conduct of others. It takes a mighty good excuse to explain why a man is in debt. I was brought up to fear debt, and as a matter of fact in the early years I always saved something every year no matter what my salary was. Having formed the habit, I have managed to conduct my business so that we have never had to borrow any money, but that is not always practical or perhaps wise. If a man is really thrifty and needs to borrow money, his reputation for thrift is his greatest asset next to honesty.'

In June, 1921, when Rochester and many other American cities were in the throes of a building trades war, Eastman endeavored, at the urgent request of the Chamber of Commerce, to bring about industrial peace.

'I don't like the word "conciliation," ' he said. 'It implies that there is some one to be conciliated. And arbitration does not strike me as the best possible way to settle such matters. Each of these words suggests antagonism in a field where there is no reason for it. We need the kind of satisfaction out of which enthusiasm grows. . . . Let us reason together.

'There are three interested parties in the building situation. These are the workers, the building contractors, and the public. There are also three objects to be attained before the business can be placed on a basis that can be regarded as permanently satisfactory. These are the reduction of seasonal labor to the lowest possible minimum, the payment of the highest possible wages that the business will justify, and a labor output that will enable local concerns to meet outside competition.

'The business of the Eastman Kodak Company is a seasonal business naturally, but by scientific management, by planning ahead, by using various devices to keep the force employed in slack times, the seasonal element has been almost entirely eliminated.' [1]

Eastman's proposal was the establishment of a Community Conference Board. This, said the 'Democrat and Chronicle,' 'anticipated by several months, so far as this community is concerned, the exhaustive report of the condition of the building industry of the nation at large prepared for Secretary of Commerce Hoover by the American Engineering Council.

'The inquirers who investigated the situation attribute much of the trouble in the industry to haphazard management in planning and controlling work, and to lack of these standards which characterize most constructive undertakings.

'Here again they were anticipated by Mr. Eastman. He not only pointed out, with amazing accuracy, where the industry was weak, but he also suggested the remedy. . . .'

It was evident by this time that in declining Governor Smith's invitation to serve on the Reconstruction Commission, Eastman's 'obligations and responsibilities' at

[1] This was the time that Secretary of Commerce Hoover began the mobilization of business statistics for the purpose of eliminating or diminishing business cycles. Five years later, in his annual report of 1926, he stated:

'We are rapidly approaching the time when a business man will be able to determine the exact position of his industry in relation to production, stocks, orders, sales, conditions of sources of supplies, the consuming market, credit, business activity and broad economic currents — both at home and abroad — which may influence the conduct of his particular occupation. Statistics are like weather reports in their relation to business conditions.

'While the causes [of the business cycle] can probably never be entirely removed, and while broad tides of increased or decreased productivity and consumption will continue to flow, it appears to the department that the violence of these phenomena have been permanently mitigated by the various forces increasingly developed during the last five years. In other words, the curve of the business cycle has, in the belief of the Department, been considerably flattened, and very large national waste has been to a considerable degree eliminated.'

home were large and varied enough to more than tax any surplus hours that he did not devote to his business. One business question in July, 1921, however, engrossed his attention. After the 2d of July, when war with Germany was declared officially at an end by Presidential Proclamation, he had company auditors make a final check of all war contracts. From the beginning of American participation in the World War, Eastman, in all his communications with the Government, had insisted that 'it is not our intention to make any profit whatever out of these materials.' On May 27, 1919, the company had refunded $23,456.70 and canceled Government bills amounting to $129,004.73, which represented a refund of $152,461.43 on all cost-plus contracts. During the war, however, there had been other contracts, upon a 'flat-price' basis, entered into at the request of the War Department. The auditor's report showed that upon these contracts the company had profited $182,-770.60, and on February 3, 1922, Eastman personally presented a check from the company for this sum to Secretary of War John W. Weeks. Including sundry small refunds, this made a total of $335,389.76, representing war profits which the company returned to the United States Treasury. In acknowledging the final adjustment of these accounts, Eastman received the following letter:

THE WHITE HOUSE
WASHINGTON

February 7, 1922

MY DEAR MR. EASTMAN:

Secretary Weeks reported to the Cabinet to-day the very unusual experience of your return to the Government, on behalf of the Eastman Kodak Company, of $182,770.00 which had been paid the company on war contracts in excess of the contemplated profit provided in the contract. I had heard of this pleasing incident informally at the time I had the pleasure of personally greeting you and some of your friends, and had also the satisfaction of seeing the incident noted in the columns of the press. I have no doubt that becoming expression has already been conveyed to you, but I cannot resist adding my own appreciation of this very prompt and considerate action on the part of your company in making a wholly voluntary adjustment after the close of a great war service.

With very best wishes, I am

Very truly yours

WARREN G. HARDING

Meanwhile, another project of national significance was under way. In the evolution of the motion picture and its recognized pronounced influence upon society, many educators and psychologists became convinced that the screen would herald the dawn of a new era in education. For many years the subject was debated, with about as much progress as the monks attained in the Middle Ages when they argued over the number of angels that could dance on the point of a needle.

In 1922, for the first time, however, a serious organized effort was made by the National Education Association to study the whole subject of motion pictures in their application to classroom practice. Dr. Charles H. Judd, Dean of the School of Education of the University of Chicago; Dr. Thomas E. Finegan, Director of the State Department of Education at Harrisburg, Pennsylvania; Dr. Frank Cody, of Detroit, and other distinguished educators served during the succeeding five years as chairmen of this committee, making contact, at times, with

Will H. Hays, President of the Motion Picture Producers and Distributors of America, Inc., representing the motion-picture industry, and with Eastman.

Between 1923 and 1926, the Eastman Company conducted a survey of this field in coöperation with these two dominant organizations.

In February, 1926, Eastman announced that the company would undertake to determine three fundamental questions:

1. Is it feasible to measure the value of films as a teaching agency?
2. Do films have a teaching value which justifies their purchase for school use?
3. Can such films be produced within cost limits that put them within the purchasing power of the schools?

By this time one of the key problems had been solved. A safety film, approximately one half the width of standard film (16 mm.), had been perfected and used by amateur cinematographers throughout the world.[1] The development of this film at Kodak Park, together with portable motion-picture cameras and home projectors, made amateur cinematography practical and paved the way for the use of similar film and equipment in the

---

[1] In August, 1923, a paper describing a new process of amateur cinematography, which had just been introduced by the company was published in the *Journal of the Franklin Institute*. 'The process depended upon the use of a narrow film, 16 mm. wide, instead of the 35 mm. of the standard motion-picture film. This film, after exposure, is not developed to a negative and printed, as is customary with 35-mm. film, but is developed by what is known as the *reversal* process. In this reversal process, the exposed image is first developed, and then the developed silver is dissolved in a bleaching bath, as it is called, which oxidizes the silver. This leaves behind the undeveloped silver bromide which was not affected by the developer, because it was not exposed to light. After a fresh exposure to light, this remaining silver bromide is developed in its turn and gives a positive.' (Dr. Mees, *Journal of the Franklin Institute*, vol. 207. no. 1, January, 1929.)

classroom at a cost far below that of standard-width (35 mm.) film and projectors. While the original classroom films were made on standard-width film, reproductions on the 16 mm. safety stock provided pictures of adequate size for classroom purposes.

Then a two-year experimental test was undertaken by Dr. Ben D. Wood, of Columbia University, and Dr. Frank N. Freeman, of the University of Chicago, who were chosen to advise on the preparation of films and assume direction and supervision of the tests, after Dr. Finegan had come to Rochester to head this division of the company's business.

The school authorities of twelve cities coöperated in the experiment to test the teaching value of the films. These cities represented all general sections of the country and thus provided a national expression of the varied interests, viewpoints, opinions, and conditions in education. Considering its general scope, the number of teachers, pupils, schools, and school systems involved, the extensive and detailed preparations for it, the funds expended, and the importance of the subject, it is probably one of the most outstanding experiments in education ever conducted.

Eight or more schools in Newton, Massachusetts; Detroit, Michigan; Lincoln, Nebraska; Oakland, California; Kansas City, Missouri; Winston-Salem, North Carolina; Rochester, New York; Chicago, Illinois; Denver, Colorado; San Diego, California; Atlanta, Georgia; and New York City participated. At least six of these were elementary schools, in which the subject chosen for the test was fifth- and sixth-grade geography. At least two were junior high schools, in which general science was the test subject. In these schools two groups of children pursued a course of study for ten weeks. One group was known as a 'control' group, or those given instruction *without* the aid of films; and the other as an 'experimental' group, or those given instruction *with* the use of films.

The children in each group came from similar home environments and social conditions. They were selected so that they would be as nearly as possible on the same intellectual level. The teachers chosen to instruct each group were, as nearly as possible, equal in training and teaching ability. In order to prevent the influence of the film from being carried by either teachers or pupils of the experimental groups to the control groups, the experimental and control classes were, with very few exceptions, chosen from different schools.

About ten thousand children were under instruction — five thousand in each group. Never before had a film experiment covered so large a number of children in regular classroom work. Furthermore, the films used had been made especially to supplement the instruction on the subjects to be taught. Each series — geography and general science — had been planned definitely for use in a particular grade.

The films were based upon carefully prepared scenarios, written by practical classroom teachers and critically analyzed by specialists in education. The whole aim was to present material rich in teaching value and adapted to the needs of the classroom.

At the conclusion of the two-year study, it was evident that visual education made possible notable improvement in regular daily classroom work by increasing and sustaining interest, by quickening originality, by creating a greater desire and ability to discuss subjects, by improving the quality of the material the pupils read, by a clearer appreciation of personal experience, by greater facility in correlating lessons with community conditions, by improving the range and accuracy of the vocabulary, and by ability to concentrate.

This study in the educational value of classroom films was the realization, also, of one of Edison's early dreams. 'I should say that in ten years,' Edison remarked in 1925,[1] 'textbooks as the principal medium of teaching will be as obsolete as the horse and carriage are now. I believe that in the next ten years, visual education — the imparting of exact information through the motion picture camera — will be a matter of course in all our schools.'

In the rapid evolution of the business there were many other new projects and new products. One of these was the development of an extensive paper mill at Kodak Park. Almost from the beginning of his business career, Eastman had urged American manufacturers to develop a photographic paper industry in the United States. For many years he had been the largest consumer of photographic paper manufactured in Germany and France. Now his own employees had realized even more than his own life ambition in this line, for they had made Rochester the center of the largest photographic paper industry in the world. Also, they succeeded in perfecting a pulp paper equal in durability and quality to rag paper, so recognized by the United States Bureau of Standards. To-day the Eastman mill is turning out sufficient photographic paper to print snap-shots of every man, woman, and child in the United States several times each year.

Down in the Cumberland Mountains of Tennessee, at Kingsport, the company had built a large wood distilla-

[1] *Collier's Weekly*, February 21, 1925.

tion plant, where chemicals were made for the Park and the chemical industry of the Nation. This insured the company of independence in any emergency and made possible the production of new products and an array of by-products which were now evolving, like magic, from the chemical research laboratories. The company was both participating in, and contributing to, the industrial renaissance of the New South.

Whether Eastman, personally, was in Europe or the United States; whether working in Rochester or camping in the Jackson Hole section of Wyoming, or on the Grand Cascapedia in Quebec, his mind was at ease, as far as the organization was concerned. For several years he had been welding human qualities into a business unit that he could leave at any time. Now he could watch the dreams of this body of men and women blossom into activities as varied and interesting as the flowers that came in endless variety from his prolific greenhouses.

Eastman maintained that every man, from the highest paid executive through the ranks to the worker occupying the humblest position, had a part in creating and building a successful profit-making organization.[1] The important thing was to make each man realize that fact, to make him see the part he should play, to make him believe that he had something valuable to contribute. Then there must be that mutual trust and respect between executives and workers that can exist only where there is an absence of favoritism, and where every man, from the top down, knows that the fair thing is to be done by everybody.

Workers must have something more than fair wages

[1] The tenure of employment in the Eastman factories and offices in Rochester, according to the 1927 annual report, revealed that 51.3 per cent of the employees had been with the company more than five years, while 27.4 per cent had been more than ten years in the service.

and decent working conditions if industrial relations are to be improved, Eastman believed, and that 'something,' in his opinion, was the knowledge and certainty that honest work and loyal interest would be recognized and rewarded by employers. He did not think it advisable to give the worker a vote in the control or direction of industries. 'It seems to me that the sound way of giving the worker a voice in the direction of industry is by the selection of the fittest for foremen and the promotion of the best foremen to superintendents,' he stated in an interview.[1] 'I do not believe that an industry run by the workers as such can prove successful. I haven't the least doubt in my mind, that if the heads of this company were to step out and turn the management and operation of the plants over to the employees, the organization would be ruined within a short time.'

'As far as possible,' Eastman stated in the same interview, 'all executive jobs in our organization are given to men who grow up in it. One of our most important plant managers started out as a carpenter. Others worked in different branches of the industry. Of course, when it comes to the technical jobs, it is the man with the most highly developed scientific mind for that particular job, who is chosen. For that we often go out into the universities to get the best brains. But that, too, is what helps make for the success of the industry; that is what helps add to the wage recognition the man on the bench gets.

'An organization cannot be sound unless its spirit is. That is the lesson the man on top must learn. He must be a man of vision and progress who can understand that one can muddle along on a basis in which the human factor takes no part, but eventually there comes a fall.'

Recognition of the 'human factor,' of the varying

[1] *New York Times*, February 4, 1923.

human qualities of individuals, was at the foundation of Eastman's policy. He built his organization, selected executives and transferred responsibilities to them, on the basis of the qualities each man contributed to the company as a whole. Eastman was convinced that an organization should be composed of men whose qualities, in the aggregrate, approximated perfection. He knew that no one individual had a monopoly of human assets. In all his own activities he had always surrounded himself with experts, men of technical training, men schooled by experience, men who were masters of details and others who had a broad general grasp of the business. He insisted, of course, upon honesty and loyalty. After satisfying himself as to the ability and capacity of an individual, he subjected him to a final test to determine whether he had any 'crooked instincts.' If there was the slightest indication of this, the individual was dropped. If this quality developed later, he was discharged instantly. It was not sufficient for a man to be honest and straight in his actions; he had to be so, instinctively.

In the course of many years of experience and observation, Eastman discovered that, while one individual might be a marvelous technician, he could be, also, a poor manufacturer; another might have wide knowledge, but lack judgment. All men were not independent thinkers; some were naturally 'yes' men, even though they had other qualities which overbalanced this weakness. Some could be stampeded by their associates; others were more patient.

A 'profit-bearing' organization, above everything else, had to have balance as well as foresight; initiative as well as caution. In developing his organization, Eastman had all of these qualities and requirements in mind, and the men who came to the top had, in his opinion, the qualities which he believed the organization, as a unit, should have.

In 1924, passing the age of threescore and ten years, he concentrated upon the selection of his successors, and in March of the following year, when he was elected Chairman of the Board, William G. Stuber was elected President and Frank W. Lovejoy, Vice-President and General Manager. This action was taken 'to make possible a division of the duties which for many years have been performed by me as President and General Manager. As Chairman of the Board,' Eastman notified the stockholders,[1] 'I shall expect to retain my supervision over matters of general policy and development, but leave the active management of affairs to Mr. Lovejoy, who for many years has had direct charge of the manufacturing. It will be Mr. Stuber's function to serve as Chairman in my absence and to perform such other duties as the Board shall prescribe. He will, of course, retain his supervision over matters of photographic quality. These changes, I feel sure, will not only be fitting acknowledgment of what Mr. Stuber and Mr. Lovejoy have done in building up the organization, but will also greatly benefit the stockholders by providing more adequately for the carrying on of the Company's management in the future.'

Stuber had been with the company thirty-one years. He was one of the first four men in the organization who was given a percentage of the profits of the business, and he had worked up from the ranks, as an emulsion maker, to a position of authority and responsibility in the company and of respect and stability in the city. For twenty-eight years, Lovejoy had grown as an executive, in Eastman's estimation, as rapidly as the business. For more than two decades, he had been at Eastman's right hand,

[1] March 6, 1925.

sharing the responsibilities of management and all business confidences. With these two men at the helm, Eastman was ready, as he wrote one of his friends, 'to fade out of the picture.'

'Of course the best thing for all of us to do is to keep busy,' he told the employees a few months later, 'but living and working as we do to-day, we need more time for recreation and reflection. I do not mean by this statement that the drudgery of work can be eliminated. There is a great deal of business that is drudgery. We must face that and not delude ourselves with the idea that work can be made play. The only antidote to drudgery is play, but the proper time for play is in our leisure hours.

'By working seriously and effectively in our working hours, much can be done to enable us to make the most of our leisure hours. What we do in our working hours determines what we have in the world. What we do in our play hours determines what we are.'

Personally, Eastman had no intention of fading out of the picture, through inactivity, for he had extensive civic projects under way in Rochester, some of which were to become models for philanthropists in other communities throughout the United States.

CHAPTER XI

NEW MOULDS FOR OLD NEEDS

'IF a man has wealth, he has to make a choice, because there is the money heaping up,' Eastman stated in an interview.[1] 'He can keep it together in a bunch and then leave it for others to administer after he is dead. Or, he can get it into action and have fun, while he is still alive. I prefer getting it into action and adapting it to human needs, and making the plan work.

'If you leave it by will, five years may pass, and the scheme you devised may be unfitting to the new circumstances. Things change while a will is waiting. Then the executors may be so hampered by the conditions of the will and the new situation that successful use of the funds is difficult. It is more fun to give money than to will it. And that is why I give.'

Adapting wealth to human needs was the motivating force, while the spirit that prompted the giving was one of 'fun' rather than duty.

The opportunities for distribution which confront men and women of wealth are incalculable. They are actively and subtilely solicited by every organized charity or social institution, by hundreds of educational groups, by clergymen from nearly every religious denomination, and by tens of thousands of individuals from Tacoma to Timbuktu. They are praised and flattered, warned and forewarned, offered honors and entertainments, even personal gifts and a galaxy of rewards. 'It is easy to be generous with other people's property.' Modern methods

[1] *Hearst's International Magazine*, September, 1923.

of communication have made this Latin proverb more applicable to-day than ever before.

As the choice rests with the giver, so does the responsibility.

While money has always been a medium of exchange, it is to-day, in the United States, largely a medium of usefulness. The generosity of the American people has made this country the most philanthropic social organization in history.[1] The art of giving is indigenous. It is one of the fundamental evidences of a national idealism. Whenever or wherever there is a genuine need or a world crisis, the generosity of the public is spontaneous. It rises above the mere mirage of money-making, shaming the skeptics who cannot see the idealism beyond any materialism. In the case of 'Mr. Smith' the spirit of giving was not born when he became a millionaire. Long before he was a rich man, he shared his income and capital to such a degree that it often appeared as if the more he gave the more he received. The first year his gifts exceeded his income, he would not believe the figures until the auditor's report proved the fact beyond question.

[1] Under the heading, 'Two Great Public Gifts,' the *Chicago Tribune* said, December 15, 1924: 'James B. Duke and George Eastman have announced gifts which will add to the vast total which rich men in the United States have contributed from their wealth to public causes. This giving is a tradition of American private wealth unequalled and unapproached in any other country, and doubtless inheritance and income taxation has strengthened it. But American men of great wealth have always shown a tendency to redistribute a generous part of their gains in the form of donations to institutions or some form of public service, an example which has impressed foreign observers as an interesting American phenomenon, if not one to be followed. John D. Rockefeller's giving has been on such a large scale and so deliberately organized and directed as to be one of the important world forces in the field to which it is limited, at first general higher education and later medical education, sanitation and research. Andrew Carnegie's giving was and is another instance, and taking the whole current of private beneficence which flows from the private wealth of Americans to fructify some field of education, philanthropy or culture, it represents one of the most important facts of American life.'

In making his 'choice,' outside the educational field, Eastman founded the Rochester Dental Dispensary, the Bureau of Municipal Research, and built a large and efficient plant for the Rochester Chamber of Commerce which rivals the stately building of the United States Chamber of Commerce in Washington, D.C. He was one of the pioneers and the largest contributor to the Community Chest and to numerous other civic organizations engaged in some form of service to 'human needs.'

'What appealed to me in connection with the Dental Dispensary,' he wrote,[1] 'was that I concluded I could get more results for my money in that expenditure than in any other philanthropic scheme I had investigated. Several years experience with its operation leaves me still with that opinion . . . money spent in the care of children's teeth is one of the wisest expenditures that can be made.'

It is not so many years ago that the public looked upon preventive dentistry with something akin to Mark Twain's skepticism of astronomy. He could easily understand, he said, how scientists could measure in millions of miles the distance between the earth and the stars, but he could not make out how they could read the names so clearly.

During the greater part of the history of mankind, the public has been as skeptical about dentistry as Mark Twain claimed he was of astronomy. 'The fathers have eaten sour grapes and the children's teeth are set on edge,' said Jeremiah, and several centuries later a French prophet observed that 'Gourmands make their graves with their teeth.' These men were good diagnosticians,

---

[1] This letter was written to Dr. D. B. Irwin, Duluth, Minnesota, September 30, 1919. Similar letters were written to Lord Riddell, Dr. Flexner, and Dr. Burkhart.

but the world was as slow to recognize the influences of heredity and the dangers of overeating as it was to realize the relationship between sound teeth and good health.

The development of a dental consciousness in Rochester dates from 1868, when the Seventh District Dental Society of New York was founded. During the succeeding half-century, education and experience here and elsewhere brought revolutionary changes in dental science, hygiene, and practice. 'Dentists are no longer only tooth carpenters,' declared Dr. W. H. Weston, President of the National Dental Association of New South Wales, when he urged the foundation of dental dispensaries in Australia. Dentistry to-day is a recognized science throughout the world, largely because of the undaunted leadership of the profession in the United States, while in the development of preventive dentistry for children two institutions in this country have served the world as models.

'Rochester will be known as the pioneer in this work,' said Dr. Woods Hutchinson, but this position rightly belongs to 'The Forsyth Dental Infirmary for Children' in Boston. Thomas B. Forsyth was the pioneer. Then came Eastman, for such is the nature of progress. 'I am simply amazed by the extent, scope, thoroughness, and effectiveness of the work that is being done in Rochester for the health of children,' said Dr. George M. Cooper, of the North Carolina State Board of Health; while Murry Guggenheim, of New York City, was 'inspired by the far-reaching benefits accruing to the residents,' after his visit to Rochester.

Eastman's active interest in dentistry began in January, 1909, when he made his first contribution to the Rochester Dental Society. This was the beginning of a series of yearly payments which had no relationship, even in his own mind, with the evolution of the use of X-ray plates or film in dental practice or diagnosis. He had long since made it a definite policy not to mix business with philanthropy. 'East is East and West is West, and never the twain shall meet.' This was true of his business and his personal interests.

In March, 1914, when his sixth yearly subscription to the Society was due, Nelson Curtis, of Boston, was visiting him. In the course of their conversation, Eastman learned of the preventive work being done in that city by the Forsyth institution. Without much ado, Curtis later obtained pamphlets from that Infirmary and sent them to Rochester. During the rest of that year Eastman reflected upon the possibilities of a similar project in Rochester without revealing his thoughts to any one. He visited also the Forsyth Infirmary without disclosing his identity.

In the spring of 1915, William Bausch, knowing of Eastman's interest in the local dental society, submitted tentative proposals for the establishment of dental clinics throughout the city which had been put forth by several dentists and citizens. For two or three months there was an exchange of ideas until Eastman's own views were crystallized, and he wrote Bausch, July 6, 1915. This, he informed Dr. Harvey J. Burkhart, was the beginning of the Rochester Dental Dispensary.

'Concerning the Dental Hospital project, I should not care to have anything to do with this affair unless a scheme can be devised which will cover the whole field and do the work thoroughly and completely, and in the best manner. Basing my opinion on all the information that has come to me up to the present time, I do not think that the work of treating the children's teeth, outside of the prophylactic work to be done by the hygienists, can be satisfactorily done and supervised at centers distributed over the city, and I do not think that I would be interested in any scheme which would involve this plan of procedure. If, however, it is decided to adopt the other plan I make you the following proposition:

‘1. You to form a corporation to be managed by say nine or more trustees; the trustees to be men who will be interested in carrying on the work of such an institution.

‘2. The trustees to provide for the raising of a sum of not less than ten thousand dollars yearly, for five years.

‘3. The city of Rochester to agree to pay the hospital the cost of the services of a sufficient number of dental hygienists, and material, to clean and examine the teeth of the school children twice a year; these hygienists to be under the control and direction of the trustees.

‘If the above can be brought about, I will build and equip a suitable central building and contribute the sum of thirty thousand dollars, for five years. At the end of the five years, if the institution is operating successfully and performing its mission satisfactorily, I will endow it with the sum of seven hundred and fifty thousand dollars, reserving the right to make any conditions at that time which I may consider advisable.

‘If it is decided that forty thousand dollars per year is not enough for the running expenses of the hospital, I will furnish the same proportion of any additional sum that is required for five years.

‘It is contemplated, of course, that there will be a nominal charge for the work done at the hospital and that suitable limits will be fixed defining the persons who are entitled to the benefit of this nominal charge.’

Within a few days of this letter, Forsyth sent Eastman blueprints and drawings of that institution, with a characteristic note:

'And when that day arrives that the United States shall be dotted with similar institutions, then I shall be content that the Forsyth Infirmary has actually accomplished ALL that it was founded for; i.e., not alone that the children of Boston be benefited, but that our cities and towns, observing the good we are daily accomplishing, should pattern similar buildings for their own use.

'The greater the number of such institutions the less need for insane hospitals, sanitariums and prisons.

'And coöperation, encouragement, should be given in large portions, to all those contemplating work such as we have undertaken.'

Events then followed in rapid succession. On July 31, the Rochester Board of Education approved the plan for taking care of the teeth of the school children and Eastman left on a trip to the Pacific Coast. Returning in the fall, he wrote his friend Babbott.[1]

'We had a bully time on our trip, enjoyed the visit to the San Diego and San Francisco Expositions, but most of all the four weeks' camping in the mountains. We had a pack train of thirty-two animals and traveled through a most delightful country, inaccessible by other means. Both Eastwood and I got elk and we had elk meat, trout, and mountain grouse in addition to the eatables we took along. I managed to work off about twelve pounds and am now twenty pounds lighter than I was a year ago, which is still as much as I ought to weigh.

'I regret that you were not available to go and look at the model of the Chamber of Commerce Building. Will send you a photograph of it. I have not seen it myself.'

[1] October 6, 1915.

Eastman was happy, as usual, to be back home and to find the Dispensary and Chamber of Commerce projects under way.

From the beginning, Eastman felt that the successes of the Dispensary would depend largely upon the director. At that time Dr. Burkhart was mayor of the neighboring city of Batavia, New York. Eastman had looked upon him from the beginning as the ideal head for the institution, but also from the beginning he declined to exert any influence with the Board of Directors in the selection. Although he was in communication with the neighboring mayor throughout the negotiations, he wrote Dr. Burkhart, November 12, 1915, that he did not show the directors any of his letters and had not replied to his recent communications, 'because I did not want to interfere in the selection,' but 'I am very glad that you are coming to Rochester and I have great faith that you will make a thorough success of the institution.' A few days before, Eastman had written Bausch: 'I understand the committee have selected Dr. Burkhart and I believe they have made the best possible choice. Under his direction and the guidance of the Board I believe that the Dispensary will fulfill all of our most sanguine anticipations.'

The following year the Dispensary, located on East Main Street, near the business section and accessible from all parts of the city by car line, was beginning to assume final form. Forsyth came to Rochester for a visit, and upon his return to Boston Eastman wrote: 'I thank you for all the nice things you say about the Dispensary. It is a source of gratification to me that it has turned out so well. We are fortunate in having a man like Dr. Burkhart as director, as the success of any such institution depends largely upon the personality of the man who is in immediate charge. I hope it is some satisfaction to you

to know that the Rochester Dispensary was benefited
greatly by having the Forsyth institution as an example
before it, and I am not at all reluctant to acknowledge
the advantage it gave us in deciding many questions.
Moreover, seeing your splendid establishment was what
suggested making the experiment in Rochester.'

On October 15, 1917, the Dispensary was opened.[1]
The dental department was provided with thirty-seven
operating units, especially designed, and provision was
made for thirty-one additional units. And, incidentally,
the construction of these units, largely designed for this
institution, served as models for the manufacture of units
which in succeeding years were in use in practically all
of the leading dental offices in the United States. The
department of Orthodontia, for straightening crooked
teeth, was one of the most important departments, while
the work of cleaning the teeth of children in the schools
was done by squads of licensed dentists and dental hygienists, the latter being trained in the school for dental
hygienists, conducted by the Dispensary. The establishment of this school opened a new vocation for young
women. The prophylactic squads were provided with
portable equipment consisting of chairs, engines, instruments, sterilizers, etc., and, under careful and strict supervision, they made the rounds of the schools twice a
year. A school lecturer was employed by the Dispensary
to deliver illustrated lantern-slide lectures on oral hygiene
and other health subjects. After the teeth were cleaned,

[1] 'Thirty of the unit equipment of the dental infirmary were given by
Mrs. Adelina Ritter Shumway and Mrs. Laura Ritter Brown, in memory
of their father, the late Frank Ritter. Mr. William Bausch, President of the
Board of Trustees, provided the furnishings and decorations of the children's
room and Mrs. Rudolph H. Hofheinz in memory of her husband, the late
Dr. Rudolph H. Hofheinz, a member of the first Board of Trustees, presented the furnishing and equipment of the Research Laboratory.' (Annual Report of the Rochester Dental Dispensary, 1928.)

ROCHESTER DENTAL DISPENSARY

a survey was made of the mouth or pathological conditions were observed, and if additional dental work was
necessary, duplicate records were made, one for the
teacher and parent, and the other for the Dispensary, so
that all these cases could be followed up.

Thousands of pamphlets on the value of clean teeth,
printed in English, Italian, Yiddish, and Polish, were
sent to parents as a means of education to induce them
to take their babies to the Dispensary as soon as the first
tooth appeared. By follow-up methods it was planned to
retain the child as a patient until the age of sixteen. A
few years' experience proved the wisdom of this procedure, which resulted eventually in the standardization
of filling materials and methods of procedure of tremendous benefit to future generations. In the department of Orthodontia, for example, not only was the appearance and comfort of many children greatly improved,
but improvements in speech were obtained by widening
the arch, and frequently children who were below normal
mentally were helped by the removal of nerve pressure
usually found in a crowded jaw.

From the beginning the Dispensary was on a 'mass
production' basis. Within three years the records were
formidable. In 1919 alone, there were 46,521 tooth
treatments; 19,593 root treatments, 1238 root fillings;
13,049 amalgam fillings; 1523 synthetic fillings; 15,268
cement fillings; 142 gutta-percha fillings; 174 silver
nitrate; 77 pulps capped; 31 crowns; 3 inlays; 4117
orthodontia treatments; 635 devitalizations; 11,997 extractions; 351 X-rays; and a total of 48,813 visits to the
Dispensary, of whom 42,994 paid the minimum fee of
five cents.

'Since the establishment of the Dispensary,' Dr. Burkhart reported (1920), 'the general hygienic conditions of

the school children of Rochester have noticeably improved. In many cases the education of the child to appreciate the comfort and benefit of a clean mouth has resulted in improved conditions in other directions. The municipal authorities, and the people of Rochester generally, strongly support the work. The Board of Education, the Health Department and physicians and dentists have heartily coöperated, and much of the credit for the results so far achieved is due to their sympathy and support.'

By the summer of 1920, the Dispensary had, in fact, been so successful that it contributed both directly and indirectly to the evolution of the idea which ultimately became the project for a great medical center in Rochester. On June 25, 1920, Eastman wrote the Trustees:

'When the Dispensary was founded I did not foresee that it might have an opportunity to become a part of a great project for a higher grade of dental education than had before been attempted. Since the opening of the Dispensary I have on several occasions discussed with our Director, Dr. Burkhart, the growing necessity for such dental education, but neither of us could see clearly any way of bringing it about. When the plan to establish a great Medical School in connection with the University of Rochester came up I welcomed the opportunity which it furnished for an alliance between the Dispensary and the University which would accomplish the much desired object. I feel that an alliance of this sort can be effected in such a way that it will not interfere with the present work of the Dispensary and will at the same time enable it to accomplish a much larger work than we had in mind when it was founded. The carrying out of such an alliance will call for a very high degree of coöperation between the Trustees of the Dispensary and the Trustees of the

University, and under present conditions I have no fear of any lack of such coöperation, but new conditions may arise which will render it more difficult. It is in view of this that I should like to put on record my wishes as far as they can be formulated.

'The main object in mind when the Dispensary was founded was the care of the teeth of children in Rochester and its vicinity. That work should not be neglected because of any enlargement of the scope and activities of the Dispensary and it is my wish that as long as the Dispensary is needed to serve that purpose it shall continue to perform that work and, if possible, extend it under such regulations as its Trustees may deem wise and reasonable.

'In connection with the Medical School of the University the Dispensary can, by enlarging its scope and activities, serve as a clinic for practical instruction of students in dentistry. To accomplish that purpose it is my wish and request that the Dispensary shall coöperate with the University to the fullest extent possible during the life of such institutions in order that the Dispensary may furnish to the University a clinic for the practical education of students in dentistry. The relations between the University and the Dispensary, in order to make the Dispensary of the greatest use possible as a clinic for dental instruction, should be, as far as the separate organization of the Dispensary will permit, the same as the relations between the University and the University Hospital which will be established in connection with the Medical School of the University.

'If at any time the need of the Dispensary is done away with, or lessened to such an extent that the Trustees think it inadvisable to maintain it as a separate institution, then I should like to have its property, real and personal, including its endowment, turned over to the University of Rochester, for the benefit primarily of dental education, but if it cannot be advantageously used for that purpose then for the benefit of general medical education.

'Let me take this opportunity to express to you my warm appreciation of the interest that you have taken in the Dental Dispensary and of the willingness that you have shown to help the Dispensary undertake the added responsibilities which this new alliance entails.'

In the mean time, plans were under way for an extensive tonsil-adenoid clinic, beginning July 26, 1920, when, four days before the opening, Eastman wrote William Bausch:

'I am anxious that the Dental Dispensary shall have plenty of money to operate its hospital for nose and throat work and especially to increase the amount of orthodontia work, and therefore I make this proposition:

'I will turn over to the Dispensary one thousand (1000) shares of Kodak common stock, the income therefrom to be used as far as may be necessary for the above purposes, providing that the contributing members of the Board of Directors will renew their subscriptions for another five years and that the vacancies on the Board will be filled by the election of contributing members.

'I know that the members of the Board of Directors are greatly interested in this work and this will insure having all the money necessary available for the additional work which is to be undertaken.

'There will be only one other condition accompanying the above gift which I propose to make, and that is that children of employees of the Kodak Company shall have a more liberal rate of family earnings per capita specified to qualify them for treatment at the Dispensary, which will enable them to more generally participate in all the work of the institution.'

At the time of the organization of the Rochester Dental Dispensary, it was recognized that there would be need of an oral surgical department to care for certain cases not within the strict scope of dentistry. These cases were those in which there was some correctible condition that interfered with proper dental development, as cleft palate, harelip, and, most notably, defective nasal respiration caused by enlarged tonsils and adenoids. If satisfactory results were to be obtained from a dental point of view, particularly as regards orthodontia, it was of paramount importance that the nose, throat, and mouth be put into as normal a functioning condition as possible before the attempt was made to straighten the teeth.

After the child had had the necessary repair done to diseased teeth, he was examined for nose, throat, and mouth defects before being passed on to the orthodontists. It was found that an astonishingly large number of the children had hypertrophied tonsils and adenoids to such a degree as to cut down nasal respiration to a point that very markedly interfered with the normal development of the jaws, with consequent narrowing of the upper arch and marked disturbance of normal tooth eruption.

The surgical department of the Dispensary was therefore created with a capacity of eighteen beds, which is sufficient to care for the cases requiring surgical care from amongst the regular dental cases coming to the Dispensary. By operating three days a week, this department was able to keep pace with the tonsil and adenoid cases which had a direct bearing in dental development. It was not the original intention to remove the tonsils and adenoids from all the Dispensary children in whom such an operation was indicated by symptoms other than those having a direct bearing on the dental work.

During the routine examination of Dispensary cases, many were found to have diseased tonsils which were not strictly obstructive, but which were detrimental to the children's general health, and which were being neglected by the families of the children. It took very little inquiry to ascertain that this condition was prevalent, not alone amongst the regular attendants at the Dispensary, but also amongst many children in the city and surrounding county with whom it was possible to get in touch.

For several years past the general hospitals of the city had been regularly conducting clinics for tonsil and adenoid removal, and in this way had disposed of a considerable number of cases. However, these comparatively small clinics became so crowded that their waiting lists had been filled up months in advance.

Knowledge, therefore, of the existence of a large and constantly increasing number of children in Rochester and surrounding rural districts suffering from the effects of enlarged and diseased tonsils and adenoids was the principal factor leading to the decision to hold the emergency clinic. Records of children treated in the Dental Dispensary, supplemented by reports from the schools, inspectors, and nurses under the jurisdiction of the Health Bureau, agents of various child welfare organizations, and from community nurses in the rural districts, as well as the testimony of physicians and surgeons, indicated that the number of operable cases had reached an alarming total. This accumulation was due, it was believed, to the following causes: Shortage of doctors in private and hospital practice, due to the World War emergency; inability of hospitals and dispensaries since the war emergency to catch up with the accumulation of cases; ignorance and indifference on the part of parents both as to the symptoms and ill-effects of adenoids and diseased tonsils, and the importance of having them removed early in the life of the child; financial inability of families of limited means to pay the fee charged by the regular practitioner.

These conditions caused Eastman and Dr. Burkhart much concern. Both realized that, unless they could be removed or measurably improved, the regular dental work of the Dispensary along preventive lines would be largely negative in the case of children who, although having been released from the handicap of bad teeth and mouth conditions, were forced, through lack of necessary throat surgery, to study, work, and grow up under the equally deplorable handicap of adenoids and diseased tonsils. It was recognized, also, that the accumulation of cases needing treatment had reached such proportions that there was little likelihood of getting the situation in hand unless emergency steps were taken. This led, after consultations and conferences with a number of leading physicians and surgeons, to the formulation of plans for the holding of an intensive clinic extending over a period of seven weeks with a definite schedule of 200 operations a week, or a total of 1400 operations. As a matter of record it may be stated that operations were performed on 1470 children.

This led to a survey of conditions in the public schools, under the direction of Dr. George W. Goler, city health officer, which disclosed that 27,748 children were in need of tonsil-adenoid operations, and plans were made for a more extensive clinic early in 1921.

'I have been so much interested lately in medical affairs that I almost feel like a doctor myself these days,' Eastman wrote J. G. Palmer, manager of the Canadian Kodak Company, Limited:

'Maybe you have heard of the tonsil-adenoid clinic that the Dental Dispensary pulled off last summer. I am sending you under another cover a booklet about it. Just now we are engaged in a bigger affair intended to clean up the town. We are going to do about six hundred cases a week for thirty weeks. I hear and see so much of the operation that I feel I can do the job myself; so if you need anything done to your tonsils, let me know and perhaps I will come over and tackle it. In addition to the tonsil affair, I am interested in the starting of a new medical school here, and last week I spent a whole day in the Johns Hopkins Hospital, Baltimore, and half a day in the Rockefeller Institute, New York. It is all very interesting.'

Dr. Rhees and Eastman had visited Johns Hopkins Hospital together, and upon his return to Rochester, Eastman wrote Dr. Winford H. Smith of that institution:

'Our new tonsil clinic is to open up on Monday, the 10th of Jan. We have fitted up to do in this clinic 80 cases a day, operating five days a week and in the four hospitals and Dental Dispensary an additional 200 cases per week, making 600 altogether; and the intention is to run for thirty weeks, if we can get the children.

'My visit to Johns Hopkins was a great pleasure to me and I think I got out of it as much as a layman could. Anyway, I enjoyed every bit of it and much appreciated the kind attentions showered upon Dr. Rhees and myself by everybody we met.'

There was no doubt but that Eastman's heart was in this project. Through the coöperation of Brulatour and the large producers and distributors of motion pictures, Eastman obtained free use of leading comedies for the 'kiddies.' 'Everything was made so attractive for the children last summer,' he wrote Hiram Abrams, of United

Artists' Corporation, thanking him for one of Douglas Fairbanks's pictures, 'that I understand some of them have attempted to qualify for a repeat operation.' 'I am feeling very vigorous,' he notified Dr. Abraham Flexner, 'so look out when you come up here'; and to his old friend Babbott he asked: 'Please let me know whether you are going to be there [in New York], as I would like to see you and bring the history of the world down to date.'

After the second successful tonsil-adenoid clinic he wrote Dr. Burkhart: 'My furnishing the plant and part of the maintenance money might have been of no, or of little, avail if you had not put the finishing touch on it and got the results. It is the end results that I am looking at and they could not have been attained without you. That these results have been attained at the cost of anxiety and effort that would have incapacitated many men I am fully aware but I think your humorous way of looking at things, as well as your picturesque vocabulary which enables you to sometimes relieve your feelings, has been a life saver and it has also been a source of great amusement and joy to me when we have discussed matters.'

During the spring of 1921, when Dr. Burkhart was away on a vacation, Eastman assumed the rôle of 'Mr. Punch' and sent him the latest news:

'Yours of March 21st from the steamer was received yesterday, and I was amused at your account of what Flexner said. He himself is the worst highwayman that ever flitted into and out of Rochester. He put up a job on me and cleaned me out of a thundering lot of my hard-earned savings. I have just heard that he is coming up here June 2d to speak at the graduating exercises of the "allied" hospitals. I have been asked to sit on the stage with him, but instead of that I shall probably flee the town for fear he will hypnotize me again.

'I have only been up to the Dispensary once since you left. It was last Monday when I took through the place Mr. and Mrs. J. Lionberger Davis from St. Louis. They were on the trip to Japan with Mulligan and me. Davis is much interested in civic affairs and they were both very enthusiastic over the Dispensary. Masse took us around, and made a very good impression. I told them about you, and they thought you must be quite a feller. I laid particular stress on the ability you have shown in taking care of the young ladies' boarding-school and picking out good-looking students. Davis told a good story about a surgeon. It seems a noted surgeon was performing an abdominal operation on a private patient before a group of hospital internes. One of them was a fresh young duck, who was always asking foolish questions. As the doctor was making the first incision, this interne said: "Doctor, what are you operating for?" The whole thing having been explained already, the doctor impatiently said, "A thousand dollars." The interne said: "Oh, no. What has he got?" The doctor answered: "Damn it, I have just told you, one thousand dollars." '

By this time inquiries and visitors were coming from all parts of the world. Among the many interested parties was Julius Rosenwald, of Chicago, who had sponsored a survey by Dr. Michael M. Davis, of the American Hospital Association Service Bureau.

'I truly hope that you will have this report printed for distribution,' Eastman wrote him, August 15, 1921. 'It seems to me that the report is admirable in every way, and if made public will perform a very valuable function in crystallizing the ideas of people interested in the development of dentistry for the masses. I agree absolutely with the conclusion of Dr. Davis with one exception hereafter referred to, and, as before indicated, I think the publication will help materially in directing future efforts along practical and efficient lines. There is only one thing that I wish he had included, and that is the reason for our preferring the centralized clinic as against the separate clinics recommended by some of the local people interested in the proposition, viz., difficulty of proper supervision.

'For your information I will say that the question as to whether we would have separate clinics or one centralized institution was very carefully gone into before the Dispensary was built, and I finally declined to have anything to do with the enterprise if separate school clinics were to be established. The reason for this was that it is impossible to properly supervise small clinics. It is necessary to have as operators young, immature dentists who cannot be allowed to work without very close supervision. No clinic, therefore, should be smaller than will warrant the employment of a first-class supervisor on the spot. Dr. Burkhart's experience in running the Dispensary has shown the wisdom of our selecting of a central clinic. Such supervision cannot be given by any one traveling from one school to another.

'There is an advantage of the centralized class which should not be overlooked, and that is the benefit of it upon the young dental graduates as a post-graduate course. As you doubtless know, the dental schools of this country are pretty much in the same condition as the medical schools were when the Flexner survey was made. The graduates turned out are lamentably lacking in knowledge and technique and need a post-graduate training before they go into general practice.

'As to supervisors, one of the most difficult problems in any scheme of extensive dental work is to get men who are competent to supervise, almost all of the competent men having practices of their own that enable them to earn vastly more than any salary that a philanthropic institution can pay.

'Dr. Davis's report in my opinion ranks with the Flexner survey, above mentioned, in the clarity of insight into the subject and wisdom of his recommendations. I congratulate you heartily on having caused to be made such a valuable contribution to the understanding of the situation.'

During succeeding years the work and influence of the Dispensary increased until nearly every child in the city under sixteen, whose parents were unable to provide for preventive dentistry for their own children, had come under the care of an institution, which, in addition to its direct services, has succeeded in abolishing in the child's mind the association of dentistry with pain and fear. To the children of Rochester, dentistry is akin to play. They frolic to and from the institution as if they were on an outing. In eleven years they have made nearly seven hundred and fifty thousand visits to the Dispensary. In addition, approximately one million prophylactic treatments have been given in the schools. Under these circumstances it is not surprising that Eastman's enthusiasm should have remained keyed to the heights of the children.

Another project which Eastman got under way simultaneously with the Dental Dispensary was the Rochester Bureau of Municipal Research. Through this body he was able to study the whole range of civic problems as well as the human needs of a cosmopolitan community.

Like most American cities, the form of Rochester's city government has been an experiment, changing from time to time to meet the varying needs of a growing community. Altogether Rochester had nine charters before the city manager plan was adopted.

Eastman became interested in the city government when he was a young man, but took no active part in local politics until, as a result of his earlier contributions to the New York Bureau of Municipal Research, he founded a similar organization in Rochester, April 20, 1915. This followed a survey of the city by the New York Bureau.

'The Rochester Bureau differs fundamentally from all the other research bureaus,' Stephen B. Story, the Director, explained.[1] 'It is the one bureau whose work with the city is done in an entirely coöperative way. The other bureaus, because they are dependent upon a fairly wide circle of friends, must, in order to raise funds with which to continue existence, advertise more or less extensively the work which they are doing and the good which they are accomplishing. The other bureaus find it necessary to supply wind for their own horns, as it were, and to call attention to their accomplishments. This can't help but militate against a fully coöperative plan of work. If a city official makes use of a suggestion of a bureau and improves the work of his department or division of the city government, and later finds the bureau advertising the fact that the improvement was a result of the bureau's work, much of the incentive for adopting these suggestions disappears. It has always been the policy of the Rochester Bureau to keep itself, its staff, and its trustees in the background, and to let all credit for improvement go to the city officials who actually make them.

'We have a staff of several men with engineering, accounting, and general experience in municipal work.

[1] February 27, 1926.

There is a tendency to call us "experts." We have come
to feel a sort of aversion for that term, because we feel
that we have no special endowment or corner on experience which enables us to be classified as authorities on
the whole gamut of subjects relating to municipal government. We are not more expert at our work than you
men are — lawyers, bankers, salesmen, advertising managers, engineers, or what not. We are simply a group of
individuals who have devoted our time to studying the
science of government. Some of us specialize in particular fields of work, for instance, engineering and public
works, public utilities, traffic and police matters, accounting and municipal finance.'

The work of the Bureau was classified by Director
Story as follows:

'1. A study of various kinds of garbage collection
equipment and their attendant systems looking toward
the most economical equipment which the city can buy
to provide improved garbage collection service.

'2. Advising with and assisting the assessors in installing a scientific system of assessing city property.

'3. A study of better utilization of the public market
and a determination of whether or not expansion of the
market is advisable at this time.

'4. Devising a system of centralized accounting and
cost finding for the hospitals of the city. This involves a
consideration of the accounting relation between the new
City Hospital and University of Rochester.

'5. Planning the movement of various offices into the
new annex on Court Street with the least disruption of
the work of the departments involved.

'6. Preparing the second part of a report on "The Volume and Cost of social work in the City of Rochester,"
which will be a collection of statistical and historical

data on the various social service organizations of the city.

'7. Acting as sort of a service agency to the Mayor's Advisory Committee on Subway Operation which involves everything from clerical and secretarial work for the committee to assisting in the preparation of its report.

'8. Study of the business operation of one of the elementary schools in order to determine whether or not a more effective arrangement of work is possible.'

Through the Bureau, experts from other cities were retained to formulate a city manager plan for Rochester. In the spring of 1922, a programme was laid out and Eastman communicated it to a few of the leaders:

'The "Democrat and Chronicle" will open the subject up, probably with an editorial, and hopes to get Mr. [George W.] Aldridge to say that if the city manager plan is better than the one in use, and if the citizens of Rochester want it, they ought to have it. This will open the subject up for discussion in the newspapers. I am confident that they will take it up with considerable interest, especially the "Times-Union," which has had a campaign outlined for more than a year, and the "Democrat and Chronicle," which is the organization paper. I hope while you are here you will meet Mr. [Herbert J.] Winn, the president of the "Democrat and Chronicle," and Mr. [Frank E.] Gannett or Mr. [Irwin] Davenport, proprietors of the "Times-Union"; also Mr. [Francis B.] Mitchell, of the "Express," and Mr. [Louis M.] Antisdale, of the "Herald." The "Express" is a Republican paper and the "Herald" independent, with Democratic tendencies; at any rate "agin" the organization. All of these men think it will take considerable time to educate the people, and it may be too early to suggest a charter committee.'

The educational process was as slow as molasses in winter, but by the time three winters had passed, the city was eager for action.

By March, 1925, the Bureau had completed a study for the City Government Plan Committee of twenty-four other cities, gathering information and ammunition for the Rochester campaign. This precipitated one of the hottest political contests in the city's history. The working draft of the charter was written by the Bureau and then submitted to four experts: Professor Howard Lee McBain, Professor of Constitutional Law and now Dean of Columbia University; to Isaac Alder and Charles L. Pierce, Rochester attorneys; and Professor A. R. Hatton, Professor of Political Science at Western Reserve University.

When the votes were counted, it was evident that the three-year educational campaign had not been conducted for naught. The manager plan was approved and Director Story was appointed city manager.

In the fall of 1917, Eastman marshaled some of the facts about the city for use in Washington when he endeavored to persuade the Government to establish a rehabilitation hospital in the city. He insisted that Rochester, 'in its industrial, educational, social, and religious life, is an ideal place for the location of a hospital that seeks to put men back on their feet as useful and productive citizens'; and supported this opinion with the following tabulated reasons:

'1. Rochester has, in round numbers, 1700 manufacturing establishments. Many of them are small. Therefore, the management can give personal attention to the introduction of new workers.

'2. There are over 325 separate commodities manufactured in Rochester. Thus there is a very wide field of activity for the worker.

'3. Most of the articles manufactured in Rochester are light in weight, small in bulk and high in value, thus calling for skill rather than strength. Illustrations: Thermometers, optical goods, cameras, photographic supplies, check protectors, clothing, shoes, carbon paper, typewriter ribbon, ivory buttons, dental supplies, in all of which Rochester leads the world or ranks very high.

'4. The conditions of labor are most favorable — sanitary factories, broad enlightened management, and good wages.

'5. The spirit of the city and the ideals of its people are high as expressed in its public education, churches, home ownership, parks and playgrounds, thus aiding materially the work of readjustment and rehabilitation.

'6. The attitude of the community is one of study and improvement. To prove this, it is only necessary to point out that over 40,000 people out of a population of 250,000 are students in some way in the public schools alone.

'7. Rochester from the beginning has fostered secondary technical education. This is shown by the tens of thousands of students who have carried on continuation work, both in day and evening classes in Mechanic's Institute.'

While Rochester is a city of diversified industries, its greatest development has taken place since it became the photographic capital of the world. Five hundred yards from the 'great fall' of the Genesee, in the heart of the city, there stands to-day a sixteen-story office building, erected in the days before such structures were named for bondholders and built by mortgages. On the roof is an electric sign of five magic letters. From the top-floor windows it is possible to survey the surrounding country in all directions. To the east, near the intersection of

Main and State Streets, commonly called the 'Four Corners,' is the old Arcade, where George W. Eastman's Commercial College was located in 1854, and where his son worked as an office boy after the close of the Civil War. One block from the corner is the Rochester Savings Bank, where Eastman was second bookkeeper when he made his first invention in the photographic industry in 1879.

Intermingled with these and other older structures are many modern stores and office buildings which comprise the business section of Rochester. Included herein are the Chamber of Commerce and Mechanics Institute Buildings, the latter covering two city blocks. Scattered in other sections of the city are the Eastman Theater, Kilbourn Hall, the Music School, Rochester Dental Dispensary, city hospitals, and a group of buildings some day to be included in a civic center. A few miles from the city, near the new Medical School and Strong Memorial Hospital, are the new buildings and grounds of the University of Rochester, rapidly nearing completion. Six miles out, with its four-mile frontage on the lake, is the Durand-Eastman Park and Zoo, extending over four hundred and eighty-eight acres.

From the sixteenth floor of the Kodak Building, looking west to the shore of Lake Ontario at Charlotte, the company's pumping station is visible. Every twenty-four hours it pumps from ten to twelve million gallons of water [1] for use at Kodak Park, which is easily within view, for it is only two and one half miles away, and now covers four hundred acres. The total floor area of its one hundred and eighty buildings exceeds four million square feet. Surrounding the Park are the homes of several thousand employees, many of them financed by the Em-

[1] The capacity is being increased to 45,000,000 gallons per day.

ployees' Saving Association. In 1890 all of this was farm land and outside the city limits.

Surrounding the office building itself, are the Camera Works and its allied buildings, extending over two city blocks and facing on State Street, not far from the deep gorge of the Genesee. Across the river, to the north, is the Hawk-Eye Works, where lenses and some scientific research instruments are made.

These are some of the Eastman landmarks in Rochester. But, after they were built and had contributed to the growth and prosperity of the city, Eastman's thoughts were no longer of landmarks but of a civic center. He was interested in the reconstruction of the heart of the city. Rochester had outgrown its century old, haphazard location of public buildings. It needed a civic center and Eastman, as usual, did what he could, in a practical way, to promote the modernization of the city. In June, 1924, when a civic center was again a theme of public consideration, Eastman purchased the old Kimball tobacco factory on the river, one of the key private properties which might be utilized in a later scheme for a more modern and beautiful city.

When the deal was concluded, he wrote Mayor Clarence D. Van Zandt the following offer:

'It [the City] can have possession of this property and occupy it temporarily as a City Hall for a period of say three years, without rent, the City to pay all taxes, assessments, and expense of upkeep during that time; and to have the privilege of making improvements and alterations such as required to carry on its business. After that the property will be available for either purchase by the City for an amount not to exceed the price paid ($500,-000), or rental for a further term, the yearly rental not to exceed 5% on that price.

'If the City accepts this offer I shall expect two things: First, that if the Planning Commission recommends the site in the middle of the river for a permanent City Hall, either in connection or out of connection with the general plan of a civic center opening on to Main Street, that the City will not proceed with the Fitzhugh Street project. And second, that the City will use the money which will be released from that project to carry out its agreement with the University of Rochester to build a new Municipal Hospital, one half of which was to be completed forthwith and the balance within five years from the date of the contract; and that the City will let the contract for the whole concrete frame in time to get it completed this fall.

'I feel very strongly that the City is obligated by every consideration to finish the Municipal Hospital according to the contract. There has already been a delay of over a year in proceeding with the first part of it. Also that nothing should be done which will block Rochester in developing a plan for the civic center which is by far the most promising that has ever been proposed. If the plan as a whole proves impracticable, the grouping of the three new buildings, the City Hall in the middle of the river, with the Soldiers' Memorial and Auditorium on one side and the Public Library on the other, will make a civic center that will be a credit to Rochester in any case, irrespective of the merits of the more ambitious plan, and entails no obligation to go farther unless it is found desirable later on.

'The main objections to the more ambitious plan that I have seen relate to the water hazard but in view of what can be done in the control of the river these will probably disappear before any move can possibly be made to carry out the project. On the other hand, has due weight been given to the great protection from a fire spreading across the river it would be to have a street opened across Main Street bridge?

'I realize the necessity you described to me of your making some immediate and definite provision for additional City Hall facilities and I hope that this proposition will meet it.'

Upon the expiration of this agreement, the City leased the building at a nominal rent. While the acceptance of the proposal did not obligate the municipality to any definite project, it is doubtless only a question of time until Rochester achieves what has been a community dream for years.

None of these civic projects, however, were as important from the standpoint of civic duty as the Community Chest. The genesis of this movement is related in a letter to Lindsay:[1]

'There is one item of real news which has not got into the newspapers yet and that is that we are considering a welfare or patriotic fund for the city, to take in all the charities and all the war charitable activities. In preparing to lay out the scheme for the forthcoming Red Cross Campaign, which has now been set down for the week beginning May 20th, I thought it would be well to dispose of the question whether we should adopt the "War Chest" scheme which has been instituted in other cities; so I called a meeting of about a dozen heads of the principal activities last Friday night. Much to my surprise after the subject had been throughly discussed every one present seemed very much in favor of instituting such a plan and another meeting has been called for Thursday night of about twenty people who will come authorized to pass upon it.

[1] March 11, 1918.

'The Chamber of Commerce had had a committee investigating the plans adopted by such cities as Utica, Syracuse, Columbus, Cleveland, and Detroit, and Mr. Woodward came to the meeting with all the facts that could be gathered. He had even made a trip to Cleveland and Detroit to get the latest information. There were present at the meeting Messrs. Eastwood, Foulkes, Miner, Todd, Woodward, Willard, James G. Cutler, Mortimer Adler, Dr. Taylor, Bishop Hickey and myself.

'There are some theoretical objections to the plan but they sink into insignificance when the main object is considered and that is that by framing up a proposition which embodies all of these activities you have something that appeals to everybody, or at least that nobody can turn down on its merits. The only question that remains is how much can each one give. As you know, there have only been a few hundred subscribers, less than two thousand, to all of the local charities in the city and to the war charities probably less than ten times that number; only twenty thousand people in this city of nearly three hundred thousand who are giving anything to charity! In Columbus they got eighty thousand subscribers out of a population of two hundred thousand. Everybody I have met who has heard of the plan since the meeting is in favor of it and I have little doubt but what it will be adopted Thursday night.

'The scheme is to invite every established organization to come into the plan and submit a budget, which will be passed on by a very comprehensive budget committee, the idea being to take as a basis for every institution their budget for the previous year and make additions or subtractions according to the needs of the institution. After these budgets have been determined the amounts for the various war activities will be added, with a certain amount for contingencies. The total sum will be the amount to be raised.

'The organization will be called the Welfare Federation, or something of that kind, and will be incorporated, with a Chairman and Board of Directors. It will have committees very much as we had in the last Red Cross campaign and in addition to that the Home Defense, under Mr. Cutler, will organize a house to house canvassing force which will be a permanent organization to do propaganda work for the Government. It will be so organized that each pair of canvassers will have not more than thirty families to visit. The city will be districted and the names of those who are approached directly by the Federation will be crossed off from the canvassers' lists so there will be no duplication but it will be arranged so that every family in the city will be approached.'

From the inception of the Community Chest in Rochester to the present, Eastman insisted, publicly and privately, that every citizen was obligated to do his 'share in making the city what it ought to be as a place for everybody to live in.'

'Because you give to churches and foreign missions does not release you from your obligations to help support the forty charities that are included in the Community Chest,' he wrote one rich, recalcitrant individual. Upon another occasion a citizen of large wealth sent in a subscription card for a few thousand dollars and asked that it be recorded as an anonymous gift. When Eastman reported the facts to his co-workers, even they voted unanimously to return the check. He had no patience with charity-slackers, or anonymous givers. In this he was supported locally and nationally.

'I have had occasion to state on several occasions,' wrote Herbert Hoover,[1] 'that after some years devoted to

[1] Letter to Eastman, January 28, 1921.

the administration of benevolent funds, my belief that
the real future of organized charity, both at home and
abroad, lies in the development of the Community Chest
idea. Conducted on keen business principles, it assures
adequate administration in our local charities, and the
influence of the Community Chest is to-day assuring
adequate application of American money in foreign charities, because of their joint support of an efficient bureau
of inquiry into these national organizations through
which their contributions pass. The Community Chest
secures a larger and more efficient giving of the whole
community and gives an assurance to continuity in charity both at home and abroad that cannot be created in
any other manner.'

In child health work, municipal government, city
planning, and charity, Eastman not only advocated but
supported, personally and financially, these new moulds
for age-old civic needs. And, in addition, he became the
dominant factor in the creation of the greater University
of Rochester, so ably administered by President Rhees.

CHAPTER XII

THE UNIVERSITY OF ROCHESTER

'IT is necessary for people to have an interest in life outside of an occupation,' Eastman maintained.[1] 'Work, a very great deal of work, is drudgery. When I was a young man I worked at a ledger eleven hours a day; by no magic could a performance such as that be made alluring. It was sheer work, unpleasant, but inescapable in civilization. This situation, I find, confronts a very large part of the population. I see no possible hope of getting away from this condition. Hours of employment will accordingly inevitably be shortened, and as production increases, as it must increase, they must be still further shortened. This tendency follows from the irksome and wearing nature of industrial employment, . . . consequently, we face the fact that working hours are going to be shortened in order that people may live full and happy lives.

'What, however, is going to be done with the leisure thus obtained? I am not at all of the opinion that people have been ground down by industry. I do not think that we have ever created enough outside interests. Leisure is unfruitful because it is not used productively. Do not imagine that I am a reformer — far from that. I am interested in music personally, and I am led thereby, merely to want to share my pleasure with others.

'For a great many years I have been connected with musical organizations in Rochester. I have helped to support a symphony orchestra. Recurrently, we have

[1] Interview in the *New York Times*, 'Philanthropy Under a Bushel,' March 21, 1920.

faced the fact that what was needed was a body of trained listeners quite as much as a body of competent performers. It is fairly easy to employ skillful musicians. It is impossible to buy an appreciation of music. Yet, without appreciation, without the presence of a large body of people who understand music and who get joy out of it, any attempt to develop the musical resources of any city is doomed to failure. Because, in Rochester, we realize this, we have undertaken a scheme for building musical capacity on a large scale from childhood.'

The first step in this programme was taken in 1918, when Eastman enabled the University of Rochester [1] to acquire the property and corporate rights of the Institute of Musical Art, 'an institution of considerable student numbers and high musical standards.' [2]

In February, 1919, the 'Democrat and Chronicle' announced Eastman's project of building a 'Concert Hall and School of Music . . . surpassed by no other in the world.' [3]

---

[1] The State Board of Regents sanctioned the establishment of the University of Rochester and granted a provisional charter, January 31, 1850. Dr. Martin Brewer Anderson was the first president, succeeded in 1888 by Dr. David Jayne Hill, later Assistant Secretary of State and Ambassador to Germany. Between the time he began his diplomatic career in 1896 and 1900, Professor Lattimore and Professor Burton temporarily assumed direction of the University. With the appointment of Dr. Rush Rhees in 1900, the modern era of the University began. Of the University, Ralph Waldo Emerson once said: 'I have watched over it in its cradle. I am very certain I shall never follow it to its grave.'

[2] Dr. Howard Hanson, Director of the Eastman School of Music.

[3] 'George Eastman's gift . . . to the School of Music of the University of Rochester, indicates a line, perhaps, which musical education in the United States is permanently to follow. It may be a pioneer deed which will determine the artistic future not only of Rochester, but of numerous other localities as well. As an example, right at the time when music is beginning to be taken up as a serious national pursuit, it can conceivably have a wide influence. Many appeals have of late been made to the conscience of Americans, that they cease regarding music as an imported plaything, and that

'Things concerning the Music School have been moving quite rapidly,' Eastman informed Dr. Rhees, who
was on a holiday. 'I will try and give you a brief chro-
nological account: While I was South, Mr. Cutler got the
options, and when I got home I had Mr. Gordon draw
some floor plans so as to find out if the lot would accom-
modate everything that we need. As soon as I found out
that it would, I gave directions to take the property. In
the mean time Mr. Cutler and Mr. Dossenbach had called
upon me and said that, in accordance with your wish,
expressed to Mr. Dossenbach, they had got up a committee headed by Mr. Todd to handle part of the underwriting and to sell the seats for the 1919–20 orchestra concerts, and asked if the plan was agreeable to me. I told
them I had some plans affecting the musical situation
here that were not quite ready to disclose, but that might
have a bearing on what should be done for the orchestra,
and that I would be able to talk about the plan in a few
days, whereupon they agreed to wait. The next day I
had Mr. Todd down to the office to luncheon and talked
with him about the plan, which is to devote the music
hall to motion pictures six days in the week, putting all of

they use it as one of their own cultural forces and as a means of self-expression. The appeals have aimed at securing an honorable place for music in
the American educational system, whether through act of Congress or
through private financial endowment. Broadly speaking they have sought
the establishment of a conservatory, where the youth of the United States
could learn authentically the theory and practice of music.

'Mr. Eastman's gift can imaginably be regarded as an answer to these
appeals. But his money, instead of being bestowed on a conservatory that
stands free and isolated from historic American institutions, is bestowed on
a department or branch of a University. It is poured, not into a vocational,
but into an academic channel, and it may cause the money of other philanthropists to flow in the same direction for a long time to come. If that should
come to pass, American music teaching will surely be inspired more with
an intellectual than with a professional ideal and American musicians will
be likely to grow into a class of thinkers, rather than into one of performers
only.' (Boston, *Christian Science Monitor*, June 28, 1920.)

the profits into the music-hall orchestra. I explained to Mr. Todd that the whole of my plan could be carried out without having a big orchestra at all, and that I thought the having of such an orchestra should depend wholly upon the support of the community; that I was willing to have the hall used in the way indicated, but the underwriting would have to be taken up by a citizens' committee such as he had formed, and I told him that it would take a lot more money than had been heretofore raised by the small group. He said he thought the town ought to have an orchestra and that he did not think there would be any trouble about raising the money. The next day the plan was explained to Mr. Sibley, Mrs. Willard, and Mrs. Mulligan. Unfortunately, you and Mrs. Watson were absent, as was also Mr. Hubbell, but he already knew about the plan. The plan was unanimously approved by those present, and I was instructed to inform Mr. Todd that the underwriting committee would go on for another year just as they have this year, by continuing their own subscriptions and sending out letters to the other old underwriters, if Mr. Todd and his committee would be responsible for the remainder of the underwriting and the selling of the tickets. He said the underwriting ought to be for three years, and I left him with the understanding that he should have an interview with Mr. and Mrs. Klingenberg this afternoon in order, as he said, to get enthused!

'I forgot to say that it is proposed to devote the hall one day a week out of the seven to musical concerts, fixing upon a day which shall be the same throughout the year, say Monday, Tuesday, or Wednesday, and crowd into that day all of the musical events that we can, concerts of the local orchestra, the visiting orchestras, and other concerts. It will, of course, be impossible to catch them all on one day, but if we are going to have the benefit of the movie scheme there cannot be any confusion about dates. I might add that the movie scheme has been discussed with Messrs. Furlong, Dossenbach, Cutler, William Bausch, and Todd, and they all think it feasible.

'I am very sorry that you have not been here to advise on all of these developments, but I have had to do the best I could and hope I have not involved the University by any indiscretions. The whole plan is known to at least two of the Trustees, and I suppose they would hang out a signal if they should see any danger on the track ahead.'

In August, 1919, when the National Association of the Motion Picture Industry was holding its third annual convention in Rochester, Dr. Rhees outlined Eastman's programme. While Eastman's interest at this time was largely in musical education it was not confined entirely to this art. He had been contributing to numerous University projects for many years, and, as we shall observe in the letters, the University was destined to become the nucleus for other extensive and useful projects.

'Mr. Eastman proposes to call in the aid of motion pictures in connection with his great enterprise for musical education', Dr. Rhees said. 'The alliance between music and pictures is not new, having been worked out on an extensive scale in a number of metropolitan picture theaters, a development in which S. L. Rothafel (better known as "Roxy") [1] has been a highly successful

[1] Brulatour, Rothafel, and Eastman had lunched together in New York City in June (1919), when these plans were discussed.

June 10, 1920, Eastman wrote McKim, Mead and White that Rothafel 'is the director who has lately been put in charge of the Capitol Theater in New York. He first came prominently into notice as the director of the Rialto and Rivoli Theaters. He is considered to be one, if not the most advanced motion-picture showman in the country. In the early stages of our enterprise we consulted him very freely, with the view of engaging him

pioneer. The success of those theaters has demonstrated not only that the enjoyment of the best motion pictures is greatly enhanced when they are interpreted by carefully selected music, but also that the people who are attracted to motion picture entertainments find interest and pleasure in music greatly enhanced. This fact indicates the possibility of greatly enlarging the number of persons in the community, who will know and value the satisfaction which good music has to offer by arranging to use the music hall in the new school for motion pictures of the best quality accompanied by music which will be furnished by a large orchestra.

'Multitudes of people who are attracted by pictures will learn what music has to give them and other multitudes attracted by music will learn new possibilities of pleasure and entertainment from motion pictures. Inasmuch as the music hall is a part of the school equipment these exhibitions will not be conducted as a commercial enterprise for profit.

'The number of people who respond to your enterprise is legion,' the President of the University continued. 'You have the public which the lovers of music would fain secure. We regard it as a happy suggestion that there should be a wedding of the motion picture and of orchestral music as nearly perfect as possible, orchestral music that will be increasingly perfect, because the proceeds from the motion pictures will go to the improvement of the music. . . . Just as music wedded to drama has made opera, which is probably one of the drama's highest forms, the time may come when the alliance of

to open our auditorium.' Eastman offered Rothafel the directorship of the Eastman Theater and also the consulting directorship, but both offers had to be declined because of his contractual obligations in New York City.

music with the motion picture will carry in its train compositions to accompany certain significant pictures and pictures that are adapted to certain musical compositions. So there may come in the development of the motion picture something comparable to the development of the opera.'

As the curtain falls on this scene, mark the silent exit of Adolph Zukor, then President of the Famous Players-Lasky Corporation (Paramount), as he slips away to visit the Dental Dispensary, where he leaves a check with Dr. Burkhart for 'some poor kiddies.' Hurrying back to the meeting, he urged his fellow producers 'to bend every effort to produce films of the highest artistic and literary merit.' This was his early solution for the censorship movement which was disturbing the development of the industry.

Early in the year, Eastman had consulted Gordon and Kaelber, of Rochester, and McKim, Mead and White, as architects, Russell B. Smith, Inc., of New York, as consulting engineers, and Professor Floyd R. Watson, of the University of Illinois, as advisor on acoustics, but he, himself, was the master architect, as the following letters reveal. In August, when McKim, Mead and White proposed a change in the floor plans, he wrote:

'This plan has been worked out after about six months of hard work and consultation with the most experienced operating experts in the country, and embodies practically all of their ideas, adapted to the shape of the lot which we have. If we had not devoted a good deal of time to the straight plan, I might perhaps be less confident that you will be able to develop that plan to a successful competition with the angular plan.

'As to the importance of a big seating capacity for this house, it may be that 3300 is a little ahead of the times, but the tendency throughout the country in the motion-picture business is toward larger houses, and it would be foolish for us to not go as far as we dare in that direction.

'In my estimation there is only one thing that we have to look out for in a house of this size and that is not to make it barny in character. I have no fears of getting the people into the second balcony, and if it is made warm and rich in color, and beautiful in proportion and detail, I believe it will be a success; and that is why I have been so much impressed with the first interior sketch which you have made. It satisfies all of these requirements and so successfully emphasizes the line of the top gallery that I am sure it will add very greatly to its attractiveness. It has been proposed by some of the operating experts that the walls of the theater should be of a neutral light tint so that color effects in the house could be made by throwing colored lights on the walls and the ceiling. The more I study this matter, the more I disagree with them. I think that the problem of the house lighting is merely one of intensity. What we want is a white, or probably a yellowish-white light, which can be regulated to give the maximum amount of indirect light in the auditorium that will not interfere with the brilliancy of the pictures. There must be no visible source of light, because that will tend to lessen the effective value of this indirect light, the chief object of which is to enable the audience to walk about without stumbling. The color effects in lighting should be concentrated on the stage through adequate provision in the "boomerang" in front of the overhead lights behind the proscenium arch. We must be just as careful to avoid visible lights in front of the occupants of the balcony as of the people under the balcony and mezzanine; in other words, we must make the balcony in every respect just as attractive a place to sit and safe to walk in as the main floor.'

To his friend Babbott, Eastman explained the difficulties he was encountering in more detail.

'I spent all day yesterday with Mr. Kendall and Mr. White discussing the rival plans for the new music hall, the result being what I feared, a deadlock. It will take too long to give you an accurate picture of the situation, but it settled down to about this: We have a lot which is acknowledged by everybody to be the best one in the city upon which to put the establishment. It is irregular in shape, and in order to get the house capacity which we must have, we found it necessary to make the axis of the auditorium at an angle which is not a right angle with the most important façade. Our plan was deliberately worked out without any reference to the design of the façade, except to get the openings arranged so that they would adapt themselves to any architectural design. These plans were shown to McKim, Mead & White when they were asked to act as architects to design the exterior and the interior, and they expressed themselves as willing to take the job, making no conditions whatever. After the terms had been arranged, they asked if there would be any objection to their trying their hand at a more regular plan, and we said "no." They knew nothing about floor plans for such a house, and the plan which they at first submitted we convinced them was wholly unsuitable. They then asked for more time, and said that, unless they could work out a plan according to their ideas, they would decline the job. As I was very anxious to retain them, I consented to their using all the time during my absence to work on a plan. Their plans were ready when I got back, and it was over them that we had the conference yesterday. The plans which they presented were drawn from a psychological standpoint, which is not in accordance with our scheme. It is the old-fashioned one that the chief effort should be to please the occupants of the best seats. Of course, it is this class who support concerts and operas, but they are not the patrons who are most esteemed in the movies and are not the ones I am after in my scheme. McKim, Mead & White, after discussion, claimed that they could modify their plans to meet those objections, but in my opinion it would result in further makeshifts. However this may be, the fundamental point of difference was that, in order to get any scheme under their plan which would work at all, they would have to have the entrance around on Main Street instead of on the main face of the building on Gibbs Street, using the very corner of the plot, which is one of the most important ones in the city, for service stairs and elevator; and making an arrangement which would cause the motor and street-car traffic to interfere with each other. Outside of everything else, this is something that no one connected with the enterprise feels should be done. Hence we will have to look for some other architects. It is the old question of utility and convenience against — appearance, I was going to say; but appearance is not the word, because the exterior architecture everybody agrees would be at least as good on our plan. It is utility against the impression of disorder which would be created on the minds of the people who glanced at the plans. The angles that McKim, Mead & White object to would never be discovered by anybody on entering the theater. They might discover it on leaving the theater, but if they did, it would not be of any importance in my estimation. We had a mighty nice interview, but I suppose right down in their hearts Messrs. Kendall and White think I am a pretty headstrong proposition, and I think they are letting their art interfere with utility. If they cannot fit their architecture to our problem, in my opinion it is a confession of weakness rather than an exhibition of strength. The fact of the matter is that where the professional architect falls down, particularly among the most cultivated artistically, is on the utility side. McKim, Mead & White are restive because the floor plans had been worked out practically to completion before the problem had been brought to them. This was my deliberate purpose, because I felt they would put the working-out of the floor plan layout into the hands of the designer, in this case Mr. White. He approached the problem purely from the architectural standpoint, which is fundamentally wrong. A floor plan is an engineering proposition, and must take precedence over the architecture in any commercial proposition.'

To Babbott fell the difficult rôle of diplomat when Eastman wrote him the following letter, and the way was paved for the selection of McKim, Mead & White as consulting architects.

'We have as yet made no decision about a consulting architect. The delay has not been on account of any hope or expectation that McKim, Mead & White would change their decision, but because we were looking up various men and wanted to take plenty of time for it. Furthermore, I have not changed my first opinion about them and their desirability from an artistic point of view, and I cannot help but feel that if their engineering department had tackled the job in the first place, they would have come to the same conclusion that [other architects] did, and there would have been no controversy over the floor plans. The trouble was they approached it first from the artistic side and got a slant on the engineering which was unfortunate.

'We do not feel that there is anything further we can do in the matter, but if you have the impression from your conversations that they have changed their views, I have no objection to your talking it over with them as a friend of both parties. The preliminary sketches which they furnished for the interior of the main auditorium and the exterior are so in line with my ideas that I would have no desire to look any further if they are willing to go on with the original agreement, but I should not want them to resume relations feeling that they had made a great concession to us, but rather that they had, on thinking it over, changed their minds about the feasibility of operating the engineering from the artistic side.' [1]

After approving the plans for the theater, Eastman joined Frank A. Vanderlip's party for his first visit to Japan,[2] and upon his return received a request from J. Lionberger Davis (chairman of the St. Louis com-

---

[1] Among the numerous indications of Eastman's careful attention to detail is the following note to the contractor, November 3, 1921:

'Tile Roof on the Music School.'

'Would it not be well to have some extra tile laid on the flat roof so that they can weather in case they are needed later on for repairs? If we had to put in a few spick-and-span new tiles some day to replace broken ones, it would ruin the beauty of the roof.'

[2] Interviewed upon his arrival in Rochester, Eastman sent the clippings to Dr. T. Dan, Director of Mitsui Gomei Kaisha, of Tokyo, one of his hosts, which Dr. Dan acknowledged on August 5, 1920, adding: 'I am simply marvelled at your masterly grasp of the situation here in spite of the comparatively brief visit. I feel sure that the candid statement of the views you entertain towards different problems in this country and America, as appeared in those papers, cannot fail to impress your people. I like particularly the conciliatory spirit in which you approach the problems. No doubt the articles have struck the psychological moment when the relations between our two countries are being discussed so much, and the good effect which they will produce upon the minds of both people is, I think, beyond dispute.

'Your interviews have been translated into Japanese, and we have had them printed in three successive numbers of one of the leading papers here in Tokyo.'

mittee to raise a guarantee fund to assure the St. Louis Symphony Orchestra) for a statement as to why music lovers, business men, and all interested 'in the life of a great city should support an orchestra.' 'An orchestra,' Eastman replied, 'can be made a big factor in education. As a matter of fact, I think very few of them accomplish as much as they ought to in this respect. As a rule they play to only 100,000 to 150,000 people in a year. We are working on an experiment here (radio broadcasting), whereby our orchestra, we hope, will be enabled to play to ten times that number. If we can do this, it is a sure thing that the ears of the populace will be so educated that they will demand good music and be satisfied with nothing else.' On September 5, 1922, the Eastman Theater[1] was

[1] 'I was saying to Mr. Eastman that a little while ago I visited the new Cervantes Theater in Buenos Aires. It was designed by Spanish architects and designed in every detail to represent the most approved and exact reproduction of the best ideals of Spanish architecture and decoration which was to be obtained. And yet, as I compare it as I saw it a few weeks ago with this Theater that I saw this morning, there is no comparison in appropriateness and loveliness of decoration between these two theaters. The ideals as represented by this building seem to me supreme in the world.' (Dr. George E. Vincent, President of the Rockefeller Foundation, July 26, 1923.)

As late as September 23, 1921, Eastman wrote Dr. Rhees: 'What would you think of calling this hall "Academy of Music," that title to go on the frieze over the portico, the advertising name for motion-picture purposes to be "Academy Theater"?' Finally, he yielded to the suggestion of his friends, and wrote L. G. White, of McKim, Mead & White, November 3, 1921: 'I agree with the conclusions of the "committee on name" that Eastman Theater is the logical one.'

Among those invited to the opening were Will H. Hays, former Postmaster-General, whose work as President of the Motion Picture Producers and Distributors, Inc., had Eastman's highest admiration. As Hays was unable to come the opening night, Eastman entertained him a few days later. 'Political censorship,' said Hays, 'is an incident. The American people are against political censorship fundamentally — against censorship of the press, pulpit, and of pictures.' To this Eastman added: 'The censorship of motion pictures demanded in some directions is all wrong. If the product emanating from the producing studios needs reformation, that reformation should be accomplished at the source, not by subsequent mutilation of the film or by damming the flow of the industry.'

opened to the public, a gala occasion for Rochester, for this theater and School of Music, according to the 'American Architect,' [1] is 'a practical solution of a purely idealistic conception.' Eastman believed, the editors wrote, 'that Music is the most satisfying and enjoyable relaxation from the grind of the average American's life. He, therefore, determined to give a thoroughly equipped School of Music to the University of Rochester; but he realized that only a small number of the population could be reached by such a school, while he wished to benefit the public at large. With a stroke of pure genius, he hit upon motion pictures, in the development and betterment of which he was also greatly interested, as the most practical and popular means of presenting good music to the people of Rochester.

'Therefore, adjoining the Music School proper, is a large theater seating over three thousand people. . . .

'The peculiar shape of the lot and the complex nature of the problem required an unusual plan, which was worked out to the last detail by Messrs. Gordon & Kaelber, in Rochester, under the constant supervision of Mr. Eastman. After the plan had been determined, Messrs. McKim, Mead & White, of New York, were called in to design the exterior of the building, and the interior of the more important rooms.

'The exterior is built of limestone in a free adaptation of the Italian Renaissance style. The dignity of a public institution is emphasized rather than the gayety of a theater. An order of Ionic pilasters, broken at the two entrances by engaged columns of Vermont marble (by a curious coincidence, known to the trade as "Eastman Green"), served to give unity to the main façade.

'The Music School proper . . . marks the highest de-

[1] Issue of February 28, 1923.

KILBOURN HALL

velopment in America in musical equipment. There are organ studios, piano studios, class rooms, rest rooms for the students, studios for the principal members of the staff, and the Sibley music library containing many rare manuscripts, besides a full working library.[1]

'On the ground floor, a wide corridor runs the whole depth of the lot, forming a connecting link between the School of Music and the Auditorium. It has, therefore, been given a monumental treatment, with a Roman Doric order supporting a segmental barrel vault with occasional penetrations. At the Swan Street end is an imposing staircase giving access to a corridor on the floor above, which, though of the same area as the one below, is lower, with a flat ceiling supported by an Ionic order. This corridor also connects with the Auditorium at the Balcony Foyer level. Its walls are lined with gray cloth forming an excellent background for exhibitions of paintings . . . [from the Watson Memorial Art Gallery of the University].

'From the upper and lower corridors, access may be had to Kilbourn Hall, a beautiful room for Chamber Music, seating 512, given by Mr. Eastman in memory of his mother, Maria Kilbourn Eastman. An effect of grandeur was not desired in this room, but rather one of intimacy, so that the attention of the listener would not

[1] 'An important accessory to any music school is its library. The Eastman School of Music is fortunate in that the Sibley Musical Library, a branch of the University library, is installed in its building. This library is a gift to the University by Hiram W. Sibley.

'It contains approximately 15,000 volumes, and is supplemented by the school's purchases of material particularly required for its work.

'The Eastman School of Music has erected a dormitory building for women students on University Avenue, adjacent to the campus of the Women's College of the University.' (Dr. Howard Hanson.)

In 1927, an eleven-story addition to the school itself was erected, providing additional practice rooms, classrooms, and recreational facilities, its practice rooms being as nearly sound-proof as engineering skill can make them.

be distracted from the music by too assertive decoration. Therefore, the polychrome ceiling and frieze of cupids and garlands, though rich in color and gold, are subdued in tone. These decorations were designed by Mr. Ezra Winter, the frieze having been modelled by Mr. C. P. Jennewein. The room is further enriched by six blue velvet hangings, stenciled in gold by the Hewlett Studios, and the lower part of the walls is panelled in walnut. The organ is located above the stage and speaks through a gilded grille in the Proscenium Arch.

'The entrance to the large auditorium is on the corner of Main and Gibbs Streets, where the curve in the façade occurs. This curve affords sidewalk space inside the building line for the sale of tickets, though they can also be bought from the other end of the ticket booth, which projects into a large, elliptical lobby, finished in Botticine marble, with black-and-gold marble columns. In the center, on a marble table, are two aquariums. Two circular panels on the ceiling are painted by Mr. Ezra Winter and Mr. Barry Faulkner, and on the walls are reproductions of the famous "Cupid and Psyche" decorations which were painted by the French artist, Lafitte, for the great Napoleon. These are printed by hand from the original wood blocks, of which over one thousand five hundred were required.

'From the lobby, access is had through a secondary vestibule to the rear of the auditorium, which has a capacity of over thirty-three thousand. There are no boxes, but a small mezzanine gallery, with an ample foyer in the rear, which will provide the choicest seats. The spectators in the large gallery above will, however, have a much better view of the great mural paintings which are the most interesting decorative feature of the room. Groups of figures, representing different kinds of music, are depicted against an Italian landscape background seen, as it were, through openings in the side walls. The paintings on the left of the stage are by Ezra Winter, and represent a music festival, lyric music, martial music and sylvan music. The corresponding decorations on the right are by Barry Faulkner, illustrating sacred music, hunting music, pastoral music and dramatic music.

'The entire color scheme of the interior of the two auditoriums was selected and supervised by Mr. Ezra Winter.

'The walls are of a tawny yellow, enriched with Corinthian pilasters. Over the two doors near the stage are heroic busts of Bach and Beethoven, and fifteen medallions on the face of the balcony rail contain portraits in relief of famous musicians. The ceiling is slightly domed and treated with coffers enriched with color and gold. From a gilded sunburst, in the center, hangs one of the largest chandeliers in existence, from which a flood of light is thrown upon the ceiling. It is not, however, entirely an indirect fixture as there is also enough direct illumination to produce brilliancy in the crystal on the fixture itself. A completely wired full-size model of this fixture, which is fourteen feet in diameter, was made for experimental purposes.

'Beneath the large gallery is the Balcony Foyer, a long curved room which is reached by stairs and ramp. At one end is a painting by Maxfield Parrish, and near by are a fountain with a figure of a cupid and dolphin, after an original by Giovanni de Bologna, and a beautiful allegorical painting of the Renaissance period, formerly in a well known collection.'

As soon as the theater and school were functioning, Eastman undertook to assist the staff in building up the departments, although he 'had various troubles in organ-

izing a staff,' he wrote his cousin Almon. 'But it has all
been very interesting and nothing to lose any sleep over,
and plenty to laugh at. I am learning a lot about psychology,' and, he might have added, 'temperament,' too.
But he permitted nothing to interfere with his object or
obscure his vision.

It was not long until the number of applicants for
courses in the School of Music was so great that students
had to be selected. This policy inspired a sensational
article in the 'Rochester Herald,' which Eastman accepted as a challenge: [1]

'Before printing an article like the enclosed, which
really amounts to an attack on the School of Music because it is using a psychological test to aid it in selecting
its students, why not investigate it? As a matter of fact,
foreseeing that the School would be overcrowded within
a few years from its opening and that it would be necessary to reject pupils, Dr. Rhees and I decided to look into
a system for testing the musical capabilities of students
which Dr. Seashore, of the University of Iowa, had been
working on for years and which he had brought to a
close of its experimental stage. After investigation, we
took it on for a demonstration trial, engaging Dr. Seashore's principal assistant, Dr. Stanton. At the end of
the first year the results were so satisfactory that it was
put into tentative use; and last year, the third year, it
was put into a little greater but not full use. When our
new Director, Mr. Hanson, came on the ground, one of
the first things he did was to thoroughly study the results
that had been achieved with it up to the end of the third
year. He found that out of one hundred and forty-nine
students who tested as low as "D" and "E," and who
would have been rejected if the test had been fully ap-

[1] November 17, 1924.

INTERIOR OF EASTMAN THEATER

plied, one hundred and twenty-nine had fallen out of the School, either of their own volition or owing to their rejection by the teachers; and that the twenty remaining were found to be unsatisfactory and unworthy musically of being retained. This showed a very much greater efficiency for the test than either Dr. Rhees or myself had anticipated. The result of the analysis was brought before the members of the Music School Faculty, and they unanimously decided to put the test in force and hereafter to reject all students testing "D" and "E."

'The object of the test, of course, is to increase the capacity of the School and save it from wasting time on useless material, thereby giving an opportunity for a large number of promising students who would otherwise have to be refused admission. The School was built with an anticipated capacity of two thousand students. It now has registered about nineteen hundred and fifty. Next year we will have to begin to reject the surplus. Surely even a rough test would be better than none.

'Fond parents are often anxious to have children with no musical capabilities taught in the Eastman School, and it is sometimes very difficult to satisfy them when they have to be rejected. If the newspapers of this city thoughtlessly publish articles such as yours, it will create a prejudice against the School and make it increasingly difficult to conduct its work on the most effective lines.

'From what I have said you can see that we have introduced the system in a very conservative way, and little or nothing has been said about it thus far for publication.'

It was Dr. Hanson's genius that persuaded the faculty, previously hostile, to voluntarily adopt the test. His versatility and his capacity for leadership made the School of Music the embodiment of the highest ideals in musical education. In fact, what Dr. Hanson has achieved since

1924, more than justifies the unusual course which Dr. Rhees followed when he discovered him.

Confronted with the desire and the necessity of selecting a new Director, suggestions in regard to qualifications, rather than individual recommendations, were solicited from various authorities. They were then embodied in a list of specifications, and a search was made for an individual who would fit the mould.

While this was under way, Albert Coates, one of the distinguished English conductors engaged to direct the Rochester Philharmonic Orchestra, brought Dr. Hanson to Rochester and introduced him to Dr. Rhees and Eastman.

Dr. Hanson had been Dean of the School of Music at the College of the Pacific, in San José, California. He had been guest conductor of the San Francisco and Los Angeles Orchestras, was also a composer, and had about completed a three-year fellowship in composition at the American Academy in Rome, having been awarded the Prix de Rome in the name of the Juillard Foundation in 1921.

He appeared to personify all of the specifications, save one, and all doubt as to that disappeared when Dr. Rhees stopped in Rome, *en route* from Egypt. Here he learned that, while at the Academy, Hanson 'ran everything without anybody knowing it,' to use one of Eastman's phrases. Dr. Hanson was, as Professor Seligman remarked, 'a find.'

In the years that intervened there was another revolutionary transition in the motion-picture industry. The foreboding prophecy of Maurice Maeterlinck in 'The Spiritual Future of America and the Movies,' [1] in 1921, was a reality two years later: 'Above all, and by its very

[1] *The Photoplay Magazine*, April, 1921.

nature, the cinema ought to be an art, but because of the enormous capital required it has become simply an industry. The business men who direct it are only now beginning to suspect that if it founders as an art, it will founder even more disastrously as an industry. And so to save this new art there must be help from the outside, intervention from above — for it is unlikely that it can save itself unaided and escape from the narrowing circle in which it will surely die of fatigue, like the unhappy marching caterpillars mentioned by Fabre, the entomologist; which, placed on the rim of a bowl, never think of climbing down, but follow each other round and round until they die of weariness and hunger.'

Cognizant of these changing conditions, Eastman consulted Rothafel again, and read his criticism 'with great interest. Of course, you may be right about the impossibility of running the Theater as an educational institution, but we have started that way and are bound to try it out. So far the results are not disheartening. With all of our mistakes, we are going to get through the year with a whole skin, and a little to the good over. This coming year we hope to earn enough to finance the opera class. If we are going to have good singing acts, it seems to me that we must depend upon this class, because we are too far away from the supply of professional talent to do it in the way you are doing it so successfully.

'Of course your experience enables you to foresee more difficulties than perhaps I can, and I would like very much to have a talk with you, as you suggest. Whether I can get down before I leave for my vacation is problematical, but if not, I will certainly make an early visit to New York on my return.

'Our orchestra is now enjoying a three weeks' vacation, this being the middle week. It will amuse you to know that apparently they are not being missed very much. For instance, yesterday was the biggest Tuesday we have had since the Theater started, with two exceptions; one during "Robin Hood" and the other during "Safety Last." '

But it was not long until conditions changed again in the realm of the cinema art. What was one day the new order was old within a few weeks. The control of the leading theaters in the country passed into the hands of a few large producing and distributing units. Pictures could no longer be selected with such discrimination by individual theaters. Presentations were becoming more elaborate and expensive than any showman had ever dreamed possible. Sound pictures were appearing, and, during this period of new orientation, attendance in all motion-picture houses decreased, so that as the curtain rises again Todd and Eastman are calling upon Zukor in New York, one of the few men in the industry 'without any frills,' stolid, cautious, but progressive. Nearly ten years had passed since Zukor listened to Dr. Rhees's prophetic words about a 'wedding' between music and motion pictures. This was now a reality. Sound pictures had literally stormed the show business. Even the new order was changing, and as Todd and Eastman foresaw an opportunity of obtaining a large revenue from a lease with the Paramount organization, they concluded an agreement with the man whose career Will Irwin dramatized in 'The House That Shadows Built.'

'The fact that I have conveyed to you the future control of the Eastman Theater indicates what I think of you,' Eastman wrote Zukor (February 1, 1929). 'You are still a comparatively young man, and I can wish for you nothing better than a continuation of your success.'

This was a *coup* for the University and for the musical

future of Rochester, for it insured the revenue required from the theater for five years 'to afford the community the highest class of [musical] recreation in an educational way at a reasonable price.' It was equally valuable to the Paramount organization, as it provided another strong link in their chain of theaters.[1]

By 1929, the old order had changed, too, with respect to the orchestra. 'What we are confronted with . . . is the preservation of our own orchestra as a part of the musical development of this city,' Eastman told the Subscribers' Association.[2] 'To that end we have devoted our thoughts. . . . What I am personally interested in, and have been from the start, is the making of Rochester a truly musical city. By that I mean where the inhabitants love to listen to good music. Everything else to my mind is secondary to this, but in order to accomplish it we must have a music school here and one of the desirable connections is a fine orchestra. . . .' [3]

[1] May 31, 1923, Eastman wrote Mrs. E. W. Mulligan: 'In discussing the overhead of the theater your question whether it would not have been better to have had a cheaper theater was so unexpected that I think I failed, in saying that it paid to have such as theater as we have, to make it clear that the overhead expenses would not have been affected in any appreciable degree by lowering the cost of the theater. The overhead expenses of a theater depend upon the size of the theater and the number of employees required to run it. . . . The only way that the public or the members of the Subscribers' Association are affected by the enormous capital expenditure in the theater is that they get the benefit of it for nothing, because they do not have to furnish any money to pay interest on that investment. The investment itself is purely a private affair of my own.' That the present and future lessees of the theater stand to benefit by the large investment is evident.

[2] January 15, 1929. The new plan for the Rochester Civic Orchestra was largely the work of Arthur M. See, Secretary of the School of Music.

[3] The distinguished conductor of the Rochester Civic Orchestra is Eugene Goossens, a famous British conductor and composer. Both as the leader of the Rochester Orchestra and as guest conductor of many famous American orchestras, Goossens is universally recognized. Eastman has always had a high regard for his genius.

But, as Eastman pointed out to the Subscribers' Association, 'All orchestras have to be supported by contributions far exceeding the amount of receipts for admission. Probably the average amount of shortage that has to be made up in this way for the big orchestras of the country is a quarter of a million dollars a year, being in some instances more. This includes New York, Boston, Philadelphia, Cleveland, Detroit, Cincinnati, Chicago, Minneapolis, San Francisco, and Los Angeles. In most places there has been one principal contributor who has borne the bulk of the burden, such men as Mackay, Flagler, Severance, Murphy, Carpenter, Clarke, and a few others. . . . The dropping out of any one of these big contributors meant disaster or confusion to the enterprise.'

Then Eastman outlined the plan for Rochester 'to create a full-time orchestra of forty-eight pieces which will play upwards of sixty concerts in the four or five high schools of the city, one half of the concerts to be played Wednesday afternoons to the children who are studying music, of course without charge, and an equal number of concerts to be played in certain high schools to adults on Sunday afternoons, to which an admission of twenty-five cents is to be charged. In addition to this, this full-time orchestra to be supplemented by city musicians outside the organization, just as our present orchestra has been supplemented, to full philharmonic size; this full Philharmonic Orchestra to play the same number of concerts in the Eastman Theater that it has heretofore played. . . . I might add that in the lease of the theater it has been provided that the theater will be available for Philharmonic concerts and series concerts, together with the performances of the Metropolitan Grand Opera Company, for a total of twenty-two days per season. Thus we will have all the concerts we have been having and at least sixty concerts more."

As provision was then made for carrying out this plan in part by public subscription, Eastman had insured another phase of his musical dream for Rochester — full orchestral music for the public schools.

Meanwhile, however, Eastman was the focal point in the development of another University project — the establishment of a Medical Department, which Dr. Abraham Flexner characterizes as 'a very important link in the chain which begins with the opening of the Johns Hopkins Medical School in 1893.'

Prior to the founding of the Baltimore institution, medical education in the United States was in the hands of groups of local physicians who formed schools, some of which were nominally affiliated with universities, while others were quite independent. No school possessed laboratories, hospital, or staff comparable to the organization which had been developed in Germany during the preceding half-century.

In establishing the Johns Hopkins Hospital, the founder wisely requested his trustees to coöperate with the University, which his will also created, whenever the University was ready to embark upon medical education. As a result the Johns Hopkins Hospital has been the laboratory of the clinical staff, and an ideal situation was created from the outset. The productivity of this institution, which has a scientific faculty for the study of the problems of disease, is attributed to the sound relationship thus established and to the wisdom of the trustees in bringing together, from all parts of the world, men who had enjoyed in this country and in Europe the finest opportunities for understanding and carrying forward research in medical sciences. Another advanced step was taken when the Rockefeller Institute for Medical Research was established in the early years of the present century. This institution, like the Johns Hopkins Medical School, scored a prompt success. Graduates and workers in the two institutions filtered into other schools, but no extensive reorganization was undertaken anywhere else.

Between 1910 and 1912, two bulletins were published by the Carnegie Foundation for the Advancement of Teaching, dealing with the status of medical education in the United States and in Europe. The first was a merciless exposure of the flagrant conditions existing in this country and Canada. The other was an appreciative but critical acknowledgment of the superior way in which medical education was carried on abroad.

In 1913, the General Education Board, of which Dr. Flexner was secretary, appropriated approximately one and one half million dollars to enable the Johns Hopkins Medical School to establish, in the main clinical branches, a group of so-called 'full-time' teachers. They were provided with excellent facilities and modest but adequate salaries. These men introduced in the clinics still more fully the same spirit which had prevailed in the laboratory subjects.

Shortly thereafter, Washington University, St. Louis, which had been reorganized, rebuilt, and reëndowed as a consequence of the first Carnegie Report, also introduced the full-time scheme. The reorganization of the Yale Medical School soon followed.

Meanwhile, it became obvious that, while bad schools could be snuffed out of existence by publicity, good schools could not be created unless adequate funds were forthcoming. In the years 1919–21, John D. Rockefeller gave to the General Education Board approximately

$50,000,000 to be expended by the Board, principal and interest, for the purpose of reorganizing and developing, as far as the funds would provide, a number of medical schools in different sections of the United States.

The Board was anxious to do something in New York City, 'but,' said Dr. Flexner, 'the medical schools in New York City, though on the laboratory side they had been reorganized, continued on the clinical side to be managed by practicing and consulting physicians who were important personages, not easily dislodged. It occurred to me that perhaps the quickest and most effective way of putting pressure upon the New York medical schools was to start something first-rate somewhere else in the State.

'In the early days of 1920, Dr. Wallace Buttrick, President of our Board, and I made one of many trips for the purpose of inspecting Southern colleges and universities. In the train, as we were leaving New Orleans, I told him that I had been thinking about the New York City situation and had concluded that the only feasible way of accomplishing anything was to build outside the city. I suggested Rochester, and when Dr. Buttrick asked why, I replied that there was an excellent college there, the University of Rochester, headed by Dr. Rhees, an extremely able and sound man, and Mr. Eastman.'

Dr. Buttrick asked why he had thought of Eastman, and Dr. Flexner replied: 'He has given the city a dental dispensary which, I am told, is a beautiful and efficient institution. It seems to me not unlikely that his interest might be extended to the medical field.'

Shortly thereafter, Dr. Rhees called at the New York offices of the General Education Board, where his conversation with Dr. Flexner naturally gravitated to the possibilities of interesting Eastman. Within a few days, Dr. Rhees submitted the suggestion to Eastman and asked if he would receive Dr. Flexner, who would personally outline his proposals. The first references to these conversations in Eastman's correspondence are found in identical letters to the daughters of Colonel Strong, Mrs. Gertrude S. Achilles and Mrs. Helen Strong Carter: [1]

'For a considerable number of years back the Rockefeller Foundation and the General Education Board have interested themselves in plans for bringing medical education throughout the country up to something like an ideal standard. They contemplate the fostering of five or six institutions of the Johns Hopkins grade.

'I was much surprised to learn a short time ago that they had picked out Rochester as a favorable location for one of the schools of the first class, and that, if they could get what they considered reasonable coöperation locally, they would spend a very large amount of money here. The other locations so far fixed I understand are Nashville, Chicago, and St. Louis. These, with Rochester and Baltimore, would make five, and I do not know where another one is contemplated. The reason that they consider Rochester such a favorable location is that, among other things, it has no medical school to complicate the development of precisely the type of school they want; it has a university which is exceptionally high class for a small one and no objectionable features; it also has in the Dental Dispensary the best clinic in the world for the dental surgery part of such an enterprise, which will make possible a combination of dental with medical education which is ideal, and will set a new standard for training in dentistry as Johns Hopkins did for training in medicine a generation ago; it is a town of about the right size and character and the right location geographically.

'It will take a considerable sum of money to finance the

[1] March 2, 1920.

affair; something in the neighborhood of $8,000,000 for the medical and dental schools and about $2,000,000 for the university proper. Dr. Flexner has been here twice, and I am so much impressed with the plan that I am going to help it all possible. No offer has been made by the Rockefeller interests, but it is believed that they will be willing to furnish half the money. I have told them that I would contribute $2,500,000. The plan includes the erection of a hospital of about 250 beds, which will cost somewhere between $1,000,000 and $1,500,000.

'I am writing this to ascertain whether you would be willing to join Helen in erecting this hospital in memory of your father. It seems to me that it would be particularly fitting for several reasons, among which are: He made his money here in an institution which will be greatly benefited by the enterprise. Although he erected memorials to his father and mother, he left no fitting memorial of himself. It would be the biggest and most appropriate memorial that you could erect to his memory, for it will probably come to be as well known over the world as the Johns Hopkins Hospital. This is rather a bold statement, but the plan certainly will develop a unique institution which must become known nationally and internationally. I have already said that it would be particularly appropriate on account of the benefit that it would be to the employees of the Kodak Company.

'The location in this town of this institution would effectually settle the health problem for all the workers, and make it a safer and more attractive place to live for everybody, because in a few years the whole standard of medicine and surgery would be raised to as high a plane as in any city in the world. For a long time, from the standpoint of making Kodak Company an enduring institution, safe against the assaults of competition for expert services and labor, I have felt that the best thing that could be done was to help make Rochester the best place in the country to live in. This has been one of the controlling ideas in my gifts to Rochester heretofore, and it is because this new project would contribute greatly to this same end that I am ready to give largely to bring it to pass. There are other concerns with more wealth than we have that are already entering our field and are trying to get away from us our skilled men. The only advantage we have over such would-be competitors is our experience and skill. We have a great staff of these experts, most of whom have families, and it will be very much harder to entice them away if they think Rochester is a better and safer place than any other for themselves and their families. Bearing on this point I enclose copy of a newspaper clipping. Don't let it frighten you into selling any of your stock. The Kodak Company can take care of itself for some time.'

Once interested in a project, Eastman never gave the grass time to grow in a new field. Writing Babbott, he explained his proposals to Dr. Flexner in greater detail: 'You will be interested to know that Dr. Flexner has been up here again. You will remember that I made him this proposition when he was here before, viz: That I would put up $2,500,000 against $2,500,000 from the General Education Board; that then the G.E.B. should add $1,-500,000 more against the endowment and plant of the Dental Dispensary, and that finally, when needed, at the end of say three years, we should each put up $750,000 more. Flexner said it was one of their rules that they would not put up money against money that was already in an enterprise; that they were willing to stretch this rule so as to allow the Dispensary endowment to be considered as fresh money, but they could not stretch it to cover the building, so he wanted me to put up $500,000 more instead of that. I told him I could not do it, but I would make him this proposition, that I would write a letter to Dr. Rhees offering to put up 5000 shares of Kodak common if he would secure the turning over of the Dispensary building and endowment to the University and get $5,-000,000 additional money, meaning, of course, $5,000,-000 from the General Education Board. I told Flexner I did not think he had provided for enough capitalization. He hesitated on the proposition, but said he would take it home to his finance committee and see what they said about the Kodak stock. I pointed out to him that $800 per share was the price Technology took it in at, and that our statement for 1919, which is just about to be issued, would show that its value had improved during the past year. There are only two grounds upon which the Education Board can turn this proposition down. One is the value of the stock, and the other is that they do not want to put so much money into any one undertaking. The stock will show an earning power of over 10% on the valuation proposed; so my guess is that they will not turn it down.'

'The medical school undertaking is progressing very favorably and the Rockefeller interests are expected to act upon it formally at their next meeting the last of April,' Eastman wrote Mrs. Achilles.[1] 'If the affair goes through as anticipated, they will put $5,000,000 into it, and the project will be announced at a dinner to be given by me to the Trustees of the University, the Dental Dispensary, and the existing hospitals. If you and Helen decide to go into it, it would be a fine thing to make the announcement at that time. Instead of the $2,500,000 which I wrote you I had agreed to give, I have agreed to give 5000 shares of

[1] March 31, 1920.

Kodak at $800 a share. The affair will be so financed and staffed that there is no question but that the hospital will be one of the most distinguished in the world, and second to none unless it be Johns Hopkins. Dr. Winford H. Smith, Superintendent of the Johns Hopkins Hospital, came here Monday at the request of Dr. Rhees and the Rockefeller interests, and looked the ground over with a view of locating the buildings, and expressed himself as not only sympathetic with the enterprise but most enthusiastic, which is the same feeling that has already been expressed by Dr. Welch and other Johns Hopkins notables.'

A few days later — Dr. Flexner, President Rhees, and Eastman were still working behind the scenes — Eastman sent Dr. Rhees the following formal commitment:

'With a view of aiding the University to establish a school of medicine, surgery, and dentistry of the highest order, I make you the following proposition:

'Providing you will secure the coöperation of the Trustees of the Rochester Dental Dispensary to the extent of turning over their plant and endowment to the University; and providing you will secure additional contributions amounting to five million dollars for the purpose of establishing and maintaining, in connection with the University of Rochester, such a school of medicine, surgery, and dentistry as has been discussed between us and other interested persons, I will thereupon turn over to the University five thousand shares of the Eastman Kodak common stock to be used for the same purpose.

'In making the above stipulation in respect to the Dental Dispensary, it is, of course, not expected that such an arrangement will interfere with the carrying out of its primary object, viz: continuing to care for the teeth of deserving children of the community. On the other hand, it is expected that its inclusion in this great enterprise will enable it to function even more effectively on that account.'

As the General Education Board had taken favorable action, the stage was set for the public announcement, which was entrusted to President Rhees and Dr. Flexner.

'Dr. Rhees belongs, in our judgment,' said the Secretary of the General Education Board,[1] 'in the small group of eminent administrators who have carefully defined their objects and who have by a substantial educational success won the confidence and esteem of all critical students of higher education in America. Pretentiousness is one of the besetting faults of American education. . . . It is because the University of Rochester is sound to the core, because it is in competent hands, because it will take no forward step unless the ground is firm beneath its feet and the necessary means absolutely assured — it is for these reasons that the General Education Board was hospitable to the suggestion that in Rochester there is an opening for the foundation of a medical school of the highest character.'

Dr. Flexner then traced the history of medical Education in the United States, and in conclusion, added:

'In one very important respect the Medical Department of the University of Rochester will try to make a novel contribution to education. We have come to see in the last few years that dentistry is a branch of medicine of the same dignity and importance as pediatrics, obstetrics, gynecology, and any other specialty. Mr. Eastman has recognized its importance by establishing and endowing the Rochester Dental Dispensary to the support of which the city of Rochester and many of its citizens are already making important contributions.

[1] Dr. Flexner, June 11, 1920.

Meanwhile training in dentistry in this country has been less highly developed than training in medicine and surgery. The new school of medicine will, it is hoped, undertake to place training in dentistry on the same academic and scientific level as training in medicine and surgery, and to this end it will seek the coöperation of the trustees of the Dental Dispensary and the practicing dental profession in the city. . . .

'The University of Rochester has already done a noble work in this community. But now it requires a larger significance, and undertakes a larger task, a task that cannot be fully achieved unless the entire University takes a forward stride. A university department of medicine in the full sense of the word . . . will thrive only if the rest of the institution, its departments of physics, chemistry, biology, mathematics, etc., its libraries and its laboratories, are conceived in the same spirit and upon the same scale. The development of the University in these directions calls for large and continuous support from the citizens of Rochester and from outside organizations interested in higher education.'

Dr. Flexner's address so impressed Eastman that he wrote John D. Rockefeller, Sr., after the dinner: 'I venture to take this occasion to say that I am proud to have my name associated with yours in a philanthropic enterprise. For many years I have considered you the foremost philanthropist of the age and have admired the wisdom with which your vast wealth is being distributed. In this case it is not only the money contribution that this community appreciates, but the coöperation of your organization, without the skilled services of which the mere money would be impotent to obtain success.'

On August 6, Eastman received a letter from Mrs. Achilles. How happy he was we may never know, for he must have reflected, if only for an instant, upon a life of memories enshrined in the name 'Strong.'

'You are quite right,' wrote Mrs. Achilles, 'in feeling that a memorial should be in the place where he [her father] was born, and lived all his life. I also *know* that he would be very glad to have you associated with Helen and me in this way, for he had a genuine fatherly affection for you. . . .

'N.B. In view of the fact that there are several Strongs who might seem to posterity to have a share in this memorial, I desire that this be known, as you first suggested, as the Henry A. Strong Memorial Hospital, the Tablet to read thus:

'Erected in Memory of Henry A. and Helen G. Strong

by

Gertrude Strong Achilles

Helen Strong Carter

George Eastman' [1]

Early in January, 1921, Eastman wrote Colonel Strong's daughters again:

'Preliminary studies looking toward the placing of the [Medical] School buildings on the present campus have opened the whole question as to whether now is not the time to change the location of the entire University to a more commodious site. It appears that if the Medical School were built on the present campus, there will not be room to make enlargements to the other departments of the University that will be necessary in the near future. As soon as this question was raised, some of our enterprising citizens, with Mr. George W. Todd at the head, began to look around the town for a suitable site.[2] I en-

[1] Eastman's name, however, was not used.

[2] Mr. Todd was the first to suggest the Oak Hill Country Club site.

close an aeroplane view which shows the property. You will remember that it is just north of the Elmwood Avenue Bridge. Now that the river down to Court Street has been made a barge canal harbor, there is a still-water pool which extends back up the river for some miles and will make the river ideal for aquatic athletics. Everybody who knows about the scheme is very enthusiastic about it; even the officers of the Oak Hill Club. . . . The view of the University buildings from the Park entrance road across the river will be most impressive. . . . Altogether it would be hard to find a university site equal to this one in the whole United States.

'It is intended to hold back the announcement of your subscriptions to such a time that will give the whole project the greatest boost. If the change is made, it will be necessary to have a campaign next fall for a lot of money, and we want to handle the affair so as to get the utmost amount of enthusiasm.'

'The University which we are considering,' President Rhees told the City Club,[1] 'is not a new institution. It has been with you and your fathers seventy-one years. Relatively small, quite conservative and honestly conscientious, it has grown with increasing rapidity in recent years alike in numbers and in recognition by the community. . . . Twenty-one years ago its students numbered 160, its faculty 18, its buildings four. This year its regular students in the College of Arts and Science, number 691, its faculty 58, its buildings eleven. In addition extension classes have furnished college instruction to busy people in the city, 851 different persons having enrolled in these classes.

'Should any one with a statistical bent plot this growth graphically and extend the curve for ten or twenty years

[1] March 5, 1921.

the prospect would be appalling. But with all allowance for factors that will limit future growth, it is wholly probable that we shall have to receive into our classes regular students to an extent which will remove Rochester from the group of smaller colleges.

'With the developments in the Eastman School of Music you are familiar. . . . That this school is to have its home in a building of palatial beauty is a source of great satisfaction to us all, and of pride to all our citizens.

'The promised School of Medicine and Dentistry will hold to similar standards of excellence, though, for obvious reasons, there will be no attempt to rival the beauty of the building equipment of the School of Music. No pains will be spared, however, to secure buildings of noble design and the most perfect adaptation to the use to which they are to be put.

'It is this new School of Medicine and Dentistry that precipitates the problem of the University's future. The Dental Dispensary will furnish the clinical facilities for the instruction in dentistry, but the hospital for the School of Medicine, and the laboratories and classrooms for both medicine and dentistry, must find a suitable place, and it should be close to the College of Arts and Science.

'The growth of that college already calls for a considerable addition to our existing plant. Mrs. Henry A. Strong [1] has promised a much-needed assembly hall as a memorial to her husband. But library, laboratories, classrooms and gymnasium are now seriously overcrowded. Can we provide for such growth and house the new Medical School on the present University campus? If we have regard for the next ten years alone, probably, yes. But when the next call for expansion comes, what can we do?

[1] Mr. Strong married Mrs. Hattie M. Lockwood, of Tacoma, Washington, after the death of his first wife.

'But is there likely to be a next call? As I said, prophecy is precarious, but experience deserves consideration. Other medical schools have had to double their hospital facilities by adding special clinics; and many universities have been convinced that schools of commerce, of education, of various engineering specialties, and of other professions are necessary to their full service to the community.

'Please do not think that Rochester proposes to change its policy, and branch out for the sake of branching out. It is folly for a university to regard it as necessary to meet the competition of all other institutions. We shall not add new schools until manifest duty points that way, and means become available to take on the work with conscientious adherence to the highest standards.

'But now is the time when we must face the problem: What shall we do when and if the call comes?

'Herein lies the significance of the proposed removal of the university to a new site, where space will be ample for all probable future growth, and where the new university may have an architectural development that will be worthy, harmonious and beautiful.

'But in all our thought we must ever bear in mind the fact that the ultimate wealth and strength of any department of a university is the men who teach and work in it for the advancement of knowledge; such wealth and strength as are happily secured for our School of Music and Medicine. A new site and new buildings will be glorious in the measure in which they furnish opportunity for students to learn from strong men, competent to guide their thought and to mould their ideals. It is because we believe that a more adequate provision for the material expansion of the whole university will bring with it also means for the constant strengthening of the immaterial forces of the college, that we are thrilled and filled with courage.'

'First of all, we must get the men,' President Rhees stated in another address before the Rochester Engineering Society, and the first of these selected was Dr. George H. Whipple, Director of the Hooper Foundation for Medical Research and Dean of the Medical School at the University of California, who was recognized as one of the leading pathologists in the United States, and enthusiastically recommended by Dr. William H. Welch, of Johns Hopkins University, and Dr. Simon Flexner, Director of the Rockefeller Institute of Medical Research. In July, 1921, Dr. Whipple came to Rochester as Dean of the new Medical School.

With the Medical School on such a sound foundation, the next step was obviously to strengthen the University as a complete unit. Todd took the initiative, inviting fifty citizens to dinner, where Dr. Rhees was asked to expand his ideals for the University of the future. Of the three proposals he submitted, Eastman suggested that he 'set his flag at ten million and see how much he could get.'

'This appeared a stupendous undertaking, but it was made possible in the fall of 1924, when a public campaign was launched, which resulted in the raising of that great sum in a surprisingly brief space of time. This campaign attracted several spectacular gifts, chief of which were one of $2,500,000 from George Eastman and another of $1,750,000 from the General Education Board. Contributions of the alumni and alumnæ also reached the unexpected total of approximately $1,500,000.

'And the remarkable stream of benefactions did not cease there. As a direct aftermath of the public's generous response in the campaign, Mr. Eastman in December, 1924, announced another gift to the University of $6,-

000,000, of which $3,000,000 were allotted to the East-
man School of Music, $1,500,000 to the School of Medi-
cine and Dentistry, and a like sum to the College for
Women. . . . Several other noteworthy gifts have since
been received, greatest of which was that of the late
James G. Culter, who bequeathed practically all of his
estate of $2,500,000 to the University.' [1]

Eastman was enthusiastic. The University development was the fruition of many of his life's experiences.

'I heartily congratulate you on the successful outcome
of the ten-million-dollar drive,' he wrote Dr. Rhees after
the campaign, 'including, as it did, five million dollars
from the citizens of Rochester and the friends of the
University. It will interest you to know that on the success of this drive depended largely the proportion I have
allotted to the University out of the stock which I have
just disposed of. The people of Rochester have repeatedly
shown their readiness to do their share in every great
civic enterprise, and that is one thing that makes it a
pleasure to do what I can to help such affairs along.'

Twelve thousand citizens of Rochester united in the
campaign, completing an undertaking which Dr. George
E. Vincent, President of the Rockefeller Foundation, said
would make Rochester one of the greatest scientific,
medical, musical, and educational centers in the world.

But it cost Eastman the bulk of his fortune to meet the
commitments which he had made, and in December,
1924, he 'signed away,' as Dr. Rhees said, the princely
portion of his wealth, dividing it between the University
of Rochester, the Massachusetts Institute of Technology,
and Hampton and Tuskegee Normal and Agricultural
Institutes.

[1] From *The University of Rochester, Past and Present*, published by the University.

Eastman's 'explanation' of this distribution of capital funds was embodied in two statements, one to the public and the other to his 'fellow employees.'

'One of the reasons why I wish this disposition of my Kodak stock,' he said in the former, 'is that it separates me from making money for myself and will give me the benefit of a somewhat more detached position in respect to human affairs. I look forward with interest to finding out how much the changed conditions will affect my outlook on current affairs.

'A friend of mine who had advanced knowledge of this transaction asked me why I selected these four institutions as the beneficiaries of this distribution. The answer was easy. In the first place, the progress of the world depends almost entirely upon education.

'Fortunately, the most permanent institutions of man are educational. They usually endure even when governments fall; hence the selection of educational institutions.

'The reason that I selected a limited number of institutions was because I wanted to cover certain kinds of education, and felt that I could get results with the institutions named quicker and more directly than if the money was spread.

'Under the best conditions it takes considerable time, sometimes years, to develop the wise expenditure of money in any line, no matter how well prepared one may be. I am now upwards of seventy years old, and feel that I would like to see results from this money within the natural term of my remaining years.

'As to Rochester, the town in which I am interested above all others, we are all set now to develop our University on the broadest lines and make it one of the outstanding universities of the country. By that I do not mean one of the largest, but one of the highest rank in all of the fields which it has entered.'

And in his second statement Eastman added:

'In view of the fact that you are, nearly all of you, now stockholders of the Kodak Company, owing to the action of myself and of the Kodak Company, and the further fact that this transaction includes the bulk of my remaining holdings in the Kodak Company, I deem it proper to inform you that it does not indicate in any way that I am about to retire from the direction of the Company, or that my interest in its success is in any way lessened by the transaction. For some time past the accumulation of money personally has lost its importance to me, and therefore my interest in the Company has not been affected by the income from its shares.

'As time goes on, I realize more clearly that I shall have to face the inevitable sooner or later, and inasmuch as my major interest in life is to guard the continued success of the Kodak Company and the welfare of those whom I have brought together as its employees, I have been shaping my plans accordingly. The distribution of stock to employees was one of the first of these plans. To make that stock more valuable every year depends largely upon you all, the humblest workmen as well as the skilled experts. Things that are outside of your control might affect the stock temporarily, such as my death and the unexpected throwing upon the market of a large block of stock. One of the objects of this transaction that I am telling you about is to guard against the latter event, my stock being the last great block in existence, as the holdings of the other big owners, my old partners, Strong and Walker, have been distributed without disturbance of the market.

'Another principal reason for this disposition of my

stock at this time is that I desire to see the money put into action during my lifetime. About sixty per cent of this particular money is to be spent in Rochester in under-takings which must inure to the benefit of Kodak em-ployees and their descendants.'

The emphasis in Eastman's mind at the time, was on the last two words.

CHAPTER XIII

WHERE EAST MEETS WEST

THE fifty-six years that intervene between March, 1868, when Eastman left school to go to work, and December, 1924, when he distributed, for the advancement of education, assets totaling several millions more than he announced publicly, there were many transformations in his personality. This was not unnatural. 'Years following years steal something every day.' But they do not take more than they leave, for the record accumulates in the features of the face of the individual and the basic qualities of character are expressed or reflected in the ome.

Rodin and Sargent expressed, what every modern artist knows, that there is a difference in the two sides of the face of men who chisel their own careers out of the marble of business competition and still retain the expressive, emotional qualities of one or more of the arts. One side of the face mirrors the aggressive qualities of achievement — cold concentration, perseverance, impersonal action and vision. The other reflects the receptive idealist, the heart and soul of the individual who is instinctively responsive to color harmonies and to music, which enrich human existence.

Eastman's features conform to this general description. He was never physically strong in an athletic sense, although at the office or in camp his endurance seems inexhaustible. Although only three and one half inches short of six feet his broad shoulders make him appear shorter than he is. He stands erect and at ease, the result of iron discipline, for he is naturally shy and retiring.

900 EAST AVENUE

Worry gave a steel-sheen to his hair before he was forty, and now it is thin and white. The eyebrows form shades over warm, blue-gray eyes, set deep under a broad, receding forehead. His eyes, the most potent of his features, function like powerful lenses capable of microscopic as well as telescopic vision. They are the inquisitive pupils of his mind. One eye appears to analyze and judge, while the other asks the question he propounds so often to his friends: 'Are you happy?' Although trained to observe in black and white, the eyes never miss the finest gradation in color values. Spectacles rest naturally on the bridge of the nose which artists and sculptors portray larger than it seems to others.

Eastman is a typical example of Disraeli's remark that Nature gave man two ears, but only one mouth. One side of the mouth is set in a half-quizzical droop: the other softens into a sympathetic tendency to smile. His chin is strong and aggressive, especially when he holds his head back to gain a perspective or leans over his desk to study a plan. Then it accentuates the lines of the mouth, which has sealed his thoughts to all except a very few intimate friends. Still people interest him individually and *en masse*. He is always entertaining friends, associates, and strangers at breakfasts, luncheons, musicales, dinners, or receptions, for he seldom dines alone. Away from Rochester he can travel almost anywhere without being recognized, for he never utilized photography to promote himself. Although the company has been an industrial mint, pouring several billions of dollars in wages, dividends, and purchases into the channels of American commerce, Eastman never attempted, or was tempted, to tell other business men how they might succeed, a rather common weakness in many prominent men.

Behind an austere exterior there is an emotional and a

carefully cloaked spiritual nature, very much the servant of his will power. Although not a member of any religious congregation, the clergy of several Rochester churches have always been counted among his closest friends.

Since 1905, most of Eastman's activities have radiated from his home in Rochester, although he has found diversion and recreation on his farm and game preserve in North Carolina, and in camp. At the office, where he is an exacting, impersonal executive, he sets in motion what he envisions while away. At home he is relaxed and receptive, isolated by music, flowers, and paintings from the worry and pressure of business. In camp he was able to fish, cook, or stalk game over the mountains, ride saddle-back and forget the problems of business, the touchy temperaments of musicians, and the insatiable needs of education. When Stevenson wrote that 'there is no duty we so much underrate as the duty of being happy,' he unwittingly described this Eastman characteristic.

In these strangely diverse situations, Eastman himself is at ease, for after many years' experience he has learned to adapt himself to his surroundings, whether self-created or imposed by circumstances. This is one of the reasons there is so little unanimity among his friends and associates as to his outstanding characteristics. Few individuals have shared all his interests. Few, indeed, have shared many of his confidences. To-day he alone bridges the abyss which separates his business from his philanthropies and both of these from his strenuous out-of-door activities.

Eastman's correspondence is replete with letters devoted to detailed discussions of camp equipment, of gun models, the culture of roses and landscaping, the arrangement of musical programmes for private recitals, the selection of portraits and paintings for different situations in the home, the qualities of Oriental rugs, the installation of an organ, the cultivation and selection of flowers and plants for private greenhouses, the amount of butter fat a Jersey cow should give, or the best time for the superintendent of his farm to market cotton. Everything he has become interested in, he has mastered, whether this involved a knowledge of the physical differences between a black and a white rhinoceros, the cultivation of orchids, or the qualities of a Corot landscape. This is the secret of the individuality of his home, which has always appealed to men and women of widely different tastes. Every detail at 900 East Avenue exists because of Eastman's own decision.

In selecting works of art, for instance, he never purchased a painting until he had 'lived with it.' The correspondence is literally punctuated with letters to his friend Babbott and to art dealers, of which the following is typical:

'My recollection is that you told me your men were going to Detroit, and I suggested that they bring the Rembrandt and the Van Dyck to Rochester and let me see them in my house. You seemed very willing to do this, and it is a common procedure with other picture dealers. I never buy a picture until I have lived with it a little while in my house. I certainly did not dream that you would think I was under any obligation to buy them if I found I did not want them. In your letter you seem to imply that I perhaps encouraged you to send the pictures here without any serious intention of purchasing either, but you must know that I went to the expense of having them examined by an independent expert before they came up here. After I had tried them in various places, I decided that I did not want either of them.

'I am not a collector of pictures simply as pictures, but each one that I buy must fit into my little collection in a way that is satisfactory to me. I found that these simply did not fit in. As a matter of fact, I came very near buying the Rembrandt, but concluded that I would rather have something else. Having decided the matter in my own mind, I did not think it necessary to go into a very full explanation of my views to your representative, as the decision was the only thing that affected you. Your letter does not indicate that you are a very good sport, but all the same I am very sorry, indeed, that you have been so much disappointed. The only thing I can do is to assure you that you will probably never have occasion to be disappointed again in any transaction with me.'

The first picture one sees upon entering the house is the portrait of a Venetian Senator, a richly toned masterpiece by Tintoretto. It has occupied the place of honor in the main hall for so many years that it is now an integral part of the house. In the music room, above and on each side of the fireplace, are three vigorous portraits of men, by Franz Hals, Rembrandt, and Van Dyck. Pastoral landscapes by painters representing later schools of art, on the side walls of this room, provide a restful background for the Sunday afternoon musicales, without detracting from the keynote which the three portraits give.

In the wide, white corridor leading to the dining-room, in the side hall where Eastman receives his guests each Sunday evening when he is at home, and in the room he uses for reading and study, are portraits by Gainsborough, Raeburn, Reynolds, and Romney. On the mantel, above the fireplace in this room, are seven photographs of his mother and one of his father; in addition to a medallion of Mrs. Eastman, a miniature of Colonel Strong, an air view of the Massachusetts Institute of Technology, and

CONSERVATORY AT 900 EAST AVENUE

one or two other photographs, which are changed from time to time. A portrait of Mrs. Eastman once hung above the mantel, but, as she did not like it, the photographs have taken its place.

Throughout the house are other paintings by Millet, Winslow Homer, Inness, Mauve, Corot, and other immortals, but each is so placed that one is not conscious of the extent or the discriminating character of the collection unless one ignores the surroundings and studies the pictures themselves. But this is not an easy task, for Eastman built and furnished this house originally as a home for his mother, the only woman who ever came into his life, and it has always retained its primary quality of comfortable habitability. To-day, more than a decade since she passed away, the home still reflects her quiet dignity, while the Kilbourn String Quartet and Eastman's love of beauty and companionship perpetuate his conception of what the most fundamental of all social institutions should be.

For more than a quarter of a century the Sunday evening musicales and suppers have made this home an informal community center. Here the East meets the West — the East and West in temperament and vocation as well as nationality. It is a home to musicians and artists as well as to sportsmen, who find in the third-floor museum, Eastman's trophies from Africa, Alaska, British Columbia, and other sections of the United States and Canada. Bankers and business men find themselves completely detached from the tense world in which they live.

After supper has been served, the guests, numbering usually about one hundred, gather in the spacious conservatory, where palms and flowers in endless succession give variety and color to the architectural details of the tall white pillars, the open stairway, and the second-floor balcony. Mounted above the door, leading to the terrace and the gardens, is the magnificent head of an elephant, its trunk and white tusks protruding above the palms.

In this setting the guests listen to the organs and the quartet, and then depart to face the next day the stern realities of human endeavor, as Eastman himself does, for the temptation to retire was never a desire to escape from work. Sometimes his friends would chide him, when he returned from a long hunting trip, by remarking that his only ambition was to have two vacations every year of six months each. Eastman's retort, however, was usually something in the nature of a letter he wrote Edward Bausch: 'I am trying to fix it so that I will have to come down to business only about every second rainy Thursday, but so many new things are continually coming up that my plan has not so far brought about the desired result. Hope springs eternal, however, and that is what keeps me going.'

CHAPTER XIV

'INSTITUTIONS ALONE CAN CREATE A NATION'[1]

'WE never reach the end of anything.' This is what East-man really believed.[2] 'You may seem to have all of the misfortunes in the world. You may think that everything has happened to you that can happen. Or, on the other hand, you may imagine that you have reached perfection — the end of the journey.

'But I hold that the man who says he is "down and out" is expressing exactly the same sentiment as the man who says, "I have attained success." It is true that they are talking of very different subjects, but the mental approach is identical. No matter what happens to one — unless it is death itself — there is always something more that may happen, fortunate or unfortunate. Neither cup is ever quite full.

'The saving grace is that if one recognizes that misfortunes are only marks, as on a thermometer, then one will know that, while the mercury can keep going down, it can just as easily go up.

'It is the same with success. The man who thinks he has done everything he can do has merely stopped thinking. He is what might be called "up and out." And, excepting that he has more money, his case really is not very different from that of the man who is "down and out." '

This philosophy was still in mind, when in 1924 he

[1] Speaking in Manchester, England, in 1866, Disraeli said: 'Individuals may form communities, but it is institutions alone that can create a nation.'

[2] From one of the few interviews Eastman authorized, published in the *American Magazine*, February, 1921.

passed the seventieth milestone in his own 'long, interesting, and eventful life.'   In December, when he distributed most of his securities to the University of Rochester
and the Massachusetts Institute of Technology, Hampton
and Tuskegee Normal and Agricultural Institutes each
received more than a million dollars, not including sums
given in previous years.[1]

After Eastman's pledges were announced, Dr. Anson
Phelps Stokes, speaking in behalf of the joint endowment
fund committee, said that the two objects of their national
appeal were 'to make Hampton and Tuskegee self-sus-
taining and to enable them to develop collegiate courses
in teacher-training, agriculture, and home economics.
Without college degrees, which require the addition of a
four-years' course, the school's graduates cannot legally
be appointed in many Southern States to high-school
principalships and other positions of leadership in Negro
education.

'When the $5,000,000 fund is raised and Mr. Eastman's
gift secured, the Institutes will be able to put into effect
their programme of training adequately a large group of
young colored men and women to be leaders and teachers
of their people. This should result in improving the
moral, social, and economic status of the entire Negro
race in America.

'Mr. Eastman sees in this programme the only hope of
the solution of the race question, America's most grave
and perplexing domestic question. In explaining his

[1] Eastman had contributed to Tuskegee for many years, although forced
to decline repeated invitations to visit the institution. December 5, 1910, he
wrote Seth Low, former Mayor of New York City, who had renewed previous invitations: 'The practical way in which Dr. [Booker T.] Washington
has dealt with his problems has appealed to me for a long time and I have
no doubt that an inspection of his plant would still further increase my
appreciation of him.'

$2,000,000 gift to Hampton and Tuskegee, Mr. Eastman said to the committee:

' "Almost the entire attention of education has been thus far devoted to the white race, but we have more than ten per cent Negro population in the United States, most of them densely ignorant. The only hope of the Negro race and the settlement of this problem is through proper education of the Hampton-Tuskegee type, which is directed almost wholly toward making them useful citizens through education on industrial lines." '

Editorial comment which followed the announcement of this gift was naturally widespread and generous. One of the leading articles from an old Southern journal, the 'Memphis Commercial Appeal,' showed that even in the South it was recognized that a new day had dawned in the education of the Negro.

'We feel satisfied that we could not have succeeded in securing the $5,000,000 in pledges but for the great impetus which your broad view, evidenced by such munificent financial support, gave to our campaign,' wrote Clarence H. Kelsey, Chairman of the Executive Committee of the Hampton-Tuskegee Endowment Fund. 'In consequence, we not only raised the $5,000,000, but secured the millions which you have so opportunely added to the fund.

'The country can hardly repay you for what you have done for it by this act, for it is not only a great service to the colored people, but still more to the white people, who are so much more numerous than the colored people and by so much more concerned in the welfare of the latter than they are themselves.'

What this New York banker was really conveying to Eastman was his gratitude for the way Eastman had joined in the spirit of the campaign. There were some hearts and purses that were hard to open, and when the problems of how to approach certain of these individuals were placed before Eastman, he so worded his conditions that what he said was quite as effective as what he gave.

As this was part of the psychology of raising money, Eastman did not mind the publicity, even though it did bring in its wake thousands of new begging letters, including one from a young relative.

'I have received your letter,' Eastman replied, 'and will say frankly that it has created an unfavorable impression on me. In the first place, you seem to have an idea that you will be helping yourself if you borrow money from me. Perhaps you have not heard the story about the man who, on signing a note for a bill, heaved a sigh of relief and said: "Well, thank Heaven, that bill is settled."

'It seems to me that if a young man wants to help himself to go through college, he should buckle in and earn some money. There is a Yale Alumni Association here of about a hundred members who select each year one or two of the most promising graduates of the high schools and give them assistance to the extent of $400 to help them through Yale. A friend of mine who is a member of this association told me the other day of one of the young men who, in addition to the $400, had earned a scholarship which netted him $250; for work on a college paper he had received $350, and $200 more for services of some kind in connection with a college restaurant. It seems to me, therefore, that if you need more than your father can give you, it is up to you to go out and earn it. I know you are using your vacation in this way, but there are opportunities for young men to increase their income during the college year.

'Another thing which creates an unfavorable impression is your inviting me to be your guest at the Colonial

Club. A young man who is trying to borrow money has no call to invite people to be his guests.

'I hope you will not think there is anything ill-natured about this letter. There is a noticeable inclination in this day and generation for young people to pass the "buck" to others, and I am only calling your attention to it, as I should be sorry to see such a bright specimen of the Eastman family fall into this habit.'

The mail was literally padded with individual appeals, including scores of letters in the handwriting of children, obviously dictated by their elders. As Eastman opened all communications addressed to him personally, he would write across the pages of these appeals with his soft-green pencil, 'Don't raise your child to be a beggar,' and return them to the senders.

During the year 1924, Eastman became interested, also, in the world-wide movement for a modern calendar, initiated by Moses B. Cotsworth.

'The possibilities of an international fixed calendar which would divide the year into thirteen months of twenty-eight days, each comprising four complete weeks, beginning on Sunday and ending on Saturday, first came to my attention in 1924,' Eastman wrote early in 1928.[1] 'Since then my interest has increased day by day as I have observed this movement gather momentum throughout the world, and it seems to me now that it is merely a question of time until all nations meet in conference to agree upon a change. There is no doubt in my mind of ultimate success, because the world moves inevitably toward the practical. When the public understands the many conveniences of a thirteen-month year, and when business in general realizes the necessity for a more

[1] 'When Thirteen Months Make a Year,' by George Eastman in *The Saturday Evening Post*, March 10, 1928.

serviceable calendar than we have to-day, all governments, religious organizations, businesses, educational institutions, and professions will welcome an international
congress such as President Arthur called in Washington,
D.C., in 1884, when standard time was officially adopted.

'As the progress of the world is determined by the progress of business, it is essential that the business minds
here and abroad comprehend the advantages of the plan
proposed by Mr. Moses B. Cotsworth, who is to-day the
recognized international authority on the history of
calendar making and the relationship of the calendar to
the peace and prosperity of mankind. Twenty years ago
the Royal Society of Canada invited Mr. Cotsworth, a
successful statistician and accountant in England, to present his calendar plan to this, the leading scientific society
in the Dominion. He suggested that the year be divided
into thirteen months and that the extra month be inserted between June and July, so that every month in
every year would be exactly alike in dates and week-day
names. The last day in every year would be dated
December twenty-ninth, as an eighth-day extra Sabbath
ending the last week. In leap-years, leap-day would be
another eighth-day extra Sabbath dated June twenty-
ninth. This plan would automatically fix a perpetual
week-day name to each date in every year.

'Mr. Cotsworth's proposals were unanimously endorsed
by this body.

'In 1922, he came to the United States to place his
ideas before a convention in Washington, D.C., called by
the Liberty Calendar and other associations. Again his
plan was unanimously selected as the best of many submitted. For the purpose of expanding international efforts to simplify the calendar, Mr. Cotsworth organized
the International Fixed Calendar League, consisting of

experts in government departments, chambers of commerce, industrial, manufacturing, trade, labor, professional and scientific organizations, because he believed that their opinions would influence the controllers of such bodies and ultimately convince governments and religious authorities that simplification was needed.

'By 1924, Mr. Cotsworth had spent all of his personal fortune; had sold his cherished and valuable collection of fine pictures, and was living in New York City, preparing and giving addresses before societies, printing pamphlets with the small subscriptions which he received from individuals here and abroad who became interested when he buttonholed them and explained his ideas.

'An associate of mine met him when he was struggling against these formidable odds. He told me that Mr. Cotsworth had been carrying on this work, single-handed, for twenty-five years. I had our statistical department make a study of his plan and I conducted an independent investigation of the whole calendar movement. The more I learned the more I became convinced that this man was unselfishly performing a great international public service.

'It seemed to me that he had already accomplished a task which appeared greater than any man could achieve alone. He was an individualist laboring in an organized world, handicapped because he lacked the financial support necessary to multiply his own efforts.

'Like all men who achieve success, he never acknowledged defeat. I thought he deserved a better opportunity and sent word to him that I would assist him for one year, during which time he was to use his own judgment in expanding and increasing the activities of the League, without disclosing my interest. In the mean time, Mr. Cotsworth went abroad to organize in as many foreign countries as possible groups of individuals and committees to carry forward his work, while I continued my study and followed his activities.

'After the British and the Canadian Governments had printed Mr. Cotsworth's thesis and given it wide circulation, it was submitted to the League of Nations through the International Chamber of Commerce. The League appointed a committee of inquiry composed of representatives appointed by the great Roman Catholic, Eastern-Orthodox, and Protestant religious authorities, astronomers, and the International Chamber of Commerce, representing business organizations throughout the world.

'The chairman of that committee requested Mr. Cotsworth to go to Geneva to analyze the 185 proposals for calendar simplification received from thirty-three nations in many languages. This one fact is an indication of the feeling throughout the world that our present calendar is not adequately adapted to modern life and business. Without receiving compensation from any organization and refusing to accept more than his necessary living and traveling expenses, Mr. Cotsworth served this committee until its report was completed and adopted by the League of Nations Assembly in September, 1927.'

When Secretary of State Frank B. Kellogg received the request of the League for the formation of a national committee in this country he addressed inquiries to the chief departments of the Government. As the replies were favorable both to the idea of a key committee and toward calendar change, the way was opened for a comprehensive investigation of American sentiment.

Following conferences between Secretary Kellogg and Eastman, the State Department forwarded the Secretary of Agriculture, W. W. Jardine, a copy of his letter to Eastman, January 4, 1928, in which it was stated:

'. . . I see no further obstacles to the formation of an unofficial committee similar to the one created in 1925 for the purpose of collaborating with the Committee on Intellectual Coöperation of the League of Nations. While this Government is not in a position actively to participate in the creation of such a committee, you are, of course, at liberty to seek the unofficial coöperation of interested Federal Departments or Bureaus in the selection of members to serve on the proposed national committee.

'I suggest that if you should desire further information as to the appointment of this committee, you communicate with Dr. Charles F. Marvin, Chief of the Weather Bureau, Department of Agriculture, Washington, D.C.'

Dr. Marvin's interest in the simplification of the calendar was both scientific and practical. He was not a recent convert, for he had been a forceful champion of a change for many years. The interest of the Secretary of Agriculture, too, was keen, and he invited other members of the Cabinet to lend their support. In a letter to his colleagues, he said:

'Wishing to assist Mr. Eastman in this matter, and because of the interest of this Department in calendar simplification, I am writing informally to request that you designate a representative from your Department to participate in the deliberations of Mr. Eastman's committee and to coöperate with the Chief of the Weather Bureau, representing this Department, along the lines of the request of the League of Nations.'

The formation of the Government group of the national committee having been accomplished, Eastman extended invitations to men and women prominent in business and social life to accept membership in the nonofficial section of the committee. This committee has endeavored to sound public sentiment in regard to an international conference without prejudice as to the plans which have been proposed.

In the mean time, at the Pan-American Conference at Havana, February 18, 1928, the following resolution was unanimously adopted by the delegates of the twenty-one nations:

'That it be recommended to the countries, members of the Pan-American Union, that they each appoint a National Committee with a view to studying the proposal relative to the simplification of the Calendar, and that they make the necessary preparation in order to participate in an International Conference to determine which is the best method of reform.'

Already more than one hundred large corporations have adopted the thirteen-month calendar for interior accounting purposes, while a formidable group of national organizations have officially endorsed the idea of a change in the present measure of time.[1]

To Eastman this movement has never been a crusade or a reform. From the beginning he has regarded it as a natural evolution in modern life, as inevitable as was Standard Time in 1884.

Throughout these years, repeated efforts were made to persuade him to accept diverse personal honors or appointment to the boards of many large national and international corporations and institutions. Frequent attempts were made to focus the spotlight of public attention upon him, but Eastman invariably escaped. Typical of his own reactions to all these efforts is a telegram to the Governors of the Society of the Genesee, many of whom

[1] Among these are: National Research Council, National Academy of Sciences, New York State Chamber of Commerce, National Retail Dry Goods Association, Institute of American Meat Packers, American Paper and Pulp Association, International Chamber of Commerce, etc.

were personal friends from Rochester, who desired to tender him a dinner in New York City.

'I deeply appreciate the honor,' he replied, 'and deeply regret that it is wholly impossible for me to accept such an invitation. I should be embarrassed beyond measure on such an occasion and do not feel that I could go through the ordeal.'

Personally, Eastman preferred the obscurity of camp life. Here he could cook, fish, shoot, ride over the mountains, and be himself without any one making a 'fuss' over him. Since the days of the World's Fair in Chicago he had been in the habit of making frequent unheralded journeys to the Rocky Mountains, to Michigan, Nebraska, and North Carolina, or to Alaska, British Columbia, Quebec, and Nova Scotia, or along the Atlantic Coast from Labrador to Panama. He believed, with the French, that 'idle people have the least leisure.' Returning one year from a fishing expedition along the Grand Cascapedia, he learned from his friend George D. B. Bonbright of the passing of a mutual acquaintance in that section of Quebec. Acknowledging the message, Eastman wrote, 'One could not wish for anything better than to keep up one's interest in fishing to the age of eighty-three and then die *en route* to the river.'

By 1925, 'life on the trail' was calling again, and this time Eastman went to Africa with Daniel E. Pomeroy, his associate in the equipping of the African Hall at the American Museum of Natural History in New York City, and his personal physician, Dr. Audley D. Stewart. While anxious to trek through the Big Game Country, Eastman had another motive. This was the year Stuber and Lovejoy were placed at the head of the company. 'When they were put in the saddle,' Eastman recalled, 'it was part of my idea to get out of the way and let them get used to the saddle.'

Before leaving for the Dark Continent, Eastman initiated another institution. For some time he had been discussing with Dr. Flexner and Dr. Burkhart the possibilities of founding a Dental Dispensary in London. At the request of Dr. Flexner, Sir Walter Fletcher had undertaken an inquiry, so that by the time Eastman passed through London on his way to Africa, where Mr. and Mrs. Carl Akeley and Mr. and Mrs. Martin Johnson were to meet him, he was able to examine the survey which Sir Walter had made.

Following conferences with Lord Riddell, president, and Sir Arthur Levy, treasurer of the Royal Free Hospital, Eastman offered to build a dispensary if the trustees of the hospital would subscribe to a maintenance fund.

Throughout the six months the Eastman party spent trailing game and obtaining specimens and photographs for the museum, Eastman wrote detailed descriptive letters to Miss Whitney (Mrs. Charles F. Hutchison) for his personal friends at home. Later the 'Chronicles of an African Trip' were published for private distribution. Then, when he found that all of his various interests had been so well administered during his absence, he was ready for a second journey to Africa.

Returning again via London and Paris, he approved Sir John J. Burnet's [1] plans for the London Dispensary.

[1] Sir John J. Burnet was the architect for the Kodak Building in Kingsway, London. March 6, 1925, Eastman wrote him: 'A clipping from the "Manchester Guardian," received to-day, mentions that you have been made an "R.A." I fully agree with the statement therein that the action is a belated one. Nevertheless, I congratulate you and want you to know I am heartily pleased that the honor has come to you. I am also puffed with pride at the mention of the Kodak and Adelaide Buildings, particularly after what you told me about the development of the latter.

'Not remembering whether I have ever sent you any description of the Eastman School of Music and Theater building, at the risk of repetition I am sending you a copy of the "American Architect" containing the best article that has been published so far. The institutions have been running

MRS. MARTIN JOHNSON WATCHING MR. EASTMAN BLOW AN OSTRICH EGG

Finally, on April 30, 1929, when Eastman was four thousand miles away on his farm in North Carolina, the foundation stone of the Dispensary was laid by the Prince of Wales. In the presence of the Prime Minister, other representatives of the Government, Frank B. Kellogg, who had recently resigned as Secretary of State, Dr. Burkhart and their friends, another Eastman institution was accepted in the community life of a great metropolis.

'I am very glad, indeed, to have been invited to perform this ceremony,' said the Prince, 'because I believe that the work which will be done in the building of which we are about to lay the foundation-stone is very important, and one which will contribute directly and materially to the health and happiness of a great many people in these districts.

'Good teeth have always been valued for several reasons. First of all, good teeth are very useful, although thanks to the development of dental art I believe that modern substitutes for the genuine article give quite satisfactory results. [Laughter.] Secondly, good teeth are essential to a good appearance, which is a matter of importance to all women and most men since the creation of the human. Thirdly, good teeth are essential from the point of view of general health and fitness, although it is only comparatively recently that this has been sufficiently realized. Even now I am sure there are many people who through ignorance or carelessness do not keep their teeth in good condition; too many people wait until they have toothache before they pay that dreaded visit to the dentist. But, ladies and gentlemen, there is another obvious, though true, reason for the neglect of the teeth among very many people, and that is

now for upwards of two years quite successfully and are having a noticeable influence upon our community life.'

inability to afford the cost of dental treatment. The dentists' bills, as we all know, are on the heavy side and there are many who cannot possibly afford to pay them.

'Here we have the Eastman Dental Clinic, which will provide free dental treatment for all. Of course, there is nothing like starting from the beginning. Prevention is always better than cure and special provision will be made for the children, but the clinic will also provide for adults. There is one point I should like to emphasize. I am told that care of the teeth is of particular importance to expectant and nursing mothers, and special provision will be made in the clinic for this form of treatment, for which, so far as I know, there is no other organized and systematic service in this great city. Of course, a clinic for children is not a new departure, and there are several dental clinics under the London County Council which provide free dental treatment for children attending the elementary schools of London. Admirable work has been, and is being done, but the provision of this Eastman Clinic will afford an opportunity of continuing and enlarging the work and doing it on a very much bigger scale, so, not for the first time, do we gladly and gratefully welcome American assistance. [Cheers.]

'Here, then, we shall have a compact institution capable of dealing with all aspects of dental healing, and devoted particularly to the preventive side for children and mothers, but I hope its ultimate influence will be even wider than that and that it will give a further impetus to the education of public opinion generally in dental matters. Our people must realize that if they want good health they must have good teeth, and if, as I anticipate and hope, the work of this clinic helps to this end it will have contributed very materially to the health and happiness of the whole nation.

'May I say a few words as to how the project came into being? Mr. George Eastman some years ago, with customary generosity and public spirit, established in Rochester, in the State of New York, a clinic for the care of children's teeth under the direction of Dr. Harvey Burkhart. It was a very great success, so great that Mr. Eastman desired to establish a similar institution in London. Lord Riddell and Sir Albert Levy, of the Royal Free Hospital, learned of Mr. Eastman's readiness to build and equip a clinic, and joined forces to provide the additional sums required to maintain the clinic after it was built.

'Ladies and gentlemen, I am to be followed by the Prime Minister, and I am well content to leave the actual acknowledgment of the very great gift of this clinic to a far more eloquent speaker than myself, but there is just one more thing I would like to say. This gift and coöperation of one American citizen and the authorities of a great hospital in London furnishes one more instance, if one were needed, of the friendship which exists between the United States and this country. [Cheers.] It is a friendship which springs from kinship of ideals as well as of blood, and it is well exemplified by this most generous and magnificent gift.'

Prime Minister Baldwin said 'that he thoroughly endorsed all that had been said about the value of teeth, and from the point of view of the statesman teeth played an important part upon which His Royal Highness did not touch. Upon teeth rested digestion, and upon digestion rested the temper; and if all people had perfect teeth there would be a great deal less rot talked, and a great deal less of those gloomy tom-fool letters to the press about England and America and half a dozen other subjects. [Laughter and cheers.] Therefore, he was all in favour of good teeth; they did not matter so much to a woman, who only held a cigarette in her mouth, but to a man who smoked a pipe, teeth were important. [More laughter.] [1]

'He was very proud to be their voice that day in thanking Mr. Eastman for that noble gift. American generosity on the part of her wealthy citizens had become proverbial, and he thought they gave their money in wise directions toward education and toward health. There was no gift which could be more welcome here at that moment than the gift of that clinic. If there was one thing which thoughtful people in this country were really keen about to-day, it was about these problems of health for children and mothers, for upon that depended the life and prosperity of the rising and future generations. Without health they could not take full advantage of education, and without education they could not play the part they should in the life of their country and the world.'

In June, 1929, announcements were made that dental dispensaries, modeled after the Rochester institution, would be built in Chicago and New York City.[2]

'Eight years ago I visited Rochester and Dr. Burkhart inoculated me with the idea of the tonsil and adenoid clinic and I established one in Chicago,' Julius Rosenwald said after another visit to the Rochester Dental Dispensary. 'Now he has given me a new inoculation and it concerns the dental clinic. The germ is working vigorously already, and I will start immediately to provide Chicago with a clinic such as has been founded in

[1] This account is taken from *The Times* of May 1, 1929.

[2] On October 7, 1929, the American Dental Association awarded Eastman the Dental Survey Medal for 1929, 'because of the far-reaching effect of his interest in the field of preventive dentistry. We feel,' said the citation, 'that the developments during the past year make his contributions of outstanding importance in the field.'

Rochester and which under Dr. Burkhart's administration has received world-wide attention and commendation.'

A few days later, the Murry and Leonie Guggenheim Foundation announced that free dental clinics would be established in New York City. The original project involved an outlay of three million dollars, with an ultimate expenditure of ten times that sum.

'This will put dental clinics on the map in this country,' Eastman wrote Lord Riddell, 'and I look for a blossoming out of the idea all over the country in the next few years.

'Julius Rosenwald spent a day with me last week and before he went away he announced his intention of tackling Chicago.

'The work, of course, ought to be done with Government money, but the rich men have got to get it started and show the right methods; and also demonstrate to the public the fact that greater returns in efficiency can be had from money spent in this way than from money spent in any other way.'

A realization of this ideal evolved more rapidly than Eastman anticipated. On June 4, following several conversations with his friend, Cesare Sconfietti, the Italian Consul in Rochester, Eastman wrote him: 'You are at liberty to tell His Excellency, Nob. Giacomo De Martino, Ambassador of H. M. King of Italy, in Washington, about your interview with me concerning the proposed dental clinic, like the one now being built in London. If the Ambassador is interested in your scheme to get me to build it and would like to come to Rochester to see our Dental Dispensary here I would be delighted, and happy to entertain him and whomever he brings with him at my house.'

Premier Benito Mussolini was quick to sense the value of such a project in Rome and cabled the Ambassador that the Italian Government would make the proposed Dental Dispensary a governmental institution. By August 22, the agreement was signed in Rochester by the Ambassador, Professor Amedeo Perna, Special Representative of the Italian Government, and Eastman. As this accorded the Italian Government the distinction of being the first to officially recognize preventive dentistry, the document itself may have an added historic value.

'After consultation with you I make the following proposition,' Eastman wrote, 'That I will furnish the Italian Government the equivalent of one million dollars ($1,000,000.00) to build and equip, on a suitable piece of ground in Rome, to be furnished by the Italian Government (to be approved by myself or my collaborator, Dr. Harvey J. Burkhart), a dental dispensary on the lines of the one in Rochester in relation to children, on the following conditions: That the Italian Government agrees to maintain the building and equipment, and to furnish the funds to operate it in a first-class manner perpetually or so long as it is necessary to have such an institution in Rome.

'My object in making this contribution is to establish in Rome a demonstration center which will be competent to care for and as far as possible rectify the teeth of all the indigent children in the city of Rome up to the age of sixteen years. Whatever is done in the dispensary for adults in the way of emergency work, such as extractions, it is not to be anything that will interfere with the full treatment of the children. It is not intended for primary education of dentists, but naturally it will serve as a post university dental school for the young dentists who are employed in the dispensary, or graduate dentists from outside.

'I learn from our conversation that there are a sufficient number of young women and men who have been educated as physicians who can be employed to serve as dental specialists at the beginning; That if more of these specialists are required than can be obtained from this group that the Government will provide laws so that the dental nurses can be educated for this particular work at the dispensary, the same as it is done here in Rochester.

'It is understood, of course, that the Government will appoint a suitable director of this institution, who will be selected solely for his ability for this purpose; the principal requirements being sympathy with and understanding of children; the ability to secure coöperation with the school authorities to carry on the work of cleaning and examining the teeth of the children in the various schools; and the ability to supervise and direct the young dentists and specialists. In doing this work he must be willing to subordinate his own immediate personal interests to the cause and devote such time as may be necessary to make the project a full success.

'The selection of the architect to be subject to my approval, as also the plans of the institution, which in general it is understood shall follow the lines of the Rochester dispensary.

'It is understood the equipment shall be selected by me or Dr. Harvey J. Burkhart after consultation with the director selected by the Government.

'It is understood that the operation of the dispensary shall be on the lines of the Rochester institution for a period of say two years before any change is made without my approval or that of my collaborator, Dr. Burkhart.

'It is also understood that the Government will send the director or a full-time assistant to this country for a period of at least two months to familiarize himself with the operations of the Rochester Dental Dispensary, and in addition to visit certain dental centers as will be recommended by Dr. Burkhart.

'Any amount remaining from the million dollar fund after paying for the building and equipment shall be invested and the income therefrom devoted to the orthodontia department.'

For nearly a year another idea had been evolving in Eastman's mind. While abroad in the early summer of 1928, Dr. Flexner wrote that he would like to present a thought in regard to education at Oxford, and Eastman invited him for a visit. Following the luncheon where the subject was discussed, Dr. Flexner submitted the following: [1]

'The suggestion which I made to you respecting a Chair of American Studies at Oxford originated in my mind from the following considerations:

'England and America must never, even in the interest of peace, endeavor to dominate the world by force of any kind (wealth, numbers, etc.): but they can give the world such an example and establish such a precedent through mutual understanding as will stimulate other nations to establish friendly and co-operative relations upon the same basis. It is the general conviction of those who have been working towards international peace, good-will, comprehension and co-operation, that more is to be expected from knowledge and intelligence respecting one another than from any other source; and obviously England and America are best fitted, through community of language, literature, etc. to set the pace or make the demonstration.

[1] August 2, 1928.

'Now the men who as journalists and statesmen and, to an increasing extent, as business men are most prominent and influential in shaping British opinion and in directing British policy are largely trained at Oxford. Oxford does for this group what Cambridge does for the scientific group. And at Oxford, those who look forward to journalistic, governmental, and other similar careers are segregated and brought together, as in no other institution in the world. It is this group which would come under the direct influence of successive Professors of American Studies who would expound and explain to them American ideals, American conditions, American problems, American experience, in co-operation with the Harmsworth Professor of American History, who deals with the historical development of the United States.

'In education, economics, and other fields, we have much to give as well as something to learn: a proper Professor of American Studies could yearly orient groups of advanced English students, among whom would undoubtedly be many men destined to be prominent in public life, in journalism, and in commerce. Great Britain would thus gain; but we too would gain, first, because it is in our interest that we should be understood, second, because successive professors of American studies, each of whom, after his term of service, return to take up his work in this country, would themselves have been enriched by their participation in the life of the great University. My own experience and that of the two Harmsworth professors of American history leave me in no doubt on that score.

'Oxford teaches annually at least two hundred Rhodes Scholars, free of all charge; they come from different states of the Union and from the Dominions. There are now over six hundred Rhodes Scholars, graduates of

Oxford, in the United States. Year by year these numbers (to which those who go independently should be added) increase. We are thus in a way to understand Great Britain. It is a fair return, in the interest of civilization, that something should be done to enable Great Britain to understand us. I believe that successive Professors of American Studies (I purposely use a vague word), chosen at intervals by a committee composed of Americans and Oxford authorities, would make a notable contribution to this end. A professorship of Spanish Studies has already been endowed at Oxford. In time a few other outstanding nations will be similarly represented; and thus something substantial will be accomplished in the way of enlightening and educating the Englishmen upon whom the burden of forming and directing opinion rests and is bound to rest. These men do not know America adequately; I believe that much would be accomplished, if they were thoroughly trained.

'An endowment of $200,000 would achieve the purpose; the income would provide salary and other necessary expenses; the principal could be held by the Association of American Rhodes Scholars, of which Dr. Frank Aydelotte, President of Swarthmore College, formerly Professor of English in the Massachusetts Institute of Technology, is the leading spirit. I am sure that all details could be easily worked out, if the sum indicated were made available.

'The object in view — the promotion of knowledge and understanding between all who speak the English language — is so important that I venture to hope you will take favorably to the idea.

'P.S. Should you care to discuss the question with him, I am sure that Dr. Aydelotte would be glad to go to

Rochester to see you. .... He is a man of excellent judgment and very great ability.'

In May, 1929, the George Eastman Visiting Professorship at Oxford was founded, following several conferences in Rochester with Dr. Aydelotte. The Eastman endowment was the first contribution for a specific purpose to the American Trust Fund of Oxford University, which was created by the Association of American Rhodes Scholars for the University of Oxford, July 5, 1928, upon the seventy-fifth anniversary of the birth of Cecil Rhodes, and the twenty-fifth anniversary of the appointment of the first American Rhodes Scholars.

These years were crowded, too, by international developments in business. The industry Eastman founded had long since assumed a world-wide character, but with the expansion in business and the larger services of photography, it was necessary to increase the manufacturing facilities in France and Germany and provide for wide distribution on the Continent and in Latin America. In 1927, the industry founded by Charles Pathé was brought into the Kodak fold. 'It is with great pride and great joy that I have signed the agreement which associates my name with yours,' Pathé telegraphed Eastman. The acquisition of this business brought together the two greatest names in modern photography.

This action in France was soon followed by the purchase of another large industry in Germany. Again photography was leading the way in foreign manufacturing and distribution for the automotive industry, while at home scientists were perfecting amateur motion pictures in natural colors, the realization of another Eastman dream.

The full fruition of this development came in the summer of 1928, when a small group of scientists and friends were Eastman's guests at his home, 900 East Avenue. In the morning of July 31, they were photographed with the new motion-picture cameras, and in the evening the guests saw themselves on the screen in natural colored pictures. 'Fine,' said Edison enthusiastically. 'It is entirely simple. I worked on it myself several years ago, but I made a failure of it. Anybody can use it now.'

'It can make new life for all of us and will be our salvation,' added Professor Michael I. Pupin. 'I consider this new process as important as motion pictures themselves,' said Major-General James G. Harbord. 'It is a remarkable achievement,' commented Dr. E. F. W. Alexanderson, one of the inventors of television, while Owen D. Young observed that 'one of the most significant features of this development is the manner in which it reflects what can be done in organized research.' 'The possibilities of this invention are unbounded,' concluded Sir James Irvine, Vice-Chancellor of Saint Andrew's University, Scotland, while Dr. Edwin E. Slosson swelled the chorus with the remark that 'this new process will give the people a new appreciation of color just as black and white photography gave the people a new conception of form.'

General John J. Pershing, however, voiced the layman's amazement by saying that 'it seems almost like a feat of legerdemain. . . . I should consider it must be the greatest development in photography.'

'The secret of the "Kodacolor" process is in the film [Dr. Mees explained to the guests]. The film surface is embossed by running it through the steel rollers with tiny cylindrical lenses composed of the film base material and extending lengthwise of the film. The lenses on the film are about seven times narrower than the dots making up the illustrations in a newspaper. They are therefore

MR. EDISON, MR. OCHS, GENERAL PERSHING, MR. EASTMAN, AND SIR JAMES IRVINE

invisible except under a microscope. They cover completely the surface of the side of the film opposite from the sensitive emulsion.

'When the trigger of the camera is pressed, light reflected from the subject passes selectively through the three-color filter, on through the camera lens, and thence through the tiny embossed lenses on the film to the sensitive emulsion coating on the opposite side, where it is recorded. The function of the lenses embossed on the film is to guide the rays of light falling upon each tiny area and lay them on the sensitive emulsion as three distinct impressions corresponding to the three filter areas, so that the three colors covering the lens are imaged behind each tiny cylindrical lens as three parallel vertical strips, because the tiny cylindrical lenses are parallel to the stripes of color on the filter. Thus the width of each of the minute areas of emulsion is subdivided into three parts related to the three filter areas and affected by light that is able to pass through the different colors. The sum of these invisibly small affected areas of film constitutes the whole photographic image.

'A red ray from an object in the front of the camera for instance, reaches the sensitive material of the film at a spot related to the red areas of the filter. The "reversal process" turns this affected spot into a transparent area, leaving opaque the adjoining unaffected areas related to the green and blue segments of the filter. So also, with the green and blue and with combinations of colors. The sum of the points on the scene containing red makes a photograph from red light on the emulsion areas related to the red filter area, the sum of the blue also makes a separate photograph, and similarly with the green. In order to project the pictures, the developed film is put in the projector which contains exactly the same optical system reversed.'

A few days before Christmas, 1928, Eastman approved
the establishment of retirement annuity, life insurance,
and disability benefit plan for all employees of the company. It was the capstone on the policy of industrial
relations which he had been encouraging since he made
his first study of pensions and insurance early in his business career.

Writing 'all employees,' scattered in every country
throughout the world, Eastman said:

'The purpose is to provide not merely a substantial
annuity for old age — this annuity to be paid by a financially solid insurance company — but also a substantial
protection in the form of life insurance and liberal treatment under the disability benefit plan.

'To put this plan into immediate effect requires a very
large investment for the liabilities which have already
accrued, covering the past services of employees. It is
proposed that this payment, which will total approximately six and one half million dollars, be made one half
by funds appropriated by the Company and one half
by the Kodak Employees' Association.

'The funds of the Kodak Employees' Association, it
will be recalled, were originally contributed by the Company and myself for the welfare of the employees. As a
matter of fact, the income from the Kodak Employees'
Association fund is now used chiefly to give a service
bonus to employees retired. The Kodak Employees'
Association fund is, however, inadequate for the purpose;
and accordingly the Management feels that this plan,
which will provide liberally for retirement annuities, life
insurance, and disability benefits, should be established.
The plan has been approved by the members and
directors of the Kodak Employees' Association, it being
their decision that the benefits to employees under the

proposed plan will be much greater than at present, and that the purposes of the Association will be better served by turning the necessary portion of these funds over to the insurance company than by having the funds administered by the Kodak Employees' Association itself.

'The Company and the Kodak Employees' Association having thus provided for the initial financing, it is necessary that the present rate of the wage dividend be reduced in order to provide funds for the future payments to be made to the insurance company.

'When the wage dividend was established, the purpose, first of all, was that it should provide employees, in a lump sum annually, with a sufficient amount of money for investment so that, after a reasonable period of service, the employee would have accumulated from these wage dividends sufficient property to produce an income during old age. Of course, it was also the intention that employees who contribute so largely to the success of the Company should, through the wage dividend, share in the profits coming from its success; yet of even greater importance in the minds of the directors was the idea that these wage dividends would enable the employees, during the active years of their life, to provide against disability and the lower earning power that might come with old age.

'The plan adopted, to a large degree, assures our employees a comfortable income in their old age. It is hoped that, in accordance with the original purpose of the wage dividend, they will supplement this income by investing for their future a substantial part of the wage dividends they will receive.

'The carrying out of the plan necessitates a change in the wage dividend formula. Beginning with the disbursement of July 1, 1929, and subject each year to favorable action by the directors, this formula will be as follows:

' "For each dollar of dividends declared during the calendar year upon shares of the common stock of the Company over and above $3.50 per share (present rule is $1.00 per share) the wage dividend rate is $5.00 per $1000 of salaries and wages paid to employees during the past five calendar years.

' "As an illustration, if the common stock dividends were $8.00 per share, the wage dividend rate would be $22.50 per $1000 of wages during the past five years instead of $35 per $100 as at present. For an employee who has been with the Company for five years and whose salary has been uniform during this period, this rate of wage dividend would represent almost one-eighth of one year's pay."

'It is expected that this reduction in the wage dividend will provide sufficient funds to pay the insurance company administering the plan the annual cost of the benefits in the future, the accrued cost having been provided for through the appropriation of $6,500,000.

'The Management has been working for some years upon a plan to provide, more liberally and reliably than at present, an income for old age, a proper protection for disability, and life insurance. Intensive study has been given to the whole plan by the Management, and I have naturally taken a deep personal interest in a matter affecting the future of the thousands of Kodak workers — a large proportion of whom I have been associated with for a score or more of years.

'The plan evolved is comprehensive, liberal, and workable. It is, in my opinion, a definite assurance for the future, and will work out to the comfort and happiness of our employees. With the wage dividend, which gives the employee a share in the profits of the Company; the sickness benefit plan, which provides a liberal allowance in case of illness; this retirement annuity, life insurance and disability benefit plan; and with the facilities offered the employees by the Kodak Employees Association for financing their homes, and the facilities offered the employees by the Eastman Savings and Loan Association for investing their savings — I feel that a comprehensive program of industrial relations has now been established. I congratulate the employes upon the work that has been accomplished.'

Developments during these years were like white caps on the sea — seemingly endless. And yet, on his seventy-fifth birthday, Eastman was thinking of the next generation. Unostentatiously, as usual, he presented all public and parochial schools in Rochester with radio receiving sets. This appeared as casual, indeed, as the building of an auditorium in a new public school in Waterville in memory of his father and mother. But these and scores of similar activities were not fortuitous. They were necessary additional details, which Eastman, the individualist, could attend to, to aid those institutions which, among many others, were helping to create a nation.

'If every one who has got pleasure from a snapshot or a movie film were to express gratitude to the man who initially made it possible, George Eastman would be the most bethanked man in the world on the seventy-fifth anniversary of his birth,' read the 'New York Times' editorial. 'The films that his factories produce each year would, it is estimated, reach ten times around the globe, and there is not a corner of the earth which has not been exposed to them, or to which they have not carried fleeting or treasured images. There would be special supplementary thanks, what the Scotch call a "bethankit" that after his three score and ten he has found a way of filling even the shadow world with colors such as objects have in God's world of nature.

'Besides all this contribution to the entertainment and enlightenment of untold millions, he has turned a vast amount of what he has gathered with one hand into philanthropic distribution by the other. His gifts have been noteworthy not only in their amount but in the wise discrimination shown in their making. He has furthered science by his for a long time anonymous gift of nearly $20,000,000 to the Massachusetts Institute of Technology; he has given other millions for the education of the Negro through Hampton and Tuskegee Institutes, and he has above all blessed his own city by his beneficence. In addition to his generous contributions to the University of Rochester in support especially of medical and dental schools, he has made his home city a center of the arts. There is nothing more that one could wish for except continued health.

'It is to be hoped that he will live long enough to see the whole world not only blossom in pictures as the rose but blossom for thirteen months in every year. While such a year would not have a greater number of days than our present Gregorian calendar contains, its added month would seem to give longer lease of life and even greater riches of time to invest in those interests which he has found in later life.'

There was an avalanche of messages on this occasion, such as always encircle the globe on an important anniversary in the lives of men whose activities never know a setting sun. But the finest of these — the one that expressed the greatest understanding, came from a friend in a neighboring State:

'On this your birthday I send you my hearty congratulations, not because you are seventy-five years old but because you have successfully fought the storms and vicissitudes of a strenuous life and have achieved great and enduring things. May the coming years bring you continued energy and strength so that your life may be enjoyable.

'THOMAS A. EDISON'

THE END

INDEX

Throughout the Index, *E.* stands for George Eastman. There were so many different companies, under names differing only slightly, that the simpler way seemed to be to cite all references to 'the Company' — after the last incorporation, in New Jersey, in which all the then existing companies were absorbed — under that heading; the earlier companies are referred to separately as far as possible.

Redwood Library

SELECTIONS FROM THE RULES

1. Three volumes may be taken at a time and only three on one share. Two unbound numbers of a monthly and three numbers of a weekly publication are counted as a volume.

2. Books other than 7-day and 14-day ones may be kept out 28 days. **Books cannot be renewed or transferred.**

3. Books overdue are subject to a fine of one cent a day for fourteen days, **and five cents a day for each day thereafter.**

4. Neglect to pay the fine will debar from the use of the Library.

5. No book is to be lent out of the house of the person to whom it is charged.

6. Any person who shall soil (deface) or damage or lose a book belonging to the Library shall be liable to such fine as the Directors may impose; or shall pay the value of the book or of the set, if it be a part of a set, as the Directors may elect. All scribbling or any marking or writing whatever, folding or turning down the leaves, as well as cutting or tearing any matter from a book belonging to the Library, will be considered defacement and damage.